Cross-Platform .NET Development: Using Mono, Portable.NET, and Microsoft .NET

M.J. EASTON AND JASON KING

APress Media, LLC

Cross-Platform .NET Development: Using Mono, Portable.NET, and Microsoft .NET

Originally published by Apress in 2004
Softcover reprint of the hardcover 1st edition 2004

Lead Editor: Jason Gilmore
Technical Reviewer: Jon Pryor
Editorial Board: Steve Anglin, Dan Appleman, Ewan Buckingham, Gary Cornell, Tony Davis, Jason Gilmore, Chris Mills, Steve Rycroft, Dominic Shakeshaft, Jim Sumser
Project Manager: Tracy Brown Collins
Copy Edit Manager: Nicole LeClerc
Copy Editor: John Edwards
Production Manager: Kari Brooks
Production Editor: Laura Cheu
Compositor: Susan Glinert
Proofreader: Liz Welch
Indexer: James Minkin
Artist: Kinetic Publishing Services, LLC
Cover Designer: Kurt Krames
Manufacturing Manager: Tom Debolski

Library of Congress Cataloging-in-Publication Data

Easton, M.J. (Mark J.), 1973–
Cross-Platform .NET development : using Mono, Portable.NET, and Microsoft .NET / M.J. Easton and Jason King.
p. cm.
Includes index.
ISBN 978-1-4302-5365-5 ISBN 978-1-4302-0746-7 (eBook)
DOI 10.1007/978-1-4302-0746-7
1. Cross-platform software development. 2. Microsoft .NET. I. King, Jason, 1970- II. Title.
QA76.76.D47E15 2004
005.1—dc22 2004018339

Dedicated to Dragon, who taught me not to fear hexadecimal and then showed me the color of nothing.
—M.J.

For my Dad, Denis.
Special thanks to all my friends and family who have supported me over the course of this endeavor—in particular, my mother Marie and my brother Tim, to whom I owe a debt of gratitude for turning me into a big fan of Martin Fowler's work and object technology. Gratitude also to M.J., for inviting me onto this project and kicking my backside when I needed it, and finally for Adèle, without whom I wouldn't be anywhere near as happy as I am.
—Jase

Contents at a Glance

Contents

Foreword by Rhys Weatherley

The Common Language Infrastructure broke new ground in virtual machine design and implementation, in that it was capable of supporting many more "write once, run anywhere" languages than previous attempts.

However, the promise of such a platform cannot be realized without portability to multiple platforms. We live in a heterogeneous and changing software environment. Today's Windows-based data-entry system may need to run on tomorrow's GNU/Linux tablet PC, for example.

Portable.NET began with the goal of bringing the CLI technology to as many platforms as possible, to give maximum flexibility to application writers and users, and it has largely succeeded at that task.

This book is an important step forward in educating programmers in the issues involved in portable CLI programming.

—Rhys Weatherley, Portable.NET Chief Architect

Foreword by Miguel De Icaza

THIS BOOK WILL BE of interest to folks with a Windows and .NET background who are interested in moving their software to other platforms. In this book, the authors have put together various elements that are worth keeping in mind when writing portable code using the .NET Framework.

As the various implementations of the ECMA Common Language Infrastructure and the C# language become more popular in the Windows platform, this book covers the basic elements on what you need to be aware of if you are planning on deploying your applications on new platforms like Linux, Mac OS, IBM's S390, or Solaris.

When building Mono, our intention was to bring the breeze of fresh air that the ECMA platform defined to UNIX. The project initially was fairly limited in scope and was only attempting a limited set of functionality, but things quickly grew, and by the time of the Mono 1.0 release, the Mono project was able to deliver two stacks of APIs: a set of APIs compatible with the Microsoft. NET Framework and another set of APIs that could be used to exploit the specifics of the open source systems. UNIX, Linux, Gtk, Gnome, Mozilla, and iFolder-specific APIs are provided to take the most advantage of a system.

—Miguel De Icaza, Mono Chief Architect

About the Authors

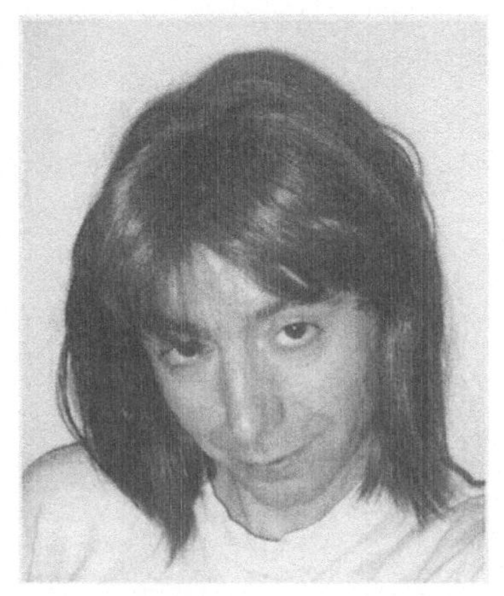

M.J. Easton suffered from a fascination with computers from the age of 7. After losing his programming virginity as a spotty teenager with some 68000 assembly code, he took a degree in artificial intelligence at London's Imperial College, before dallying away the remnants of his youth developing enterprise systems and writing sporadic articles for sporadic Web sites.

He currently works as a consultant for Avanade (`http://www.avande.com`), where he bores colleagues by bemoaning the human condition, and droning on about the wonders of object-relational persistence.

Jason King first cut his teeth as a teenager in the '80s learning BBC Basic. After spending his early 20s flirting with fruit picking and deciding whether to complete his degree in electronic engineering, Jason opted for a career in teaching, gaining qualifications in teaching subjects as diverse as English as a foreign language, computer literacy, and IT. Jason started his first small business teaching IT to office staff, before moving into technical support followed by programming, which has kept him busy since 1996. Jason now runs .NET residential training courses in the beautiful North Cornwall town of Bude in the UK and is director of Profox Systems Limited (`http://www.profox.co.uk`), a development company that specializes in writing customer relationship management software for call centers.

About the Technical Reviewer

Jon Pryor started working with .NET Beta 1 in 2000, focusing on C#, .NET Reflection, and `System.Windows.Forms`. In 2002, Jon contributed Trace and Debug support to the Mono Project. Jon maintains the Managed and Unmanaged Code Interop Guide in Mono's documentation, and he frequently is a FAQ-o-matic on the Mono mailing lists, particularly with Platform Invoke issues. Jon holds a master's degree in computer science from Virginia Tech.

Acknowledgments

ALTHOUGH WRITERS GENERALLY TRY to avoid clichés, one that's worth embracing is the one about how tortuous a task it is getting a book into print. We'd therefore like to offer our sincerest thanks to everyone who has been part of this process, and more specifically, to those who follow.

Liz Stafford at Apple for helping us work Apple's bargain-basement system.

All those who have developed technologies for us to write about and who have answered our questions, including Bob Ippolito, Brian Ritchie, Brian Lloyd, Gomi Kapoor, Gopal Vijayaraghavan, Gowri Kumar, Jack Jansen, Jay Freeman, Jeroen Frijters, Julio C. Silva, Rafael Teixeira, and Randy Ridge. We'd also like to thank Benjamin Wootton, Sébastien Pouliot, James Chambers, Jaroslaw Kowalski, Gert Driesen, Bernhard Spuida, Volker Hilsheimer, Susie Penner, Tonje Sund, Mark Summerfield, Bryan Bulten, Julian Smart, Richard Torkar, and James Duncan Davidson.

Microsoft, for developing such a great technology in the first place, and the Mono and Portable.NET teams for proving the technical proficiency of altruism. In particular, our deepest gratitude to Miguel De Icaza and Rhys Weatherley, who have both spent a lot of time answering our questions, giving us feedback, and wasting their time for our benefit.

All the staff at Apress for being supportive and not throttling us, including Beth Christmas, Chris "The Nude Trapeze Artist" Mills, Gary Cornell, James Cox, and Sarah Neidhardt.

Special thanks to Martin Streicher, for not slamming the door in our face; Jason Gilmore, for keeping the copy show on the road; John Edwards, for applying Band-Aids to our sloppy writing; Liz Welch, for actually reading the damned thing; Laura Cheu, for pulling it all together; and Tracy Brown Collins, for holding our hands and not wincing at the endless disorganization we dreamed up for her.

Finally, Mono guru Jon Pryor deserves our deepest gratitude, not only for smoothing over our technical deficiencies but also for keeping hold like a rabid pit bull and shaking the book viciously. If you find spittle between the pages, it's probably Jon's—treasure it.

Preface

AS EVERY GOOD journalist knows—as do most bad journalists—a good news story starts with the five Ws: *Who, What, Where, Why,* and *When*. Because this formula works, it's with little ceremony that we borrow such a trusted profession's schema in a brazen attempt to excuse and clarify the crazy ramblings that haunt this book's subsequent pages.

"Okay," we hear you cry, "but this is a computer book and not a news story." Perhaps you've even decided the copy of *Crossword Programs with .NET* that first caught your eye in the bookshop might have been a safer purchase, and perhaps it would have been—but only if you don't mind your crossword programs being chained to the hegemony of Windows.

So while this is most definitely a technical book for computer professionals (and any so-inclined freakish amateurs), it's also the biggest software story since the last biggest story: the coming of age of Microsoft's premier cross-platform development tool, .NET.

Who Should Read This Book

This is a book for anyone who dreams about the grail of platform independence or for anyone who longs to use one of the most advanced development platforms on his or her OS of choice. The book is primarily aimed at developers and software architects who are familiar with building Windows solutions using .NET and are interested in creating solutions for non-Windows platforms; as a corollary, it's also aimed at those who prefer non-Windows platforms and have an interest in building .NET solutions.

Consequently, this book assumes certain proficiency with programming, the C# language, and the .NET Framework. It is by no means a programming book for beginners and is unlikely to solve the problem of what to buy Grandma for Christmas. If you have some .NET experience and know your IL from your GAC, you should find it a breeze; if you're not too sure about separating your C# from your D flat, you might want to read it in conjunction with a good C# book.

NOTE Although the principles in this book are demonstrated on Windows Server 2003, GNU/Linux 2.4.20, and Mac OS X 10.2, the techniques they describe are generic, and they should apply just as well when running .NET on your operating system and hardware of choice.

What to Do with This Book

The first thing that comes to mind is to read it. Sure, you can place it on your shelf to impress your friends, use it to prop up a lopsided table, or if, like us, you've got an overactive imagination, you could murder it, mull over it, or marry it—although there are cheaper ways of doing all those things, with the exception of marriage.

On a more serious note, while the book does have certain reference-like qualities—for example, Appendix B is ideal for determining which bits of .NET rely on platform-specific services—you'll find the book is generally best read on a chapter-by-chapter basis. Although the chapters follow a pseudo logical order and tend to build on material presented in preceding chapters, if you come across a chapter that holds absolutely no interest to you, you should be able to move on to the next chapter without scuppering your chances of following the flow of the book.

Where to Read This Book

By presenting the material in the portable format of a book, you'll be able to delve into the chapters wherever it takes your fancy. Whether you're on the way to a job interview, sitting at your desk trying to get some apparently faultless code working, or lying in bed trying to tire yourself to sleep, it could be the ideal location for jumping into a chapter and tackling some pesky cross-platform issues.

Why You Should Read This Book

Whether you're already using .NET as a cross-platform development tool or considering it for the first time, this book describes what you need to know to get started, before focusing on the mixture of simple and more complicated issues that you will undoubtedly encounter on cross-platform projects.

Demonstrating how to build cross-platform software with a variety of techniques and tools, this book should help you to avoid the potential pitfalls, allowing you to develop robust, professional software while impressing your colleagues with the breadth of your esoteric .NET knowledge.

When to Read This Book

The ideal time to read this book would be before you start your first cross-platform .NET project, or during the technical portion of a feasibility study.

Failing that, we'd recommend that you read this book during a cross-platform project, because it might just save you from making a show-stopping decision, or perhaps it will help explain why that earlier design decision has transmogrified into one of those all-singing, all-dancing show-stoppers.

Content Outline

Although you can certainly read this book from cover to cover, in the real world of software development, most developers exist in a perennial struggle to keep on top of the new and sometimes not-so-new technologies. Deciding on a suitable amount of time to learn a new technique can often be the difference between getting that bonus and bearing the humiliation of being chased naked through the streets by your birch-wielding boss.

Assuming that you might be in such a "bonus or birch" situation (or perhaps you already know everything there is to know about all the hidden complexities of *Hello World*), the following high-level overview of each chapter should allow you to plot as hasty a route through the book as necessary.

Chapter 1: Introducing .NET

This chapter introduces .NET as a development platform that is suitable for cross-platform development, examining how the standardization of the Common Language Infrastructure (CLI) architecture lends itself to implementation on different operating systems, and how the underlying technical concepts of .NET provide a highly portable, advanced runtime environment. It also describes the various CLI implementations that are currently available and the platforms that they currently run on.

Chapter 2: A First Cross-Platform Program

Chapter 2 describes how to download and install working CLI implementations onto Windows Server 2003, GNU/Linux, and Mac OS X. The chapter then discusses the subsidiary issues of how to prepare a cross-platform laboratory and ensures that the reader has enough knowledge of the three platforms to run through the book. A simple C# program is then introduced, compiled, and run on the three platforms to demonstrate the basic cross-platform features of .NET.

Chapter 3: Cross-Platform Pitfalls

This chapter starts by discussing CLI binary portability and Intermediate Language (IL), before disassembling a program to compare the IL that is generated by different CLI implementations. It then investigates how to deal with platform-specific assemblies by analyzing how Portable.NET mimics the registry, before suggesting some alternative ways of avoiding the registry. The chapter finishes by defining some terminology to use when developing cross-platform .NET software.

Chapter 4: The .NET Framework Dissected

Chapter 4 documents which Microsoft .NET Framework features are intrinsically cross-platform and which are based on Windows-specific features. After describing the functionality that is available in the CLI-defined libraries, the chapter differentiates between architecturally independent and architecturally dependent namespaces to allow the reader to determine which .NET features are most suitable for his or her cross-platform projects.

The second half of the chapter introduces the bridge design pattern and demonstrates how it can be used as part of a strategy for developing robust, cross-platform software.

Chapter 5: The Spice of Life: GUI Toolkits

This chapter delves into the vast array of options for creating cross-platform GUI applications. It starts with a description of an ideal managed GUI, before contrasting how the different CLI implementations handle the `System.Windows.Forms` namespace. The chapter then describes a number of other GUI toolkits that are usable with .NET, including Gtk#, QT#, #WT, Ticklesharp, and wxWidgets. The final section of the chapter shows how the classic Model-View-Controller pattern can be used to develop applications in a toolkit-agnostic fashion.

Chapter 6: Developing Distributed Applications

Chapter 6 describes the issues revolving around distributed cross-platform applications. It starts by describing how to use ADO.NET for database access and demonstrates a cross-platform database application using the open source MySQL database server. The chapter then introduces ASP.NET, describing how to install ASP.NET on various platforms, and then contains an example Web application that is followed by an example Web service.

Chapter 7: Using Native Code

This chapter discusses how native code should be approached when developing cross-platform software. It starts by investigating how the different CLI implementations rely on native code before introducing the `NativeProbe` tool, which can be used to analyze assemblies' native dependencies. The chapter then demonstrates how P/Invoke can be used to call native functions, discusses how conditional compilation can be used to call different C functions on different platforms, and shows how an abstract factory pattern can be used to good effect. The chapter finishes with an example of a cross-platform program that plays sound using an OpenAL native library and the `Tao.OpenAL` assembly.

Chapter 8: Remoting, Components, and Interoperability

Chapter 8 shows how .NET can be used to interoperate with existing software and how to port existing code to .NET. It starts by discussing the Common Language System and then shows an example of how to bridge Java to .NET using IKVM. The chapter then demonstrates how VB6 code can be ported to .NET, before discussing Remoting with a simple cross-platform example. It finishes by showing how .NET can be integrated with component technologies; this is backed up with an example of CORBA integration using the `Remoting.Corba` assembly.

Chapter 9: Testing and Building Strategies

This chapter describes some best practices for developing robust, professional software. It starts by demonstrating how unit testing and the open source NUnit tool can be used to promote quality software. The chapter then demonstrates techniques for building cross-platform software using NAnt.

Chapter 10: Summary

Chapter 10 concludes the book by discussing the future of .NET as a cross-platform technology, and the summary finishes with a little food for thought.

Appendix A: The Unified Modeling Language

Because the Unified Modeling Language (UML) is the de facto diagramming tool for modeling object-oriented software, it is used almost exclusively throughout the book. For readers who are not familiar with UML, Appendix A contains a précis of the key concepts and various diagram types that are defined within the UML.

Appendix B: .NET Framework Map

To allow you to quickly determine which .NET features and namespaces are cross-platform, platform-independent or platform-dependent, a complete map of Microsoft's .NET Framework Class Library is presented, as first described in Chapter 4.

Appendix C: Additional Portable.NET Features

This appendix provides a list of the additional assemblies and tools that are available with Portable.NET.

Appendix D: Additional Mono Features

The various assemblies and tools that are unique to Mono appear in Appendix D.

CHAPTER 1

Introducing .NET

"Linux sure is rising . . ."

—Steve Wozniak, Apple designer

"Microsoft isn't evil . . ."

—Linus Torvalds, Linux creator

"To create a new standard, it takes something that's not just a little bit different . . . And the Macintosh, of all the machines I've seen, is the only one that meets that standard."

—Bill Gates, Microsoft CEO

FROM THE EDIFICE of the American judicial system to the liberal coven of the open source community, it is a widely accepted fact that Microsoft's business is to write software that is tied to its Windows operating system. Although Windows is often disparaged as being technically inferior, difficult to use, and expensive, by consistently coupling its software products to the operating system, Microsoft has managed to grow into one of the most successful business empires that the world has ever seen.

This book demonstrates how .NET, the next-generation technology that Microsoft famously "bet the company on," can be used as a tool for developing software that not only runs on Windows but also runs on a variety of competing operating systems. Before we delve into the fun-filled code examples and technical nuances that litter the later chapters, we start by introducing .NET and describing the historical, regulative, and technical background that positions it as the ideal cross-platform tool for the new millennium.

A Brief History of .NET

When Microsoft's grand vizier, chairman, and chief software architect, Bill Gates, first announced the company's next-generation Windows software to the public on Thursday, June 22, 2000, a modest ripple of excitement lapped through the technical media, the technical stock exchanges, and then the IT industry at large. The announcement certainly sounded like Microsoft was doing something exciting and provocatively suggested that the company was preparing to further expand its domination of the world's computers—after all, Bill Gates's speech-writers aren't paid to bore the audience—but as with many announcements regarding the IT industry, the revelation lacked any real technical substance.

Was the next-generation Windows software, the so-called .NET, another Microsoft marketing gimmick? Was it just another rebranding of the existing phalanx of Microsoft technologies—something that Microsoft's marketing department tries every few years—or was it an attempt to further capitalize on the success of the Internet, a bandwagon that Microsoft had very nearly missed out on in the first place?

After all, for an industry that is often joked about as being built on Fear, Uncertainty, and Doubt, it is not uncommon for marketing one-upmanship to subsume technical innovation. As the Ultimate Success Story of the IT industry, Microsoft is often touted as being a company whose success is better understood as a marketing phenomenon rather than as an example of strategic intelligence, operational prowess, or technical brilliance.

Having described Microsoft's vision of how .NET would build on the explosion of Internet-based computing and how it would revolutionize the building of next-generation Internet experiences, the world was given a weekend to let its hair down. The real .NET story, backed with a tirade of technical details, was then released in an act of marketing profundity on Monday, June 26, 2000, when Microsoft announced the C# language as the flagship of the .NET vision. In the world's technical media, technical stock exchanges, and IT industry at large, the ripple rose to a crescendo.

The initial announcement of C# carried with it a heady air of excitement. Apart from offering a number of standard object-oriented features, C# also included a number of exciting features, such as object-oriented function pointers, garbage collection, and a mechanism for defining extensible metadata. Even though the language clearly contained a feature set that was familiar to users of other modern programming languages, the following three important features immediately stood out:

- The language built on the success of the C family of languages, which would allow swaths of developers to leverage their existing skills and thereby ensure a relatively quick uptake of C# in the Windows development community.

- It was the first new language that Microsoft had championed since the launch of Visual Basic in 1991, which proved that .NET was more than a mere marketing exercise.

- C# promised modern features, such as object orientation and automatic memory management, which ensured that it would be ideal for Rapid Application Development (RAD), an essential requirement in the increasingly competitive commercial marketplace.

While C# was the central pillar to Microsoft's announcement, the really innovative parts of the C# language belonged to a broader technology platform, the .NET Framework, of which C# was merely one part. Commentators were quick to point out how similar the .NET Framework was to Sun's Java platform. When coupled with Sun's J2EE specifications, the Java platform had been fiercely competing against Microsoft's strategy for building enterprise applications, the *Windows Distributed interNet Applications* architecture—or Windows DNA. Of course, with both companies' platforms being similar, both the C# and Java languages were highly comparable, with both languages being members of the C family, providing object-oriented syntax and garbage collection.

While neither company could decide whether to play down or capitalize on the similarities between their languages, the most important point for the legions of loyal Windows developers was that .NET was moving away from a stalwart part of Windows development, the Component Object Model (COM) technology.

COM had originally evolved from the Object Linking and Embedding (OLE) technology of 1990 and had become the most important technology for Windows application developers. The most popular programming language for Windows, Visual Basic 6.0, was based on COM, as was the Windows application integration framework and the Windows DNA architecture. Apart from being the major tool in any Windows developer's toolkit, COM had also caused a mixture of heartache and inspiration to Microsoft's competitors. COM had been involved in a drawn-out and highly debated conflagration with the Object Management Group's middleware standard, Common Object Request Broker Architecture (CORBA), and COM's original transactional manager, the Microsoft Transaction Server, had reportedly formed the basis for the transactional services in Sun's J2EE specifications.

With C# and the .NET Framework promising such a fundamental change to Windows development, there was little surprise that Microsoft was also going to target the next version of Visual Basic at .NET. What was surprising, however, was how innovative .NET's architects had been in ensuring that language interoperability was central to .NET. While CORBA had provided language interoperability through defined interface standards and COM had provided interoperability through a binary specification, .NET takes advantage of a virtual instruction set that can be efficiently converted to native code, known as Intermediate Language, or IL.

JK I hear that you can use many languages with .NET, even COBOL, so why are we using C# and not a more established language?

MJ Well, C# is the de facto language for .NET development. With a good mix of high- and low-level features and its own ECMA standard, C# is ideal for writing cross-platform software. Additionally, currently more C# compilers are available for non-Windows platforms than for other languages, so it's going to be the most popular language for cross-platform .NET development in the foreseeable future.

JK Okay, so we're going to stick to C#, but will this book be useful for readers who prefer a different language?

MJ Absolutely. Syntax has been relegated in .NET, and while we use C# for the majority of the examples, these examples should be easily transferable into different languages.

JK So, are you saying that .NET's language agnosticism is great for interoperability and not just another creation from the Microsoft marketing machine?

By ensuring that a variety of languages—including C#, VB.NET, C++, and JavaScript—can be compiled into IL, .NET provides an excellent environment for allowing developers with different skill sets to cooperate. For a number of years, as the client–server paradigm has slowly been replaced by n-tier development, the complexity of enterprise applications—and especially the multitude of languages that are used for different subsystems—has hindered many otherwise successful projects. A typical COM-based Windows DNA application can rely on JavaScript for Web browser scripting, VBScript for server-side scripting, Visual Basic for a COM middle-tier layer, and possibly C++ for low-level COM components. Managing such projects and ensuring that developers can communicate and agree on implementation details can be increasingly difficult. In retrospect, it was perhaps unsurprising that when .NET first arrived, it came with support for C#, VB.NET, C++, and JavaScript, with IL being the glue that helped hold the technologies and the development team together.

Introducing a level of interoperability that Windows DNA developers had previously only dreamed of, IL offers the promise of simpler interoperability with non-Microsoft languages, such as COBOL, Delphi, Eiffel, Perl, Python, and even Java. While this certainly provides a simple migration path by which non-Windows developers can approach .NET, it also has the important job of simplifying the porting of existing applications to .NET, a feat that COM had carefully shied away from. In effect, Microsoft has not only provided a next-generation development tool for Windows developers, but it has also thrown open the doors and invited the rest of the world's developers to the party.

Of course, if that's all there was to the story, you wouldn't be holding this book in your hands. In fact, you might only remember .NET as one in a long line of Microsoft's marketing exercises. No, apart from .NET being a language-neutral platform that enhances and extends the principles of COM, Microsoft intelligently placed C# and .NET outside of its legendary shroud of technical obscurity and instead put them into the hands of two international standards bodies, ECMA and ISO. While Microsoft detractors have had a hard time racking their brains to belittle an act of such transparent technical benignity, the majority of the development community, from Microsoft to its nemesis—the open source community—have seen the gesture for what it really is: a flirtatious move that promises many things and—believe it or not—the ability to use a term that has never been associated with Microsoft: *cross-platform*.

NOTE In the traditional world of Windows development, developers only expect the operating system to run on hardware that's based on the *x*86 architecture; they might consider *cross-platform* to imply software that can run on different operating systems. However, for alternative operating systems, such as GNU/Linux, the operating system is not necessarily tied to a particular machine architecture, and the term *platform* refers to a specific operating system that runs on a specific hardware architecture.

In the world of .NET, there are different implementations of .NET. These implementations can also be considered as *platforms*, and therefore defining the term *cross-platform* becomes somewhat more complex. Although we will return to defining our terminology in Chapter 3, in the meantime, when we use the term *cross-platform*, we imply platform in the broadest sense. With this in mind, *cross-platform software* implies software that not only runs on a variety of different hardware architectures but also runs on different operating systems and for a variety of .NET implementations.

Setting the Standards: ECMA and ISO

"The nicest thing about standards is that there are so many of them to choose from."

—Ken Olsen, founder of Digital Equipment Corp.

After announcing .NET and C# to the public, Microsoft was quick to hand over the specifications for the C# language and the core parts of its .NET Framework, known as the Common Language Infrastructure (CLI), to the European Computer

Manufacturers Association (ECMA) for standardization. Following a year-long process of refining the specifications into standards—which involved representatives from a number of organizations, including Microsoft, Hewlett-Packard, Intel Corporation, IBM, and Fujitsu Software—the C#[1] and Common Language Infrastructure[2] standards were finally ratified in December 2001.

Following the ratification of C# and the CLI at ECMA, the standards were submitted to the International Organization of Standardization (ISO) and were subsequently ratified as ISO standards in April 2003.

NOTE While a thorough discussion of the C# and CLI standards is outside the scope of this book, it should make for enthralling reading when you're on your summer vacation, soaking up the sun by the beach and sipping a Monkey Gland cocktail. For more information on the ECMA, ISO, and C# and CLI standards, visit the following Web sites:

ECMA: `http://www.ecma-international.org/`
ISO: `http://www.iso.org/`

Putting a Smile in Your Work: The Monkey Gland Cocktail

- 2 oz. gin
- 1½ oz. orange juice
- 1 tsp. Benedictine
- 1 tsp. grenadine

Half-fill a shaker with cracked ice, pour in the ingredients, and give the concoction a vigorous shaking. Strain the mixture into a cocktail glass, and drink with a wink and a smile. Coding has never been so much fun!

Of course, submitting technical specifications to international standards bodies is by no means a new practice, but allowing regulatory bodies to govern C#'s and the CLI's technical standards was a good way to ensure that .NET is

1. C# Language Specification, ECMA 334, European Computer Manufacturers Association, 2001, `http://www.ecma-international.org/publications/standards/Ecma-334.htm`.
2. Common Language Infrastructure (CLI), Partitions I to V, ECMA 335, European Computer Manufacturers Association, 2001, `http://www.ecma-international.org/publications/standards/Ecma-335.htm`.

constrained within a formal set of guidelines. Not only does the standardization of C# and the CLI benefit the user by ensuring that precise technical details of the technology are kept freely available, but the thorough review process that preceded the standards also helped to stabilize the technologies and demonstrate that .NET was ready for the big time.

The C# standard is defined as "A simple, modern, general-purpose, object-oriented programming language . . . ." The language's syntax is then explained with a detailed description of the language's behavior. The standard makes almost no mention of .NET and serves as little more than a blueprint for the creation of a C# compiler.

In comparison to the lean C# standard, the .NET CLI standard is positively obese. Based on a normative description of the CLI architecture, the IL instruction set, and an overview of standard CLI libraries, the standard is separated into the following five partitions:

- **Partition I: Concepts and Architecture**—Describes the CLI architecture, the Common Type System, the Virtual Execution System, and the Common Language Specification.

- **Partition II: Metadata Definition and Semantics**—Discusses the physical layout, logical content, and semantics of the CLI's metadata.

- **Partition III: CIL Instruction Set**—Contains details of the Common Intermediate Language's instruction set.

- **Partition IV: Profiles and Libraries**—Presents an overview of the CLI libraries, with details of the classes, value types, and interfaces in each of the libraries.

- **Partition V: Annexes**—Provides sample CIL programs and a set of guidelines that are used in the design of the CLI libraries.

Apart from containing a number of mind-boggling details about the functioning of the CLI, the CLI standard also allows interested parties to analyze the fundamental operational mechanisms of .NET. In essence, the CLI specifications not only serve as technical guidelines to the CLI, but they also provide detailed enough information for anyone with ample spare time and a Herculean urge to implement their very own version of the CLI.

While it's unlikely that lone developers will be crazy enough to code their own version of the CLI—with the notable exception of Rhys Weatherley—the key point of interest for those developing cross-platform software is that a number of initiatives to implement the CLI are already under way. As long as these initiatives adhere to the standards, they should produce implementations that are interoperable with Microsoft's implementations of the CLI, namely the .NET Framework, the .NET Compact Framework, and the Shared Source CLI.

The Architectural Foundations of .NET

While the standardization of C# and the CLI were undoubtedly important steps in the development of .NET as a cross-platform technology, the real story about .NET's cross-platform aspirations begins with the CLI architecture, which provides a robust technical foundation on which secure, managed code can be run. Not only does the CLI architecture provide a modern, language-agnostic environment for running code in a secure and verifiable manner, but it also provides a mechanism for running unmanaged code, with excellent support for accessing the features of the underlying machine architecture.

NOTE Some industry analysts have suggested that the main difference between Java and .NET is the outstanding support that .NET provides for calling native code. While Java proponents argue that reducing support for native code is a highly desirable quality for cross-platform development, it invariably makes it harder to take advantage of specific platform features. While providing a good native code invocation mechanism can be problematic for cross-platform development, it is a useful feature for platform-dependent development, and when used carefully, it can also simplify cross-platform development by taking advantage of existing libraries. This is almost certainly why you will not see a Java book that focuses on cross-platform issues, and it is the central theme that this book hopes to address.

While anyone with a reasonable understanding of .NET will already be familiar with the architectural concepts underlying it, anyone who is attempting to build cross-platform .NET software should have a cursory understanding of the CLI's architecture and a very brief overview of the key concepts that allow it to function as a cross-platform tool. If you're interested in system architecture and want to learn more, we would recommend that either you pick up a good book on .NET or—if you're feeling particularly determined—you could always read the source code for any of the CLI implementations that are discussed later in this chapter.

The Virtual Execution System

Unlike traditional programming environments, and in a manner that is similar to Java, .NET doesn't intrinsically run machine code on the underlying hardware; instead, .NET runs code in a managed runtime environment. The managed runtime environment for .NET is defined in Partition 1 of the CLI standard and is known as the Virtual Execution System (VES).

Before code can be loaded into the VES, it must first be compiled into an intermediate format that is called, sensibly enough, *Intermediate Language (IL)*. Consisting of virtual machine instructions, Intermediate Language can be efficiently compiled into native machine code by the VES's Just-In-Time (JIT) compiler.

NOTE While it's entirely justifiable to use the term *Intermediate Language*, attentive readers will notice that we previously used the more formal term *Common Intermediate Language*, or *CIL*. It's a fact of .NET life that you will come across three different terms for the same thing: Intermediate Language (IL), Common Intermediate Language (CIL), and Microsoft Intermediate Language (MSIL). Strictly speaking, MSIL is the IL that's created from a Microsoft compiler, CIL is the standardized embodiment of IL, and IL is a shorthand form that slips off the tongue and is perfect for lazier developers. Because we're prone to a little laziness, we will use the term *Intermediate Language* for the rest of the book, unless we specifically need to distinguish it from one of the other forms.

Although C# is arguably the cleanest language for writing .NET programs, and it is the language that we will use for the majority of this book, one of the most exciting consequences of .NET's use of Intermediate Language is the ability to write .NET components in a number of different languages, with such components then being capable of interoperating with each other. Although language interoperability had long been dreamed of by system integrators, .NET goes further than previous technologies, such as COM and CORBA. .NET not only allows code that is written in one language to call methods that are written in another, but it also allows types that are written in one language to inherit from types that are written in another. Suffice it to say that language agnosticism has never been this good.

The use of Intermediate Language and the VES does add an extra layer and a slight performance overhead to the runtime process, but apart from providing language agnosticism, the VES has the significant advantage of providing a highly controlled environment in which code can run. Not only can the VES act as a sandbox, which in itself provides a level of code security that is unattainable in unmanaged environments, but it also provides a number of advanced features, including automatic memory management, type management, and dynamic loading, all of which help to simplify software development.

To reduce the performance overhead of compiling IL code into native code whenever a call is made to IL code, the VES essentially checks a native code cache to see whether it already has a compiled copy of the IL, as shown in Figure 1-1. If it has a copy, the VES makes a direct call to the native code. If it doesn't have a copy, the VES calls the Just-In-Time compiler to translate the IL into native machine code. After native code has been produced by the JIT compiler, it can be called by the VES and is also stored in the VES's native code cache for future use.

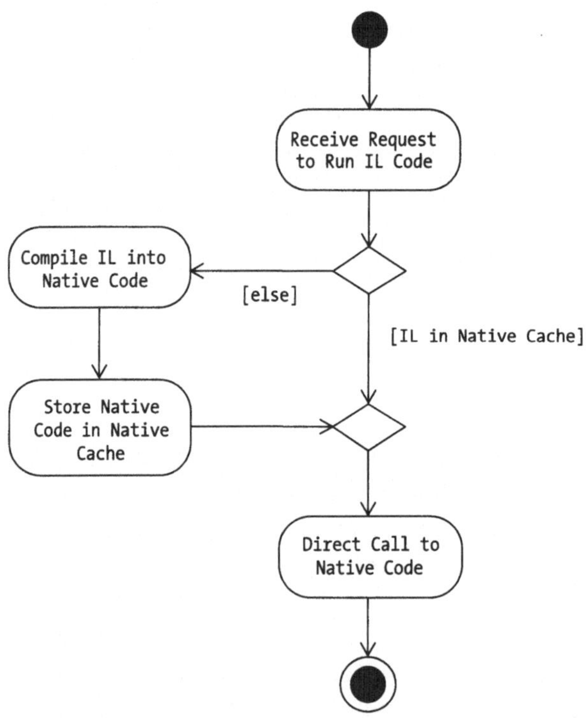

Figure 1-1. An activity diagram of the VES dealing with a call to IL code

Intermediate Language

No description of the VES can avoid mentioning the Intermediate Language (IL), which is not only central to the functioning of the .NET CLI but is also, above all, the main mechanism that allows .NET to be considered a cross-platform tool.

As discussed earlier, IL is the instruction set for the Virtual Execution System, and as such, it is the target language that all .NET compilers must produce. By virtue of the Intermediate Language being a virtual instruction set rather than a native instruction set, IL is not associated with a particular machine architecture and is therefore intrinsically portable. Figure 1-2 shows the relationship between C# source code, IL, and native code, which in this case is for the *x*86 architecture.

```
C#
namespace CrossPlatform.Net.Chapter1
{
   public class CompileMe
   {
       public static void  Main()
       {
            System.Console.WriteLine("Compile Me!");
       }
   }
}
```

Preliminary Compilation

```
IL
.method public static void  Main() cil managed
{
  .entrypoint
  // Code size       11 (0xb)
  .maxstack  1
  IL_0000:  ldstr      "Compile Me!"
  IL_0005:  call        void [mscorlib]System.Console::WriteLine(string)
  IL_000a:  ret
} // end of method CompileMe::Main
```

JIT Compilation

```
Native Code
...
0040200C 0200      add al, byte ptr [eax]
0040200E 0000      add byte ptr [eax], al
00402010 7C20      jl 00402032
00402012 0000      add byte ptr [eax], al
00402014 2402      and al, 02
00402016 0200      add byte ptr [eax]. al
...
```

Figure 1-2. The metamorphosis of C# into native code

Although IL is not targeted at a specific physical machine architecture, it does contain a number of *base instructions*, which are very similar to those that are found in most native instruction sets, such as those that handle control flow and arithmetic and logical operations.

Apart from the base instructions, IL also contains a number of object-oriented instructions, the *object model instructions*, which carry out a variety of higher-level operations, such as calling a virtual method on an object, converting value types to and from objects (via the processes of boxing and unboxing), and handling exceptions.

By basing IL around a core set of instructions that are very similar to those found in native instruction sets, Microsoft ensured that the runtime overhead of JIT compilation is minimized, because the translation of IL instructions into native instructions is relatively simple when compared to the translation of high-level code into native instructions.

Although the *object model instructions* aren't directly analogous to native instructions, they help to simplify the compilation of higher-level languages, such as C# or VB.NET, by providing a consistent set of object-oriented services. In practice, a number of the *object model instructions* can be converted into a series of *base instructions* during an initial phase of JIT compilation. This, in turn, simplifies the architecture-specific portion of JIT compilation, which converts basic IL instructions into native machine instructions. This is the approach that is used by Ximian in its CLI implementation, which is known as Mono.

For all our rhetoric about IL, the main advantage offered by IL is that by creating a JIT compiler for a new machine architecture, IL can be run on that architecture, therefore allowing cross-platform .NET programs to be created. Because all .NET languages are, by definition, compiled into IL, it is possible for programs that are written in different high-level languages, such as JavaScript and C#, to not only call methods in each other but also to take advantage of inheritance and other techniques.

Metadata

During the compilation of source code to IL, the compiler also produces some declarative information about the code, which is called metadata. Once created, the metadata is either stored in memory for dynamically created code, or, more commonly, it is incorporated into the binary file that stores the IL, as described in the section "Assemblies," later in this chapter.

After the VES has loaded some IL at runtime, the VES then reads the metadata that is associated with the IL; the metadata is finally used to verify the code's type safety and security restrictions. The metadata contains several types of predefined, declarative information that describes various facets of the code, as follows:

- The code's versioning information
- The culture or locality of the code
- The security permissions that the code requires to run
- A complete description of each type that is defined in the code, which includes the signatures for each of the type's members
- A list of the external types that the code references
- Developer-defined metadata, called *Custom Attributes*

Apart from the predefined types of metadata, one of the frequently touted advantages of .NET's metadata system over earlier metadata mechanisms—such as COM's type libraries and CORBA's Interface Description Language—is the attribute mechanism that allows developers to add custom bits of metadata to their code. Based on a programming paradigm called *declarative programming*, .NET's attributes make it easy to associate arbitrary declarations with code. These attributes have a number of uses, such as for making code-manipulation tools or for generative programming.

Generative programming makes use of a powerful, ancillary feature of the CLI's metadata system called *Reflection*, which provides the facility for code to reference metadata at runtime and is accessible through .NET's `System.Reflection` namespace and `System.Type` type. Not only does Reflection allow metadata to be analyzed at runtime, but it also caters for late-binding, or runtime-binding, to types. This helps make .NET metadata a flexible and expressive way of implementing certain types of extensible functionality.

The Common Type System

Unlike a number of bygone programming languages, the CLI defines a strongly typed environment in which every variable must be declared with a specific *type* and in which functions and methods can be readily associated with these types. Not only does this allow a number of assumptions to be made about variables at runtime, but it also guarantees that all code is given a clearly defined scope. This can significantly reduce complexity in large programs.

The CLI type system, called the *Common Type System*, provides an object-oriented framework in which classes, structures, interfaces, and intrinsic data types are all said to be *types*. The CLI defines types as either value types or reference types, and it specifies how these *types* can be declared with fields, methods, and a variety of object-oriented features, such as accessibility and inheritance. All types are defined as a mixture of IL and metadata, and it is the binary representation of a program's types that forms a CLI program.

Assemblies

Having discussed the CLI's two types of binary code, Intermediate Language and metadata, we haven't mentioned how either is stored for loading into the VES. Like all types of binary code, IL and metadata often need to be stored in a physical location, and the fundamental unit of storage for IL and metadata is called an *assembly*.

Assemblies come in two varieties: dynamic and static. Dynamic assemblies are created at runtime and are stored in memory; static assemblies are more common than dynamic assemblies and, once compiled, are persisted to the file system.

Rather than storing an arbitrary collection of IL and metadata, assemblies contain a collection of .NET modules, types, and global functions, and assemblies only store the IL and associated metadata required to implement this collection of entities. Apart from being the standard packaging unit for binary code, assemblies can optionally store a variety of data resources, such as bitmaps or strings. This allows .NET code to be easily packaged with the static data that it references, as shown in Figure 1-3. Assemblies also contain metadata called the *assembly manifest*, which describes various aspects of the assembly and is used to define the assembly's boundaries for code reuse, version control, and security.

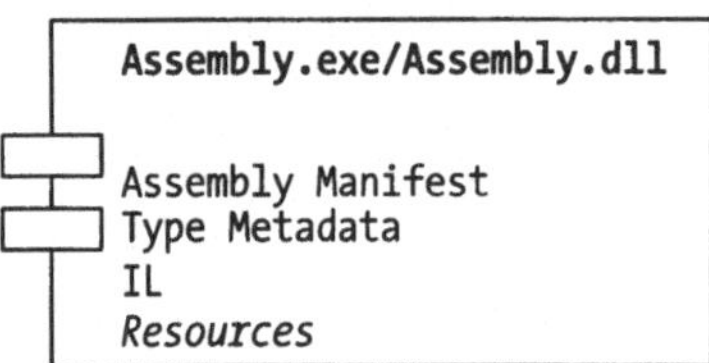

Figure 1-3. A single file assembly

When an assembly is loaded into the VES, the manifest is read, thereby allowing the VES to check version numbers, validate type information, calculate security permissions, and verify which external assemblies are referenced by the assembly's types.

A static assembly can therefore be construed as consisting of four elements: an assembly manifest, the metadata and IL for a number of types, and optionally, some resources.

Multifile Assemblies

While static assemblies are very similar to an operating system's shared libraries and executables, these assemblies have one major difference: They are under no obligation to be stored in a single file, as depicted in Figure 1-4. Although an assembly still requires the three mandatory elements that were discussed earlier, the elements can be split into a number of different files, with the assembly's manifest containing links to all the files that make up the assembly and the assembly's code being split into a number of modules.

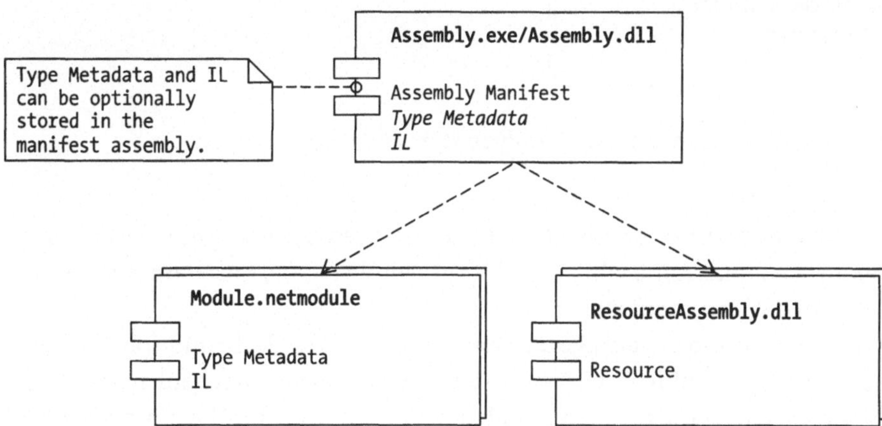

Figure 1-4. A multiple file assembly

The ability to separate assemblies into modules is essential for the creation of multiple language assemblies, because the modules can be compiled with their relevant compilers and then referenced from the assembly's main file. Using multifile assemblies is also a useful technique for larger development teams, because it gives developers the ability to compile their code independently of each other.

One of the main advantages that multiple file assemblies offer to the cross-platform developer is the ability to segregate platform-specific functionality in a single module.

Satellite Assemblies

Apart from the multiple file assemblies that were described in the previous section, you can also separate culture-specific resources, such as foreign language text strings, from the main assembly and store the resources in satellite assemblies. The relationship between a main assembly and a number of satellite assemblies is shown in Figure 1-5.

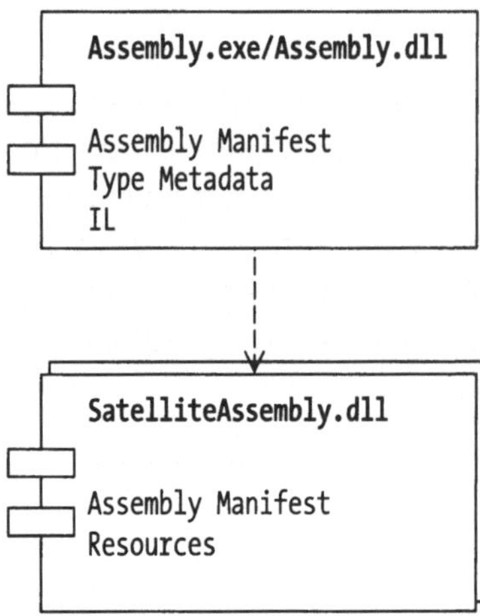

Figure 1-5. Using a satellite assembly to store resources

When the main assembly needs to access a resource at runtime, the main assembly can determine which satellite assembly to load based on the culture settings of the host machine.

With the option to package an assembly in a single file, in multiple files, or by using satellite assemblies, .NET provides a highly flexible mechanism for storing binary code and static resources, and, most importantly for the cross-platform developer, the binary format that is used for assemblies is specified in the CLI standards. In practical terms, this means that an assembly that is compiled on one implementation of the CLI can not only be used in a different CLI implementation but also on a different operating system and on a different machine architecture.

.NET Clichés

"The computing field is always in need of new clichés."

—Alan Perlis

With the .NET architecture providing a managed runtime environment and being ratified by two international standards bodies, Microsoft's .NET strategy was always that alternative CLI implementations would be produced and that .NET would subsequently grow beyond being a Windows-only technology. Although such a move is at odds with the traditional Microsoft approach of tying users to Windows, it nonetheless improves the scope of .NET as a development tool and opens the possibility that companies that are using alternate operating systems might opt for using .NET as their development tool.

JK .NET is a real break from tradition for Microsoft, isn't it?

MJ I wonder if it has anything to do with all those court cases that the company has been fighting?

JK Are you saying that .NET is Microsoft's attempt to stop playing hardball?

MJ Well, I guess if I were His Billness, I wouldn't mind introducing a standard for other people to adopt. It would mean porting my own software onto Mac and Linux would be all the more easy, while helping to stem the rush toward Java.

JK One of the other benefits of .NET is that it can simplify moving existing software and users from the Mac and Linux markets to Windows.

MJ This means that .NET is not only a powerful development technology but also a well-crafted marketing tool.

JK Is this nothing other than the traditional Microsoft approach?

With this in mind, a variety of CLI implementations are currently available, each of which runs on a different set of operating systems, has different objectives, has different licensing conditions, and has a different set of features that extend the CLI specifications. While this book's later chapters concentrate on using a subset of these CLI implementations, for everyone who is seriously considering .NET as a cross-platform tool, it makes sense to contrast the different CLI implementations so that you can choose the most suitable CLI implementation for the specific needs of your project or organization.

Microsoft .NET Framework

The first available implementation of the CLI was unsurprisingly Microsoft's commercial .NET Framework, with version 1.0 released in February 2002 and version 1.1 released in April 2003.

The Microsoft .NET Framework is much more than a CLI implementation and provides a number of enhancements to the CLI in an extensive class library. Microsoft .NET is often described as consisting of two main parts: the .NET Common Language Runtime (CLR) and the .NET Framework Class Libraries. Although the CLR is often touted as Microsoft's implementation of the CLI, a one-to-one correspondence does not exist between the CLR and the CLI, because the CLI libraries are technically implemented as a subset of the Framework Class Libraries.

As a companion to the .NET Framework, Microsoft also released a developer toolkit called the .NET Framework SDK, which provides a number of development tools that simplify the development of .NET solutions. While the majority of these tools, such as the IL disassembler, `ildasm.exe`, are not intrinsically tied to Windows, some of the tools, such as the Type Library Importer, `tlbimp.exe`, deal specifically with integrating .NET with the Windows operating system.

One of the most exciting features of Microsoft .NET is the availability of compilers for a number of different languages, such as C#, C++, Visual Basic .NET, Java, and JavaScript. This allows programs that are written in a variety of languages to be compiled into IL, as shown in Figure 1-6. Another particularly useful feature of MS.NET is the Native Image Generator (`ngen.exe`). This is a command-line tool that compiles IL into native code, thereby removing the overhead of JIT compilation and improving the startup time of frequently used assemblies.

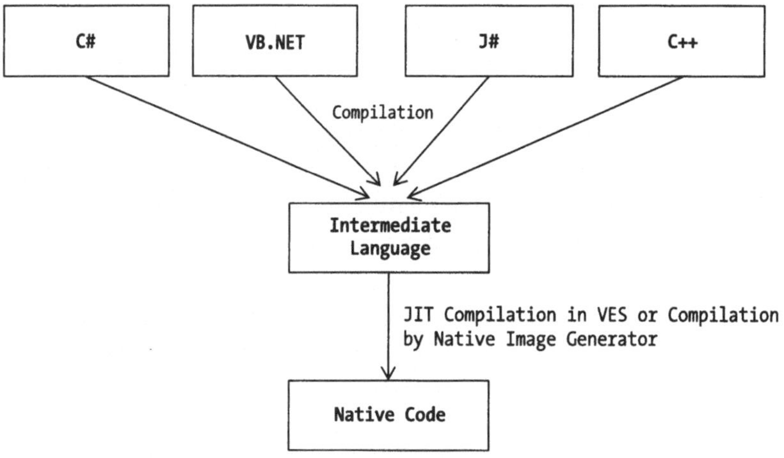

Figure 1-6. The Microsoft .NET compilation chain

If Microsoft had implemented the .NET Framework without extending the CLI standards, there would be quite a bit less to say on cross-platform .NET development, but as it stands, the .NET Framework Class Libraries provide a large number of highly useful features, which position MS.NET as an advanced solution to meet the tricky requirements of software development.

A number of the enhancements are not intrinsically tied to the Windows operating system, such as the `System.Data` namespace or the enhancements to the `System.Xml` namespace, and might well be included in future revisions of the CLI standards. Some of the other enhancements, such as the `System.EnterpiseServices` or `System.Management` namespaces, provide facilities that are tightly coupled to

Windows and are unlikely to be much use to cross-platform developers, except when coupled with software that emulates Windows services.

The Microsoft .NET Framework is the obvious choice for running .NET programs on the Windows family of operating systems. Because a number of the .NET Framework's features rely on calls to the Win32 API and its license only allows it to be run under a Windows operating system, it is legally of little use to those who are developing software to run on a non-Windows operating system.

NOTE More information and a download of the .NET Framework is available from `http://www.microsoft.com/net/`.

Microsoft .NET Compact Framework

Apart from the full-blown .NET Framework, Microsoft has also released a slimmer version of MS.NET called the .NET Compact Framework, which has a lower memory overhead and is suitable for developing for hardware that runs either Microsoft Pocket PC or Windows CE operating system. The target platforms of the .NET Compact Framework are often referred to as *smart devices.*

With the variety of smart devices rapidly on the increase—from PDAs and mobile phones to digital TV set-top boxes and computer game consoles—the marketplace for smart devices is increasingly competitive, and the .NET Compact Framework allows .NET developers to easily target their development skills at such devices.

NOTE More information and a download of the .NET Compact Framework is available from `http://www.microsoft.com/mobile/developer/`.

Mono

Started in July 2001 by the open source software champions, Ximian Inc., Mono was created to provide a quality tool for developing enterprise software on GNU/Linux. Mono not only includes a C# compiler and an implementation of the CLI, but it also contains some Mono-specific enhancements, such as a number of additional libraries, and is attempting to implement many of the extensions that are available in MS.NET.

In a similar vein to MS.NET, Mono also includes a currently unstable Visual Basic .NET compiler, which should one day cut the umbilical cord between the Visual Basic language and the Windows operating system.

One significant advantage that Mono holds over Microsoft .NET is that Mono's source code is open source, which means that, should the need arise, the inner workings of Mono can be prodded, poked, tested, and analyzed. Different parts of Mono are available under three different licenses, as follows:

- The compilers are being released under the GNU General Public License.
- The runtime libraries are available under the GNU Library General Public License.
- The class libraries are available under the MIT X11 License.

For more details about the various licenses, refer to the sidebar "CLI Licensing Issues."

As shown in Figure 1-7, the Mono project has two distinct runtimes, `mono` and `mint`. The `mono` runtime uses JIT compilation to convert IL to native code and provides maximum performance, while the `mint` runtime uses interpretation to provide maximum platform portability at the cost of performance.

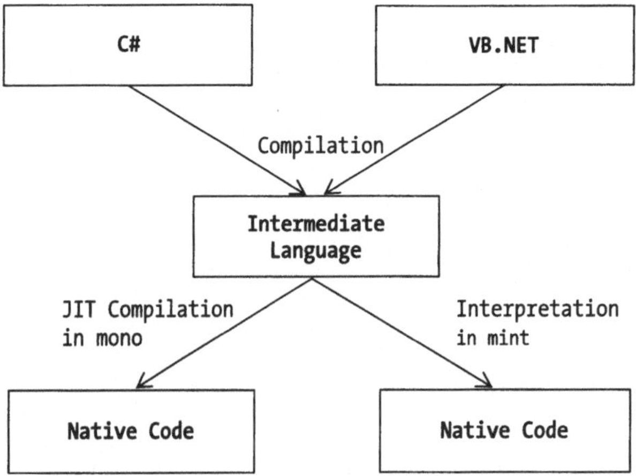

Figure 1-7. The Mono compilation chain

Although `mono` outperforms `mint`, because `mono` contains a significant portion of platform-dependent code, `mono` is only available for a subset of the architectures that are supported by `mint`, as shown in Table 1-1.

Table 1-1. Platforms That Are Supported by Mono

Platform	**mono Supported**	**mint Supported**
FreeBSD (*x*86)	Yes	Yes
GNU/Linux (HPPA)	No	Yes
GNU/Linux (PPC)	Yes	Yes
GNU/Linux (S390)	Yes	Yes
GNU/Linux (StrongARM)	No	Yes
GNU/Linux (*x*86)	Yes	Yes
Mac OS X (PPC)	Yes	Yes
Solaris (SPARC)	Yes	Yes
Windows (*x*86)	Yes	Yes

You should use `mono` whenever possible and only use `mint` when absolutely necessary, but because Mono was intrinsically designed to be cross-platform, the number of platforms that are supported is likely to change relatively quickly. As a result, check the Mono Web site frequently for the latest list of supported platforms.

NOTE More information on Mono, including source code and binary downloads for Windows and GNU/Linux, is available from `http://www.go-mono.com/`.

Because one of Mono's goals is to implement the majority of the .NET Framework, it is the ideal choice of CLI when porting an application that is written for Microsoft .NET to a non-Windows platform. Similarly, because it includes large chunks of functionality that are above and beyond that defined by the CLI standards, Mono is also a good choice for carrying out general cross-platform .NET development.

However, while Mono attempts to mimic the functionality of the .NET Framework as faithfully as possible, some good arguments exist for avoiding some of Mono's features for greenfield cross-platform projects. In particular, greenfield projects should generally avoid the Mono functionality that relies on the emulation of Windows-specific services, because pure cross-platform software should make as few assumptions about the target platform as possible.

For example, while Mono provides two different implementations of the `System.Windows.Forms` namespace—one that relies on the lower-level GTK# toolkit and another that relies on the Windows emulator, WINE—the design of `System.Windows.Forms` is based on underlying features of the Windows GUI. This means that any application that uses `System.Windows.Forms` is forced to implement a Windows-style GUI. A better alternative for developing a cross-platform GUI is to use one of the alternate GUI toolkits that are mentioned in Chapter 5. This could help to maximize the application's decoupling from a specific platform.

Open CLI Library

The Open CLI Library (OCL) is an implementation of the CLI standard, which was created by Intel for its Open Runtime Platform (ORP). Intel's ORP is a managed runtime environment that can host multiple coexisting JIT compilers for languages such as Java and C#. The ORP was designed as a flexible environment in which to carry out experiments on managed runtime environments.

ORP runs under both Windows and GNU/Linux and is licensed under the Intel Open Source License; OCL is licensed under a BSD license. ORP and OCL are primarily used to carry out research on managed environments and are therefore unlikely to hold much appeal to anyone without an academic interest in managed code, or a penchant for CLI implementations in general.

NOTE More information and the source code for ORP can be found at the following Web site:

`http://sourceforge.net/projects/orp`

More information on the Open CLI Library can be found at the following Web site:

`http://sourceforge.net/projects/ocl`

Portable.NET

Started in 2001 by Southern Storm Software, Portable.NET (PNET) is the CLI implementation for the DotGNU meta-project, which aims to build a free software environment for running Web services that can fully replace the .NET Framework.

As suggested by its name, Portable.NET was designed foremost to be a highly portable implementation of the C# and CLI standards. Portable.NET contains a number of standard tools such as a C# compiler, an IL assembler, an IL disassembler, and a CLI runtime engine. It also includes a variety of unique tools, such as the PNetMark benchmarking tool and compilers for a variety of languages, including Java, Visual Basic .NET, and even traditional C.

One interesting benefit that Portable.NET holds over other CLI implementations is that it compiles source code using Southern Storm Software's Tree Compiler, `treecc`. This allows source code to not just be compiled into IL but also into Java bytecode.

However, the most outstanding feature of Portable.NET—and indeed the crux of its inherent portability—is the unique and ingenious architecture of the runtime environment. Rather than JIT compilation of IL into native code, the runtime starts by translating IL into the runtime's own internal format, Converted Virtual Machine (CVM), in a process known as *bytecode JIT compilation*, before the CVM is finally translated into native code by an interpreter. The compilation process for PNET is shown in Figure 1-8.

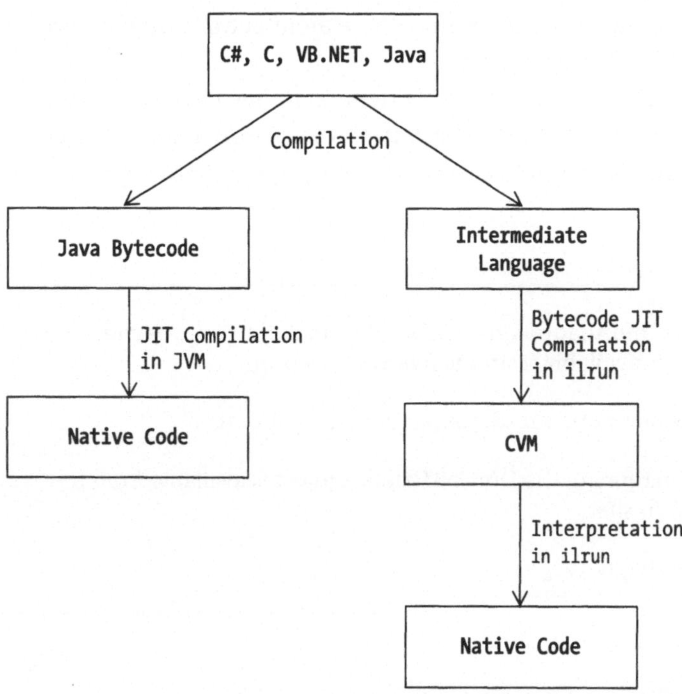

Figure 1-8. The Portable.NET compilation chain

Although the use of an interpreter has a slight performance overhead at runtime, it has the advantage of minimizing the platform-specific parts of the runtime engine. This makes it comparatively easy to port the runtime engine to work with new machine architectures.

NOTE Although Portable.NET currently relies on CVM-native code interpretation, a recent addition to the DotGNU meta-project is the libjit library, which implements Just-In-Time compilation functionality. Unlike other JIT compilers, libjit is independent from any specific virtual machine bytecode format and, as an added bonus, if it's run on a machine architecture that doesn't have a native code generator, it falls back to interpreting the code. While libjit is likely to be an indispensable tool for developing new virtual machines, plans are already afoot to migrate PNET to libjit, which means that it's highly likely that PNET's compilation architecture will become even richer in the not-too-distant future.

While Portable.NET was originally targeted at GNU/Linux, it currently runs under a variety of operating systems, including Windows, Solaris, FreeBSD, and Mac OS X, and on a variety of machine architectures, including *x*86, PowerPC, SPARC, and IA-64. Because the runtime environment uses an interpreter, Portable.NET is likely to be ported to new machine architectures much more quickly than other CLI implementations.

Portable.NET is available under the GNU General Public License. It is an ideal CLI implementation to use as an alternative to Microsoft .NET or Mono, or when running .NET applications on esoteric and less popular hardware platforms.

NOTE More information on Portable.NET, including source code and downloads, is available from the following Web site:

`http://www.southern-storm.com.au/portable_net.html`

More information on the DotGNU meta-project is available from the following Web site:

`http://www.dotgnu.org/`

Shared Source CLI

Also known as Microsoft Rotor, Corel Rotor, or simply Rotor, the Shared Source CLI (SSCLI) was first released to the public in November 2002. The SSCLI is an implementation of the CLI, with a C# compiler and some extra class libraries and development tools.

The development of the SSCLI began when Microsoft approached Corel and asked Corel to convert the CLI portions of the .NET Framework so that .NET could run on different platforms. This would duly serve as a demonstration of the cross-platform nature of .NET and as an example implementation for CLI implementers. The SSCLI is essentially a copy of the Microsoft CLR, with a more portable JIT compiler, a simplified garbage collector, and a Platform Abstraction Layer that replaces all the function calls to the Win32 API.

TIP While the Microsoft SSCLI's shared source license stipulates that it is only for noncommercial use, the license also states that developers can retain "nontangible" goods, essentially allowing developers to use the ideas that are contained within the SSCLI. This is why the SSCLI is often described as an ideal research tool for developers who are implementing their own CLIs.

Rotor is available with a shared source license. This means that while the source code is available for noncommercial purposes, such as teaching and research, it cannot be used in commercial projects. Although the license makes the SSCLI less useful than the other CLI implementations, the SSCLI shares a significant portion of its source code with Microsoft's commercial .NET Framework and thus provides an invaluable chance to investigate how the .NET Framework functions. Also, note that the SSCLI is used by Microsoft for research, and as such it has the added benefit that Microsoft makes certain research tools—such as Gyro, the preliminary implementation of C# 2.0—available for the SSCLI.

NOTE More information and a download of the Shared Source CLI source code is available from `http://www.microsoft.com/net/`.

CLI Licensing Issues

Because a variety of CLI implementations are available, both with and without source code, it is important to understand how the different implementations are licensed before choosing which implementation is right for a specific project. When you consider that assemblies shipped with one implementation can be used with different implementations, as demonstrated in Chapter 3, it is especially important to consider the overall licensing implications for the project.

Whereas both the Microsoft .NET Framework and the .NET Compact Framework require a Windows license on every machine on which they are installed, none of the other CLI implementations have such licensing requirements, although the SSCLI's shared source license expressly forbids its use in commercial applications.

The three remaining implementations—Mono, Portable.NET, and OCL—all have open source licenses, with different parts of the implementations being available under a variety of different licenses.

The OCL's BSD license is equivalent to the Mono class library's MIT X11 license, and the BSD license implies that you can use the source code as you see fit. However, the original copyright notice must be included whenever a substantial portion of the code is used.

The Mono compilers and applications use the GNU General Public License (GPL) and contain a long list of conditions that ensure that if you use any of the source code or binary files in your own software, your software must also be licensed under the GPL. This is why detractors of the open source software movement have labeled the GPL as a viral license. Portable.NET uses a modified version of the GPL that allows your own software to use the PNET library without itself being licensed under the GPL.

Finally, the Mono runtime library uses the Lesser GPL (LGPL), which is similar to the GPL but without the requirement that a program that uses it needs to be released under the Lesser GPL.

While the complexities that are associated with licensing can be confusing, the open source licenses should allow the open source CLI implementations to be used in most development projects with little hindrance. More details about open source licenses can be found at `http://www.opensource.org`.

Summary

Now you've struggled through the rather sober introductory chapter, you should have a rough idea of the background on which the rest of the book carefully teeters.

In the following chapters, we ditch some of the formalities and move on with some code examples, coding techniques, and random assorted tidbits. You'll find that each chapter culminates in a quick summary, much like this one, which serves as a sanity check for you, the reader, and just as importantly, for us, the authors. Not only does each summary stop us from barking obsessively at the moon, but for those of you who dozed off midchapter, it also serves as a polite reminder of what has been covered and suggests potential research avenues that particularly keen readers might want to pursue.

This chapter started with a brief history of .NET, in which we mentioned some of .NET's core features and fleetingly contrasted .NET and C# to a number of technologies, including COM, CORBA, and Java. Because no technology is an island, the issues that are associated with interoperating .NET with some of these alternate technologies are covered in Chapter 8.

We then discussed ECMA and ISO standardization and took a cursory glance at the contents of the CLI standards, although any developer who wants to impress someone with his or her .NET knowledge should take the time to understand the CLI. The chapter then briefly covered some fundamental aspects of the .NET architecture and finished by looking at the various CLI implementations that are currently available.

NOTE The CLI implementations are likely to change quickly—probably too quickly for even the modern printing press. For the latest cross-platform news, links, and code samples, visit `http://www.cross-platform.net`.

CHAPTER 2

A First Cross-Platform Program

"There is no meal that cannot be improved by the addition of cheese."

—Unknown

BY NOW, YOU ARE either enjoying the refreshment offered by the hallowed Monkey Gland or reeling from the after-effects of several. If you're suffering, perhaps you should have stuck with just one beast, not the whole troupe. From here on in, the learning in earnest really begins, starting with installation instructions for our chosen CLI implementations and culminating in our first cross-platform application—Woo-hoo! Breaking with the tradition that was set forth in many highly esteemed programming books, our first code sample deviates from the rather tired and, some might say, cheesy `helloworld` and instead concentrates on something a little more complex. En route, we investigate the platform differences when executing programs on the command line.

Let's Get Ready to Rumble!

Before stumbling headlong into cross-platform nirvana, you need to get tooled up for your journey.

Just as various operating systems can run on a variety of hardware platforms, several CLI implementations are also available, as mentioned in Chapter 1, that run on a variety of operating systems. Combining the three factors of hardware, operating system, and CLI gives a number of configurations—which would be restrictively expensive and logistically impractical to demonstrate in this book. So we have decided to use a laboratory that provides good coverage of the most popular platforms and CLI implementations.

I Spy CLI

JK One of the complexities of cross-platform .NET development is that developing for Windows with Microsoft's .NET Framework is a subtly different development experience than developing for Windows using a different CLI implementation, such as Mono or Portable.NET.

MJ Sheesh! A "subtly different development experience"? You sound like a marketing executive.

JK This might be better than sounding like a geek. Anyway, why have we chosen to use three different CLIs for this book? After all, Mono works on our three chosen operating system platforms, so wouldn't it be easier to stick to Mono?

MJ While Mono runs on our three chosen operating systems—and yes, it probably would be easier to stick to one CLI implementation—we're using three differing CLIs to show the whole spectrum of cross-platform .NET development, which means showing how to deal with different CLI implementations.

If your setup differs from ours, don't worry. Just throw away your old kit and buy the same equipment as we have. Your boss/wife/kids will thank you, and we will be happily in your debt, particularly as we have shares in all the relevant companies. Can't do that? Well, this book still has value for you, because all the issues that we deal with are abstracted to as high a level as possible. All the techniques and tips that we discuss are generic solutions to cross-platform problems. Although we may occasionally demonstrate a solution to a common configuration problem that you may not have, you should take heed nonetheless, because you might find that the solution is relevant in other circumstances.

A Simple Laboratory

Before proceeding with cross-platform development, it pays to have a usable and comfortable setup. Realistically, even an alpha male code monkey can find writing and testing software for multiple platforms on a single machine a little daunting. The ideal setup is a laboratory that contains a variety of machines, with different hardware architectures running different operating systems and CLI implementations.

For the purposes of this book, our laboratory evolved to include the following equipment:

- Windows Server 2003 with Microsoft .NET Framework 1.1 and Microsoft .NET SDK. (See the section "Installing Microsoft .NET 1.1 on Windows," later in this chapter.)
- SuSE Linux 8.2 with Mono 0.31 installed.
- Apple iMac with Mac OS X 10.2 operating system and Portable.NET 0.6.4.
- One long table and a chair on wheels.

However, our laboratory has more than this. All three machines are networked, and we use a shared folder for writing and compiling code; this folder is accessible by all our platforms.

Networking and File Sharing

Networking your operating systems and sharing files across them is too large a topic to be dealt with in this chapter—and arguably too off-topic for this book. Operating systems that are produced by large corporations, such as Microsoft and Apple or some of the larger GNU/Linux distributors, are provided with plenty of help features in an attempt to make networking straightforward. Certain GNU/Linux distributions, or *distros*, can present a more difficult problem to newcomers. To start reading about GNU/Linux networking, visit `http://www.justlinux.com` or `http://www.samba.org`.

You may feel happy using compact discs or floppies to move your code from one computer to another, and maybe you need the exercise, but you will soon tire of it. We encourage you to take the operating system that you are most comfortable with and host the shared folder on that platform. After all, any administrative tasks that you carry out need be as easy to achieve as possible—you don't want to destroy all your hard work accidentally.

You'll probably find cross-platform development to be reasonably arduous. For example, some code that produces a beautiful interface under one platform may look totally out of place on another. It therefore pays to have all your machines close together, so unless you have a problem with wandering basilisks, do not be tempted by an arrangement of mirrors for looking at screens in other rooms. Additionally, at least one of your platforms—again, we recommend your preferred platform—should have access to the Internet. You can always download anything you need into the shared folder, and thus you can provide all platforms with whatever they need. See Figure 2-1 for a schematic of our laboratory.

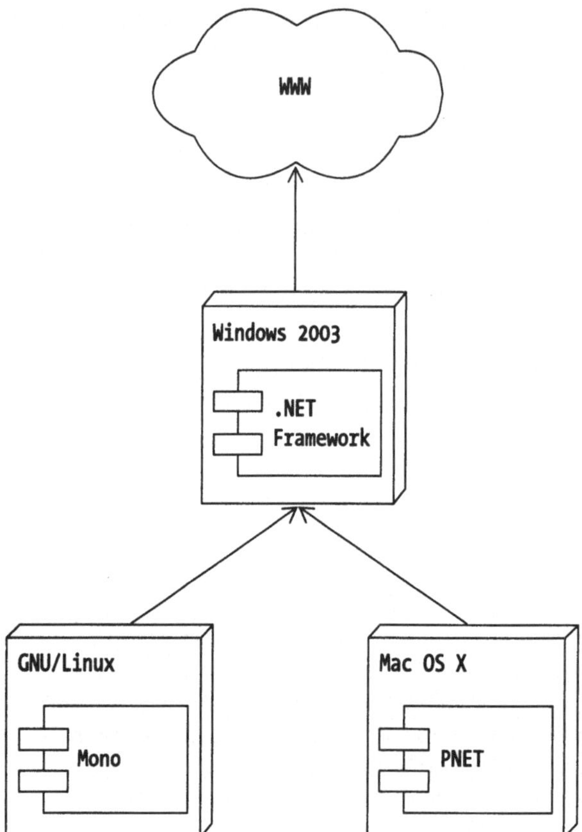

Figure 2-1. A deployment diagram of our laboratory

Of course, our setup is only one of a myriad possibilities, and it's the most expansive configuration that could fit onto our table. If space is at a premium, or if you want to stop the finance director from scowling at you over the boardroom or breakfast table, you can always reduce the hardware overhead by running more than one operating system on a single machine.

One way to carry this out is to install two or more operating systems on the same machine and configure the machine to dual-boot between the operating systems. Although dual booting is a particularly simple and cheap way to set up a cross-platform laboratory, it has the disadvantage of only allowing one operating system to be run at a time, disallowing concurrent testing and making it impossible to test distributed cross-platform programs. A subsidiary problem with dual booting is that it does not allow programs to be tested on more than one machine architecture.

Code-Access Security and Shared Folders

Those cross-platform programmers who want to take advantage of .NET's code-access security (CAS) might have to sit patiently for a while or contribute their own efforts to the open source projects. Portable.NET has a lot of code in place to support CAS. However, a significant portion of code is still needed for both the compiler and the Portable.NET runtime. For Mono, there has been much discussion among the cognoscenti, and CAS is unlikely to be implemented for some time, due to the large amount of work necessary to carry out a method-by-method audit of the entire class library.

On Microsoft .NET platforms, security permissions within Microsoft .NET frequently prevent code being executed from a network share/drive, because .NET security treats the local network with the same security rights as the Internet. As a result, the CLR cannot read local network files. However, security can be relaxed by using the Microsoft .NET Framework Configuration tool. This tool allows you to alter the security policies at the machine, user, or assembly level.

If you feel confident that no malicious code exists on your network, you could alter the security policy under the `Runtime Security Policy/Machine/Code Groups/All Code/LocalIntranet_Zone` node. Right-click the `LocalIntranet_Zone` node, and choose Properties. Click the Permissions Set tab, and change the value in the combo box from `LocalIntranet` to `FullTrust`.

A slightly more expensive alternative to dual booting is to use virtual machine or emulation software to run a variety of guest operating systems on a host operating system. Not only does this allow concurrent testing, but it also potentially allows multiple hardware architectures to be tested on a single computer. The main disadvantage of using virtual machines compared to using multiple physical machines is that virtual machines cannot be used for performance testing due to the processing overhead that is incurred by the virtual machine or emulation software.

An increasing variety of virtual machines, emulators, and portability layers are available; some of the more popular choices are as follows:

- Virtual PC from Microsoft (`http://www.microsoft.com/mac/products/virtualpc/virtualpc.aspx?pid=virtualpc`): For hosting Windows operating systems on Mac OS 9 or Mac OS X
- VMWare (`http://www.vmware.com`): For hosting a variety of operating systems on both GNU/Linux and Windows
- Cygwin (`http://www.cygwin.com`): A portability layer that provides a number of GNU/Linux facilities on top of Windows

The geek-masochist in you might even consider using a Mac to host Windows, in turn hosting Linux, to allow you to try developing on all three platforms on just a single machine—although scarification may be a more suitable pastime for you.

TIP Another emulator to watch for is the Bochs project, which is an up-and-coming portable *x*86 PC emulator written in C++. Bochs can currently emulate 386, 486, Pentium, Pentium Pro, and AMD64 processors, and it supports a number of operating systems, including GNU/Linux, Windows 95, DOS, and Windows NT. Bochs can be found at `http://bochs.sourceforge.net/`.

Basic UNIX Skills

To anyone who is unfamiliar with UNIX commands, the following installation processes may be a little painful. Readers who are familiar with MS-DOS console commands might have a small battle with habit because the equivalent UNIX commands are similar, but different enough to cause a few problems at first. Table 2-1 presents a short list of the commands and elements of the commands that are used in the installation instructions.

Table 2-1. Console Commands

Microsoft DOS	GNU/Linux and UNIX	Purpose
`dir`	`ls`	Lists the contents of a directory
`cd..`	`cd ..`	Moves up one directory to parent directory
`cd`	`pwd`	Displays current directory name
`cd myDirectory`	`cd myDirectory`	Changes current directory to `myDirectory`
`\`	`/`	Directory delimiter
`help <DOS command>`	`man <command or program name>`	Displays help text for command or program, if available
`help <DOS command>`	`info <command or program name>`	Displays help text for command or program, if available
`md myDirectory`	`mkdir myDirectory`	Creates `myDirectory` directory

What Is a Tarball?

The most popular distribution medium for UNIX variants is the *tarball*, which is an archive that contains a collection of files required for distribution. Frequently, tarballs not only collect files, but they also compress the contents.

A tarball with compressed files has a file extension of `.tar.gz`, where the `gz` denotes the use of GNUZip for the compression. Similar to a WinZip file, a tarball may also contain path information for each file that is contained therein. This information is used during the unpacking process for delivering files to intended locations.

To unpack a tarball, type **tar -xzvf myTarFile.tar.gz**. This is demonstrated in the following Mono installation section. To learn more about the options that are available for `tar`, use the `man tar` command or, alternatively, use `info tar`.

Using vi

Those readers who come from a background steeped in graphical user interfaces may find console-based text editors unfamiliar at first. The `vi` editor, a commonly distributed text editor, works in two modes: command mode and edit mode. Keystrokes issued while in command mode instruct the editor, while keystrokes issued in edit mode are echoed in the current document.

The best advice is to use the `man` command to gain a fast-track explanation of using `vi`. Open a terminal—for Mac users, if you already have a terminal open, choose File ➤ New Shell to open another—and switch to it. If you are unfamiliar with `vi`, it pays to have the manual open every time you are using `vi` to edit a file. The `man vi` command opens the manual for you. Press the spacebar to move to the next page of the manual, press B to take you back a page, and press Q to exit the manual.

Set Your Monkey Free: Installing Mono on Linux

> *"'Ave you a lie-sonse fur that minkey?"*
>
> —Inspector Clouseau

The Mono Web site is the ideal starting point for finding out more about the Mono project. It is crammed full of information. This information ranges from the informative Frequently Asked Questions (FAQs) page to details of how to subscribe to the various e-mail lists and a number of suggestions about how you can contribute to the ongoing development of the project.

NOTE You can find the Mono Web site at `http://www.go-mono.com`.

You have essentially three ways to install Mono on GNU/Linux. The typical hard-core GNU/Linux user will probably enjoy downloading the source code and building it himself, whereas the less-hardcore reader will probably want to install the binaries for her particular flavor of GNU/Linux.

For the ultimate in luxury installation, take a walk down the Ximian Red Carpet, a tool that allows easy installation of Mono. All budding starlets in need of a little red carpet treatment should trot their browser over to the following Web site:

```
http://www.ximian.com/products/redcarpet
```

Because the more difficult route of building source code is more generically applicable than the simpler binary route, we demonstrate the more complex approach. By demonstrating the process that is involved in building Mono from source code, we can avoid showing a distro-centric installation of Mono and thus cater to the greater masses.

NOTE GNU/Linux is distributed by a variety of companies, RedHat and SuSE being just two of the more popular examples. Although the merits of the various distros are vocally debated in a number of popular forums, the underlying GNU/Linux operating system is essentially the same, and for our purposes, there is little difference between one distro and another.

Like many open source projects, Mono follows the maxim of making frequent releases, and as a result, its version numbers are likely to change rapidly. Therefore, the versions that we list are unlikely to match the version numbers that you find. Similarly, the packages on the Web site that are available for distribution are likely to change in content as the version numbers increase. The net result of these factors is that imparting precise instructions from the static medium of this book is next to impossible, so we will try and describe the common principles that are needed for a Mono installation. Essentially, you need three basic parts for a working Mono installation: the garbage collector, the compiler, and the runtime. Any particular release of Mono may package all three elements together, while a subsequent release may not.

If you plan to install Mono for use by all of a computer's users, you should log in as the *root user*, because you need a number of administrative privileges to install Mono in the correct location. Start a console or terminal—we will use these terms interchangeably from now on—and issue the following command to create a folder for the files from the Mono site:

```
mkdir /usr/local/MonoDownload
```

Because we cannot second-guess where your shared folder is, or which machine you use for Internet access, you must make your own choices at this point, including whether you use a file manager or console commands. Navigate to the Mono Web site in your browser, and find the download area. Look for the section titled Source Code, and download the Mono runtime; this is listed with a version number, for example, `Mono Runtime 0.31`. Although strictly speaking, you only need the Mono runtime, those with an interest in such items could also download the source code for the Mono class libraries and the C# compiler.

The source code makes for an interesting read on a rainy day, and it's an excellent resource for hardcore cross-platform .NET developers to learn how things work.

Building the Mono Runtime

Now that you have your hot little tarball sitting expectantly on your hard drive, extract all the files from it using the following command, being careful to substitute your version numbers where appropriate:

```
tar -xzvf mono-0.31.tar.gz
```

This process should have produced a directory with all the required files for your build. Type **cd mono-0.31** to move into that directory, remembering to substitute your own version numbers. Then, execute the following commands to configure the installation, rebuild the source code, and finally install the end results:

```
./configure
make
make install
```

As each stage performs for you, you may occasionally see error messages as the screens whiz by. You only need to pay attention to error messages at the end of each process.

NOTE In addition to producing the Mono runtime, this process also gives you the C# complier, `mcs`.

GNU/Linux Installation Problems

JK Grrrr! When I tried to install Mono, I could not get the Mono to build without throwing an error—my make just kept on bombing out!

MJ Well, that's news to me. It worked absolutely fine on my machine.

JK I guess that makes me a Linux newbie. How can I get around this? I am not that concerned about rebuilding Mono from source code or fiddling with the build process; I just want to get the thing working.

MJ Well, you could check the Mono mailing list archive to see whether anyone else has the same problem, or you could install the Mono binaries.

JK Indeed. but we forget the easiest solution . . .

MJ . . . which is swishing in our high heels down the red carpet. Check out `http://www.ximian.com/products/redcarpet`.

Now that the installation is complete, a quick test for success is to issue the commands `mono --version` and `mcs --version`. If these two commands return version numbers to match your expectations, you are in business! At this point, you are either smiling or cursing. If you are cursing, you can seek further help from the Mono community, a Mono book, or the Mono Web site. If you have no interest in installing Portable.NET on a Mac and cannot wait to start coding, you can skip the next section.

Installing Portable.NET on Mac OS X

If you have reached this point *and* read the Linux installation section, award yourself two big, fat cross-platform crusader points! Congratulations! Your masochism/spirit of adventure (delete as applicable) can lead you to a brighter and more enlightened future—or not.

If you have never used Mac OS X, allow yourself an afternoon to play with it and take a system tour. Networking a Mac to a Windows network is relatively pain free, and connecting a Mac to a shared folder that's hosted on Windows is also pretty straightforward.

TIP The Apple Web site (`http://www.apple.com`) is a great place to find additional resources and help for Mac OS X. Additionally, the Applecare section of the Sherlock application can be useful for finding alternative Mac help online.

Before beginning the installation of Portable.NET, a Mac OS X 10.2 machine requires further work, that is, the installation of the Apple developer tools. Without installing the developer tools, you cannot configure, build, and install Portable.NET. Open the Finder, and navigate to your Applications folder (look for a shortcut button on the menu along the top of the Finder window), where you can find the Installers folder. Choose Installers ➤ Developer Tools, and look for the `Developer.mpkg` file. Double-clicking this file starts the installation of your prerequisite developer tools. A copy of these tools is also available, along with the latest updates, from the Apple Web site.

Portable.NET, or PNET as it is frequently referred to, is distributed via the Southern Storm Web site. On the Web site, you can find the usual Frequently Asked Questions section, complete with comprehensive answers and discussions. Similar to the Mono distribution, PNET is available as a set of tarballs. The Download and FAQs sections of the Web site describe how to install the software on a Linux platform. Because of Mac OS X's BSD roots and UNIX heritage, we now have enough instructions to hack the code into place. The main files that you need for installing are `treecc`, `pnet`, and `pnetlib`, although the site lists other available items.

TIP You can find the Southern Storm Web site at `http://www.southern-storm.com.au`.

In a routine that should be familiar to you if you followed the GNU/Linux instructions earlier in the chapter, you need to log in to Mac OS X as the root user.

Enabling the Mac OS X Root User and Logging In

If you're a Mac OS wizard, you can enable the root user by navigating the GUI to `Finder/Go/Applications/Utilities/NetInfo Manager`. If you're not a Mac wizard and you don't have the Finder running, click the Finder icon on the Dock (the toolbar at the bottom of the screen). Then, using the menu bar at the top of the desktop, choose Go ➤ Applications. Open the `Utilities` folder, and start the NetInfo Manager utility.

In the lower-left corner of the NetInfo Manager window, click the padlock icon once to allow edits. This opens another window, and you are prompted to enter the name and password of a user with administrative rights.

If you have Mac OS X 10.0 or Mac OS X 10.1, choose Domain ➤ Security ➤ Enable Root User. This step prompts you to set a password for the root user.

If you have Mac OS X 10.2, choose Security ➤ Enable Root User. This step prompts you to set a password for the root user.

To log in as the root user, follow these steps:

1. Log out.
2. Choose the Other option from the login screen.
3. Enter **root** as the username, and enter the password that you set up earlier.

From the download page, grab a copy of the `treecc`, `pnet`, and `pnetlib` tarballs. You should download them to your Home folder while logged in as root. For those who are interested, we are using `treecc-0.3.0.tar.gz`, `pnet-0.6.4.tar.gz`, and `pnetlib-0.6.4.tar.gz`, although you are unlikely to be using the same version numbers. The next stage involves opening a terminal and unpacking these three files into the relevant folders.

TIP To start a Mac OS X terminal, switch to (or launch) the Finder. Then, from the menu bar at the top of the Mac desktop, select Go ➤ Applications ➤ Utilities ➤ Terminal.

Switch to your terminal window, and type **ls** to get a listing of the contents of the current directory. Because building `pnetlib` depends on `pnet`, which in turn depends on `treecc`, the correct installation order, as shown in Figure 2-2, is `treecc` followed by `pnet` followed by `pnetlib`.

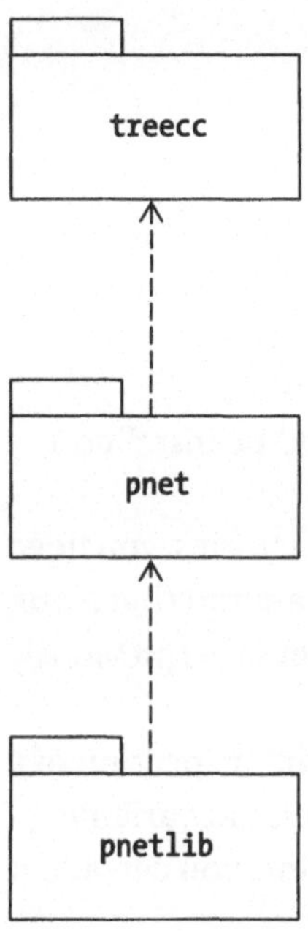

Figure 2-2. Portable.NET package dependencies

treecc

The treecc file is required by the Portable.NET compiler and should therefore be the first PNET package that you install. Remember to substitute your own version numbers, and use the tar command to unpack the files from the archive. Therefore, type **tar -xzvf treecc-0.3.0.tar.gz** . This process creates a directory of a similar name, treecc-0.3.0. Type **cd treecc-0.3.0** to move to the new folder. The following three lines of code configure, build, and install treecc, with each stage taking some time to complete:

```
./configure
make all
make install
```

Before proceeding with a similar routine for pnet, check the PATH environment variable. If treecc isn't in PATH, pnet will not install. Type **echo $PATH** to display the PATH in the terminal window. It should consist of at least the following paths:

- `/bin`
- `/usr/bin`
- `/sbin`
- `/usr/sbin`
- `/usr/local/bin` (This is the directory where `treecc` should be installed.)

If your `PATH` environment variable doesn't contain these directories, you need to add them. You can do this in several ways; one way is to edit a script that is run every time a login event occurs. To do so, we will use the text editor `vi`, as previously described, to edit the `/etc/csh.login` file.

To launch the editor and open the file, type **vi /etc/csh.login**. Inspection of a typical `csh.login` file reveals a line that sets up the `PATH` environment variable using a string of colon-delimited paths. If you do not find this line, you can add it by using the following command:

```
setenv PATH "/bin:/usr/bin:/sbin:/usr/sbin:/usr/local/bin:~/bin
```

If the line already exists, edit it to include the paths that are listed in the previous bullet points. Save and exit the file. Type **rehash** in your terminal window to refresh the `PATH` environment variable, which can be confirmed by again executing the `echo $PATH` command.

TIP In `~/myFolder`, the tilde symbol (~) is used as a substitute for the path to the current user's Home directory, so adding ~/myFolder to the path would add the current user's `/myFolder` directory. When written to the screen using the `echo` command while user JasonKing is logged in, it will appear as `/Users/jasonking/myFolder`.

To determine whether `treecc` is installed, type **treecc --version**. If you receive an error message, something has gone wrong. If you get a message that displays the version number, congratulations! You have successfully installed `treecc` and set up the `PATH` accordingly. Make yourself a cup of your favorite beverage and then proceed to install `pnet`.

Portable.NET: Runtime, Compiler, and Other Tools

As previously stated, PNET requires treecc to be installed successfully. Navigate back to your home folder and expand the pnet tarball by issuing the following command:

```
tar -xzvf pnet-0.6.4.tar.gz
```

As before, move to the new folder that has been created and type **cd pnet-0.6.4**. Then configure, build, and install, using the following commands:

```
./configure
make all
make install
```

If this process is successful, you should now have the Portable.NET runtime ilrun. Again, you can check the version by typing **ilrun --version**. If the installation process has failed, you can get further help by typing **madcow** (**./madcow**) from the pnet-0.6.4 directory. This command attempts to analyze your system and produces a log file for submission to the pnet user groups.

pnetlib: The PNET Library Package

Installing this package follows the same routine: Navigate to your Home folder, unpack the tarballs, and then configure, make, and install by issuing the following commands:

```
tar -xzvf pnetlib-0.6.4.tar.gz
cd pnetlib-0.6.4
./configure
make
make install
```

To conclude this section on Portable.NET installation, it is worth looking back and comparing the installation process with that of Mono. Both processes require root user permissions and follow similar steps. Although to the newcomer, these processes can feel a little daunting, it only takes one or two repeat performances before the principles stay with you. For continued development using these tools, familiarity is essential, because the open source community frequently releases new versions.

Building with Portable.NET Profiles

When building the Portable.NET packages, you have the option to build the packages in a variety of different configurations by calling the `configure` script with various switches. The most important switch is the `--with-profile=`*`profilename`* profile switch.

Each package directory contains a `profiles` directory that contains a configuration file for each available profile. By choosing a profile other than the default profile, that is, the *full* profile, you can customize the installation of Portable.NET to suit your own requirements, reducing the memory overhead and tweaking performance by reducing Portable.NET's feature set.

For example, by configuring `pnetlib` with the `./configure -with-profile=ecma` switch, you can build a fully ECMA-compliant version of the Portable.NET class libraries with no extra functionality. While using the `ecma` profile significantly reduces the available functionality, and might not be suitable for your general needs, it is perfect for exploring the ECMA specification or for ensuring that your programs only rely on functionality as defined in the ECMA standards.

Installing Microsoft .NET 1.1 on Windows

Microsoft .NET 1.1 is installed as part of Windows Server 2003. That works for us, but what if you have a previous version of Windows, such as Windows XP? Well, the Microsoft .NET Framework is freely available from the Microsoft Web site, as is the .NET Software Development Kit (SDK). The SDK contains the necessary tools, documentation, and samples for developing applications with the .NET Framework.

TIP To download version 1.1 of the Microsoft .NET Framework and the .NET SDK, point your browser to `http://www.microsoft.com/downloads`, where a search facility can take you to the framework version of your choice.

The site instructs you to download the redistributable set first as it provides the .NET Framework that the SDK then works with. The downloads are both large—the Framework is approximately 23 MB, and the SDK is approximately 100 MB. If you don't have a fast Internet connection, consider sourcing these files elsewhere; they are occasionally available with industry magazines.

The install processes may well reboot your machine several times as it updates the operating system. The usual warnings apply: Save your current work, and exit any applications before attempting the installations. When the installation is complete, you need to run either the `sdkvars.bat` or `corvars.bat` batch file from the SDK's `bin` directory, depending on your version of the SDK. The batch file adds the path of the various SDK tools to the relevant environment variables.

Goodbye Hello World

Itching to cut some code now that you've chosen your platforms and set them up? Good work; hold that enthusiasm! For this exercise, we introduce the bare-bones approach to .NET development, discussing the fundamental tools and the most common build options for three different CLI implementations. Rather than making our coding efforts easy for ourselves by using an integrated development environment (IDE), we are going to follow the simplistic approach of using plain-vanilla text editors and command-line build tools as follows:

- **Notepad:** We use Notepad for our Windows coding, Microsoft's `csc` for compiling (provided as part of the SDK installation), and Microsoft's CLR for the runtime environment.
- **KWrite:** We use KWrite for SuSE GNU/Linux coding, Mono's `mcs` for compiling, and `mono` for the runtime environment.
- **TextEdit:** We use TextEdit for Mac OS X coding, Portable.NET's `cscc` for compiling, and `ilrun` for the runtime environment.

Compiling a Simple Program

To start with, we get you familiar with the basic use of the compilers in our setup, and we set the scene for code later in the chapter.

NOTE The source code for these exercises can be found in the Downloads section of this book's Web site (`http://www.cross-platform.net`) and the Apress Web site (`http://www.apress.com`). On the Apress site, select this book from the list of titles and then look in the `Chapter_02/GetInfo` directory.

Create a new file called `GetInfo.cs`, and open the file using your editor. This simple class uses the console to write out a few simple strings: the operating system name, the version number of the operating system, and the current date. We define it to be a member of our own namespace with an appropriate no-nonsense name, `Crossplatform.NET.Chapter02`, as follows:

```
//Filename: GetInfo.cs
using System;

namespace Crossplatform.NET.Chapter02
{
    class GetInfo
    {
        static void Main()
        {
            GetInfo info = new GetInfo();
        }

        public GetInfo ()
        {
            Console.WriteLine("---------------------------------------");
            Console.WriteLine("Code in Main file.");
            Console.WriteLine("Operating system: " +
                                  Environment.OSVersion.Platform.ToString());
            Console.WriteLine("OS Version: " +
                                  Environment.OSVersion.Version.ToString());
            Console.WriteLine("Today's date is: " +
                                   DateTime.Today.ToString());
        }
    }
}
```

Now, depending on how much you want to play, you could either compile your code once or compile it on each of your target machines to familiarize yourself with each platform. We will be using `csc.exe` for Microsoft .NET, `mcs` for Mono, and `cscc` for Portable.NET, as follows:

```
C:\MS.NET> csc GetInfo.cs
mono@linux:~ % mcs GetInfo.cs
pnet@macosx:~ % cscc GetInfo.cs
```

Console Prompts

When showing code examples, we have elected to use prompt styles that make it easy to determine which operating system and CLI combination we are referring to. Although your prompts will undoubtedly be different than ours, the prompts we will use for the rest of the book are as follows:

- **For Windows:** `C:\MS.NET>`
- **For GNU/Linux:** `mono@linux:~ %`
- **For Mac OS X:** `pnet@macosx:~ %`

If you used Portable.NET's `cscc` compiler, as shown in the previous code, you will find that the compiler has given you a file called `a.out.exe`. Do not be alarmed; this is normal behavior for `cscc`. Later you will see how to specify a name for your executable file. If you used Mono's `mcs` or Microsoft's `csc`, you should now have a file called `GetInfo.exe`.

Regardless of how many times you have compiled your code on however many platforms, you should now run the resultant CLI code on each of them; after all, that is what this book is all about. Under the Windows console, type in the name of the executable file, optionally including the `.exe` file extension. The operating system passes the file to the CLR, so you don't need to specify anything additional. Screen output from running the program should appear as follows:

```
C:\MS.NET> GetInfo.exe
--------------------------------------
Code in Main file.
Operating system: Win32NT
OS Version: 5.2.3790.0
Today's date is:
08/07/2003 00:00:00
```

For both Mono and Portable.NET, you must pass the name of the CLI executable to the respective runtime program, as follows:

```
mono@linux:~ % mono GetInfo.exe
-----------------------------------------------------
Code in Main file.
Operating system: 128
OS Version 5.1.2600.0
Today's date is:
07/08/2003 00:00:00
```

Implicit Invocation of IL Programs on GNU/Linux

As you have seen, running your code under Mono or Portable.NET is pretty straightforward: Invoking `mono mycode.exe` or `ilrun mycode.exe` does the trick. However, it is not quite as straightforward as using the .NET Framework on Windows, where you simply type the executable file's name to explicitly invoke the runtime engine.

The good news is that if you're running a recent version of GNU/Linux, you can register either `mono` or `ilrun` to automatically execute PE/COFF executables files. This allows you to run your IL binaries without explicitly invoking the runtime engine. For details on how to configure GNU/Linux to work implicitly with Portable.NET, visit the PNET web site, or for Mono, drop by `http://www.atoker.com/mono`.

Finally, a quick peek at Portable.NET under Mac OS X reveals the following:

```
pnet@macosx:~ % ilrun a.out.exe
--------------------------------------
Code in Main file.
Operating system: Unix
OS Version: 5.1.2600.0
Today's date is:
07/18/2003 00:00:00
```

"Success!" you cry—or something similar. Taking a closer look through the output from each CLI implementation, however, reveals some interesting points:

- **When running Mono on GNU/Linux, the operating system is usefully listed as 128.** Although this is obviously not as helpful as Microsoft .NET and PNET, which respectively displayed `Win32NT` and `Unix`, it is due to the limited number of values in the `System.PlatformID` enumeration. Because Microsoft's implementation of the enumeration only contains values for `Win32NT`, `Win32S`, `Win32Windows`, and `Win32CE`, the Mono project decided not to break binary compatibility with Microsoft .NET and therefore didn't add extra entries to the enumeration. In contrast, PNET's `PlatformID` enumeration has an extra value, `Unix`, which means a more helpful platform can be shown, although code that is written against the `PlatformID.Unix` value only works on PNET.

- **When running the program on PNET and Mono, the OS Version is listed as 5.1.2600.0.** Because we're running PNET and Mono on different operating systems, it's odd that they display the same version number. In fact, 5.1.2600.0 is the version number for Windows XP; both Mono and PNET have their `Environment.OSVersion` property hard-coded to this value. While this means that PNET and Mono display the same version number regardless of the operating system that they're running on, they have been implemented like this because the concept of a four-part version number is a Windows concept that doesn't cleanly translate to other operating systems. This means that while you can use the `OSVersion` property, it is practically meaningless in a cross-platform context, and its use should generally be avoided.

- **Both PNET and Mono display a different date format than Microsoft .NET.** Despite the three operating systems being configured to display dates in the British format of `dd/mm/yyyy`, PNET and Mono displayed the date in `mm/dd/yyyy` format. This is due to the current versions of PNET and Mono not implementing environment-based date formatting; they use U.S.-formatted dates unless specifically asked to do otherwise.

So, are we just finding fault where there is no need to find fault, or are these serious problems with real consequences? Not really, on both counts. Although these issues are potentially problematical, like most open source software, frequent release cycles mean that issues such as these are often resolved in a short timescale. Mono and Portable.NET will almost certainly have progressed by the time you read this, and the date formatting issue may well have been fixed.

The issue of the `PlatformID` enumeration is a different type of beast. In an ideal world, you would never need to determine which platform a .NET program was running on, but as you'll see in a number of the later chapters, it's often a very useful facility to have. Ensuring that the `PlatformID` enumeration can handle all the different platforms that .NET will one day run on, while maintaining binary compatibility between different CLI implementations, is a difficult issue that must be addressed by all the major players, including Microsoft, PNET, and Mono. This issue may need to be addressed in a future version of the ECMA standards.

The PlatformID Enumeration

With the current state of the `PlatformID` enumeration, you can only differentiate between Windows-based and non-Windows-based operating systems. Making this distinction programmatically across all CLI implementations is a useful technique, and it can be achieved in a couple of different ways. One way is to use the `IsWindows()` method, as follows:

```
bool IsWindows()
{
    PlatformID platform = Environment.OSVersion.Platform;
    return (platform == PlatformID.Win32NT ||
               platform == PlatformID.Win32S ||
               platform == PlatformID.Win32Windows  ||
               platform == PlatformID.WinCE);
}
```

One problem with this approach is that it can fail as additional versions of Windows are released. To see a different way of achieving the same effect, Chapter 4 demonstrates an alternative approach to solving this problem.

To conclude this section, we illustrate the use of the `/out:` option with each of the compilers to specify a new filename for our compiled code, as follows:

```
C:\MS.NET> csc /out:MyNewName.exe GetInfo.cs
mono@linux:~ % mcs /out: MyNewName.exe GetInfo.cs
pnet@macosx:~ % cscc /out: MyNewName.exe GetInfo.cs
```

From this point forward, we will be using the `/out:` option for most of our builds. A number of advanced options are also available for each compiler, which can be viewed by running each of the compilers with the `/?` switch.

Figure 2-3 shows a comparison of the building and running process for a piece of code.

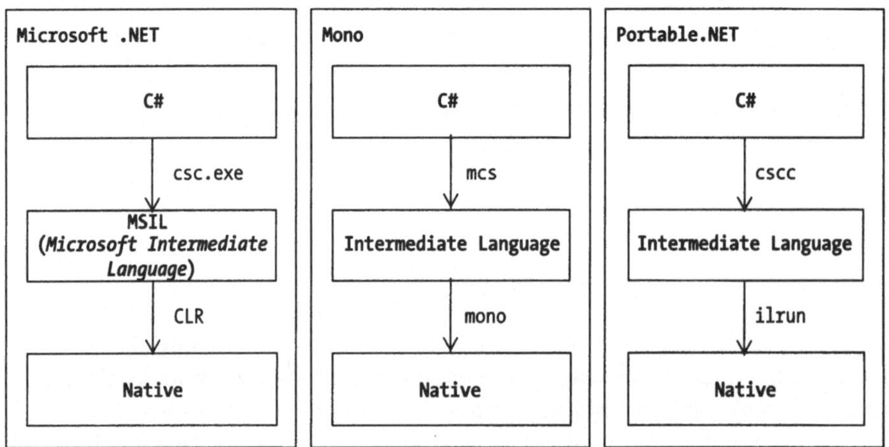

Figure 2-3. A comparison of the build and run processes

Compiling Two or More Files

For users of integrated development environments, the concept of the project file will be familiar. Essentially, a project file is a way of grouping details of a project, such as source code filenames, resource filenames, and so on.

NOTE The source code for these exercises can be found in the `Chapter_02/GetInfo2` directory.

When using the command-line interfaces for the compilers, there are no easy-to-use project files, so we must examine how to compile code from more than one file into a single executable file. To achieve this, we add some simple code to another file. Inspecting the following code, we can see that it is just a minor variation on the previous code:

```
//Filename: TimeInfo.cs
using System;
namespace Crossplatform.NET.Chapter02
{
    class TimeInfo // code that resides in a different file
    {
        public TimeInfo()
        {
            Console.WriteLine("--------------------------------------");
            Console.WriteLine("Code residing in a separate .cs file:");
            Console.WriteLine("The time now is: " + DateTime.Now.ToString());
        }
    }
}
```

To call this code, open the `GetInfo.cs` file and edit the constructor. Then add a new `callOthers()` method, as follows:

```
//Filename: GetInfo.cs
...
        public GetInfo()
        {
            Console.WriteLine("--------------------------------------");
            Console.WriteLine("Code in Main file.");
            Console.WriteLine("Operating system: " +
                              Environment.OSVersion.Platform.ToString());
            Console.WriteLine("OS Version: " +
                              Environment.OSVersion.Version.ToString());
            Console.WriteLine("Today's date is: " +
                              DateTime.Today.ToString());
            Console.WriteLine("About to call other methods...");
            this.callOthers();
        }

        private void callOthers() // new method
        {
            TimeInfo time = new TimeInfo();
        }
```

To compile both files into one executable file (.EXE), we simply list them both at the end of the command line, as follows:

```
C:\MS.NET> csc /out:GetInfo2.exe GetInfo.cs TimeInfo.cs
mono@linux:~ % mcs /out:GetInfo2.exe GetInfo.cs TimeInfo.cs
pnet@macosx:~ % cscc /out:GetInfo2.exe GetInfo.cs TimeInfo.cs
```

The general form for compiling multiple files is as follows:

```
<compiler> /out:<DesiredExeName> <source1.cs> <source2.cs> <source3.cs> // etc
```

You can also use wildcard compilation in the following manner:

```
<compiler> /out:<DesiredExeName> *.cs
```

Using this wildcard technique, the following compilation commands are now a bit simpler:

```
C:\MS.NET> csc /out:GetInfo2.exe *.cs
mono@linux:~ % mcs /out:GetInfo2.exe *.cs
pnet@macosx:~ % cscc /out:GetInfo2.exe *.cs
```

Feel free to run your shiny new code using your choice of CLR.

Compiling Two or More Files and a Library

This exercise builds on the previous two to demonstrate how to reference an external library from our finished executable file. Once again, the code is simple but further demonstrates the points that were already made about a platform's date format, and the code serves as a mechanism to illustrate the use of libraries.

NOTE The source code for these exercises can be found in the `Chapter_02/GetInfo3` directory.

To realistically emulate real-life library usage, we create a new namespace for this library, `Crossplatform.NET.Chapter02.Library`, as follows:

```
//Filename: LongShortDates.cs
using System;
namespace Crossplatform.NET.Chapter02.Library
{
    public class DateStringLibrary
    {
        public static void GetTestString()
        {
            Console.WriteLine("---------------------------------------");
            Console.WriteLine("Library code in DLL:");
            System.DateTime dt = new DateTime(2003,12,25);
            Console.WriteLine(dt.ToLongDateString());
            Console.WriteLine(dt.ToShortDateString());
        }
    }
}
```

Now that we have the code for the library, we must compile it into a DLL file. We give the resultant `dll` file a sensible name, `LongShortDates.dll`, using the `/out:` option, and we specify that the compiler should build a library by specifying the `/target:library` option, as follows:

```
C:\MS.NET> csc /out:LongShortDates.dll /target:library LongShortDates.cs
mono@linux:~ % mcs /out:LongShortDates.dll /target:library LongShortDates.cs
pnet@macosx:~ % cscc /out:LongShortDates.dll /target:library LongShortDates.cs
```

As with executable files, you can combine more than one file into a library by listing the files that you want to combine or by using wildcards.

To take advantage of the library, we must include the correct namespace in the client code. The complete listing for `GetInfo.cs` is then as follows:

```
//Filename: GetInfo.cs
using System;
using Crossplatform.NET.Chapter02.Library;

namespace Crossplatform.NET.Chapter02
{
    class GetInfo
    {
        static void Main()
        {
            GetInfo info = new GetInfo();
        }

        public GetInfo ()
        {
            Console.WriteLine("--------------------------------------");
            Console.WriteLine("Code in Main file.");
            Console.WriteLine("Operating system: " +
                              Environment.OSVersion.Platform.ToString());
            Console.WriteLine("OS Version: " +
                              Environment.OSVersion.Version.ToString());
            Console.WriteLine("Today's date is:" +
                              DateTime.Today.ToString());
            this.callOthers();
        }

        private void callOthers() // new method
        {
            TimeInfo time = new TimeInfo();
            DateStringLibrary.GetTestString();
        }
    }
}
```

The final piece in this jigsaw puzzle is for us to build the latest code and reference the new library. Calling library methods is not as simple as just including the correct namespace in the client code; the compiler also needs to know how to link to the library. We instruct the compiler to reference an external library by using the `/r:` (reference) option for all three compilers, as follows:

```
C:\MS.NET> csc /out:GetInfo3.exe /r:LongShortDates.dll GetInfo.cs TimeInfo.cs
mono@linux:~ % mcs /out:GetInfo3.exe /r:LongShortDates.dll GetInfo.cs TimeInfo.cs
pnet@macosx:~ % cscc /out:GetInfo3.exe /r:LongShortDates.dll GetInfo.cs TimeInfo.cs
```

For brevity, we only show the results on one platform—Portable.NET on the Mac—although running the executable file on your chosen platform should give a similar screen output. Use the following code to launch your freshly baked program:

```
pnet@macosx:~ % ilrun GetInfo3.exe
-----------------------------------------
Code in Main file.
Operating system: Unix
OS Version: 5.1.2600.0
Today's date is:
02/17/2004 14:12:01 PM +0
About to call other methods...
-----------------------------------------
Code residing in a separate .cs file:
The time now is:
02/17/2004 14:12:01 PM +0
-----------------------------------------
Library code in DLL:
Thursday, 25 December 2003-12-25
12/25/2003
```

Summary

You're basking in the flickering light of three or more monitors. Lightning strikes, thunder roars, and your eyebrows cast ominous, arched shadows across your forehead like cerebral trademark stigmata, reminiscent of a fast-food empire. You have experienced the simplicity of .NET cross-platform development in your own laboratory.

"Igor, another mouse, quickly now!"

Give yourself a fat slice of pizza for each environment that you have set up—a whole pizza, with extra cheese, if you have all three environments on one machine. So far, you have learned how to compile an executable file from a single source code file and again from multiple files. You have learned how to instruct the compiler to give your efforts the name that you want. This was followed by compiling code into a library, followed by building an executable file that then used the resultant DLL file.

It is not quite complete though, is it? Surely it cannot be that simple? Although that code you snacked upon was satisfying, you are hungry and you want the next meal. The truth is, of course, that it's not that simple. You've already seen issues with .NET implementations—such as the limited return values for `System.Environment.OSVersion.Platform`—that could be the waiter's blistered thumb in your cross-platform soup. You may need better eatin' irons for your next chow down: What about debuggers and development environments?

Of course, numerous IDEs are available that can drastically simplify your .NET development efforts. They are well worth hunting down, although your choice is likely to depend as much on your personal preference as on your development platform.

If you're using Windows as your main development platform, Microsoft's Visual Studio .NET is an advanced and convenient environment for programming and debugging code.

A popular alternative is the open source and highly extensible Eclipse IDE, which runs on a variety of platforms. Although Eclipse is best known as a Java IDE, when used with the Improve C# plug-in, it becomes an excellent tool for developing C# code on your platform of choice. One useful aspect of Eclipse is that it is highly configurable and relatively easy to set up to interact with different CLI implementations. This is a real boon for developing and testing .NET programs on more than one CLI implementation.

NOTE More information and downloads for the Eclipse IDE can be found at the following Web site:

`http://www.eclipse.org`

The Improve C# plug-in can be found at the following Web site:

`http://www.improve-technologies.com`

Another choice for developers who are using Windows is the open source SharpDevelop IDE, which is written in C# and includes a number of advanced features, such as a graphical forms designer for C# and VB.NET, code completion for C# and VB.NET, and a C#-to-VB.NET code converter.

NOTE A Windows installer and source code for SharpDevelop can be downloaded from `http://www.icsharpcode.net/OpenSource/SD/`.

For those who prefer to use UNIX-based operating systems, the MonoDevelop project is a port of SharpDevelop that replaces the use of `System.Windows.Forms` with Gtk#. Although MonoDevelop is only in its infancy, its reliance on Gtk# means that it is likely to become the most popular IDE for Mono developers.

NOTE More details on MonoDevelop can be found at `http://www.monodevelop.com`.

TIP If you want to read an excellent case study on developing complex GUI applications using .NET, *Inside SharpDevelop*, by Bernhard Spuida and Christoph Wille (Apress, 2004), serves as an excellent investigation into what makes a modern IDE tick.

CHAPTER 3

Cross-Platform Pitfalls

"If, for some reason, you want to feel completely out of step with the rest of the world, the only thing to do is sit around a cocktail lounge in the afternoon . . . ."

—Lizabeth Scott in *Pitfall* (1948)

EVERYTHING YOU'VE SEEN so far might make .NET look like the quintessential cross-platform tool, but is it really that easy to write cross-platform programs for .NET? While we would love to say yes and tell you that you now know everything there is to know about cross-platform .NET development, the simplicity of Chapter 2's cross-platform programs is a bit of an illusion that's generated by the simplicity of the programs themselves. After all, we don't want you to run screaming into the sunset—perhaps by the next chapter or the end of the book, but definitely not just yet.

So having given a brief overview of the .NET architecture, described the installation of three different CLIs on three different platforms, and introduced some very simple cross-platform programs, it's now time to delve a bit deeper into the workings of the CLI implementations and trawl them to see how certain incongruities can manifest themselves in ways that discerning cross-platform developers should probably avoid. Along the way, we look at some intermediate language, some Portable.NET source code, and a cool feature that's offered by Mono. We finish by presenting a simple solution for application data storage.

Examining IL Code

Although you've now read about cross-platform this and cross-platform that, we haven't fully defined what we mean by *cross-platform software*, which is an omission we will now correct before digressing too far into an opaque medley of verbiage. Sure, we noted in Chapter 1 that cross-platform suggests something that works with a variety of CLI implementations, operating systems, and hardware architectures, but what exactly do we mean by the word *software*?

Microsoft's Encarta dictionary defines software as *"Computer programs and applications . . . that can be run on a particular computer system."*[1] This is a fine definition, but even although Microsoft achieved dominance through a particular operating system, given the title of this book and the nature of .NET, "particular computer system" is perhaps a little short-sighted. Of course, computer programs can usually be considered in one of two forms: source code or binary code. In the case of .NET, you have three forms to consider: Source code begets IL binary code, or assemblies, which in turn begets native binary code. Native binary code is, for obvious reasons, not what we mean by cross-platform software, so when we say *cross-platform software*, are we talking about cross-platform source code or cross-platform assemblies?

The beauty of .NET is that we can mean both source code and IL binary code. While source code can generally be moved between platforms and compiled by different compilers for different CLI implementations, as demonstrated in Chapter 2, .NET assemblies can also be created with one CLI and then run inside a different runtime environment.

Writing Portable Code

As shown in the previous chapter, writing portable source code is as simple as opening your chosen text editor and banging away at the keyboard until you have some valid C# code. To begin this exploration of portable binary code, we introduce some rather simple source code that, when compiled, returns the name of the host computer.

NOTE The source code samples for this chapter can be found in the Downloads section of this book's Web site (`http://www.cross-platform.net`) and the Apress Web site (`http://www.apress.com`). The code for this section can be found in the `Chapter_03/ComputerName` directory.

The code for this example is then as follows:

1. *Encarta® World English Dictionary* ©, 1999 Microsoft Corporation. All rights reserved. Developed for Microsoft by Bloomsbury Publishing PLC.

```
//Filename: ComputerName.cs
using System;
using System.IO;
using System.Net;

namespace Crossplatform.Net.Chapter03
{
    class ComputerName
    {
        public static void Main()
        {
            //Could have used Environment.MachineName
            String hostName = Dns.GetHostName();
            Console.WriteLine(hostName);
        }
    }
}
```

It's extremely unlikely that this is the most complex of C# programs you've ever seen, and the code's most interesting feature is the use of the static `System.Net.Dns.GetHostName()` method to carry out the program's real work.

To compile the source code using Mono under GNU/Linux, use the following command:

```
mono@linux:~ % mcs /out:mono_ComputerName.exe ComputerName.cs
```

To compile the same program using Microsoft .NET under Windows, use the following command:

```
C:\MS.NET> csc /out:msnet_ComputerName.exe ComputerName.cs
```

Finally, for those fruity readers who have a preference for all things Apple, you can compile the code under Portable.NET on Mac OS X as follows:

```
pnet@macosx:~ % cscc /out:pnet_ComputerName.exe ComputerName.cs
```

As should be expected, the code compiles quickly under each platform, but before we run the programs, we take a little detour.

While some readers might think this is indeed rocket science at its finest, you're more likely to have a nagging doubt circling 'round the back of your mind. After all, we promised portable IL binary code at the beginning of this section and proceeded to demonstrate how to compile some source code. As they would complain in England: "That's not cricket!" But fear not. Having compiled the source code, we can now get on with the matter at hand, and more importantly, we can do it with no further references to boring, archaic sports.

A .NET by Any Other Name

JK Why do you keep using the phrase *CLI implementation* instead of *.NET*?

MJ Because the ECMA standards describe the Common Language Infrastructure with no mention of .NET. Because Microsoft's implementation of the CLI is called the Microsoft .NET Framework, the term *.NET* is often used to refer to Microsoft's CLI implementation.

JK So are you saying that we should only use *.NET* when referring to Microsoft's implementation?

MJ Ideally yes, but because *CLI* is a little formal, I reckon it's okay to use .NET to refer to all the CLI implementations. After all, as Shakespeare noted, what's in a name?

Disassembling Portable Code

Now that you've seen and compiled the source code on each platform, it is time to halt the cogs of creativity and do a little reverse engineering to help us analyze what happens to source code behind the scenes.

Each of our chosen CLI implementations comes with a tool to disassemble assemblies into human-readable IL, which makes it easy to do a quick comparison. While this is not something that most .NET developers are likely to do on a frequent basis, it is an ideal way to see how the different compilers generate IL code.

To disassemble the `mono_ComputerName.exe` assembly on GNU/Linux, use the `monodis` tool with the following command:

```
mono@linux:~ % monodis --output=Mono.il mono_ComputerName.exe
```

To carry out the disassembly on Windows, use the `ildasm` program that comes with the .NET Framework SDK and that can be invoked as follows:

```
C:\MS.NET> ildasm /out:MS.NET.il msnet_ComputerName.exe
```

Finally, to disassemble on Mac OS X, use the Portable.NET disassembler, which is also called `ildasm`, as follows:

```
pnet@macosx:~ % ildasm /out:pnet.il pnet_ComputerName.exe
```

Although each of the disassemblers has a variety of switches, for our simplistic purposes, it is sufficient to just specify the name of the output file.

Now before we peek at the output files, it is worth reminding ourselves that assemblies do not just contain IL, but they are full of metadata. For the purposes of our investigation, we ignore the majority of the metadata declarations—which means that you'll have to skip the initial smattering of lines when inspecting your `.il` files—and we instead concentrate on the program's payload.

So here's the first chunk of code from the `Mono.il` file, which consists of the declaration of the `Crossplatform.NET.Chapter03` namespace and the `ComputerName` class:

```
.namespace Crossplatform.NET.Chapter03
{
  .class private auto ansi beforefieldinit 'ComputerName'
      extends [mscorlib]System.Object
```

The `MS.NET.il` file contains the following code:

```
.namespace Crossplatform.NET.Chapter03
{
  .class private auto ansi beforefieldinit ComputerName
      extends [mscorlib]System.Object
```

Finally, the `pnet.il` file contains the following code:

```
.namespace Crossplatform.NET.Chapter03
{
  .class private auto ansi ComputerName extends [mscorlib]System.Object
```

These fragments look very similar—indeed the code fragments that are generated by Mono and Microsoft .NET are identical—but the code fragment from Portable.NET is ever so slightly different. Apart from a missing carriage return, which is just a minor aesthetic difference, the class declaration is missing the `beforefieldinit` attribute, which is present in both of the other files.

What's in a Name: Apple Macintosh

Legend has it that Apple gained its corporate name when Steve Jobs threatened to name the young company unless the employees could think of a name by the end of the day. None of them dared. But while Steve Jobs' choice certainly showed some marketing savvy, it was by no means a harmonious moniker. When the Macintosh computer was first promoted as having music-playing capabilities, the company was promptly sued for $43 million by the Beatles' record company, Apple Records, because Apple had earlier promised not to use the name Apple for marketing any music-related products.

With one expensive legal wrangling under its belt, Apple was lucky that the Macintosh's creator, Jef Raskin, had been shrewd enough to avoid enraging the audio manufacturing company McIntosh, by creatively reworking the name of his favorite eating apple and naming his creation the Macintosh. The company's marketing department and shareholders were probably quite lucky that Jef's taste buds did not have a preference for Granny Smiths or Winter Bananas.

While it's not the place of a technical book to moralize on the legal dynamics of the world, the moral of this story is that a Macintosh a day won't keep the money-grabbing hippies at bay.

At first sight, this difference will not mean much to anyone apart from the odd programmer with an intimate knowledge of IL. According to the CLI standard,[2] the `beforefieldinit` attribute determines whether the runtime needs to call a type's type initializer (the C# `static` constructor) before any members of the type are used. The presence of this attribute indicates that the runtime has some leeway in when it calls the type's initializer, so this attribute can be interpreted as a performance enhancement.

Indeed, looking at the source code for our class, you can see that it only has one `static` method, `Main()`, and no `static` fields. Because type initializers are used to initialize `static` field values, the runtime must guarantee that it is called before any other code that references the `static` fields is executed. This means that while the different IL code fragments have slightly different semantics, in this case, the fragments are functionally equivalent, and the presence of `beforefieldinit` in Mono and Microsoft .NET's code can be considered a minor optimization.

While it would be easy to think negatively of Portable.NET for the lack of `beforefieldinit` optimization, it is worth noting that each compiler carries out different optimizations depending on switches that are specified on the command

2. *Common Language Infrastructure (CLI), Partition II, section 9.5.3, ECMA 335* (European Computer Manufacturers Association, 2001).

line. It would be pointless to start judging the performance of the different compilers without carrying out an in-depth, objective analysis.

The point worth remembering is that although the CLI standard provides a uniform blueprint that each implementation must adhere to, the standard does not precisely indicate the implementation details—or if you'll excuse a spiritual analogy, there is always more than one path up the mountain.

Now take a look at the IL code for the `Main()` method. You can see a similar situation, with the code being fundamentally the same, albeit with some minor deviations.

We start with the `Mono.il` file, as follows:

```
.method public static
    default void 'Main' ()  cil managed
    {
        // Method begins at RVA 0x20f4
        .entrypoint
        // Code size 13 (0xd)
        .maxstack 3
        .locals init (
              string V_0)
        IL_0000: call string class [System]'System.Net.Dns'::'GetHostName'()
        IL_0005: stloc.0
        IL_0006: ldloc.0
        IL_0007: call void class [mscorlib]'System.Console'::'WriteLine'(string)
        IL_000c: ret
    } // end of method ComputerName::default void 'Main' ()
```

We won't go into too much detail about the IL commands, but the feature that's worth keeping an eye on is the `.maxstack` declaration. In this case, this declaration has a value of 3 and defines the maximum number of items that the method might push onto the evaluation stack.

The code in the `MS.NET.il` file is similar to Mono's code, but it has a `.maxstack` value of 1. In a similar vein to the `beforefieldinit` declaration, the lower `.maxstack` value is a performance tweak, instructing the runtime that at most one item will be pushed onto the evaluation stack. The `MS.NET.il` file is as follows:

```
.method public hidebysig static void
    Main() cil managed
    {
      .entrypoint
      // Code size       13 (0xd)
      .maxstack  1
      .locals init (string V_0)
```

```
    IL_0000:  call       string [System]System.Net.Dns::GetHostName()
    IL_0005:  stloc.0
    IL_0006:  ldloc.0
    IL_0007:  call       void [mscorlib]System.Console::WriteLine(string)
    IL_000c:  ret
  } // end of method ComputerName::Main
```

Finally, the code in pnet.il is almost identical to the two previous examples, but it deviates by initializing the string in the .local init declaration with some slightly different but functionally equivalent syntax, as follows:

```
.method public static hidebysig void Main() cil managed
    {
        // Start of method header: 2050
        .entrypoint
        .maxstack  1
        .locals    init (class System.String)
    ?L205c:
        call    class System.String [System]System.Net.Dns::GetHostName()
        stloc.0
        ldloc.0
        call    void [mscorlib]System.Console::WriteLine(class System.String)
        ret
    }
```

Having now looked at IL that was produced by three different compilers, we know that each can produce some remarkably similar-looking code. This is exactly what we wanted, and it's the reason that Microsoft wanted the .NET CLI to be standardized.

NOTE Those readers who have actively been following this chapter by looking at their own IL code will probably have noticed that the code contains another method that we neglected to mention; this method is the default constructor for the ComputerName class. While we don't want to belittle the importance of constructors, we leave a comparison of the IL code for interested readers.

Testing the Code

Following our quick diversion through the realms of reverse engineering, it is time to feel the crackle of programming power emanating from your fingertips and run the compiled programs on their associated CLI implementations.

To run the `mono_ComputerName.exe` program using Mono under GNU/Linux, use the following command:

```
mono@linux:~ % mono mono_ComputerName.exe
linux
```

To run the `msnet_ComputerName.exe` program using Microsoft .NET, run the following command, which in this case reveals our personal penchant for single-malt Scottish whisky:

```
C:\MS.NET> msnet_ComputerName.exe
GLENBURGIE
```

To run the `pnet_ComputerName.exe` program under Portable.NET on Mac OS X, use the following command:

```
pnet@macosx:~ % ilrun pnet_ComputerName.exe
macosx
```

Although the results of running the programs are different on every machine, you can relax in the knowledge that it is neither due to significant differences in the IL code that's generated by the compilers nor is it due to operational differences in the runtime implementations. The results are simply different because each of our laboratory computers has a different name.

Porting Portable Code

Having compiled, disassembled, analyzed, and tested the code, we have done every sensible thing that we could think of, apart from moving the assemblies between the different platforms. Nonetheless, while we have shown how each CLI implementation generates and runs IL code, we have so far neglected to mention the physical format of the assemblies themselves. This is obviously of some significance when moving binary files from one platform to another.

The CLI standard[3] specifies that assemblies should be stored in an extended form of the Microsoft Portable Executable (PE) format. This format, which is used for Windows exe and dll files, is often referred to as the *PE/COFF format*. By relying on a format that extends the PE/COFF format, .NET assemblies are also de facto Windows modules. On the one hand, this simplifies .NET integration with Windows, but on the other hand, it complicates integration with non-Windows operating systems.

The Portable Power of Prophesy

Although the word *Portable* in the name *Portable Executable* refers to architecture agnosticism, the file format was never originally intended to be portable across different operating systems.

When PE files were first introduced in Windows NT, it was Microsoft's intention that the file format be portable across all 32-bit versions of Windows that ran on a variety of architectures, including *x*86, Alpha, and MIPS.[4] As 32-bit Windows grew to dominate the operating system marketplace, the *x*86 architecture gradually became ubiquitous. This situation not only led to the coining of the name *Wintel* but also to the demise of Windows support for the more exotic hardware architectures.

However, with the recent growth in popularity of portable computers, Windows CE has become available on a number of architectures, and with 64-bit architectures on the horizon from both AMD and Intel, the number of architectures that run Windows—and therefore rely on PE files—is set to increase significantly.

Coupling the growth of Windows CE with the cross-platform aspirations of the CLI, it would appear that fate has decreed that the PE format lives up to its name and will fittingly be used on far more operating systems and architectures than its designers could have ever dreamed.

Even with the checkered past of the PE/COFF file format, assemblies can generally be copied from one platform to another with no notable side effects, because each CLI implementation is designed to load assemblies that are stored in the extended PE/COFF file format.

---

3. *Common Language Infrastructure (CLI), Partition II, section 24*, ECMA 335 (European Computer Manufacturers Association, 2001).

4. Prasad Dabak, Sandeep Phadke, and Milind Borate, *Undocumented Windows NT* (New York: Wiley Publishing, 2000).

To demonstrate that the assemblies created earlier in the chapter are portable, we will copy each of the assemblies onto a different platform as follows:

- The mono_ComputerName.exe file is copied from the GNU/Linux machine to the Windows computer.
- The msnet_ComputerName.exe file is copied from the Windows computer to our Mac OS X machine.
- The macos_ComputerName.exe file is copied from the Mac OS X machine to the GNU/Linux machine.

Although this only covers three of six possible permutations, it nevertheless suffices for the purpose of this demonstration.

The pnet_ComputerName.exe program can then be run using Mono under GNU/Linux with the following command:

```
mono@linux:~ % mono pnet_ComputerName.exe
linux
```

To run the mono_ComputerName.exe program using Microsoft .NET, use the following command:

```
C:\MS.NET> mono_ComputerName.exe
GLENBURGIE
```

Finally, to demonstrate the msnet_ComputerName.exe program running under Portable.NET on Mac OS X, use the following command:

```
pnet@macosx:~ % ilrun msnet_ComputerName.exe
macosx
```

Once again, the results of running the programs are different depending on the name of the machine that they are running on, but more importantly, they are the same as when we previously ran the programs.

Although we just ran each of the programs in a CLI environment that is different from the one in which they were compiled, they still worked as expected. This proves that assemblies can be used across operating systems, machine architectures, and CLI implementations, and that IL binary files are therefore inherently portable.

Using Native Image Files

While we're on the subject of portable IL binary code, we want to mention *native image files*, which are binary files containing native code that has been precompiled from .NET assemblies.

CAUTION The original phrase for generating native image files was *prejitting* as the compilation to native code occurs before Just-In-Time compilation. You should be aware that some .NET literature and advocates still use this term.

Because the files have been precompiled, you don't need to translate them from IL code at runtime. This helps reduce application startup time and potentially allows the compiler to perform optimizations to increase runtime performance. However, because native image files contain machine code, they are obviously tied to a specific platform and are therefore something that cross-platform developers should be particularly aware of.

Although the native image files are stored in the file system, it's still necessary to keep the original assembly file, because the native image files won't contain the assembly's metadata, as shown in Figure 3-1.

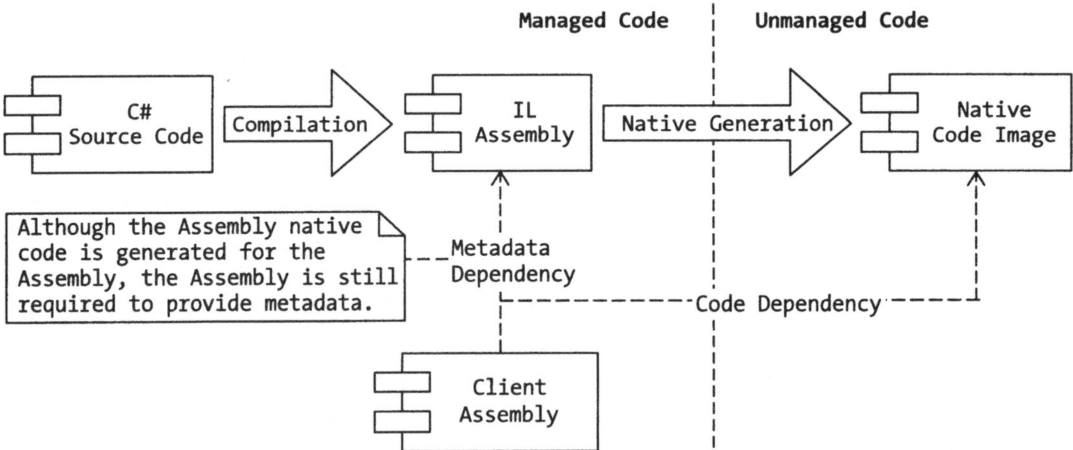

Figure 3-1. Native image generation

Furthermore, precompiled assemblies are presently not tied to a particular Application Domain instance, and while this minimizes memory requirements, it also inhibits a number of the JIT optimizations. This means that precompiled assemblies may execute slower than their JIT–compiled counterparts.

NOTE Native image files can be created on Microsoft .NET using the Native Image Generator program, `Ngen.exe`, that comes with the .NET Framework SDK, or they can be created on Mono using `mono`'s Ahead Of Time compilation switch; see the mono(1) man page for details.

Because the PNET runtime currently uses interpretation rather than compilation, there's currently no way for Portable.NET to create native image files, although Southern Storm's new `libjit` project might help provide PNET with this functionality in the future.

Neither of these issues means that cross-platform projects cannot use native image files but only that particular care should be taken when considering their use. One useful guideline is to never copy native image files from one machine to another, but rather to copy the underlying assemblies and then create the native image files on the target machine. This is good practice because assemblies are .NET's fundamental unit of deployment. This practice also ensures that the latest version of the assembly is present on each machine, which is important, because native image files still rely on assemblies for storing their associated metadata.

A best practice for enforcing these guidelines is to ensure that native image files are only generated as part of an assembly's installation process. This can check for the presence of native image facilities on a host machine and only generate native image files where appropriate, otherwise relying on the eminently reliable and platform-friendly virtues of assemblies.

Another useful practice is to avoid system designs that rely on the performance benefits that are promised by native image files. Although native image files can be useful for tweaking performance, you should always be able to reduce an application's startup time by factoring the application intelligently and then using a custom assembly loading strategy.

Coping with Assembly Differences

In the previous section, you saw that no fundamental difference exists between the IL that's generated from different C# compilers. This means that the choice of compiler does not determine whether a program is cross-platform. However, as mentioned in Chapter 1, all the CLI implementations extend the CLI standards by containing extra functionality that is implemented in a mixture of new and existing assemblies, and it is this functional mismatch that creates the first cross-platform pitfall.

Because we have defined the term *platform* to include the CLI implementation and each CLI can potentially have some exclusive functionality, it is particularly easy for an unwary developer to use nonstandard features without realizing that the features are not available in other CLI implementations. You have three different approaches for dealing with this situation. The one that you use depends on the scope of the program that is being developed, as follows:

- **Develop for a specific CLI implementation:** This has the advantage of guaranteeing the availability of functionality, but it assumes that the chosen CLI implementation will be installed on all the computers that will host the application. This is the simplest approach and is adequate when developing an application for a single platform within a controlled environment. However, this approach is unsuitable if the environment is likely to change in the future, or if the environment is uncontrolled—such as for a consumer audience, where it is not possible to determine which CLI implementations the program might be run under.

- **Develop for CLI compliance:** By only using functionality that is available in the CLI standard's libraries,[5] you can make an application highly portable and interoperable with future CLI implementations, but it has the disadvantage of severely reducing the functionality available and potentially increasing the development time and cost. This approach is ideal when creating small applications that need maximum portability, but due to the restricted functionality, it is likely to be unjustifiably expensive for most projects.

- **Develop for hybrid CLI implementations:** Although this may appear to be a subset of the first approach, it is subtly different. By packaging all required assemblies with your program, you can ensure that the application will run on .NET implementations that do not contain the requisite functionality. This has both the advantages of being highly portable and guaranteeing functionality, but it has the disadvantage of requiring extra assemblies to be included with the application from a suitably licensed source, essentially meaning one of the open source offerings. This is an ideal solution when neither of the previous two options is acceptable and when high functionality, portability, and CLI independence are required.

5. *Common Language Infrastructure (CLI), Partition IV,* ECMA 335 (European Computer Manufacturers Association, 2001).

Because the first approach is strictly platform dependent and the second is simply a matter of using a restricted set of features, we now focus on how a hybrid CLI implementation can be used to take advantage of some functionality that is available in Mono, partially available in Portable.NET, but not available in the Microsoft .NET Framework.

NOTE The functionality can be considered "partially available in Portable.NET" because the PNET development team has begun its own hybridization, by testing and building a selection of Mono libraries with PNET and by making the assemblies available in the optional Mono Library, or `ml-pnet`, package.

For the sake of demonstrating a hybrid CLI application, we now look at a simple program that parses a number of options that are set on the command line. .NET does some of the work by splitting the command line for us and by passing the contents as a parameter array into the `Main()` method.

NOTE The code for this section can be found in the `Chapter_03/Hybridization` directory at this book's Web site (`http://www.cross-platform.net`) and the Apress Web site (`http://www.apress.com`).

While it would be simple to write some code to process the parameter array, we instead rely on the functionality of the `Mono.GetOptions` assembly, which provides a number of advanced features for handling command-line options.

CAUTION Before implementing any software using a hybrid CLI approach, you must understand the licensing of the CLI implementation that you intend to "borrow" assemblies from. Although Mono and Portable.NET both contain open source licenses that allow class libraries to be freely used by your applications, the Microsoft. NET Framework has a strict license that does not allow its constituent assemblies to be used on non-Windows operating systems.

Our simple program prints out the current user's username and is created from a single source file, UserName.cs. The file starts by declaring the required namespaces and then contains a number of assembly attributes, as follows:

```
//Filename: UserName.cs
using System;
using System.Reflection;
using Mono.GetOptions;

[assembly: AssemblyTitle("UserName")]
[assembly: AssemblyDescription("Determines the logged in username.")]
[assembly: AssemblyCopyright("(C) 2003 M.J. Easton & Jason King.")]
[assembly: Mono.UsageComplement("")]
```

We then declare a simple class that inherits from the GetOptions.Options class and that contains a single field that is declared with an Option attribute, as follows:

```
namespace Crossplatform.NET.Chapter03
{
    class UsernameOptions: Options
    {
        [Option("Display the username in uppercase", 'u')]
        public bool DisplayUppercase = false;
    }
```

Note that UsernameOptions inherits from Options. This means that by declaring the DisplayUpperCase field with an Option attribute and the 'u' parameter, the field value is set to true if the program is called with /u on the command line; it otherwise retains its default value of false.

Finally, a Username class is declared. This class contains the bulk of our program in the ubiquitous Main() method, as follows:

```
    class Username
    {
        static void Main(string[] args)
        {
            //Process the application's command-line options
            UsernameOptions options = new UsernameOptions();
            options.ProcessArgs(args);
```

```
            string name;
            if(options.DisplayUppercase)
            {
                name = Environment.UserName.ToUpper();
            }
            else
            {
                name = Environment.UserName.ToLower();
            }

            Console.WriteLine("{0}", name);
        }
    }
}
```

The `Main()` method starts by creating an instance of `UsernameOptions` and calls the `ProcessArgs()` method. This method is inherited from the `Options` class and uses reflection to process all the instance's members that have been declared with an `Option` attribute.

After processing the command-line options, the program prints the username of the current user in uppercase if `/u` is specified on the command line; otherwise, it prints in lowercase.

So now we make sure everything works. To compile the program using Mono on GNU/Linux and run it with no command-line options, use the following commands:

```
mono@linux:~ % mcs /r:Mono.GetOptions.dll UserName.cs
mono@linux:~ % mono UserName.exe
mjeaston
```

Perhaps you are particular about the case that your username is displayed in. In this case, we build the program on Windows and use the `/u` option to set the display of the username in uppercase. Remember, the `Mono.GetOptions.dll` assembly is not part of Microsoft .NET, so we must first copy the `Mono.GetOptions.dll` file from our GNU/Linux machine into the same directory as our source code.

After you have copied `Mono.GetOptions.dll` onto your Windows machine, type the following commands to compile and run the program:

```
C:\MS.NET> csc /r:Mono.GetOptions.dll UserName.cs
C:\MS.NET> UserName /u
MJEASTON
```

One of the neatest touches of Mono.GetOptions is its ability to display a list of usage instructions for your program, with the basic functionality being inherited from the Options superclass and extensible through the use of Options attributes. Before you try this with PNET, you must remember to either install the ml-pnet package or copy the Mono.GetOptions.dll file from Mono. Compiling the program and displaying the usage instructions is then as simple as running the following commands:

```
pnet@macosx:~ % cscc /r:Mono.GetOptions.dll /out:UserName.exe UserName.cs
pnet@macosx:~ % ilrun UserName /?
UserName  0.0.0.0 - (C) 2003 M.J. Easton & Jason King
Determines the logged in username.

Usage: UserName [options]
Options:
  -? --help              Show this help list
  -u --DisplayUppercase  Display the username in uppercase
     --usage             Show usage syntax and exit
  -V --version           Display version and licensing information
```

You can see from the program's output that including the /? switch displays a description of our /u switch and prints the information from the assembly attributes, adding a professional sheen to the program for very little coding effort.

The most important point to remember is that as long as the Mono.GetOptions.dll file is distributed with the UserName.exe program, the program should work as expected on all CLI implementations.

TIP One common feature of command-line processing is the need to process file paths. Because different platforms use different separators for file paths, whenever you want to handle file paths in .NET, you should use the System.IO.Path class to ensure that the file paths are cross-platform.

Although the username program is certainly a bit on the artificial side—especially considering that unlike Windows, most operating systems treat case with enough respect to not require a program like this—it nonetheless serves as a simple demonstration of how features that are unique to one CLI implementation can be used with other implementations and is a good starting point for own experiments in cross-fertilization.

Taking Command of the Command Line

JK Did you know that apart from using `Mono.GetOptions.dll` to parse command-line switches and set `boolean` fields, you can also use it to pass in ad hoc values and also call methods?

MJ And next you'll be saying that it can make the tea while giving an Indian head massage?

JK Well, as long as you can put an `Option` attribute on it . . . .

Coping with Shared Assemblies

While we're on the subject of moving assemblies between CLIs, we want to briefly consider the broader subject of sharing assemblies between .NET applications. Although the usual .NET practice is to include required assemblies in the application's binary directory, in some cases, assemblies are used by numerous applications, in which case it makes sense to store the assembly in a centralized directory. In addition, to allow different applications to use different versions of a shared assembly, a mechanism is required that allows more than one version of a shared assembly to be installed.

In Microsoft .NET, these issues are dealt with by the concepts of strongly named assemblies, which define a unique names for assemblies, and the Global Assembly Cache (GAC), which is a centralized assembly store that allows strict versioning of assemblies and allows the same assembly to be shared between applications.

Mono also supports strong names and contains a GAC for sharing assemblies between applications. At the time of this writing, Mono's GAC implementation is in a state of flux. Check the Mono Web site (`http://www.go-mono.com`) for the latest details of Mono's GAC.

Meanwhile, in the Portable.NET camp, versioning and sharing assemblies are supported by the `ilgac` program, which manipulates subdirectories per version under the `/usr/local/lib/cscc/lib` directory. Further details about PNET's support for shared and versioned assemblies are available in the manual pages for `ilgac`. However, in keeping with PNET's philosophy that the user is *King* and should be free to make his own choices about these matters, assemblies can be found as long as the path environment variable is set appropriately.

As mentioned in the previous section, when developing applications for hybrid CLI implementations, you must include the hybrid assemblies with the application, although you should be aware that if a shared version of the assembly is already available for the host CLI, it will be neglected in favor of the assembly that's included with the application.

To ensure that an application uses a particular version of a shared assembly, a <dependentAssembly/> entry can be added to the application's configuration file, as shown in the following example code:

```
<configuration>
 <runtime>
  <assemblyBinding>
   <dependentAssembly>
    <assemblyIdentity name="SharedAssembly"
                      publicKeyToken="12cb3ba51f0177a2"
                      culture="neutral" />
    <bindingRedirect oldVersion="1.0.0.0"
                     newVersion="2.0.0.0" />
   </dependentAssembly>
  </assemblyBinding>
 </runtime>
</configuration>
```

Using Platform-Specific Assemblies

Having seen how to borrow assemblies from one CLI implementation and package them with your own applications, you might have a niggling doubt lingering in your mind: Surely there is more to borrowing functionality from other CLI implementations than just copying a required assembly and packaging it with your own application? In fact, a large piece of the picture remains to be discussed, and without further ado, we now sketch out the issues that surround platform-specific assemblies.

As mentioned in Chapter 1, the .NET CLI provides outstanding support for calling native code. With this in mind, a number of .NET platform-specific assemblies rely on native shared libraries that are frequently only available for a single operating system. Because of this, using platform-specific assemblies can be fraught with difficulties.

To demonstrate some of the difficulties that you can face when using platform-specific assemblies, we now introduce a simple Windows program that needs to store a small amount of transient application data. The program stores the details of the time and date that it was last run as well as the username of the user who last ran the program.

NOTE The code for this example can be found in the `Chapter_03/LastRun` directory at this book's Web site (`http://www.cross-platform.net`) and the Apress Web site (`http://www.apress.com`).

Because the program is intended to be run on Windows, we follow good Windows development practice by storing the data in the system registry. Although the program is not particularly useful in its own right, it nonetheless demonstrates some of the cross-platform issues that can arise when attempting to store application-specific data—a common requirement for many applications. The Windows program is as follows:

```
//Filename: LastRun.cs
using System;
using Microsoft.Win32;

namespace Crossplatform.NET.Chapter3
{
    class Lastrun
    {
        //We should ideally place this in a resource file
        private const string errorMessage = "Error '{0}' occurred in '{1}'";

        //Let's not embed any strings in the program's guts.
        private const string registryKey = "Software\\Crossplatform.NET";
        private const string userNameValue = "userName";
        private const string lastRunValue = "lastRun";
```

The file begins by referencing the `System` and `Microsoft.Win32` namespaces, which contain the external functionality that we need for the program.

TIP While any program that uses the `Microsoft.Win32` namespace is prone to relying on underlying features of the Windows operating system, we shall see later that it is by no means the only namespace that relies on features of Windows. Learning which namespaces contain platform-specific code and which are fully cross-platform is essential for all serious cross-platform development and is the subject of the next chapter.

Following the ubiquitous `using` directives and `namespace` declaration, some `string` constants are declared. These constants define a generic error message and the key and value names that the program uses in the registry.

The program has a fairly simple `Main()` method that contains some generic exception handling code and calls on a method called `DisplayUsageDetails()` to carry out all the real work, as follows:

```
static void Main(string[] args)
{
    try
    {
        //Leave the real work to be done somewhere else
        DisplayUsageDetails();
    }
    catch (Exception e)
    {
        //Writing error messages directly to the console is bad practice!
        Console.Error.WriteLine(errorMessage, e.Message, e.Source);
    }
}
```

TIP Although using `try...catch` statements is a standard practice for exception handling in C#, you often—and incorrectly—see error messages written using `Console.WriteLine()` rather than `Console.Error.WriteLine()`. By using the `Console.Error` property, you ensure that error messages are written to the error stream rather than the standard output stream. This, in turn, allows the user to separate error output from any standard output by using stream redirection.

The `DisplayUsageDetails()` method starts by attempting to open the registry key that is specified by the `registryKey` constant, creating the key if it does not exist. The code then attempts to retrieve data values from the registry key's values before writing out a wonderfully useful message to the console. If the values do not exist under the key, the calls to `GetValue()` return `String.Empty`, and the displayed message contains two pairs of empty single quotes. The following code shows the `DisplayUsageDetails()` method:

```
        private static void DisplayUsageDetails()
        {
            RegistryKey rk = Registry.LocalMachine.OpenSubKey(registryKey, true);

            //Try and create the key if it doesn't exist
            if (rk == null)
            {
                rk = Registry.LocalMachine.CreateSubKey(registryKey);
            }

            //Retrieve data from values
            string userName = (string)rk.GetValue(userNameValue);
            string lastRun = (string)rk.GetValue(lastRunValue);

            Console.WriteLine("Last run by user '{0}' at '{1}'",
                              userName, lastRun);
```

Finally, the method attempts to update the values with some new data, and if the values do not exist under the key, they are automatically created before being populated. The updates are shown in the following code:

```
            //Update data into values
            rk.SetValue(userNameValue, Environment.UserName);
            rk.SetValue(lastRunValue, DateTime.Now);
        }
    }
}
```

To compile and then run the program on Windows, use the following commands:

```
C:\MS.NET> csc LastRun.cs
C:\MS.NET> LastRun
Last run by user '' at ''
```

As expected, the output doesn't contain any data for the username and the time that the program was last run. (This is a good thing, because the program has not been run before!)

To confirm that the program created the key in the registry and saved the two values, you can open the registry by running the `Regedit.exe` program and navigating to the `My Computer\HKEY_LOCAL_MACHINE\SOFTWARE\Crossplatform.NET` key by using the following command:

```
C:\MS.NET> Regedit
```

As shown in Figure 3-2, your system registry should now contain the `Crossplatform.NET` key with three values: an empty `(Default)` value, a `lastRun` value containing the time that you ran the program, and a `userName` value containing your username.

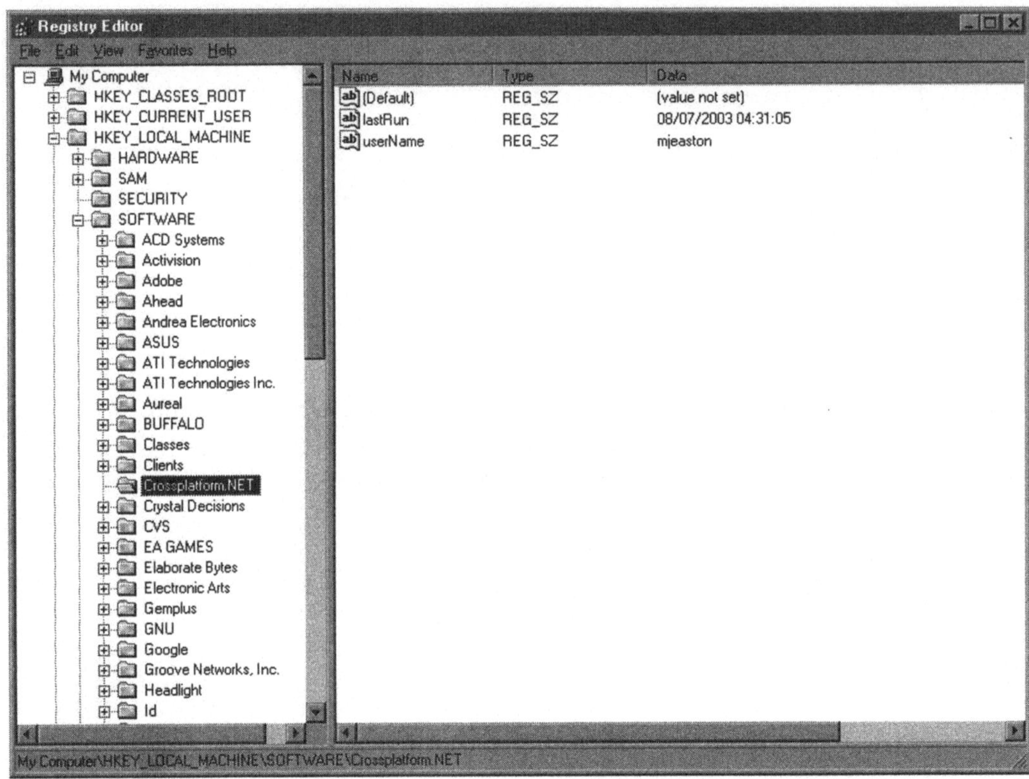

Figure 3-2. Using the Windows registry

To check that the program can also retrieve previously stored data correctly, run the program again and confirm that the output message contains the details that were recorded during the last run. Use the following command:

```
C:\MS.NET> LastRun
Last run by user 'mjeaston' at '08/07/2003 04:31:05'
```

So there you have it: a simple program that stores its own data in the Windows system registry, just like a traditional Windows program.

Of course, Windows is the only operating system that uses the registry for storing application data. This begs the question of what will happen if we compile and run the program on another operating system.

Putting Mono and GNU/Linux to one side for a moment, we try to compile the program on Mac OS X using Portable.NET, as follows:

```
pnet@macosx:~ % cscc /out::LastRun.exe LastRun.cs
```

While it is a good sign that the program compiles the first time without error, what happens if we run the program a couple of times, as shown in the following code?

```
pnet@macosx:~ % ilrun LastRun.exe
Last run by user '' at ''
pnet@macosx:~ % ilrun LastRun.exe
Last run by user 'pnet' at '17/02/2004 15:04:05'
```

As you can see, the program runs without a hitch, returning exactly what we wanted. The problem is that Mac OS X doesn't have a registry, so why did the program work? Has .NET magically pulled a registry out of its hat, or is something more sinister going on behind the scenes?

TIP At the time of this writing, Mono's implementation of the registry classes is little more than an empty stub on all non-Windows platforms. To get the `LastRun` example working with Mono, a simple solution would be to compile PNET's implementation into a stand-alone assembly and then reference that assembly from the `LastRun` program.

Although this would usually be the ideal situation in which to use hybridization, because the registry classes are part of `mscorlib.dll`, it is not as simple as just including PNET's assembly with the application.

To answer this question, we need to rummage through the Portable.NET source code that we installed in Chapter 2 and see exactly how the implementation of the `RegistryKey` works on Mac OS X. This can help us understand how PNET's Registry code works.

Browsing Portable.NET Source Code

The first thought to assail many small-town developers when faced with the tidal wave of source code for a large software project is often one of running away, fainting, or giving birth to a figurative kitten. Although it is certainly not the largest CLI implementation available, Portable.NET's core and library packages contained over 4,000 files and 30 MB of source code. However, before you put your legs to good use, flop onto the ground, or feel the pull of that first, figurative contraction, we would urge you to close your eyes, take a couple of deep breaths, and focus on instilling some inner tranquility. After all, it's only code, and just because a broad expanse of it is split into many files and spread across many directories, it is quite simple to find your way around the source tree with a little thought and a modicum of practice.

TIP Looking through the source code for any of the open source CLI implementations is not only useful for diagnosing cross-platform issues, but it's also the ideal way of learning what goes on behind the .NET curtains. While looking through the code is unlikely to become part of the daily routine for most .NET developers, it's particularly useful when you want to impress your colleagues with your esoteric knowledge of the rituals that occur inside .NET's inner sanctum.

You should start by navigating to the location in the file system where you unpacked the PNET tarballs. As mentioned during the installation section in Chapter 2, the `pnetlib` package contains Portable.NET's library of assemblies, so you can instantly ignore the other directories and concentrate on the `pnetlib` directory.

Although the source code for most of PNET's assemblies can be found in a directory that follows the assembly's filename, to locate PNET's registry code, you must navigate to the `runtime` directory, which contains the source code for the `mscorlib.dll` assembly.

Drilling down through the `runtime` directory, navigate into the `Microsoft` directory and finally the `Win32` directory, where you can find the various source code files that make up the registry classes. Use the following commands:

```
pnet@macosx:~ % ls -al /usr/src/pnetlib-0.6.6/runtime/Microsoft/Win32/
total 76
-rw-r--r--   1 root     wheel       12870 Jul  1 22:32 FileKeyProvider.cs
-rw-r--r--   1 root     wheel        2818 Jul  1 22:32 IRegistryKeyProvider.cs
-rw-r--r--   1 root     wheel        8840 Jul  1 22:32 MemoryKeyProvider.cs
-rw-r--r--   1 root     wheel        3271 Jul  1 22:32 Registry.cs
-rw-r--r--   1 root     wheel        1357 Jul  1 22:32 RegistryHive.cs
-rw-r--r--   1 root     wheel       11850 Jul  1 22:32 RegistryKey.cs
-rw-r--r--   1 root     wheel       23625 Jul  1 22:32 Win32KeyProvider.cs
```

Having located the source code files, you've completed the first step of the journey and can afford yourself a pat on the back.

If you recall the first line of the `LastRun` program, which attempts to access the registry and is shown as follows, it provides a good clue about which source code file we should look in first.

```
RegistryKey rk = Registry.LocalMachine.OpenSubKey(Key, true);
```

The code retrieves an instance of the `RegistryKey` class by calling the `OpenSubKey()` method on the `Registry` class's `LocalMachine` field. So what better way to start this investigation than by looking at the declaration of the `LocalMachine` field in the `Registry.cs` file, as follows:

```
public sealed class Registry
{
    // Constructor.
    private Registry() {}

    // Standard registries on the local machine.
    public static readonly RegistryKey ClassesRoot;
    public static readonly RegistryKey CurrentUser;
    public static readonly RegistryKey LocalMachine;
    public static readonly RegistryKey Users;
    public static readonly RegistryKey PerformanceData;
    public static readonly RegistryKey CurrentConfig;
    public static readonly RegistryKey DynData;
```

As you can see, the `LocalMachine` field is declared along with a number of other fields as a `static readonly` field of type `RegistryKey`. Because it is a `static readonly` field, we know that its value can only be initialized with the declaration or in a type initializer. Because `LocalMachine` is not initialized with the declaration, we need to look in the `Registry` class's type initializer, which is as follows:

```
static Registry()
{
    ClassesRoot = RegistryKey.OpenRemoteBaseKey
                                        (RegistryHive.ClassesRoot, String.Empty);
    CurrentUser = RegistryKey.OpenRemoteBaseKey
                                        (RegistryHive.CurrentUser, String.Empty);
    LocalMachine = RegistryKey.OpenRemoteBaseKey
                                        (RegistryHive.LocalMachine, String.Empty);
```

```
    Users = RegistryKey.OpenRemoteBaseKey
                                (RegistryHive.Users, String.Empty);
    PerformanceData = RegistryKey.OpenRemoteBaseKey
                               (RegistryHive.PerformanceData, String.Empty);
    CurrentConfig = RegistryKey.OpenRemoteBaseKey
                                (RegistryHive.CurrentConfig, String.Empty);
    DynData = RegistryKey.OpenRemoteBaseKey
                                (RegistryHive.DynData, String.Empty);
}
```

Scanning down a few lines, you can see that the `LocalMachine` field is initialized by passing details of the `LocalMachine` hive to the `RegistryKey` class's static `OpenRemoteBaseKey()` method. Rather than wasting time trawling through the rest of `Registry.cs`, we can jump from the `Registry.cs` file and burrow into the `RegistryKey.cs` file, as follows:

```
public static RegistryKey OpenRemoteBaseKey(RegistryHive hKey, String
machineName)
{
    // Validate the parameters.
    if(hKey < RegistryHive.ClassesRoot || hKey > RegistryHive.DynData)
    {
          throw new ArgumentException(_("Arg_InvalidHive"));
    }

    if(machineName == null)
    {
        throw new ArgumentNullException("machineName");
    }

    // Get the name of the hive to be accessed.
    String name = hiveNames [((int)hKey) - (int)(RegistryHive.ClassesRoot)];

    // Is this a remote hive reference?
    if(machineName != String.Empty)
    {
        //The real file contains some real code
                ...
    }

    // Open a local hive.
    return new RegistryKey(Registry.GetProvider(hKey, name), true);
}
```

The OpenRemoteBaseKey() method starts with a couple of validation checks before retrieving a hive name from the class's hiveNames array. Because we are only interested in accessing a local registry, we ignore the remote registry access code and focus on the last line, which retrieves a reference to a RegistryKey instance from the Registry class's GetProvider() method.

Putting RegistryKey.cs aside for a moment, it's time to delve back into the Registry.cs file and find the GetProvider() method.

```
// Get a registry key provider for a particular hive.
internal static IRegistryKeyProvider GetProvider(RegistryHive hKey, String name)
{
    int index;

    lock(typeof(Registry))
    {
        // Allocate the "providers" array if necessary.
        if(providers == null)
        {
            providers = new IRegistryKeyProvider[7];
        }

        // See if we already have a provider for this hive.
        index = ((int)hKey) - ((int)(RegistryHive.ClassesRoot));
        if(providers[index] != null)
        {
            return providers[index];
        }

        // Create a Win32 provider if we are on a Windows system.
        if(Win32KeyProvider.IsWin32())
        {
            providers[index] = new Win32KeyProvider(name,
                                        Win32KeyProvider.HiveToHKey(hKey));
            return providers[index];
        }
```

Although the method starts with some fairly provocative foreplay, including locking the Registry type, conditionally allocating an array, and attempting to retrieve a cached provider, the code that we are interested in once again occurs in the later part of the method.

Just considering the name of the Win32KeyProvider.IsWin32() method tells us that the code is conditionally dependent on whether we are running on a Windows system. Although we'll look into the implementation of the salient Win32KeyProvider class later in the chapter, we first analyze what is happening on Mac OS X.

After failing the check to see whether the code is being running on Windows, the method attempts to create a `FileKeyProvider`, and if the creation of the `FileKeyProvider` fails, the method finally resorts to using a `MemoryKeyProvider`, as follows:

```
            // Try to create a file-based provider for the hive.
            try
            {
                providers[index] = new FileKeyProvider(hKey, name);
                return providers[index];
            }
            catch(NotSupportedException)
            {
                // Could not create the hive directory - fall through.
            }

            // Create a memory-based provider on all other systems.
            providers[index] = new MemoryKeyProvider(null, name, name);
            return providers[index];
        }
}
```

The names of the key providers give a good indication of what is happening. If PNET does not detect that it is running on Windows, it attempts to use a file-based data store, and if that fails, as a last-ditch precaution, it uses a memory-based provider.

To confirm that the `LastRun` program is storing its registry values in the file system, you only need to take a quick look at the comments at the top of the `FileKeyProvider.cs` file, as seen here:

```
// FileKeyProvider.cs - Implementation of Microsoft.Win32.FileKeyProvider class.
//
// This class implements a file-based registry on disk. The registry
// is stored within the "$HOME/.cli" directory. This can be overridden
// with the "CLI_STORAGE_ROOT" environment variable.
//
// Each registry key is stored as a subdirectory within the file system.
// Subkeys are represented as subdirectories underneath their parent.
//
// Values are stored in a file called "values.reg" within the subdirectory
// that corresponds to the registry key. The format is XML-based, with
// the following structure:
//
```

```
//    <values>
//      <value name="foo" type="bar">...</value>
//      ...
//    </values>
```

Voilà! Not only does the `FileKeyProvider.cs` file confirm our earlier suspicion about using a file-based registry, but it also tells us where the registry files are stored and it provides details of the format that is used. We now know what is going on and how Portable.NET is storing our registry values between runs.

Having covered a lot of code snippets from numerous files in the last few pages, Figure 3-3 serves as a quick recap and shows the sequence of messages that occur when instantiating the `LocalMachine` `RegistryKey` on Mac OS X.

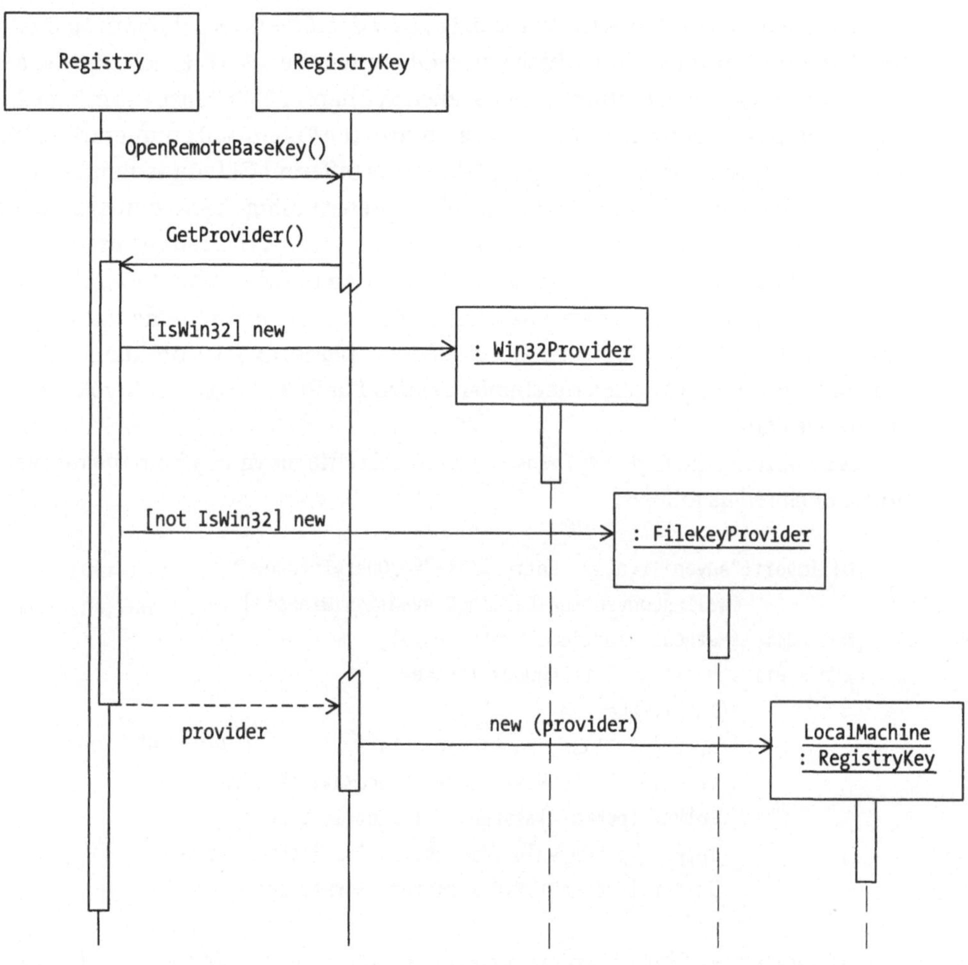

Figure 3-3. A sequence diagram showing the instantiation of the `LocalMachine` `RegistryKey`

Invoking Platform-Specific Services

Although we have solved the riddle of how the LastRun program works on Mac OS X, we deliberately avoided tracing through the Win32KeyProvider.IsWin32() method that is used to determine whether the program is executing on Windows.

Looking in the Win32KeyProvider.cs file, the IsWin32() method consists of three lines of code and determines whether the program is running on Windows:

```
// Determine whether we should use the Win32 registry.
public static bool IsWin32()
{
    return (Environment.OSVersion.Platform != PlatformID.Unix);
}
```

The method compares the value of Environment.OSVersion.Platform against the PlatformID enumeration, which you might remember was the technique used for determining the operating system shown in Chapter 2. Because the other CLI implementations don't include Unix as a value of the PlatformID enumeration, it's worth noting that this code isn't portable across different CLI implementations, and that the code in Chapter 2 is preferable for determining the operating system.

Browsing through the rest of the Win32KeyProvider.cs file, hiding after a number of standard C# methods, you can also see a number of methods that are declared with the DllImport attribute but do not contain an implementation. These are the root cause of the majority of cross-platform .NET problems and they indicate .NET is using a mechanism called Platform Invoke (P/Invoke) to call native code.

For example, the RegQueryInfoKey() method retrieves values from the registry and is declared as follows:

```
    [DllImport("advapi32.dll", EntryPoint="RegQueryInfoKeyW",
              CallingConvention=CallingConvention.Winapi)]
    [MethodImpl(MethodImplOptions.PreserveSig)]
    extern private static int RegQueryInfoKey
               (IntPtr hkey,
                byte[] lpClass, IntPtr lpcbClass, IntPtr lpReserved,
                out uint lpcSubKeys, IntPtr lpcbMaxSubKeyLen,
                IntPtr lpcbMaxClassLen, out uint lpcValues,
                IntPtr lpcbMaxValueNameLen, IntPtr lpcbMaxValueLen,
                IntPtr lpcbSecurityDescriptor, IntPtr lpftLastWriteTime);
```

The presence of the DllImport attribute is an ominous sign that stands as a frontier post, demarcating the boundary between IL code and native code, and warns of the dangers that lurk just out of sight. This attribute signifies that the implementation of a method is not in managed code, but rather is native code in the named library. In the case of `RegQueryInfoKey`, it is in one of the Windows Win32 API libraries, `advapi32.dll`.

While we won't worry about the exact syntax of the `DllImport` attribute or the use of Platform Invoke until Chapter 7, the point of interest for our registry example is that when PNET runs the `LastRun` program on Windows, rather than using managed code, it instead relies on a function that is implemented in a Windows-specific library.

We can now step back and look at the structure of the whole `LastRun` program, which is shown in Figure 3-4.

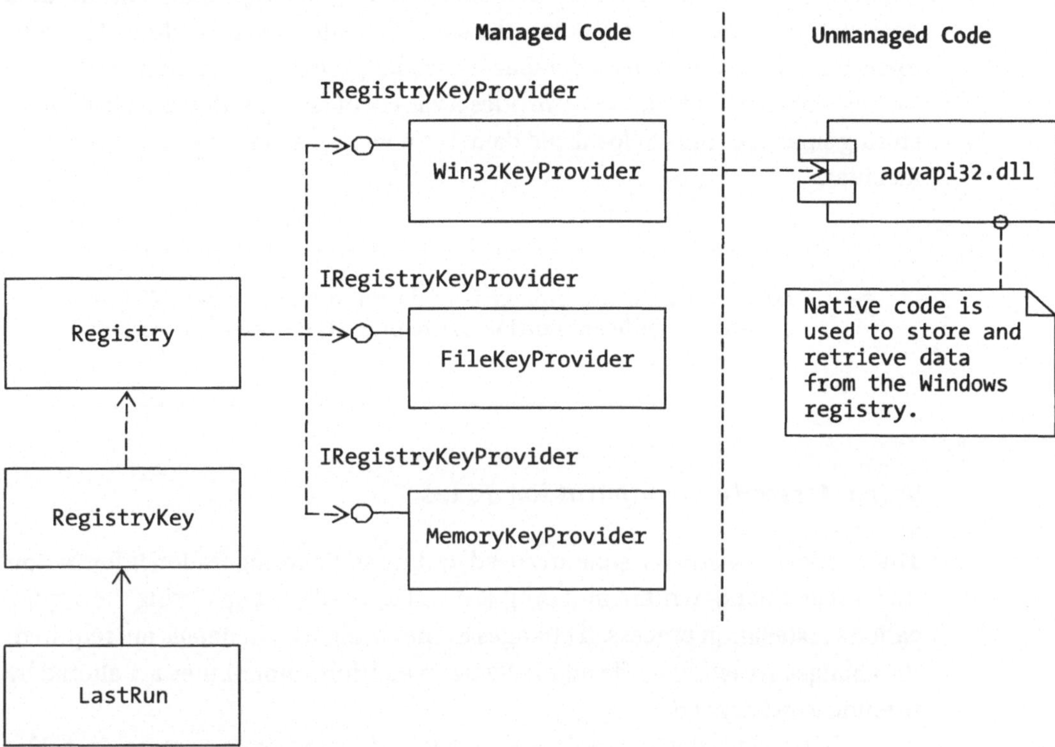

Figure 3-4. A class diagram of the `LastRun` *program*

By relying on native code, the registry classes suffer from the weakness that lies at the heart of most cross-platform problems. This weakness is reliance on code that, by its very nature, is restricted to a single platform.

Avoiding the Registry

Although you've now seen how cross-platform .NET programs can get around the platform-specific pitfall of the registry, because it is an innate feature of the Windows operating system, the registry should automatically be a suspicious implementation choice when developing cross-platform software from scratch. While anyone who is porting existing Windows .NET applications might have to tackle some registry-manipulation code, there are a couple of alternative methods for storing data that are philosophically preferable for writing clean cross-platform .NET applications.

When dealing with larger amounts of data, or when more advanced storage features are required, such as transactions, indexing, and replication, the de facto data-storage standard is, of course, the database. Although no technical reason exists for `LastRun` not to use a database, it would probably be overkill for the `LastRun` program. In fact, .NET provides a variety of facilities that are ideal for storing small amounts of localized data. We now take a look at some of these facilities.

NOTE Because data storage is vitally important to many .NET applications, a significant portion of Chapter 6 is devoted to covering databases.

Using Assembly Configuration Files

The Windows registry is frequently used to store static configuration information that is read but not written by a program and is usually set up during the application's installation process. If changes to the configuration details are required, the changes are either made manually by an administrator or they are altered by running a registry script.

.NET provides the `System.Configuration` and `System.Configuration.Install` namespaces for exactly this purpose, and .NET allows configuration information to be stored on a per-assembly, per-machine, and per-organization basis.

.NET configuration files are stored in the file system with an extension of `.config`, and, because they are implemented as XML files, they are inherently cross-platform. These files also have the advantage of allowing .NET applications to be deployed by using *Copy and Paste* or *xcopy* deployment, which is as simple as copying the application's directory to a new machine.

Despite the benefits that are offered by assembly configuration files, they only apply to executable assemblies. As an extension, Mono permits library configuration files, but only to specify the native libraries that are used in Platform Invoke; see Chapter 7 for more details. This means that configuration files can only be used for per-application configuration data. They are not suitable for per-user or per-organization data or for general configuration data that's required by library assemblies (DLLs).

Using Isolated Storage

Another frequent use of the Windows registry is to store data on a per-user basis. The .NET mechanism for securely storing personal data is called *isolated storage* and is accessible through the `System.IO.IsolatedStorage` namespace.

Apart from providing a secure mechanism for storing user data, isolated storage acts as a virtual file system, and because it is technically little more than a managed wrapper over the actual file system, it is inherently cross-platform to boot.

The main difference when using isolated storage on different platforms is that the storage location within the file system is different. The storage location depends on a number of factors such as the CLI, the operating system, and the system configuration that are being used.

To illustrate, isolated storage on Mono and GNU/Linux stores its data in `$HOME/.mono/isolated-storage`, whereas Portable.NET for UNIX-based systems maps isolated storage to `$HOME /.cli/isolated-storage`. In contrast, assuming roaming profiles are not enabled, Microsoft's .NET Framework stores data in `C:\Documents and Settings\`*`UserName`*`\Local Settings\Application Data\IsolatedStorage`.

However, because isolated storage is user-scoped, it isn't suitable for application-scoped data that must be shared among users and it therefore wouldn't suffice for storing the data of our `LastRun` example, which must be accessible to all the users of the program.

Using an XML-Based File Storage

The final use of the Windows registry is for storing transient application data that is both readable and writable by one or more programs and various users. While .NET does not include a specific mechanism for storing such data, the `System.Xml.Serialization` namespace makes it easy to use an XML file for storing application data. Not only is the data stored in a human-readable form, but it is also easy to process in code and, because the file is stored in the file system, it is intrinsically cross-platform.

Because XML serialization is simple to use and an XML file is the ideal data store for the simple needs of our `LastRun` program, we now revisit the `LastRun` program to demonstrate a clean solution to the original problem that avoids the registry and all the platform-dependent baggage that goes with it.

The start of the program is similar to the previous implementation, with the notable difference being that the reference to `Microsoft.Win32` has been replaced by references to the `System.IO` and `System.Xml.Serialization` namespaces. The file then declares a new `struct` called `LastRunData` that is used for storing the program's data at runtime, and can be written to and read from the XML file by using XML serialization. The code for the new class, `LastRun3`, is as follows:

```
//Filename: LastRun3.cs
using System;
using System.IO;
using System.Xml.Serialization;

namespace Crossplatform.NET.Chapter03
{
    //Provide a structure for storing data
    public struct LastRunData
    {
        public string userName;
        public DateTime lastRun;
    }

    class LastRun3
    {
        //Embedding strings in a program's guts is not good practice.
        private const string fileName = "lastRun3.xml";
        private const string errorMessage = "error '{0}' was raised from '{1}'";
        private const string msg = "Last run by user '{0}' at '{1}'";

        static void Main(string[] args)
        {
            try
            {
                //Leave the real work to be done somewhere else
                DisplayUsageDetails();
            }
            catch (Exception e)
            {
                Console.Error.WriteLine(errorMessage, e.Message, e.Source);
            }
        }
```

As you can see, the Main() method is identical to the previous version, with all the real differences being in the DisplayUsageDetails() method. This method has had all the registry-manipulation code ripped out and replaced with equivalent XML serialization code.

DisplayUsageDetails() starts with the declaration of a LastRunData variable, before instantiating an XmlSerializer for carrying out the serialization and deserialization of data, as follows:

```
private static void DisplayUsageDetails()
{
    LastRunData data;
    XmlSerializer serializer = new XmlSerializer(typeof(LastRunData));
```

The code then checks for the existence of the XML file. If the code finds the file, it attempts to deserialize the contents of the file into the data variable; otherwise, it merely instantiates the data variable for use later, as shown in the following code:

```
    //Deserialize the data
    if (File.Exists(fileName))
    {
        using(FileStream fs = new FileStream(fileName, FileMode.Open))
        {
            data = (LastRunData)serializer.Deserialize(fs);
        }
    }
    else
    {
        data = new LastRunData();
    }
```

The code then outputs the tried-and-tested message to the console before updating the data variable with some new values, as follows:

```
    //Display the output and update the data
    Console.WriteLine(msg, data.userName, data.lastRun);
    data.userName = Environment.UserName;
    data.lastRun = DateTime.Now;
```

Finally, the code attempts to serialize the data variable back to the XML file by instantiating a StreamWriter and then calling the XmlSerializer's Serialize() method, as follows:

```
            //Serialize the data
            using(StreamWriter writer = new StreamWriter(fileName))
            {
                serializer.Serialize(writer, data);
            }
        }
    }
}
```

If you have not worked with XML serialization before, you might be surprised at how little code is actually required. You now have a fully working replacement for the registry example that has no dependencies on native code. As shown in Figure 3-5, the class diagram for `LastRun3` is significantly simpler than the class diagram for `LastRun`.

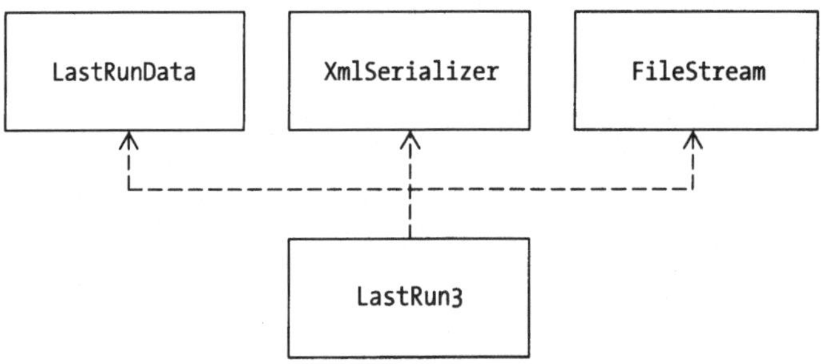

Figure 3-5. A class diagram of the `LastRun3` *program*

To test whether the program works, compile the program and run it using the following commands on Mono and GNU/Linux:

```
mono@linux:~ % mcs LastRun3.cs
mono@linux:~ % mono LastRun3.exe
Last run by user '' at 'Monday, 01 January 0001 00:00:00'
```

Unlike the previous version, because the `data` variable's `lastRun` field is of type `DateTime`, our initial message is populated with a rather early date and time. To engage in a bit of time travel and check that the program really stores and retrieves data, run the program one more time, as follows:

```
mono@linux:~ % mono LastRun3.exe
Last run by user 'mono' at 'Thursday, 10 July 2003 16:18:49'
```

As you can see, we now have a program that can store and retrieve its own data. Rather than relying on specific operating system services, it is truly cross-platform, and because it also creates its own XML file when needed, it is also perfect for *xcopy* deployment. Of course, the program is still a long way from being production-quality code. In particular, it doesn't address the subtle issue of where the XML file should be stored in the file system, instead relying on the current working directory. For a production version, you would not only need to ensure that the XML file was placed in a well-known location—where users had permission to access the file—but you would also need to vary the location depending on which operating system the program was running under. As you'll learn by the end of this book, the road to cross-platform bliss is fraught with twists and diversions.

Apart from demonstrating how to avoid the registry, the `LastRun3` program is a reasonable demonstration of how to approach cross-platform .NET development in general: Avoid as much platform-specific functionality as possible—which is probably based on an antiquated design that harks back to the platform's distant youth—and concentrate on using .NET's extensive class libraries to produce clean and elegant solutions that would not go amiss on any self-respecting platform-dependent project.

Cross-Platform Nomenclature

Having shown that some assemblies rely on operating system–specific features and that a simple solution to a specific platform-dependent problem often exists, it is time to clarify the terminology that we are using to refer to different types of cross-platform .NET development.

Although in Chapter 1 we defined *cross-platform* to imply development for different combinations of operating systems, machine architectures, and CLI implementations, this chapter has blurred our earlier definition somewhat. Table 3-1 further formalizes the terminology to provide some naming conventions for the different combinations of target platforms.

Table 3-1. Target Platform Terminology

CLI	**OS**	**Machine**	**Terminology**
Single	Single	Single	Platform-dependent
Multiple	Single	Single	CLI-independent
Single	Multiple	Single	OS-independent
Single	Single	Multiple	Machine-independent
Single	Multiple	Multiple	CLI-dependent
Multiple	Single	Multiple	OS-dependent
Multiple	Multiple	Single	Machine-dependent
Multiple	Multiple	Multiple	Platform-independent

From this we can now say that any program that is tied to a particular CLI, operating system, and machine architecture is *platform dependent*. This might include software that is written for Microsoft .NET and uses the Windows-specific features of Microsoft .NET.

A program that relies on a single CLI implementation but can work on any operating system and machine architecture is called *CLI dependent*. This could be a Mono program that uses features that are only available in Mono.

A *platform-independent* program is then one that runs on any combination of CLI implementation, operating system, and machine architecture, and as such it includes all programs that are CLI compliant.

To help visualize how these different distinctions relate to one another, it's worth looking at the Venn diagram shown in Figure 3-6.

Returning to the examples in this chapter, we can now say that CLI hybridization is a mechanism for converting *CLI-dependent* applications into platform-dependent applications, and that an application that uses the registry classes is at best *OS dependent* and at worse *platform dependent*. The implementation of `LastRun3` was platform independent, and because its implementation was intrinsically cross-platform, we prudently call it a better cross-platform implementation than its ancestors.

Apart from clarifying the different types of target platforms, redefining the terminology also forces us to reappraise our definition of cross-platform. If cross-platform retained its previous definition, it would be equivalent to *platform independent*, and while nothing would be eminently wrong with such a definition, we will be less wasteful by redefining *cross-platform* to imply software that is not platform dependent. Conversely, following good cross-platform practices implies creating software that is as far along the platform-independent continuum as possible.

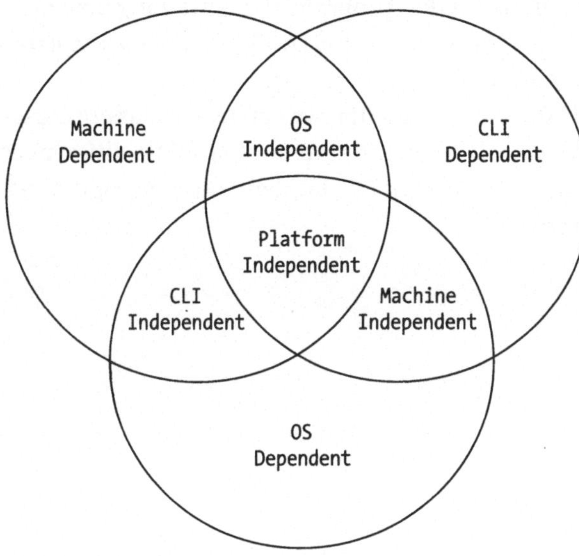

Figure 3-6. Target platforms for .NET programs

Summary

After the lolling quietude of the first two chapters, Chapter 3 has covered a lot of ground, containing a number of concepts that highlight various cross-platform intricacies, and it has arrived dangerously close to the precipice that drops into the bowels of cross-platform .NET development.

The chapter started by introducing the simple `GetComputerName` program. This was followed by a brief, comparative analysis of the IL code that is generated by each CLI implementation. We then discussed the PE/COFF binary format before demonstrating the porting of assemblies from one platform to another, and the inherent platform independence of the CLI.

A CLI-dependent program was then introduced that relied on the command-line processing functionality that is available with Mono; the program was duly converted into a platform-independent program in the process called hybridization. This process involved packaging the requisite `Mono.GetOptions.dll` assembly with the program's assembly.

The chapter then introduced the OS-dependent `LastRun` program, which used the Windows registry for some minor data persistence and, by browsing through the Portable.NET source code, investigated how the program was implemented on non-Windows operating systems. Not only did this serve as an example of how OS-dependent code can be written for production systems, but it also introduced how P/Invoke plays a pivotal role in utilizing native code.

We finished the discussion of the `LastRun` program by mentioning how to avoid using the registry in .NET applications by using configuration files, isolated storage, and finally XML serialization.

Finally, the chapter refined the vocabulary that we can use to classify cross-platform software. This helps empower discussions about the subtle differences that are raised by writing software for different CLI implementations, operating systems, and hardware architectures.

CHAPTER 4

The .NET Framework Dissected

". . . come up to the lab, and see what's on the slab . . ."

—Dr. Frank N. Furter

IN CHAPTER 3, we discussed, among other topics, the issue of the Windows registry, and we saw that while Portable.NET mimics Microsoft .NET's functionality, its implementation is something of a false friend.

In fact, a number of the namespaces in Microsoft's .NET Framework are fundamentally based on features of the Windows operating system, and you should be aware of the issues that relate to these namespaces before you use them in cross-platform development. Although Mono is attempting to implement all the .NET Framework class libraries, this is more a question of portability than a green light to use all the namespaces in a cross-platform project. So, now it's time to get to know our friends better by reflecting on their underlying characteristics, and in doing so, we discover who to invite to our party.

"If your namespace ain't on the list, you ain't gettin' in."

The first part of this chapter maps out the Microsoft implementation of the .NET Framework class libraries, and by the end of this chapter, you should have a thorough understanding of how these class libraries fit together—which namespaces are fundamental to a CLI implementation, which namespaces can be freely used without raising cross-platform issues, and those evil namespaces that are plagued by Windows-isms.

This is essential knowledge for the cross-platform developer. After all, without an understanding of the underlying technologies that these namespaces are built on, you could be coding yourself the wrong way down a one-way street.

The second part of the chapter introduces a strategy for coping with those situations where you are forced to tailor your solution differently for each deployed platform. Crucially, in this chapter, we start to develop some cross-platform best practices in earnest, but to start with, we get back to basics.

A .NET Love Story

MJ I admit it: I love .NET. I love her name and her nuances, and I take great pleasure in sneaking glances at her curvaceous libraries while . . .

JK Steady on MJ; remember, this is a family book.

MJ Sorry, I forgot myself there for a moment.

JK Well, there's nothing wrong with sharing your emotional delectations, but surely your infatuation hasn't blinded you to the ugly warts that your beloved sports?

MJ A flaw? You're mad! She's perfection incarnate; a work of empyrean splendor; the end to all developer suffering . . .

JK So why's she named after a fishing receptacle? And what about the Windows-specific functionality that's dotted across her like a torrent of teenage acne?

The CLI Libraries

At the heart of .NET are seven libraries that are defined in Partition IV of the ECMA standards, and these libraries contain no platform-specific idiosyncrasies, forming a solid cross-platform foundation.

These libraries provide the basic building blocks of a CLI implementation, and they contain a wealth of core functionality, such as basic types, collection classes, and IO classes. The libraries are as follows:

- Base Class Library
- Runtime Infrastructure Library
- XML Library
- Network Library
- Reflection Library
- Extended Numerics Library
- Extended Array Library

However, before examining these libraries in detail, it makes sense to give them a context, and that, ladies and gentlemen, introduces the concept of the CLI Profile.

The CLI libraries are grouped into two standard profiles, the *Kernel Profile* and the *Compact Profile.* The Kernel Profile is the minimal implementation of the CLI standards and contains the fundamental types and classes that are needed by the simplest CLI programs. The Compact Profile is a superset of the Kernel Profile and provides additional types for dealing with XML, reflection, and networking. Table 4-1 shows how the libraries are grouped to make the two profiles.

Table 4-1. The Relationship Between CLI Libraries and Profiles

Library Name	**Kernel Profile**	**Compact Profile**
Base Class Library	Yes	Yes
Runtime Infrastructure Library	Yes	Yes
XML Library	No	Yes
Network Library	No	Yes
Reflection Library	No	Yes
Extended Numerics Library	No	No
Extended Array Library	No	No

Neither the Extended Numerics Library nor the Extended Array Library is included in either of the defined profiles, although CLI implementations typically build on the compact profile to include them. The Extended Numerics Library provides support for floating-point number types, such as `System.Single` and `System.Double`, and for extended precision types, such as `System.Decimal`. The Extended Array Library provides features for handling multidimensional and non-zero-based arrays.

Presenting a Fine Profile

Although Portable.NET contains a broad range of functionality that isn't defined in Partition IV, it also allows its libraries to be built in a number of slimmer versions, one that matches the Kernel Profile and another that matches the Compact Profile. By providing the option to limit the libraries in this way, PNET not only makes it easy to build versions of PNET that adhere to differing levels of the ECMA standards, but it's also useful for reducing PNET's storage overheads. This is ideal when targeting resource-hungry environments, such as embedded systems.

To build Portable.NET to take advantage of profiles, alter the configuration stage of the installation process—as mentioned in Chapter 2—to use the `--with-profile` option, as follows:

```
./configure --with-profile=compact
```

When the `--with-profile` option is not specified, the default profile is `full` and includes all of PNET's features, although several other options are available, as follows:

- Kernel: The smallest possible ECMA-compatible configuration. No support exists for floating-point, reflection, networking, P/Invoke, multidimensional arrays, and so on. The default text encoding is hard-wired to Latin1.
- kernel-fp: The Kernel Profile, with the addition of floating-point support.
- compact: The Kernel Profile, with the addition of reflection and networking.
- compact-fp: The Compact Profile, with the addition of floating-point support.
- tiny: The Kernel Profile, without runtime infrastructure or file system support.

Further information about Portable.NET's profiles can be found in the `/profiles/readme` file of the `pnet` package's source code.

So why should you be interested in the CLI libraries and profiles? Well, knowledge of these libraries is crucial when developing on a restricted-resource platform, such as a handheld device like a mobile phone. Furthermore, a solid grounding in what the .NET Framework contains can serve as an aid for finding sources of trouble in the cross-platform development process and provides you with a starting point for building a list of trusted libraries.

Partition IV of the CLI standard is distributed in the following two parts:

- A document that describes the CLI-compliant libraries and profiles
- An XML file that provides details of each class, value type, and interface in the CLI libraries

The CLI Library Parser Program

Because the CLI standards are likely to slowly expand to encompass more namespaces and types, keeping track of the contents of the CLI-defined libraries could become increasingly difficult. Fortunately, the ECMA standards come with a handy XML file that documents the libraries, and with the help of the trivial CLI Library Parser program, you can output a list of classes for categorization when required.

NOTE The source code samples for this chapter can be found in the Downloads section of this book's Web site (`http://www.cross-platform.net`) and the Apress Web site (`http://www.apress.com`). The code for the CliLibraryParser can be found in the `Chapter_04/CliLibraryParser` directory.

The `CliLibraryParser.cs` file starts by declaring a number of namespaces and then contains the static `Main()` method. This method checks whether at least one argument has been passed in and then ensures that a full file path is available before calling the `GenerateFiles()` method, as follows:

```
//CliLibraryParser.cs
using System;
using System.IO;
using System.Xml;
using System.Xml.XPath;
using System.Reflection;

namespace Crossplatform.NET.Chapter04
{
    class CliLibraryParser
    {
        static void Main(string[] args)
        {
            //Check for a filepath
            if (args.Length != 1)
            {
                Console.WriteLine("Please specify the XML file to parse.");
                return;
            }
```

```
        //Rationalize the filepath
        string filePath;
        if (Path.IsPathRooted (args[0]))
            filePath = args[0];
        else
           filePath = Path.Combine(Directory.GetCurrentDirectory(), args[0]);

        //Let's cut to the chase!
        try
        {
            GenerateFiles(filePath);
        }
        catch (Exception ex)
        {
            Console.Error.WriteLine("An error occurred: {0}.", ex.Message);
        }
    }
```

Inspecting the XML CLI Documentation

The XML document is broken down into six major nodes, which the `CliLibraryParser` uses to generate the text files, as follows:

```
<Libraries>
    <Types Library="BCL"/>
    <Types Library="ExtendedNumerics"/>
    <Types Library="Networking"/>
    <Types Library="Reflection"/>
    <Types Library="RuntimeInfrastructure"/>
    <Types Library="XML"/>
</Libraries>
```

Each of the `<Types/>` elements contains a child element for each type that's contained in the library. For example, the `<Types Library="BCL"/>` element contains a child element for the `Object` type, which contains the following data:

```
<Type Name="Object" Fullname="System.Object" FullNameSP="System_Object">
    <TypeSignature Language="ILSASM" Value=".class public serializable Object"/>
    <TypeSignature Language="C#" Value="public class Object"/>
    <MemberOfLibrary>BCL</MemberOfLibrary>
    <AssemblyInfo>
    <ThreadingSafetyStatement>All public...</ThreadingSafetyStatement>
    <Docs/>
    <Base />
    <Interfaces />
    <Attributes />
    <Members />
    <TypeExcluded>0</TypeExcluded>
</Type>
```

The CliLibraryParser program makes minimal use of this data, because it only needs to generate a list of types in each library, but by examining the XML in more depth, you can find out exactly what is defined in each of the CLI libraries.

The `GenerateFiles()` method creates a series of files by loading the specified XML document. The method then creates an `XPathNavigator` to traverse the data and an `XPathExpression`, which is used to select the XML file's `<Types/>` elements and to sort them by the `Library` attribute, as follows:

```
public static void GenerateFiles(string filePath)
{
    //Load the ECMA CLI document
    XmlDocument xmlDoc = new XmlDocument();
    xmlDoc.Load(filePath);

    //Sort the document to split the sections into a file per library
    XPathNavigator navigator = xmlDoc.CreateNavigator();
    XPathExpression expression = navigator.Compile("//Types");
    expression.AddSort("attribute::Library ", XmlSortOrder.Ascending,
                    XmlCaseOrder.None, String.Empty, XmlDataType.Text);
```

The method then iterates through all the <Types/> elements, creating a text file for each library and calling the GenerateFileContents() method to extract the types that are present in the library and to write their names to the newly created file. The code is as follows:

```
        XPathNodeIterator nodeIterator = navigator.Select(expression);
        while (nodeIterator.MoveNext())
        {
            string target;
            target = Path.Combine(Directory.GetCurrentDirectory(),
                  nodeIterator.Current.GetAttribute("Library",String.Empty) +
                    ".txt");

            using (StreamWriter stream = File.CreateText(target))
            {
                GenerateFileContents(nodeIterator.Current, stream);
            }
        }
    }
```

The implementation of the GenerateFileContents() method sorts the <Type/> elements from the XML file based on their type name and then iterates through the nodes, writing the full name of each type to the stream for the output file, as follows:

```
    //Write the contents for a single library...
    private static void GenerateFileContents(XPathNavigator navigator,
                                            StreamWriter stream)
    {
        //Sort the nodes to create an ordered file
        XPathExpression expression = navigator.Compile("child::Type");
        expression.AddSort("attribute::FullName ", XmlSortOrder.Ascending,
                          XmlCaseOrder.None, "", XmlDataType.Text);

        XPathNodeIterator nodeIterator = navigator.Select(expression);
        while (nodeIterator.MoveNext())
            stream.WriteLine(nodeIterator.Current.GetAttribute("FullName",
                                                         String.Empty));
    }
  }
}
```

To compile and run the CliLibraryParser on Windows using the .NET Framework, use the following commands:

```
C:\MS.NET> csc CliLibraryParse.cs
Microsoft (R) Visual C# .NET Compiler version 7.10.3052.4
for Microsoft (R) .NET Framework version 1.1.4322
Copyright (C) Microsoft Corporation 2001-2002. All rights reserved.
C:\MS.NET> CliLibraryParser All.xml
```

If you prefer to build and run the program on GNU/Linux using Mono, use the following commands:

```
mono@linux:~ % mcs CliLibraryParser.cs
Compilation succeeded
mono@linux:~ % mono CliLibraryParser.exe All.xml
```

Finally, to compile and run the program on Mac OS X using Portable.NET, use the following commands:

```
pnet@macosx:~ % cscc /out:CliLibraryParser.exe CliLibraryParser.cs
pnet@macosx:~ % ilrun CliLibraryParser.exe All.xml
```

Although the CLI libraries are split into seven distinct libraries, you might notice that running the program only produces six files—five files for the libraries that make up the Compact Profile and one file for the Extended Numerics Library. Because the Extended Array Library doesn't specify any additional types and merely provides extensions to the Array class, it has been omitted from the CLI XML document. Table 4-2 shows example classes from the Kernel Profile.

Table 4-2. Example Classes from the Kernel Profile

Base Class Library (BCL)	Runtime Infrastructure Library
System.ApplicationException	System.MissingMethodException
System.Collections.ArrayList	System.Runtime.InteropServices.DllImportAttribute
System.Int32	System.Runtime.CompilerServices.MethodImplAttribute
System.IO.File	System.UnhandledExceptionEventArgs

As its name suggests, the Base Class Library contains the fundamental classes of the CLI, incorporating value types, exceptions, and classes for handling file input and output, and so on. The Runtime Infrastructure Library provides services and classes that are required by compilers that are targeting the CLI and includes classes such as `DllImportAttribute`, which is used for interoperability. Table 4-3 shows a selection from the Compact Profile.

Table 4-3. Example Classes from the Compact Profile

Networking Library	Reflection Library	XML Library
System.Net.Dns	System.Reflection. MethodAttributes	System.Xml.Formatting
System.Net.IPAddress	System.Reflection. TypeAttributes	System.Xml.NameTable
System.UriBuilder	System.Reflection.EventInfo	System.Xml.ReadState
System.Net.HttpVersion	System.Reflection.PropertyInfo	System.Xml.WhitespaceHandling

In addition to the contents of the Kernel Profile, the Compact Profile adds functionality for network access, XML processing, and reflection, which significantly extends the core .NET functionality while providing support for communication and data interchange. Table 4-4 lists the extensions to the numerics and array libraries.

Table 4-4. Extended Numerics and Extended Array Libraries

Extended Numerics Library	Extended Array Library
System.Decimal	System.Array
System.Double	--
System.Math	--
System.NotFiniteNumberException	--
System.Single	--

The Extended Numerics Library does what it says on the tin by enhancing the number-processing capabilities of .NET. The Extended Array Library doesn't add any extra types, but it does extend the array-handling mechanism.

A quick count of the types in the seven libraries gives a total of 295 types, which is a small fraction of the 3,500 types that are contained in the Microsoft .NET Framework. To duplicate the additional functionality that's available in the Microsoft .NET Framework, the open source community not only has a lot of ground to cover, but it also has to cope with 3,000-odd extra types, each of which is a potential source of hijinks.

Noticeably absent from the seven libraries are the higher-level types that deal with graphical user interfaces, data access, and Web development, which are staple requirements in many commercial ventures. Wouldn't it be useful if someone compiled a list of the namespaces that cross-platform developers could use with confidence? Let's go!

Categorizing Microsoft's .NET Framework Class Libraries

By definition, the Kernel and Compact Profiles contain namespaces that are safe to use in a cross-platform project. Nonetheless, the namespaces that are encompassed by these profiles have been extended to include types that don't fall within the CLI specifications, and this is where you meet the first hurdle.

Just because a namespace is defined in the CLI standards, it doesn't necessarily mean that all of its types are similarly defined or safe to use in a cross-platform context, and because Microsoft has also added members to the CLI-defined types, you can't even assume that it's safe to use all the standardized types' members.

TIP Appendix B contains a list of the types that are defined in the ECMA standards, but for more thorough coverage, read *C# in a Nutshell*, by Peter Drayton, Ben Albahari, and Ted Neward (O'Reilly, 2003).

So how do you distinguish between the types that are *safe* for cross-platform development and those that are not so safe? The namespaces that are available in Microsoft .NET is a suitable place to start making informed choices, even if you have no intention of using Microsoft's offering. It also makes sense to decide on a means to categorize the cross-platform applicability of the namespaces. This can be done using the following distinct groups:

- **CLI Defined:** Any type that's listed in the CLI standards can reasonably be called a CLI-defined type, and the namespaces that house these types are therefore referred to as CLI Defined. These CLI Defined namespaces are shown in Table 4-5.

- **Architecturally Sound:** Represents the namespaces that don't contain CLI-defined types, but that provide functionality that is likely to be duplicated in different .NET implementations, and are potential candidates for inclusion in future versions of the CLI standards. The Architecturally Sound namespaces are shown in Table 4-6.

- **Architecturally Dependent:** These are any namespaces that build on the underlying architecture of an operating system. A good example is the scapegoat from Chapter 3, the `Microsoft.Win32` namespace, which contains types that deal with the Windows registry. The Architecturally Dependent types are shown in Table 4-7.

Furthermore, these categorizations could be equally applied to Mono, Portable.NET, or any other CLI implementation. For example, Mono and PNET include the `Mono.Posix.dll` assembly. This assembly provides access to features that are defined by the Portable Operating System Interface (POSIX), which is a set of portability standards that are implemented by UNIX-based operating systems.

NOTE Although POSIX compliance is generally considered to be a feature of UNIX-based operating systems, a POSIX subsystem is available for Windows as part of Microsoft's Windows Services for UNIX, which is available from `http://www.microsoft.com/windows/sfu/default.asp`. The Cygwin environment, mentioned in Chapter 2, also provides a number of POSIX features for Windows.

Bear in mind that these categorizations do not represent a qualitative judgment, but more of a quantitative classification as an aid for avoiding pitfalls.

NOTE Although these categorizations can equally be applied to types, the huge number of types makes categorizing at the type level a fruitless task. Even so, it's worth remembering that just because a namespace is classified in one category, it might well contain individual types that fall in a different category.

While perfectionist cross-platform developers might want to restrict themselves to only using the CLI Defined and Architecturally Sound types, some projects will always be aimed at a specific platform and invariably use a wealth of Architecturally Dependent features. One best practice to use on new cross-platform projects is to avoid Architecturally Dependent types when possible, although as shown in Chapter 3, you can sometimes use abstraction to make Architecturally Dependent features work in a cross-platform fashion.

CLI Defined Namespaces

In the ideal cross-platform world, all the types in the CLI Defined namespaces would have been intrinsically cross-platform, but alas, the Redmond Brethren have added some extensions, and as useful as they are, some of the extensions are not directly suitable for non-Windows platforms. Perhaps it's too easy to comment with hindsight, but it would have been far easier for cross-platform developers if "embrace and extend"—or another suitably named namespace—had been factored into the `Microsoft` namespace. The CLI Defined namespaces are shown in Table 4-5.

Table 4-5. CLI Defined Namespaces

Namespace	**Notes**
`System`	Contains the `CLSCompliant` attribute, as mentioned in Chapter 8, which must be declared in all CLS Framework libraries. Also contains the `DllNotFoundException` class, which is discussed in Chapter 7 and is vital when dealing with P/Invoke. As you saw in Chapter 2, `System` contains the `PlatformID` enumeration, which in turn is used by the `System.Environment` class. Microsoft's implementation of `PlatformID` defines four values that encompass various Windows platforms, while Portable.NET defines an additional `Unix` value and Mono has an additional internal value of `128` to represent UNIX. The `Environment` class defines a diverse set of cross-platform members, although the `Environment.SpecialFolder` enumeration contains values that indicate special operating system directories, and some of these values are unique to the Windows operating systems.
`System.Collections`	Contains additional collection types such as `Queue`, `Stack`, and `BitArray`—good finger food.
`System.Collections.Specialized`	--
`System.Diagnostics`	The CLI only defines one type for this namespace, `ConditionalAttribute`. The namespace has been heavily extended and contains a number of potential cross-platform pitfalls that are described later.
`System.Globalization`	--

Table 4-5. CLI Defined Namespaces (Continued)

Namespace	Notes
System.IO	Contains the FileSystemWatcher, which is not supported in Microsoft .NET for Windows 95/98/Me. Portable.NET provides the class and allows the client code to subscribe to file system events but does not currently raise the events to clients for security reasons. Mono has three implementations: a default implementation that's written in pure managed code, a UNIX-based implementation that requires File Alteration Monitor (FAM) to be installed, and a Windows-only implementation. The default implementation works for all platforms, but there is a caveat: It cannot reliably raise Renamed events. Because the default implementation doesn't perform nearly as well as the others, it should only be used as a fallback mechanism.
System.Net	--
System.Net.Sockets	--
System.Reflection	--
System.Runtime.CompilerServices	--
System.Runtime.InteropServices	Used for interacting with unmanaged libraries, as discussed in Chapter 7, but also contains types for COM interoperability, which is heavily reliant on Windows, as mentioned in Chapter 8.
System.Security	--
System.Security.Permissions	Contains the RegistryPermission and FileDialogPermission classes. The RegistryPermission class secures access to the Windows registry and was investigated in the previous chapter. The FileDialogPermission class secures access to the Windows FileDialog, which is part of the Architecturally Dependent System.Windows.Forms namespace. This namespace is described in detail in Chapter 5.

Table 4-5. CLI Defined Namespaces (Continued)

Namespace	Notes
`System.Text`	Provides various types for handling strings. The `Encoding` and `ASCIIEncoding` classes both have a `WindowsCodePage` property that returns the Windows code page that is most similar to the given character encoding.
`System.Threading`	--
`System.Xml`	--

As you can see from Table 4-5, just because a namespace is listed in an ECMA profile, that doesn't mean that all the namespace's types are an integral part of the standard. While most of the namespaces have indeed been extended beyond the ECMA standards, thankfully only a few types raise cross-platform issues.

System.Diagnostics.EventLog

The `EventLog` class is used for interacting with the Windows operating system's Event Log. The Microsoft .NET Framework implementation is obviously fine when run on versions of Windows that support the Event Log; this includes Windows NT 4, 2000, XP, and Server 2003. However, because the implementation can't be used on all versions of Windows, this raises the interesting question of how it is handled by Mono and Portable.NET.

In fact, Mono has implemented the `EventLog` class, which allows existing code that targets the Windows Event Log to work—but only to a certain degree. While events are indeed logged to the class, they are only stored in memory and are not persisted as of yet; this means that no useful degree of data resilience exists. However, plans are being made to add a Windows implementation that uses the Windows Event Log and an XML implementation for other operating systems.

Along similar lines to the Mono implementation, Portable.NET also has an implementation of `EventLog` that uses an in-memory data store for recording the events that have occurred in the host Application Domain.

While the non-Microsoft implementations currently emulate the Windows Event Log and are likely to soon provide persistence mechanisms, in keeping with the tenet of avoiding features that are based on the operating system's architecture, you should consider your needs carefully. If you merely need a basic mechanism to record application events, you could write a simple custom solution, although a popular alternative is the open source `log4net` library. This library is a .NET port of the established `log4j` library.

TIP The `log4net` project can be found at `http://log4net.sourceforge.net`.

The `log4net` library offers a wide range of features that include logging to various data stores, such as text files, databases, NetSend, memory streams, e-mail, and others, including the Windows Event Log.

System.Diagnostics.PerformanceCounter

The `PerformanceCounter` class backs onto another architectural feature from Windows, the operating system's Performance Counters, which are typically used to monitor metrics related to the operating system or hardware's operational status. Examples of performance counters include one that determines the percentage of time that a processor isn't idle and one that tallies the number of bytes received across a network connection.

Although both Portable.NET and Mono include `PerformanceCounter` and its associated types, they are only placeholders that ensure binary compatibility with Microsoft's .NET Framework. Because the Windows Performance Counters don't have obvious equivalents in other operating systems, the `PerformanceCounter` types are likely to be of little use in cross-platform projects.

TIP Although `PerformanceCounter` and its related types aren't suitable for cross-platform development, those who are desperate to measure performance metrics could investigate the Performance API (PAPI), which is a C shared library for accessing the hardware performance counters that are available on many modern CPUs. PAPI is known to work under a variety of processors and operating systems, including Windows, GNU/Linux, Solaris, and AIX, and although it is C API, there is no reason it couldn't be called from a .NET wrapper using P/Invoke, which is described in Chapter 7.

The Performance API can be found at `http://icl.cs.utk.edu/projects/papi`, and a full list of hardware and operating systems that PAPI supports is available at `http://icl.cs.utk.edu/projects/papi/software`.

Architecturally Sound Namespaces

The Architecturally Sound categorization groups those namespaces whose types are inherently compatible across platforms, because their types don't rely on unique architectural features from the operating system or underlying hardware.

With managed code being easy to move between different CLI implementations and platforms, it's tempting to suggest that the Architecturally Sound namespaces should only be implemented in pure managed code, without relying on native code via .NET's Platform Invoke mechanism. Nonetheless, the good availability of functionality within native code and the lure of certain performance advantages mean that some Architecturally Sound namespaces depend on native code.

However, as long as the native code doesn't itself rely on unique architectural features of the operating system, there's no reason why the namespace cannot be used on different platforms, although the requisite shared libraries must exist on different platforms. Calling native functions in shared libraries is covered in depth in Chapter 7. The Architecturally Sound namespaces are shown in Table 4-6.

Table 4-6. Architecturally Sound Namespaces

Namespace	**Notes**
`System.CodeDom`	--
`System.CodeDom.Compiler`	--
`Microsoft.CSharp`	--
`Microsoft.VisualBasic`	--
`System.ComponentModel`	Contains classes that define .NET components and is predominantly cross-platform, with the exception of the `Win32Exception` class, which embodies Windows errors.
`System.Configuration`	--
`System.Configuration.Assemblies`	--
`System.Configuration.Install`	--
`System.Data`	--
`System.Data.Common`	--

Table 4-6. Architecturally Sound Namespaces (Continued)

Namespace	Notes
`System.Data.Odbc`	Provides access to ODBC data sources but requires unmanaged implementations of ODBC and ODBC drivers, as described in Chapter 6.
`System.Data.OleDB`	Provides access to OLEDB data sources. Because OLEDB is based on COM, it is not primarily supported on non-Windows platforms, although Mono has a clever implementation that is discussed in Chapter 6.
`System.Data.OracleClient`	Provides access to Oracle databases but requires an unmanaged Oracle driver, as mentioned in Chapter 6.
`System.Data.SqlClient`	--
`System.Data.SqlTypes`	--
`System.Diagnostics.SymbolStore`	--
`System.Drawing`	Provides types for drawing graphical artifacts. Microsoft's implementation uses the native GDI+ library on Windows, while Mono's implementation uses GDI+ on Windows and Cairo on non-Windows operating systems. Cairo is a cross-device vector graphics library that can be found at `http://www.cairographics.org/`. Portable.NET's implementation uses a toolkit-based approach and forms the foundation on which PNET's implementation of `System.Windows.Forms` is built, as discussed in Chapter 5.
`System.Drawing.Design`	Allows the development of design-time behavior of components.
`System.Drawing.Drawing2d`	--
`System.Drawing.Imaging`	--
`System.Drawing.Text`	--
`System.Drawing.Printing`	--

Table 4-6. Architecturally Sound Namespaces (Continued)

Namespace	Notes
`System.IO.IsolatedStorage`	Provides types to securely store data on a user, assembly, and domain basis. The implementation in Microsoft's .NET Framework provides support for Windows roaming profiles, while PNET and Mono do not. Isolated Storage was discussed briefly in Chapter 3.
`System.Reflection.Emit`	--
`System.Runtime.Remoting`	--
`System.Runtime.Remoting.Activation`	--
`System.Runtime.Remoting.Channels`	--
`System.Runtime.Remoting.Channels.Http`	--
`System.Runtime.Remoting.Channels.Tcp`	--
`System.Runtime.Remoting.Contexts`	--
`System.Runtime.Remoting.Lifetime`	--
`System.Runtime.Remoting.Messaging`	--
`System.Runtime.Remoting.Metadata`	--
`System.Runtime.Remoting.Metadata.W3cXsd2001`	--
`System.Runtime.Remoting.MetadataServices`	--
`System.Runtime.Remoting.Proxies`	--
`System.Runtime.Remoting.Services`	--
`System.Runtime.Serialization`	--
`System.Runtime.Serialization.Formatters`	--
`System.Runtime.Serialization.Formatters.Binary`	--
`System.Security.Cryptography`	--
`System.Security.Cryptography.X509Certificates`	--
`System.Security.Cryptography.Xml`	--
`System.Security.Policy`	--
`System.Text.RegularExpressions`	--
`System.Timers`	--

Table 4-6. Architecturally Sound Namespaces (Continued)

Namespace	Notes
`System.Web`	--
`System.Web.Configuration`	--
`System.Web.Security`	Mono doesn't support Microsoft's Passport API or authentication for the Windows Internet Information Server (IIS). Because both IIS and Passport are proprietary Microsoft technologies, it is unlikely that they will ever be supported on Mono or PNET, although a call to arms has gone out to the Mono community to provide functionality that encompasses other authentication servers.
`System.Security.Principal`	Contains a number of types for dealing with Windows users, including `WindowsAccountType`, `WindowsBuiltInRole`, `WindowsIdentity`, `WindowsImpersonationContext`, and `WindowsPrincipal`. Portable.NET currently provides a binary-compatible but nonfunctional implementation, while Mono provides an implementation that works on all platforms, with the Windows-specific features only working on Windows. As discussed in Chapter 2, Code Access Security is in the cards for both Mono and Portable.NET but is not currently supported in either CLI implementation.
`System.Web.Services`	--
`System.Web.SessionState`	Microsoft .NET currently supports three modes of session storage: in-process, in an SQL Server database, and in a special Windows service. Mono currently supports the preservation of state in the ASP.NET process, but the intention is to provide options to use a database or an operating system daemon (for UNIX-based operating systems) that effectively mimics the options that are available under Microsoft .NET.

Table 4-6. Architecturally Sound Namespaces (Continued)

Namespace	Notes
System.Web.Caching	--
System.Web.Hosting	--
System.Web.Mail	--
System.Web.Services.Description	--
System.Web.Services.Discovery	--
System.Web.Services.Protocols	--
System.Web.UI	--
System.Xml.Schema	--
System.Xml.Serialization	--
System.Xml.XPath	--
System.Xml.Xsl	--

With the majority of namespaces falling into the Architecturally Sound category, the fact that the vast majority of their types also fall into the same category is a testament to .NET's cross-platform suitability. If the CLI Defined namespaces are the foundations, the Architecturally Sound namespaces are the walls, fittings, and luxury fixtures that turn .NET into a truly deluxe development tool. Pushing the analogy further, it's now time to take a look at the leaky roof.

Architecturally Dependent Namespaces

A type can be defined as Architecturally Dependent if it encapsulates a feature, technology, or philosophy that's unique to a particular platform. Similarly, a namespace is defined as Architecturally Dependent if the majority of its types are Architecturally Dependent or if the main technology it encapsulates is unique to a specific platform. This doesn't mean that Architecturally Dependent namespaces should not be used in a cross-platform context, but rather that their use should be carefully considered.

Examples of Architecturally Dependent technologies are Microsoft's COM, the Windows Start button, and Apple's menu bar. Because most operating systems have a graphical user interface (GUI) with a particular branded style, GUIs can also be considered Architecturally Dependent, and as you will see in Chapter 5, cross-platform GUI development presents its own range of complex configuration, deployment, and design issues. The Architecturally Dependent namespaces are shown in Table 4-7.

Table 4-7. Architecturally Dependent Namespaces

Namespace	Notes
`Microsoft.Win32`	Provides types that deal with Windows operating system events and the Windows Registry. Chapter 3 discussed the Windows Registry in-depth and proposed a number of alternatives. Mono's implementation of the Registry types merely provides binary compatibility, and both Mono and PNET only provide binary compatibility for the types that deal with system events.
`System.ComponentModel.Design`	Contains types for specifying design-time behavior of controls for integration with design-time environments. Because the functionality is geared toward the `System.Windows.Forms` namespace, it is coupled to the Windows GUI.
`System.ComponentModel.Design.Serialization`	Provides types for handling component persistence at design time and the loading of components by designers. See `System.ComponentModel.Design` for more details.
`System.DirectoryServices`	Contains types that encapsulate Microsoft's Active Directory technology, which is Microsoft's implementation of a Lightweight Directory Application Protocol (LDAP) server and provides enterprise directory-management facilities. Mono's implementation wraps the `Novell.Directory.Ldap` assembly, which is included with Mono. Because the assembly is not Architecturally Dependent, it is a good replacement for `System.DirectoryServices`.
`System.EnterpriseServices`	Provides types that implement an enterprise service infrastructure, which provides various facilities, such as transaction management, role-based security, and object pooling. Microsoft's implementation is based on COM+, which is tightly coupled to Windows, although Mono has plans to implement a fully managed solution. See the next section for more details.

Table 4-7. Architecturally Dependent Namespaces (Continued)

Namespace	Notes
System.EnterpriseServices.CompensatingResourceManager	See the previous entry, System.EnterpriseServices.
System.Management	Provides access to management information about the system and applications that subscribe to the Windows Management Instrumentation (WMI) infrastructure. The WMI infrastructure is Microsoft's implementation of Web-Based Enterprise Management (WBEM). Further information about WBEM is available from http://www.dmtf.org/standards/wbem. Although Mono and PNET contain a stubbed implementation of System.Management for binary compatibility, there are no plans to implement a working version. Currently, the best alternative would be to use a different WBEM implementation, such as the WBEM Services project. This is an open source Java implementation of WBEM and is available from http://wbemservices.sourceforge.net/.
System.Management.Instrumentation	Contains classes for exposing applications to the Windows Management Instrumentation infrastructure by providing events for WMI consumers. See System.Management for more details.
System.Messaging	See the section "Message Queuing," later in this chapter, for more details.
System.ServiceProcess	Provides types to install and control Windows Service applications. Although both PNET and Mono currently only contain a minimal implementation for binary compatibility, because Windows services are equivalent to UNIX daemons, a future implementation will probably use daemons when running on UNIX-based systems and Windows Services when running under Windows.
System.Windows.Forms	Provides types for creating a Windows-style graphical user interface but is set to be surpassed by WinFX in Windows Longhorn. See Chapter 5 for further details on building cross-platform graphical user interfaces.
System.Windows.Forms.Design	Extends the design-time support for System.Windows.Forms.

Enterprise Services

The System.EnterpriseServices namespace provides a number of common services to simplify the implementation of .NET components, including transaction management, Just-In-Time Activation, object pooling, Synchronization, and role-based security. By separating these logistical services from application logic, it is theoretically easier and quicker to create robust enterprise systems.

Microsoft implements the System.EnterpriseService namespace by wrapping COM+, which is a complex unmanaged system with strong roots in COM. Because it would be unrealistic for either Mono or PNET to create a cross-platform implementation of COM+, the Mono project has plans to implement a completely managed version, although it is in the preliminary design stage and will not be available for a substantial period of time.

TIP More information on Mono's implementation of System.EnterpriseServices is available from http://www.nullenvoid.com/mono/wiki.

Message Queuing

Another .NET namespace that implements functionality that's useful in enterprise application development is the System.Messaging namespace, which contains a thorough asynchronous messaging framework. Microsoft's implementation encapsulates the Microsoft Message Queue Server (MSMQ). Message queues—which are often known as e-mail for applications—are useful for enterprise applications because they can guarantee delivery of interapplication messages, even though the connection between the sending and receiving applications might be unreliable.

Because MSMQ is a large and complex unmanaged product, the Mono project intends to implement a fully managed message queue system called Mono Queue Server Lithe Engine (MonoQLE). When MonoQLE is completed, the System.Messaging namespace will be functionally compatible with the implementation in Microsoft's .NET Framework.

TIP For details on the progress of MonoQLE, go to http://sourceforge.net/projects/monoqle.

Following the Leader

While Tables 4-5, 4-6, and 4-7 show that the majority of assemblies from the Microsoft .NET Framework are being implemented by Mono and PNET, it's worth considering that some of the assemblies are only implemented to be binary compatible and don't realize the requisite functionality. This leads to the following warning: Just because an application that runs on the Microsoft .NET Framework appears to work on Mono or Portable.NET, the application could fail in some unseen way or might not work exactly as expected.

TIP The key to ensuring that applications written for one platform work on another is to run extensive unit tests on each platform at which they are targeted. A good tool for carrying out these unit tests is NUnit, which is discussed in depth in Chapter 9.

While in Utopia, Architecturally Dependent namespaces wouldn't exist, with each CLI implementation exhibiting functional as well as binary compatibility. For those of us who are used to the dystopian travails of the real world, these namespaces not only exist, but they're also important parts of numerous projects.

With this in mind, the next section describes a technique that allows these namespaces to be used in a fashion that isolates their usage and patterns to encapsulate the solution. A .NET native solution allows Architecturally Dependent functionality to be bolted on, maintained, or swapped out with minimal overheads.

Bridging Platform Differences

Having dissected the available namespaces and decided that certain namespaces are only suitable for certain platforms, it would be convenient to be able to tailor solutions so that Architecturally Dependent features can be used when appropriate, with alternative implementations being used on different platforms.

Fortunately, an object-oriented solution to this problem exists, in the form of a design pattern called the *bridge*. This flexible pattern allows you to tailor as many different implementations as you want and, with minimum fuss, reconfigure your software to use the right implementation for the platform that it's deployed on.

Design Patterns

If you're new to the concept of design patterns, some explanation is in order. A design pattern is essentially an arrangement of classes that solve a particular problem in object-oriented design. Because patterns are used to solve specific issues that occur frequently, by identifying and naming patterns, it becomes easy to communicate design issues to other developers.

By way of analogy, the architect of a shiny, tall, new building will, at some stage, have to consider the problem of moving people among the building's numerous floors. Referring to blueprints of other large buildings, she can see that staircases, elevators, and escalators all serve as good examples of solutions. The adventurous architect finally settles on an elevator that's mounted to the outside of the building and proceeds, happy in the knowledge that others have found it to be a good solution.

A typical example of such a scenario is the use of the `System.Diagnostics.EventLog` class, which was mentioned earlier in the chapter. Under Microsoft .NET, this class interacts with the Windows Event Log, but Mono and Portable.NET only have partial implementations that cannot persist events past the lifetime of the program's application domain. To ensure that applications persist their events as expected when using PNET or Mono, a different mechanism is needed.

This situation occurs repeatedly as you look through the table of Architecturally Dependent namespaces. As a case in point, Portable.NET's implementation of the registry classes, which was discussed in Chapter 3, uses a bridge pattern by implementing different Key Providers to implement the registry-storage mechanism on different platforms.

The Bridge Design Pattern

The bridge pattern serves to "decouple an abstraction from its implementation so that the two can vary independently,"[1] which involves breaking a solution into two parts. The first part of the solution is the *abstraction*, which is used by the client code; the second part is the *implementation*, which is used by the abstraction to carry out the requisite functionality. Figure 4-1 illustrates the basic bridge design pattern.

1. Gamma, Helm, Johnson, and Vlissides, *Design Patterns: Elements of Reusable Object Oriented Software* (Reading, MA: Addison-Wesley, 1995).

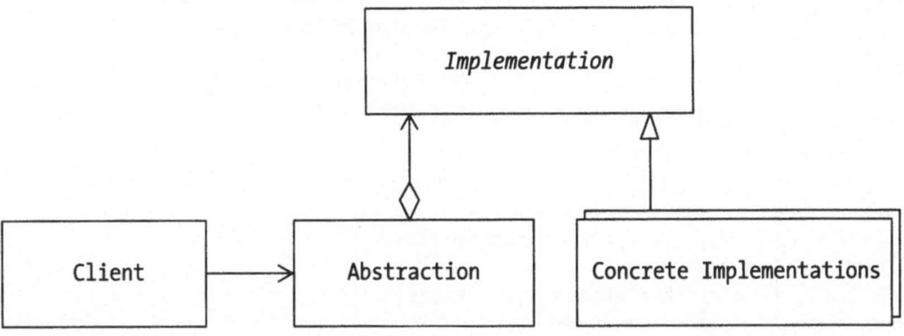

Figure 4-1. The bridge design pattern

Because the whole purpose of the bridge is to provide multiple implementations, the implementation is usually embodied as an abstract base class, with a number of concrete implementation classes providing the actual implementations.

We can clarify things by way of an example and apply the bridge pattern to a project that needs to record program events. While the program will use the Windows Event Log when running on the Microsoft .NET Framework, it will need a different implementation when running on other CLI implementations and operating systems.

NOTE The code for this example can be found in the `Chapter_04/LogClient` directory at `http://www.cross-platform.net` and `http://www.apress.com`.

To start with, we create a couple of classes for the abstraction and base implementation. Because we merely want to record program events for our simple example, a little brain rattling suggests that both the abstraction and base implementation need a single `public` method, `Record()`, which takes a string as a parameter, as illustrated in Figure 4-2.

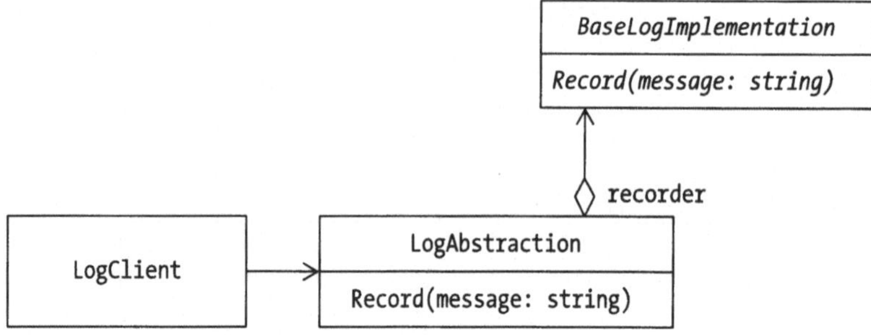

Figure 4-2. Applying the bridge pattern

We first look at the LogAbstraction class, which apart from the Record() method, also requires a private field to store a reference to an instance of the actual implementation class. We've called this field recorder, as shown in the following code:

```
//LogAbstraction.cs
using System;
using System.IO;

namespace Crossplatform.NET.Chapter04
{
    public class LogAbstraction
    {
        private BaseLogImplementation recorder;

        //No constructor yet...

        public void Record(string text)
        {
            this.recorder.Record(text);
        }
    }
}
```

Because the class is acting as an abstraction, the only thing that its Record() method does is to forward its parameter to the Record() method on the BaseLogImplementation instance that is referenced by the recorder field.

Also, notice that no constructor is shown yet; this was done on purpose. The bridge pattern raises several questions about how to choose the concrete implementation, which part of the project instantiates it, and when it should be created. We ignore these questions for now and return to them later, when we implement the class's constructor.

The `BaseLogImplementation` class is even simpler and is implemented as an `abstract` class with one `abstract` method, `Record()`, as follows:

```
//BaseLogImplementation.cs
using System;

namespace Crossplatform.NET.Chapter04
{
    public abstract class BaseLogImplementation
    {
        protected BaseLogImplementation(){}

        public abstract void Record(string message);
    }
}
```

To complete the bridge pattern, we need to implement one concrete implementation to use with the Microsoft .NET Framework and another to use with the other CLI implementations, as shown in Figure 4-3.

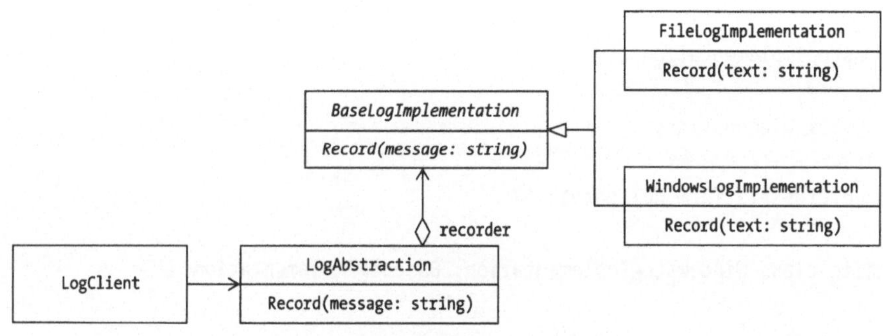

Figure 4-3. The bridge with concrete implementations

The code for the `FileLogImplementaion` class is straightforward, with the class being declared as an `internal` class that inherits from `BaseLogImplementation`.

The `Record()` method uses the `File.AppendText()` method to return an instance of a TextWriter, which is subsequently used to write the message to the `SimpleTextFile.txt` file in the application's current working directory. While we haven't provided a mechanism to specify the path to the log file, a production system could easily include some extra functionality for setting the file's path.

```
//FileLogImplementation.cs
using System;
using System.IO;

namespace Crossplatform.NET.Chapter04
{
    internal class FileLogImplementation: BaseLogImplementation
    {
        public FileLogImplementation(){}

        public override void Record(string message)
        {
            using(TextWriter writer = File.AppendText("SimpleTextFile.txt"))
            {
                writer.WriteLine(message);
            }
        }
    }
}
```

This code for the `WindowsLogImplementation` is just as simple as the `FileLogImplementation`, but instead of writing to a file, it instead uses the `EventLog` class to write a message to the Windows Event Log, as follows:

```
//WindowsLogImplementation.cs
using System;
using System.Diagnostics;

namespace Crossplatform.NET.Chapter04
{
    public class WindowsLogImplementation: BaseLogImplementation
    {
        //Could create "sources" here
        public WindowsLogImplementation() {}

        public override void Record(string message)
        {
            EventLog.WriteEntry("WindowsLogImplementation", message);
        }
    }
}
```

Now that we have the classes that implement the actual bridge, it's time to create a basic client program to test the code. The `LogClient` class contains a single `static` method, `Main()`, which creates an instance of the `LogAbstraction` class and then concatenates the command-line arguments together, passing the resulting string for posterity to the `LogAbstraction` class's `Record()` method, as follows:

```
//LogClient.cs
using System;

namespace Crossplatform.NET.Chapter04
{
    public class LogClient
    {
        static void Main(string[] args)
        {
            LogAbstraction recorder = new LogAbstraction();
            recorder.Record(string.Join(" ", args));
        }
    }
}
```

While the program is almost ready to go, as we mentioned earlier, we haven't implemented a constructor for the `LogAbstraction` class yet; we now address that issue. We left the constructor until the end, because we need a mechanism to decide which concrete implementation to use. The ideal place to do this is in the `LogAbstraction`'s constructor.

As you will see later in the chapter, you can use a number of different strategies when deciding what implementation to use. In this instance, we opt for a bit of self-determination and allow the abstraction to decide, depending on whether it's running on Windows, as follows:

```
public LogAbstraction()
{
    if (IsWindows())
        this.recorder= new WindowsLogImplementation();
    else
        this.recorder = new FileLogImplementation();
}

private bool IsWindows()
{
    return (Path.DirectorySeparatorChar == '\\');
}
```

If you've been paying attention, you will have noticed that `LogAbstraction` uses a slightly different `IsWindows()` method than the example shown in Chapter 3, which used the `PlatformID` enumeration.

NOTE Although this version of `IsWindows()` differentiates between operating systems by checking which character is used for separating directories in a path, it's just as effective as using `PlatformID` and should work for the foreseeable future—until other operating systems start using backslashes to separate directories, that is.

Before compiling and running the program, we briefly recap the whole code for `LogAbstraction`, as follows:

```
//LogAbstraction.cs
using System;
using System.IO;

namespace Crossplatform.NET.Chapter04
{
    public class LogAbstraction
    {
        private BaseLogImplementation recorder;

        public LogAbstraction()
        {
            if (IsWindows())
                this.recorder= new WindowsLogImplementation();
            else
                this.recorder = new FileLogImplementation();
        }

        //Are we running on Windows?
        private bool IsWindows()
        {
            return (Path.DirectorySeparatorChar == '\\');
        }
```

```
        //Forward calls to the implementation
        public void Record(string message)
        {
            this.recorder.Record(message);
        }
    }
}
```

All that's left to do is to compile and run the program. Assuming that you've saved all your files in their own directory, you can do it on GNU/Linux using Mono, as follows:

```
mono@linux:~/LogClient % mcs *.cs
Compilation succeeded

mono@linux:~/LogClient % mono LogClient.exe This is a message

mono@linux:~/LogClient %
```

To compile and run `LogClient.exe` on Windows using the Microsoft .NET Framework, use the following commands:

```
C:\MS.NET\LogClient> csc *.cs
Microsoft (R) Visual C# .NET Compiler version 7.10.3052.4
for Microsoft (R) .NET Framework version 1.1.4322
Copyright (C) Microsoft Corporation 2001-2002. All rights reserved.

C:\MS.NET\LogClient> LogClient This is also a message

C:\MS.NET\LogClient>
```

Finally, on Mac OS X and Portable.NET, use the following commands:

```
pnet@macosx:~/LogClient % cscc /out:LogClient.exe *.cs
pnet@macosx:~/LogClient % ilrun LogClient.exe This is still a message

pnet@macosx:~ %
```

Because both PNET and Mono should have used the `FileLog` implementation, which was hard-coded to write to the `SimpleText.txt` file, you can use the `cat` command to display the output, as follows:

```
cat SimpleText.cs
```

To check that the program ran as expected on Windows, you can look in the Windows Event Viewer, which is available from the Start menu's Administrative Tools directory and is shown in Figure 4-4.

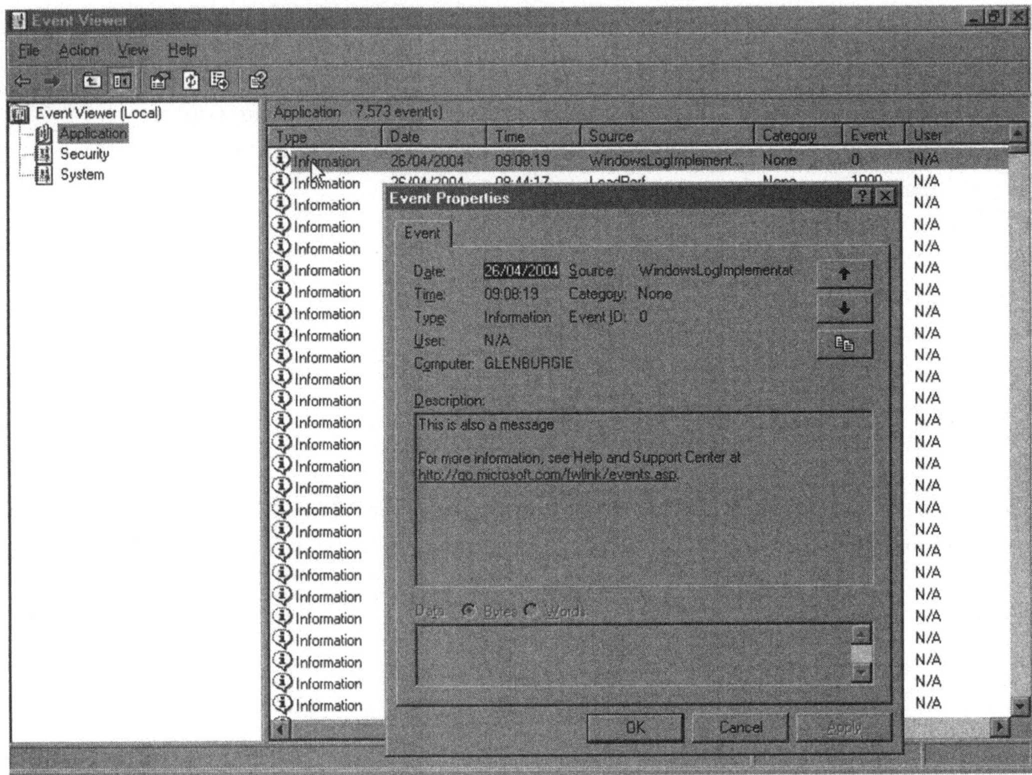

Figure 4-4. The Windows Event Viewer

TIP Rather than using the decidedly simple `FileLogImplementation`, a more robust implementation might have included a concrete implementation that used the `log4net` library, which was mentioned earlier in the chapter.

Manually Choosing an Implementation

Although the `LogClient` program seemed to work pretty well, it contained a glaring error. Because the program decided which concrete implementation to use based on the operating system, it doesn't work if we run it with either of the non-Microsoft CLI implementations on Windows. In effect, this means that we need a different mechanism for deciding which concrete implementation to use.

NOTE The code for this example can be found in the `Chapter_04/LogClient2` directory at `http://www.cross-platform.net` and `http://www.apress.com`.

Because the previous program automatically determined which concrete implementation to use, the simplest fix is to allow the client code to specify which implementation to use, which we now do in the `LogClient2` program, as illustrated in Figure 4-5.

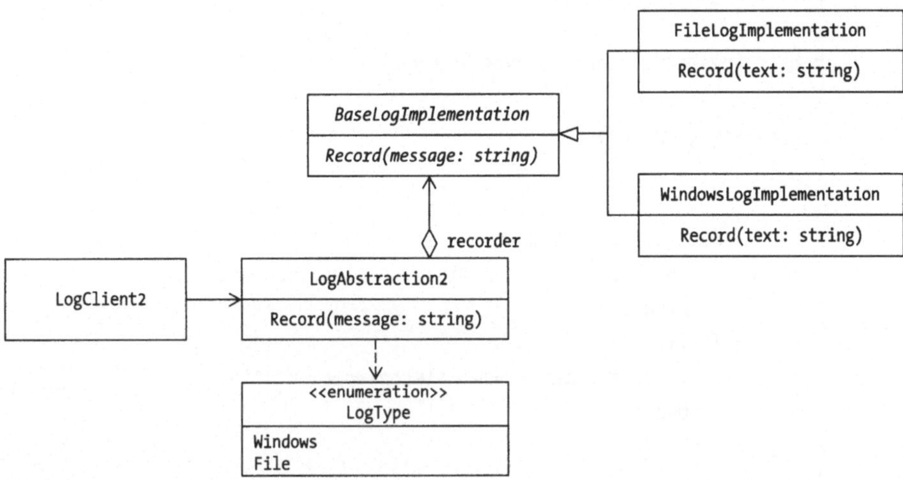

Figure 4-5. The `LogClient2` *program*

To allow the client code to specify which implementation it wants to use, we add a `LogType` enumeration, which contains a value that represents each type of `LogImplementation`, as follows:

```
//LogTypes.cs
public enum LogType
{
    Windows,
    File
}
```

We now need to modify the LogAbstraction class so that it allows client code to specify one of the LogType values in calls to the constructor. We also provide an overloaded constructor so that if the client doesn't specify a Logtype value, it falls back to use the FileLogImplementation, as follows:

```
//LogAbstraction2.cs
using System;

namespace Crossplatform.NET.Chapter04
{
    public class LogAbstraction2
    {
        private BaseLogImplementation recorder;

        //Use the file implementation by default
        public LogAbstraction2(): this(LogType.File){}

        public LogAbstraction2(LogType logType)
        {
            switch (logType)
            {

                case (LogType.Windows):
                    this.recorder= new WindowsLogImplementation ();
                    break;
               default:
                    this.recorder = new FileLogImplementation();
                    break;
            }
        }

        public void Record(string message)
        {
            this.recorder.Record(message);
        }
    }
}
```

Finally, we need to modify the client code to allow it to choose which implementation to use. To do this, we modify the previous LogClient's code to use the LogAbstraction2 class and get it to additionally ask the user which implementation to use, retrieving his response using the Console.Read() method, as follows:

```
//LogClient2.cs
using System;

namespace Crossplatform.NET.Chapter04
{
    public class LogClient2
    {
        static void Main(string[] args)
        {
            LogAbstraction2 recorder;
            Console.WriteLine("Enter '1' to use the WindowsLogImplementation.");
            Console.WriteLine("Enter '2' to use the default implementation.");

            if ((char)Console.Read() == '1')
                recorder = new LogAbstraction2(LogType.Windows);
            else
                recorder = new LogAbstraction2();

            recorder.Record(string.Join(" ", args));
        }
    }
}
```

All that's left to do is to compile and run the program. This can be done on GNU/Linux using Mono, for example, as follows:

```
mono@linux:~/LogClient2 % mcs *.cs
Compilation succeeded

mono@linux:~/LogClient2 % mono LogClient2.exe The variety of life
Enter '1' to use the WindowsLogImplementation.
Enter '2' to use the default implementation.
2
mono@linux:~/LogClient2 %
```

While the `LogClient2` program resolves the issue with the first incarnation of always choosing the same implementation for an operating system, two problems still exist with this approach.

First, you can now run the program with the wrong implementation. This means that it is not only prone to misbehave on Windows, but it's also equally likely to misbehave on other operating systems. Second, if new concrete implementations are created, not only does the `LogType` enumeration need to be extended, but the main `LogAbstraction2` constructor also needs to be updated.

This is one reason why many object-oriented aficionados suggest that the presence of case statements is a sign of trouble ahead.

So, if either of these problems sticks in your craw like a misshapen tiger prawn, you may need the Heimlich maneuver. Read on, and breathe a bit easier.

Using Configuration Files

To resolve the issues that are raised by the `LogClient2` program, we need a mechanism that minimizes the chance of using the wrong concrete implementation while allowing new implementations to be added with minimal code changes. A good candidate for this mechanism is the .NET configuration file. This is an XML file that can be associated with a .NET executable assembly, and it can be used to store arbitrary application data that is read when the assembly is first loaded.

To associate a .NET configuration file with an assembly, the configuration file must be stored in the same directory and have the same name, with `.config` appended. At its most basic level, a configuration file must contain a `<configuration/>` element. This element, the top-level XML element, can contain a number of child elements, including the `<appSettings/>` element, which provides a simple way to store application data as key/value pairs, as shown in the following example:

```
<configuration>
    <appSettings>
        <add key="GUIColor" value="Red">
    </appSettings>
</configuration>
```

.NET Configuration Files

Apart from storing program-specific data in the `<appSettings/>` section, configuration files are also used by many fundamental parts of .NET, and as such, a number of predefined sections can be used under the domain of the top-level `<configuration/>` element.

For example, the `<configSettings/>` section allows new configuration sections to be defined, allowing the section name and the type that processes the section to be declared. While `<appSettings/>` can handle most simple application configuration requirements, you always have the option to define a custom section in `<configSettings/>` and then write a class to process the section.

As a cross-platform developer, something to be careful of is that the different CLI implementations don't currently predefine all the same configuration sections, so always check whether a particular section is supported by all the CLI implementations that you're targeting your program at.

To demonstrate a configuration file in action, we return to the `LogClient` program and create a configuration file that stores the name of the type to instantiate as the concrete implementation that's used by the `LogAbstraction` class. Because this is the third version of `LogClient`, we call the program `LogClient3`; the XML file is therefore named `LogClient3.exe.config`. The code for this configuration file is as follows:

```
<?xml version="1.0" encoding="utf-8" ?>
<configuration>
    <appSettings>
        <add key="LogImplementation"
           value="Crossplatform.NET.Chapter04.FileLogImplementation,LogClient3"/>
    </appSettings>
</configuration>
```

The value of the `LogImplementation` entry contains the type name in the format *namespace.typename,assemblyname*, which is known as a *Fully Qualified Type Name*. Because Fully Qualified Type Names additionally allow the culture and version number to be specified, they are the ideal way to accurately refer to types by name.

We then need to modify the implementation of the abstraction class to allow it to read the value from the configuration file. Because configuration files are only read once during an application's lifetime, we can read our `LogImplementation` setting in a `static` constructor and store the result in the `static` field, `typeName`.

NOTE The code for this example can be found in the `Chapter_04/LogClient3` directory at `http://www.cross-platform.net` and `http://www.apress.com`.

The `static` constructor simply needs to create an instance of the `AppSettingsReader` class and then call its `GetValue()` method to retrieve the value that's associated with the `LogImplementation` key, as follows:

```
//LogAbstraction3.cs
using System;
using System.Configuration;
using System.Runtime.Remoting;
```

```
namespace Crossplatform.NET.Chapter04
{
    public class LogAbstraction3
    {
        private static string typeName;

        private BaseLogImplementation recorder;

        static LogAbstraction3()
        {
            AppSettingsReader appSettings = new AppSettingsReader();
            string key = "LogImplementation";
            typeName = (string)appSettings.GetValue(key, typeof(string));
        }
```

The class constructor then needs to create an instance of the type whose name is stored in the `typeName` field, which is done by calling the `Activator.CreateInstance()` method. This method has several overloads, and it can create objects given the details of the type to instantiate and, if required, the constructor's parameters.

Because `CreateInstance()` returns an `object`, the final task of the constructor is to cast the returned `object` into a `BaseLogImplementation` and store it in the instance's `recorder` field, as follows:

```
        public LogAbstraction3()
        {
            object obj = Activator.CreateInstance(Type.GetType(typeName));
            this.recorder = (BaseLogImplementation) obj;
        }

        //Forward calls to the implementation
        public void Record(string message)
        {
            this.recorder.Record(message);
        }
    }
}
```

Finally, the `LogClient3.cs` file is practically identical to the original `LogClient.cs` file, although the former uses the `LogAbstraction3` class instead of the `LogAbstraction` class, as follows:

```
//LogClient3.cs
using System;

namespace Crossplatform.NET.Chapter04
{
    public class LogClient3
    {
        static void Main(string[] args)
        {
            LogAbstraction3 recorder = new LogAbstraction3();
            recorder.Record(string.Join(" ", args));
        }
    }
}
```

The architecture of the `LogClient3` program is illustrated in Figure 4-6:

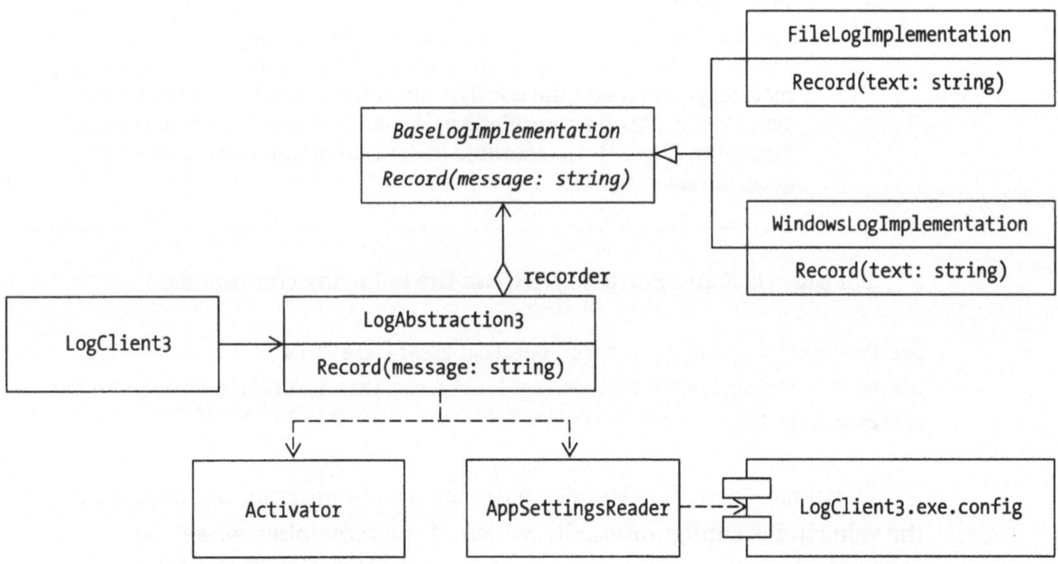

Figure 4-6. The `LogClient3` *program*

Now all that's left to do is to compile and run the program. For GNU/Linux using Mono, use the following commands:

```
mono@linux:~/LogClient3 % mcs *.cs
Compilation succeeded

mono@linux:~/LogClient3 % mono LogClient3.exe This is a configured message
mono@linux:~/LogClient3 %
```

For Windows and the Microsoft .NET Framework, use the following commands:

```
C:\MS.NET\LogClient3> csc *.cs
Microsoft (R) Visual C# .NET Compiler version 7.10.3052.4
for Microsoft (R) .NET Framework version 1.1.4322
Copyright (C) Microsoft Corporation 2001-2002. All rights reserved.

C:\MS.NET\LogClient3> LogClient3 This is also a configured message

C:\MS.NET\LogClient3>
```

TIP Users of Visual Studio might notice that when compiling, it has a nasty habit of deleting configuration files that are in the project's `bin\Debug` and `bin\Release` directories. To avoid this rather annoying feature, you can add the configuration file to your project and call it `app.config`. During compilation, Visual Studio will then copy the configuration file to the executable file's build directory and rename it accordingly.

For Mac OS X and Portable.NET, use the following commands:

```
pnet@macosx:~/LogClient3 % cscc /out:LogClient3.exe *.cs
pnet@macosx:~/LogClient3 % ilrun LogClient3.exe This is still a configured message
pnet@macosx:~ %
```

Of course, each of these calls to the `LogClient3` program will have used the value in the configuration file, which, if you remember, we set to `FileLogImplementation`. To take advantage of the Windows Event Log when using Microsoft .NET, you can easily change the value in the configuration file. This essentially means using different configuration files, depending on the target platform.

NOTE Although using a configuration file still allows the application to use the wrong concrete implementation if the application is misconfigured, it's easy to correct configuration mistakes, and even better, it's also possible to create additional concrete implementations without changing one line of the application's code.

Summary

We started the chapter by examining the XML CLI document and saw how it defines profiles, which are made up of libraries of types.

Because the CLI document forms part of the ECMA standard, the types that are contained therein form a solid foundation for developing cross-platform solutions. The chapter then defined three categories for classifying namespaces: CLI Defined, whose types are almost exclusively safe for cross-platform development; Architecturally Sound, whose types are theoretically safe for cross-platform development; and Architecturally Dependent, whose types encapsulate features that are highly unlikely to be suitable for cross-platform development. Although we only applied the classifications to the Microsoft .NET Framework, they are, nonetheless, equally applicable to the other CLI implementations, such as the `Mono.Posix.dll` assembly.

A map of the .NET namespaces, consisting of diagrams of the ECMA profiles and the three namespace classifications from this chapter, is included in Appendix B. Although the classifications are certainly open to interpretation, they by no means form a definitive list of what to use and what not to use in cross-platform projects but instead serve as a line in the sand. Ah, the joy of lists. Run your finger down them one more time—go on, we won't tell. Get a feel for the smooth, safe namespaces as well as those nasty ones that snag under your nails.

After a visit to Crazy Joe's Pattern Warehouse, the chapter introduced the bridge design pattern, which was used to divide a problem into an abstraction and an implementation of the solution. Finally, we introduced .NET configuration files and demonstrated how they can enhance the bridge pattern.

CHAPTER 5

The Spice of Life: GUI Toolkits

"There are two major products that came out of Berkeley: LSD and UNIX. We don't believe this to be a coincidence."

—Jeremy S. Anderson

SPAWNED IN THE EARLY 1970S, the decade of sartorial flamboyance that brought us sequined jump suits, ridiculously flared trousers, and the expression "Fat Elvis phase," the graphical user interface (GUI) has grown from a hacker's convenience tool into the public facade of the multibillion-dollar business that we all know and love. The impact that a good user interface has on an application should not be underestimated, and many projects, careers, and fortunes have been lost and found in the twinkling of a treeview.

So, the world is full of shallow aesthetes, but so what? It's fun to pander to them, and the best thing about graphical interfaces is that they provide a chance to make manifest the underlying artistry that is software development. For those of you who don't think that software is art, take a moment when you finish your next project to remind yourself that you've created something that didn't previously exist. If creation—even when infused with logic—isn't art, then call me a sandal-wearing, beard-chewing techie (brown kaftan and disastrous personal hygiene included).

TIP To read more about the history of the GUI, visit the excellent Web site `http://www.toastytech.com/guis`.

Philosophical ramblings aside, it's time to delve into the exciting jumble of GUI tools that are available for .NET and that can help make the difference between a professional, cross-platform GUI application and a jarring profusion of pixel soup.

Topography of a .NET Graphical User Interface

Because this book deals with a variety of CLI implementations and operating systems, a good place to start is to figure out how an ideal managed GUI might work. After that, we'll take a look at how each of the CLI implementations shapes up to the ideal implementation.

An Ideal Managed Windowing System

For the cross-platform developer dreaming of effortless portability, the ideal .NET rendering system would be written entirely in managed code.A sensible approach would involve the following steps:

1. Creating a basic rendering system for displaying primitive items—such as lines and rectangles—on a device such as a screen, printer, or file.
2. Developing a higher-level drawing library that encapsulates more-advanced functionality by using the basic rendering system.
3. Designing a class hierarchy that uses the high-level rendering library and catches the user input to produce a windowing system.

Although there's nothing wrong with this approach, it raises the question of when to leave the safe haven of managed code for the dangerous world of unsafe code and memory addresses. If this approach were taken to the extreme, the rendering system would depend on video drivers written to a managed interface, say `IVideoDriver`, and hardware vendors would release video drivers that conformed to the interface, as illustrated by Figure 5-1.

Of course, if hardware manufacturers wrote part of their video drivers in managed code, it wouldn't just be a performance disaster but it would seriously overstep the boundaries of user code, and it might irreparably sour the relationship between kernel and user code.

In contrast to the managed approach, from a performance point of view, it would be ideal if all the code were tightly written assembler code, without a whiff of managed code.

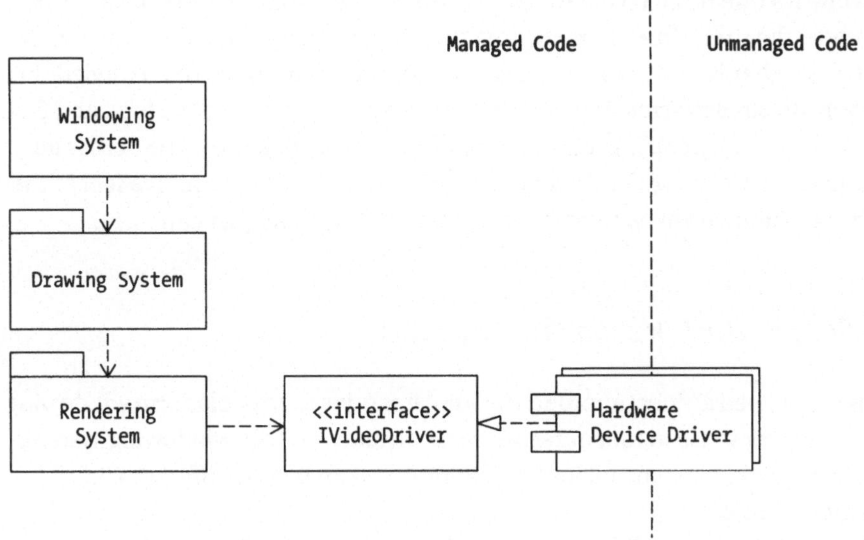

Figure 5-1. How slow does your system go?

Treading the fine line between these two approaches involves carefully separating functionality between managed and unmanaged code to deliver a compromise in performance and portability. Because device drivers are intrinsically linked to the host operating system and most operating systems provide some common rendering functionality, a more realistic split would use managed windowing and drawing systems, with an unmanaged rendering system calling to the device drivers, as shown in Figure 5-2.

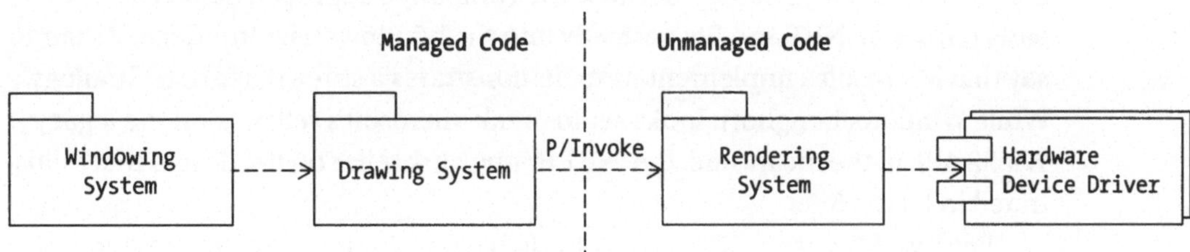

Figure 5-2. A managed windowing system

While it's one thing trying to balance tip-top performance with easily portable code, the main complaint against the managed approach that's shown in Figure 5-2 is that it invariably leads to a standardized interface that is styled the same way on all platforms, but is contrary to each platform's native look and feel.

Because some people prefer their applications to look the same across all platforms and others prefer their applications to fit in with the native feel of the operating system, frankly, a cross-platform GUI developer just can't win.

The Basic .NET Windowing System

Having considered an ideal approach for implementing a cross-platform windowing system, it makes sense to root ourselves in the realities of .NET windowing systems and take a quick, conceptual look at the route taken by the different CLI implementations.

Because Microsoft .NET provides the `System.Drawing.dll` assembly for drawing and the `System.Windows.Forms.dll` assembly for windowing, it should come as no surprise that the other CLI implementations have also chosen to implement these assemblies. What's interesting is to see how each CLI implementation has taken a significantly different approach to achieve this goal.

Microsoft .NET Framework

The .NET Framework currently implements both low-level rendering and higher-level controls by using Platform Invoke (P/Invoke) to call the Win32 API.

While it would be tempting to condemn Microsoft for reusing and extending the life of legacy technology, because the company's approach helped achieve an early release of .NET and fits perfectly into the Windows user interface, it's fair to say that Microsoft's implementation demonstrates a shrewd use of technology. While Windows Longhorn looks set to break Microsoft's reliance on the legacy Win32 API, in the meantime, the .NET Framework relies on the design that's illustrated in Figure 5-3.

Because Microsoft .NET is only available for Windows, its use of Windows native functionality should come as no surprise, because it provides good performance with little concern for portability.

However, while it's perfectly acceptable that Microsoft's implementation isn't portable, because `System.Windows.Forms` encapsulates the Windows GUI rather than a generic windowing system, one common complaint is that it should really be called `Microsoft.Windows.Forms`, with anything scoped within the `System` namespace being platform independent.

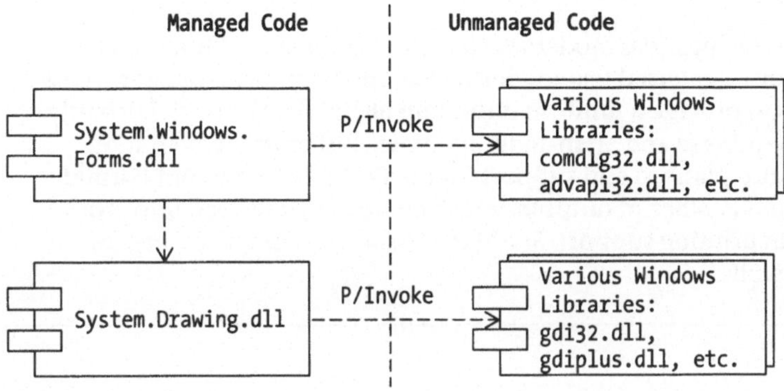

Figure 5-3. Microsoft's implementation of `System.Windows.Forms` *and* `System.Drawing`

Mono

Mono's approach to providing GUI functionality has evolved over time, and with multiple rendering back ends and multiple deployment platforms, the world of the GUI has been a tricky route to negotiate. It remains to be seen exactly where it will all end.

For its implementation of `System.Drawing`, Mono uses GDI+ on Windows, and Cairo on platforms running X Windows. As shown in Figure 5-4, while Platform Invoke is used to call directly into `Gdiplus.dll` on Windows, on non-Windows platforms, a library that mimics GDI+ is used. This library in turn passes all calls on to the Cairo library.

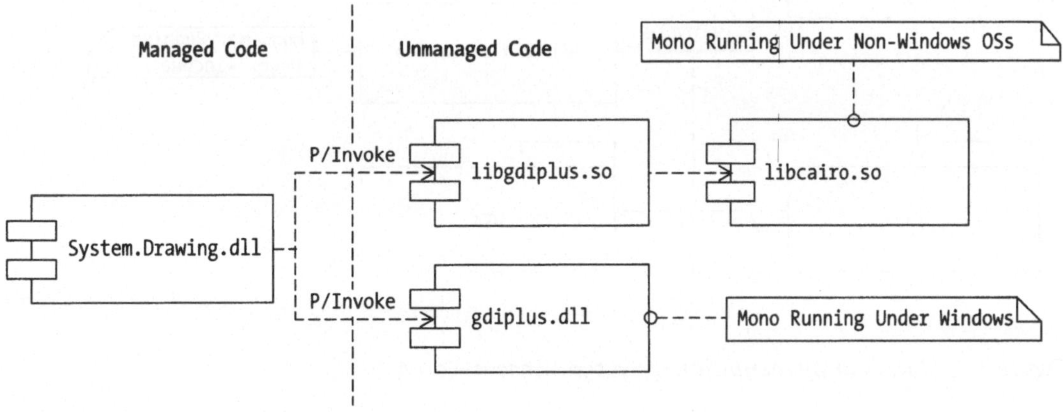

Figure 5-4. Mono's implementation of `System.Drawing`

NOTE Cairo provides modern vector graphics functionality and features, including antialiased text rendering and mathematical transforms. Its ethos is to provide a uniform output on all media, although currently only X Windows and an in-memory image buffer implementation exist. Cairo plans to add support for the Portable Document Format (PDF) and PostScript outputs, which could elegantly lead into cross-platform printing support. See `http://www.cairographics.org` for more details.

While Mono's implementation of `System.Drawing` is relatively straightforward, things are not so simple in regard to GUI toolkits. While we discuss a number of alternative GUI toolkits later in the chapter, three GUI implementations are currently directly related to Mono: `System.Windows.Forms`, implemented using Winelib; `System.Windows.Forms`, implemented using Gtk#; and Gtk#, a managed code wrapper for GTK+ that can be used as an alternative for `System.Windows.Forms`. Figure 5-5 shows these strategies in action.

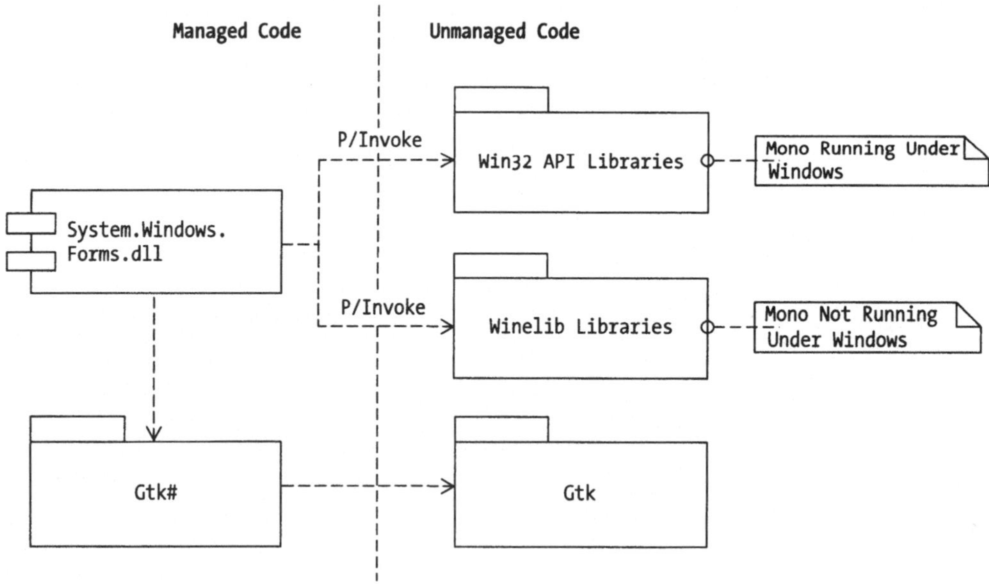

Figure 5-5. Mono's implementation of `System.Windows.Forms`

Drowning Your Sorrows: Wine

While it often seems that a bottle is the answer to your cross-platform development woes, some help is at hand in the form of the Wine project.

Wine is an adaptability layer for Windows programs and provides an environment that allows Windows programs to be loaded on different operating systems and executed with varying degrees of success. Wine consists of the following two separate parts:

- The `wine` program, which loads Windows binaries and marshals calls to the Windows API functions
- The `Winelib` library, which implements an ever-increasing subset of the functions from the Win32 API libraries

Although the `wine` program only runs on *x*86 hardware and can only be used for running native Windows applications, the `Winelib` libraries can be used as replacements for their Windows counterparts and can be accessed from .NET applications by using Platform Invoke.

For more information on the Wine project, visit `http://www.winehq.com`.

TIP Because both of Mono's `System.Windows.Forms` implementations are currently heavily in development, they aren't as reliable as Gtk#, and therefore our advice is to use Gtk# where possible.

Because Gtk# has a strong following in the open source community, choosing between Gtk# and `System.Windows.Forms` is both a political and a practical dilemma, not made any easier by the fact that both namespaces will eventually work on a variety of platforms. As you would expect, the Gtk# namespace is not directly interchangeable with `System.Windows.Forms`. This means to effectively use Gtk#, you need to learn all about its types and peccadilloes, although that's a small price to pay if `System.Windows.Forms` doesn't meet your needs.

As you can see from Figure 5-6, a number of supporting assemblies are required for the Gtk# namespace. Each Gtk# assembly not only calls directly into the equivalent GTK+ shared library, but each Gtk# assembly also calls into a C shared library that acts as *glue code* and exposes some higher-level facilities that are not provided by the GTK+ libraries.

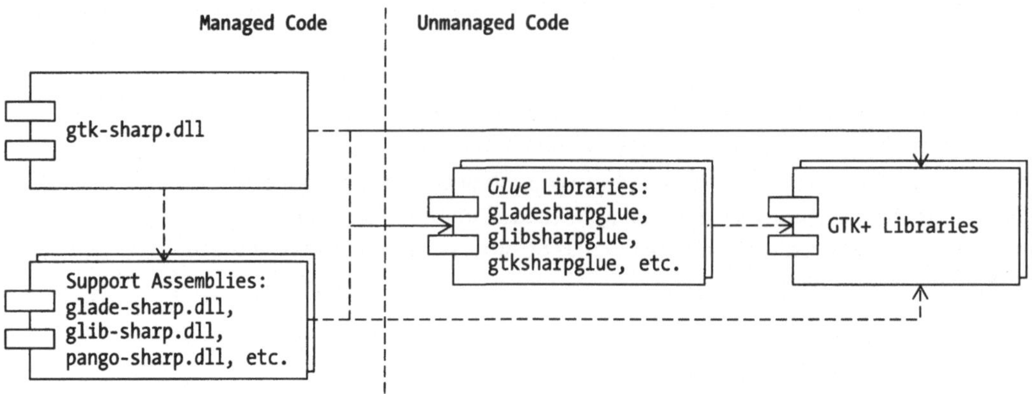

Figure 5-6. The Gtk# *implementation*

Portable.NET

Unlike Microsoft .NET and Mono, Portable.NET's graphical architecture tends toward the linear design that was advocated in Figure 5-2, with System.Windows.Forms building on the rendering functionality that is provided by System.Drawing. This results in all the controls being written in managed code.

To provide a portable rendering system, System.Drawing uses a helper namespace, System.Drawing.Toolkit, that defines a number of interfaces that can be used when wrapping arbitrary rendering engines. To date, Portable.NET has created wrappers for Win32, which provides Windows portability, and for X Windows, which provides portability to GNU/Linux, Mac OS X, and other UNIX-based operating systems. This architecture is illustrated in Figure 5-7.

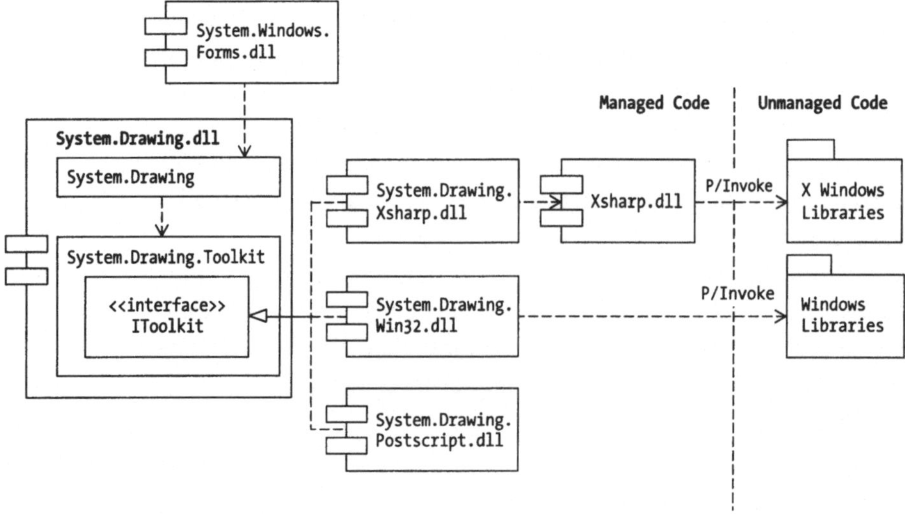

Figure 5-7. Portable.NET's GUI implementation

This architecture could well prove to be the purist's choice, because it strives to accommodate a good, portable design. As other rendering systems are brought into the fold, the core of the `System.Drawing` and `System.Windows.Forms` namespaces will remain uncluttered, and the Portable.NET community has started discussing wrapping up the Mac OS X Cocoa APIs for a more Mac-native feel on Mac OS X.

TIP For those who are concerned with authoring controls or who have a general interest in how widgets work, the source code for Portable.NET's implementation of `System.Windows.Forms` is an invaluable resource, although should you choose to use it as the basis for your own controls, the usual licensing rules apply.

Alternative GUI Toolkits

Having examined the standard graphical systems that are included with Mono, Portable.NET, and Microsoft .NET, it's now time to investigate a range of alternative GUI toolkits, each of which provides its own set of features and challenges, while helping to spice up the already colorful life of the cross-platform developer.

While developers from a stringent Windows background might be inclined to shun these toolkits and stick with `System.Windows.Forms`, you have a number of good reasons to embrace these alternative GUI toolkits.

Not only are some of toolkits easily portable across different platforms, but they also offer different feature sets, and some of them can provide a native look and feel on any platform that they are deployed on. It's also worth noting that when Microsoft releases Windows Longhorn in 2006, it will herald the arrival of a new Windows GUI system, Avalon, and will undoubtedly replace `System.Windows.Forms` as the preferred tool for developing Windows GUIs.

NOTE Promising the latest in vector graphics–based GUIs and using its own XML language, XAML, Avalon is set to be the future of GUI development on Windows. Luckily, an open source vector graphics library, VG.NET, is already available for .NET. While VG.NET is not identical to Avalon, it offers a number of similar features—such as exporting to MyXaml, an open source implementation XAML—and unlike Avalon, it's available for use today.

Downloads and more information on VG.NET are available from `http://www.vgdotnet.org`, and details of MyXaml can be found at `http://www.myxaml.com`.

The one advantage of investing in `System.Windows.Forms` is that although its days are numbered, because Mono and PNET are both implementing their own version, `System.Windows.Forms` is likely to be the most popular .NET GUI toolkit for the foreseeable future.

Gtk#

Sounding like the branding for a toy racing car—you can just picture the logo's speed blur and italic styling—Gtk# was created as a managed wrapper for the GTK+ toolkit, which is the cross-platform GUI toolkit that's used by GNOME, one of the most popular desktop managers for GNU/Linux.

NOTE Details about Gtk# are available from the project's Web site, `http://gtk-sharp.sourceforge.net`. More information on GTK+ is available from `http://www.gtk.org`.

While the original intention of Gtk# was only to wrap GTK+, the source parser and C# generator that are used to create Gtk# from the GTK+ API were found to be suitable for wrapping other GNOME APIs. As a result, Gtk# now encompasses much more than just GTK+ but retains the historical moniker. Because this chapter primarily deals with graphical user interfaces, investigating the other features of Gtk# is left to your own discretion.

Gtk# Libraries and GNOME

Although Gtk# is a useful GUI toolkit in its own right, a number of advocates from the open source community see Mono as the perfect development tool for furthering GNOME in the future. While there's by no means a consensus that the relationship between Mono and GNOME will blossom, Gtk# might be the first sign of a highly fruitful future between GNOME and Mono.

Gtk# currently wraps the following libraries:

- GTK+: gtk, gdk, atk, and pango
- gda
- gnomedb
- gconf
- libgnomecanvas
- libgnomeui
- libglade

For further details on these libraries and for a developer's eye view of the GNOME project, tutorials, and API references, go to `http://developer.gnome.org`.

To use Gtk#, the required core technology is the underlying GTK+ libraries. Consisting of three main libraries, as shown in Figure 5-8, GTK+ is built on GLib, a low-level core library at the heart of GTK+; Pango, which provides text rendering and font handling for GTK+–2.0; and ATK, which is a set of accessibility interfaces.

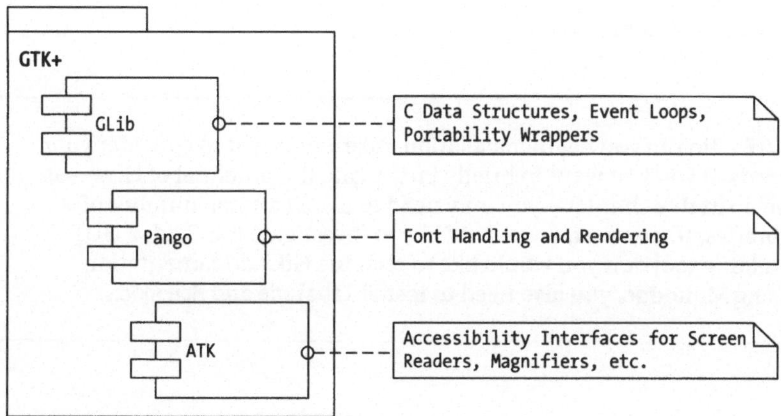

Figure 5-8. The core GTK+ libraries

The core GTK+ libraries are described by the GTK+ Web site as follows:

- **GLib:** Forms the basis of GTK+ and GNOME. It provides data structure handling for C, portability wrappers, and interfaces for runtime functionality, such as event loops, threads, dynamic loading, and an object system.
- **Pango:** Implements facilities for the layout and rendering of text, with an emphasis on internationalization. It forms the core of text and font handling for GTK+–2.0.
- **ATK:** Provides a set of interfaces for accessibility. By using the ATK interfaces, an application can support a number of accessibility tools, such as screen readers, magnifiers, and alternative input devices.

Installation and Prerequisites

Because building from source code is the most broadly applicable way of installing Gtk#, we demonstrate this approach on GNU/Linux, but if such strenuous manual efforts aren't your particular flavor of masochism, you have a number of easier ways to install Gtk#, depending on your operating system. To install Gtk# on Windows, an installer is available from the Gtk# Web site, and if you're a GNU/Linux user, you could always use Red Carpet, as mentioned in Chapter 2. If you decide to use either of these techniques, you can skip the remainder of this small section about installation.

NOTE Before you begin installation, take a moment to consider your needs. If you just want to briefly investigate the potential of Gtk#—as we do in this chapter—you only need to install a small number of libraries. If, however, you would like to investigate the Glade# GUI building tool or if you would like to read the Gtk# documentation using Monodoc, you also need to install `libglade` and `Monodoc`.

Table 5-1 lists the package dependencies and build order that are required for a minimum installation of Gtk# for use with Mono on GNU/Linux. Some optional extras are included in italics. For each package, the building instructions follow the following familiar routine:

```
./configure
make
make install
```

TIP Refer to Chapter 2 for a description of unpacking archives, or *tarballs*.

Table 5-1. Gtk# Installation Order

Order	Package Name	Download Location	Installation Tips
1	Glib	`http://www.gtk.org/download`	In the download directory, the latest versions are listed as empty files with the corresponding name (for example, LATEST-GLIB-2.2.3). For further building instructions and troubleshooting assistance, check out `http://developer.gnome.org/doc/API/2.2/gtk/gtk-building.html`.
2	Pango	`http://www.gtk.org/download`	Installation of any of these libraries may result in error messages when the configuration process is unable to locate certain files with a `.pc` file extension. The error messages are suitably verbose, but for further help, refer to the gtk-building link mentioned in the previous item for explicit instructions.
3	ATK	`http://www.gtk.org/download`	Use your distribution's file-search facility to locate missing files.
4	GTK+	`http://www.gtk.org/download`	You may need to install `libpng`. This can be downloaded from the `dependencies` link at `http://www.gtk.org/download`.
5	Libglade	`http://ftp.gnome.org/pub/GNOME/desktop/2.4/2.4.0/sources`	Required for using Glade# to graphically build GUIs.

Table 5-1. Gtk# Installation Order (Continued)

Order	Package Name	Download Location	Installation Tips
6	Gtk#	`http://gtk-sharp.sourceforge.net`	The configure and install process for GTK# can take a long time. Because you are not installing the other supported libraries, you can expect to see the occasional warning as the script attempts to create and install wrappers for libraries that you do not have.
7	Monodoc	`http://www.go-mono.com`	Optional but recommended for browsing the GTK# documentation.

TIP To reinstall or uninstall any of these libraries, navigate to the source code directory from where you built them; then issue `make clean` followed by `make distclean`.

Hello Gtk#

For our first foray into the world of Gtk#, we create a minimal GUI application, which consists of a form that contains a single button for closing the application. So, put the kettle on and dig out your favorite fingerless coding gloves—it's time to put Gtk# through its paces.

NOTE The source code samples for this chapter can be found in the Downloads section of this book's Web site (`http://www.cross-platform.net`) and the Apress Web site (`http://www.apress.com`). The code for this example can be found in the `Chapter_05/HelloGtk` directory.

We start the application by creating a simple class that inherits from Gtk#'s `Window` class, which is equivalent to the `Form` class from `System.Windows.Forms`. Because it's a little annoying using different terminology for discussing the same concepts in different GUI toolkits, we will use the terms *form* and *window* interchangeably throughout the rest of this chapter.

The class's code begins with a couple of `using` statements to reference the `System` and `Gtk` namespaces and then declares a couple of `private` fields to store references to two Gtk controls, as follows:

```
//Filename: MainWindow.cs
using System;
using Gtk;

namespace Crossplatform.NET.Chapter05
{
    class MainWindow: Gtk.Window
    {
        private Gtk.VBox buttonBar;
        private Gtk.Button closeButton;
```

To add several widgets, which we do in a later example, a container needs to be provided to house the controls. In this example, the `Button` is hosted in a `VBox`. `VBox` is an invisible container that lays out its widgets vertically, from top to bottom or bottom to top, depending on whether the controls are added with the `PackStart()` or `PackEnd()` method.

NOTE `VBox` has a horizontal equivalent, `HBox`, which provides the same kind of functionality, and again uses `PackStart()` and `PackEnd()` to control left and right positioning of the aggregated widgets.

After the two field declarations, a basic constructor calls the class's `Initialize()` method. The code has been written in this way to mimic the style that is imposed by Visual Studio when developing `System.Windows.Forms` applications, in a deliberate bid to ease comparisons between the two technologies. The code is as follows:

```
        public MainWindow(string caption) : base(caption)
        {
            Initialize();
        }
```

The `Initialize()` method is then responsible for setting the size of the form and then instantiating the `closeButton`, with the button's text being set to `Close` in the constructor. The `Button`'s `Click` event is then wired up to an event handler—in the same manner as `System.Windows.Forms`—before the `VBox` is created and packed with the `closeButton` container by calling the `PackEnd()` method. Finally, the `buttonBar` is added to the form, as follows:

```
        private void Initialize()
        {
            SetDefaultSize(350, 200);

            //Create the button
            this.closeButton = new Gtk.Button("Close");
            this.closeButton.Clicked += new EventHandler(closeButton_Click);

            //Create a container and add the button to it
            this.buttonBar = new Gtk.VBox(false, 5);
            this.buttonBar.PackEnd(this.closeButton, false, false, 5);

            // Finally, add our single top-level container to the form
            Add(this.buttonBar);
        }
```

We finish the class with a method to handle the Button's Click event, with the body of the method calling the class's inherited Destroy() method, as follows:

```
        private void closeButton_Click(object sender, EventArgs args)
        {
            Destroy();
        }
    }
}
```

Now that we have the MainWindow class, the program just needs an entry point, which we add by creating a new class, HelloGtk. HelloGtk contains the Main() method and is responsible for creating an instance of MainWindow and then starting and ending Gtk#'s message loop.

The class starts by declaring a static field MainWindow, which is used to store a reference to the application's window. The Main() method then writes to the console (which will help us see how Gtk# fires its events a little later), after which it calls the static Init() method on the Application class. This initializes the Gtk# environment, as follows:

```
//Filename: HelloGtk.cs
using System;
using Gtk;
```

```
namespace Crossplatform.NET.Chapter05
{
    class HelloGtk
    {
        private static Gtk.Window mainWindow;

        public static void Main()
        {
            Console.WriteLine("Starting Gtk engine...");
            Gtk.Application.Init();
```

When the Gtk# environment is ready, an instance of `MainForm` is created and a method is connected to the instance's `Destroyed` event, which will be fired when Gtk# deletes the `MainForm` object, as follows:

```
            mainWindow = new MainWindow("Hello from Gtk#");
            mainWindow.Destroyed += new EventHandler(MainWindow_Destroyed);
```

The `Main()` method finally calls `MainForm`'s `ShowAll()` method, which displays the application window, and then control is passed to the Gtk# message loop by calling the `Application.Run()` method, as follows:

```
            mainWindow.ShowAll();
            Gtk.Application.Run();
            Console.WriteLine("Codeflow back in GtkDemo.Main()");
        }
```

The class is topped off with a method to act as an event handler for the `Destroyed` event, which writes to the console and then shuts down the Gtk# environment by calling the `Application.Quit()` method. When `Quit()` has been called, control returns to the line immediately after the initial call to `Application.Run()`, as follows:

```
        public static void MainWindow_Destroyed (object sender, EventArgs e)
        {
            Console.WriteLine("Quitting Gtk engine...");
            Gtk.Application.Quit();
        }
    }
}
```

Theme Engine Trouble?

When you run the `HelloGtk` example, you might receive the following error:

```
(<unknown>:24180): Gtk-WARNING **:
Unable to locate theme engine in module_path:"qtpixmap "
```

This occurs because the Gtk# cannot locate the theme engine. This is due to incompatible installation locations of GTK+ and Gtk# or if more than one set of GTK+ libraries is installed.

To resolve this problem, locate your GTK+ directory (possibly `/usr/lib/gtk-2.0/2.2.0`) and then reinstall Gtk# in the same parent directory (for example `/usr`) instead of in `/usr/local`.

To test whether the program works, compile and run it on GNU/Linux and Mono using the following commands:

```
mono@linux:~ % mcs /out:HelloGtk.exe *.cs -pkg:gtk-sharp
Compilation succeeded
mono@linux:~ % mono HelloGtk.exe
Starting Gtk engine…
```

Assuming that the program compiles and runs correctly, it should create a one-buttoned window titled "Hello from Gtk#" which should look similar to the one depicted in Figure 5-9.

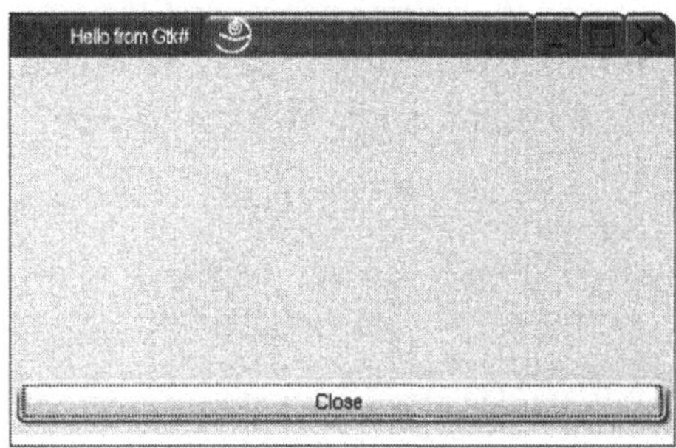

Figure 5-9. The Hello Gtk# program

When you click the button, the window should disappear, and the following lines are written to the console:

```
Starting Gtk engine...
Quitting Gtk engine...
Codeflow back in HelloGtk.Main()
mono@linux:~ %
```

So there you have it—a basic demonstration of Gtk# in action on GNU/Linux. While this example has only shown a minimal GUI application, it's hopefully been enough to show some of the similarities between Gtk# and `System.Windows.Forms`. Indeed, both toolkits have an `Application` class, they both use a `Run()` method to give control to the application's message loop, and Gtk#'s `Application.Quit()` method serves the same purpose as the `Application.Exit()` method in `System.Windows.Forms`.

Although the object models share some similarities and the general principles of application design are readily transferable between Gtk# and `System.Windows.Forms`, as you see in the next example, a number of significant differences can catch hasty developers by surprise.

A Modal Example

To demonstrate some of the differences between Gtk# and `System.Windows.Forms`, we use an example that opens a modal form. Consider the following code:

```
Console.WriteLine("About to launch modal form...");
ModalForm modalForm = new ModalForm("It's a Modal World");
Console.WriteLine("Modal form has been launched");
```

If you're used to developing exclusively for Windows, you would expect the code execution to pause after the form has been launched and to resume when the form is destroyed. In effect, the second message is only written to the `Console` after the modal form has closed.

Under GTK#, things are a little different. After the form has been launched, the code continues to execute. This means that the second message is written to the console as soon as the modal form has been displayed. Despite this fact, the handling of the modal form continues in a modal manner, that is, once the form has been launched, no other form can accept user input until the modal form is destroyed.

NOTE The code for this example can be found in the `Chapter_05/ModalWorld` directory at `http://www.cross-platform.net` and `http://www.apress.com`.

Another difference is that under Gtk#, a modal window is not guaranteed to stay in front of its parent window. To ensure that the modal form stays in front, two additional steps need to be taken: The window's `Modal` property must be set to `true`, and the `TransientFor` property must be set to the parent window, as follows:

```
this.TransientFor = parentWindow;
```

To demonstrate a modal form in action, we create a new class, `ModalWindow`, that inherits from `MainWindow`. The class contains a single, `private` field for storing a reference to the parent window, which is passed in through the constructor along with the window's title. The code is as follows:

```
//Filename: ModalWindow.cs
using System;
using Gtk;

namespace Crossplatform.NET.Chapter05
{
    class ModalWindow : MainWindow
    {
        private Gtk.Window parentWindow;

        public ModalWindow(string caption, Gtk.Window parentWindow) : base(caption)
        {
            this.parentWindow = parentWindow;
            Initialize();
        }
```

The `Initialize()` method ensures that the window is modal by setting the `Modal` property to `true` and the `TransientFor` property to reference the parent window, as follows:

```
        private void Initialize()
        {
            //Ensure the window is modal
            this.Modal = true;
            this.TransientFor = this.parentWindow;
        }
    }
}
```

Of course, to show a modal window in action, the application needs at least two windows, so we modify the `MainWindow` class to include an extra button that displays a modal window.

Alter the `MainWindow` class by adding an extra `private` field for the new button, and then ensure that the new button is instantiated and set up in the `Initialize()` method, as follows:

```
//Filename: MainWindow.cs
using System;
using Gtk;

namespace Crossplatform.NET.Chapter05
{
    public class MainWindow : Gtk.Window
    {
        private Gtk.VBox buttonBar;
        private Gtk.Button closeButton;
        private Gtk.Button modalButton;

        public MainWindow(string caption) :base(caption)
        {
            Initialize();
        }

        private void Initialize()
        {
            SetDefaultSize(350, 200);

            //Create the buttons
            this.closeButton = new Gtk.Button("Close this Window");
            this.closeButton.Clicked += new EventHandler(closeButton_Click);

            this.modalButton = new Gtk.Button("Open a Modal Window");
            this.modalButton.Clicked += new EventHandler(modalButton_Click);

            //Create a container and add the button to it
            this.buttonBar = new Gtk.VBox(false, 5);
            this.buttonBar.PackEnd(this.closeButton, false, false, 5);
            this.buttonBar.PackEnd(this.modalButton, false, false, 5);

            //Add our top-level container to the window
            Add(this.buttonBar);
        }
```

```
        private void closeButton_Click(object sender, EventArgs args)
        {
            Destroy();
        }
```

Finally, a new method, modalButton_Click(), is added to act as the event handler for the Clicked event of the new button, as follows:

```
        private void modalButton_Click(object sender, EventArgs args)
        {
            Console.WriteLine("Launching a modal form...");
            ModalWindow modalWindow = new ModalWindow("A Modal Window", this);
            modalWindow.ShowAll();
            Console.WriteLine("Modal form launched.");
        }
    }
}
```

Because the MainWindow class hasn't changed its external interfaces, we can use the same client class, HelloGtk, but to differentiate between the previous example, we've taken the opportunity to rename the class ModalWorld and updated the title of the main window accordingly. The code is as follows:

```
//Filename: ModalWorld.cs
using System;
using Gtk;

namespace Crossplatform.NET.Chapter05
{
    class ModalWorld
    {
        private static Gtk.Window mainWindow;

        public static void Main()
        {
            Console.WriteLine("Starting Gtk engine...");

            Gtk.Application.Init();
            mainWindow = new MainWindow("It's a Modal World");

            //Setup event handling
            mainWindow.Destroyed += new EventHandler(MainForm_Destroyed);
```

```
            mainWindow.ShowAll();
            Gtk.Application.Run();

            Console.WriteLine("Codeflow back in Main()");
        }

        public static void MainForm_Destroyed(object sender, EventArgs e)
        {
            Console.WriteLine("Quitting Gtk engine");
            Gtk.Application.Quit();
        }
    }
}
```

The example can now be compiled and run on Mono and GNU/Linux, using the following commands, and should produce a window that is similar to the one produced by `HelloGtk`, but with an extra button.

```
mono@linux:~ % mcs /out:ModalWorld.exe *.cs -pkg:gtk-sharp
Compilation succeeded
mono@linux:~ % mono ModalWorld.exe
```

To see the modal window in action, click the Open a Modal Window button, which responds by opening a modal window with the same layout and controls, as shown in Figure 5-10.

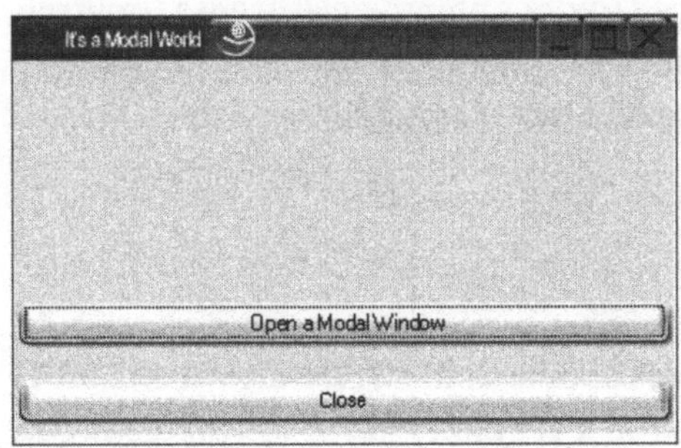

Figure 5-10. It's a Modal World in action

If you're feeling particularly enthusiastic about modal windows, you can recursively open modal windows until you get bored or until your finger drops off. If you prefer to play around with the "modalness" of the windows, try commenting out the line in `ModalWindow.cs` that sets the `TransientFor` property. You'll notice that the modal form can now slip behind its parent window.

So there you have it—a simple introduction to the world of Gtk#. While this chapter's sole focus is GUIs, it's worth remembering that Gtk# encompasses much more than GTK+ and even includes a GUI building tool in the guise of Glade. Time will tell exactly how the future of Gtk# and .NET will transpire, but you can bet your lunch that Gtk# will continue to mature and that it will be an increasingly important part of building good-looking cross-platform .NET applications.

Qt# & Qt

As is the case with most products with a sharpened moniker, Qt# bases itself on an existing product, Qt, which is a C++ toolkit that is specifically geared to producing cross-platform applications. Qt is currently supported on a number of platforms, including Windows, GNU/Linux, and Mac OS X, and it is well supported, documented, and maintained.

TIP Qt# can be found at `http://qtcsharp.sourceforge.net`. Qt is developed by Trolltech and can be found at `http://www.trolltech.com`.

Qt is also famously used by the open source Kool Desktop Environment (KDE), one of the most popular desktop environments for GNU/Linux. As such, Qt's libraries are distributed with a number of GNU/Linux distributions.

Although Qt was originally only released under a commercial license, Trolltech now releases Qt under a number of licenses, including the GPL. This means that Qt is equally suited to commercial and open source projects.

Using Qt# with .NET

Qt# is an open source project that provides access to the Qt libraries from .NET.

Qt# is currently written to work with the X Windows flavor of Trolltech's Qt, and—because Qt is written in C++—its design requires an extra layer of C code, called QtC. QtC allows the `qtcsharp.dll` assembly to use Platform Invoke, as shown in Figure 5-11.

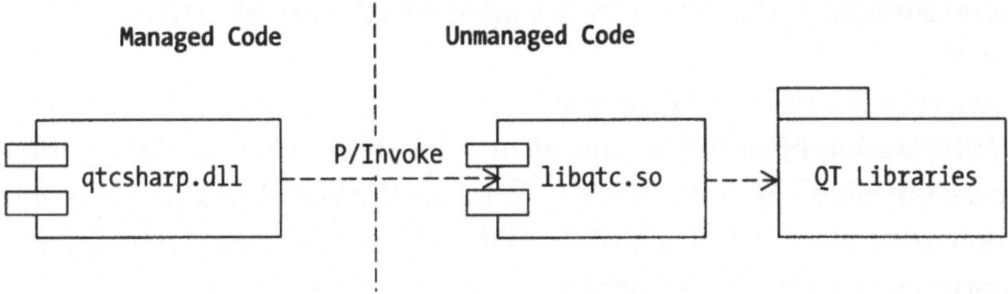

Figure 5-11. Qt#'s dependencies

Because Qt# currently only works with the X Windows version of Qt, it's not yet suitable for general cross-platform development projects (unless you're prepared to install X Windows on all and sundry platforms). The other flavors of Qt are likely to be supported in due course.

Although Qt#'s current version, 0.7.1, is very much an alpha release, because it's based on the solid foundation of Qt (which has an excellent track record), it has a lot of potential to become a firm fixture in the cross-platform .NET arena.

Using Qt with .NET

Because Qt# is currently available as an alpha release, it's not particularly suitable for production systems, but if Qt floats your boat, all's not lost, because you can also call Qt directly from .NET code.

The mechanism that Trolltech currently recommends for using Qt from .NET involves using the ActiveQt framework. This framework allows Qt to be accessed through .NET-COM interoperability, as shown in Figure 5-12, and ActiveQt is available under a commercial license.

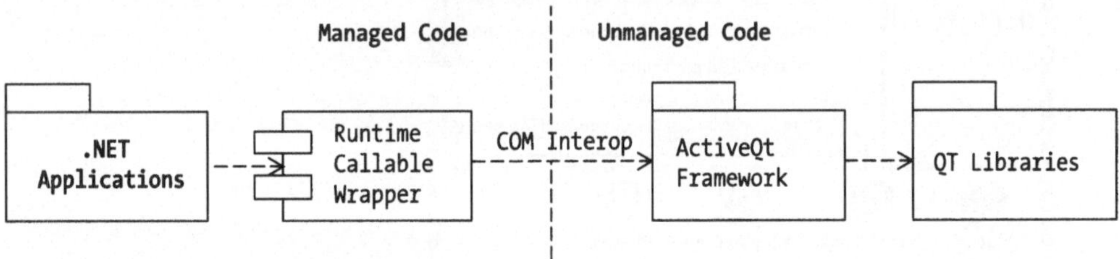

Figure 5-12. Using ActiveQt to access Qt from .NET

Apart from only being available under a commercial license, the main disadvantages of using the ActiveQt framework are that it only works with Windows and it has a reasonable performance overhead due to the use of .NET-COM interoperability.

While ActiveQt is a possibility for developers using the Microsoft flavor of .NET, if COM interoperability isn't an option or if you demand ass-kicking performance, a more portable option for using Qt is to use the Simplified Wrapper and Interface Generator, also known as SWIG. SWIG, which can create C# wrappers for C++ libraries, is mentioned in Chapter 7.

If your development requires professionally authored, cross-platform controls, such as those shown in Figures 5-13 and 5-14, or if you're an existing Qt developer, Qt may well be the way forward.

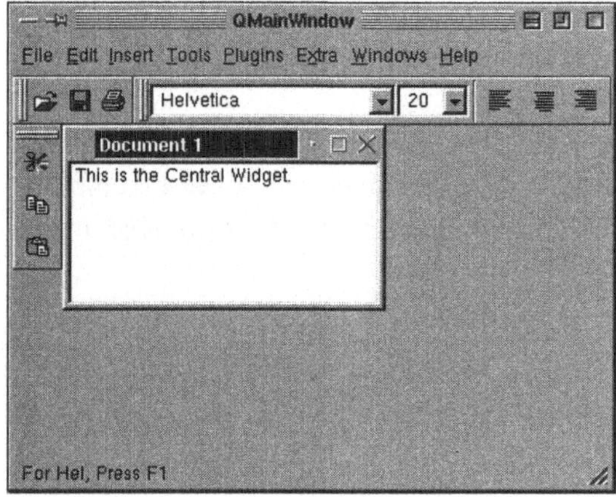

Figure 5-13. A Qt MDI application

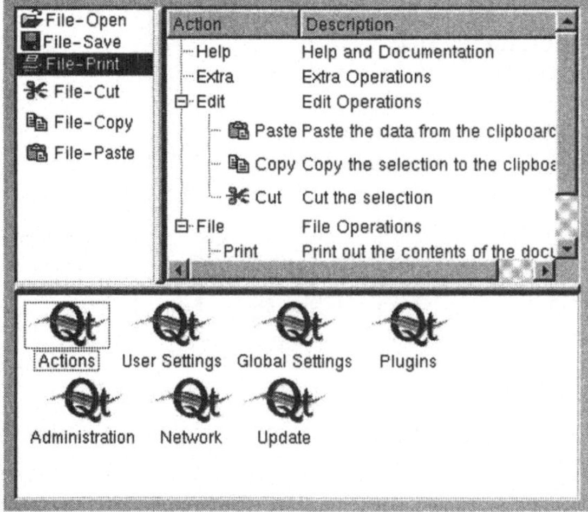

Figure 5-14. Assorted Qt widgets in action

TickleSharp

TickleSharp is a binding to the Tool Command Language, or Tcl, which is a popular, open source, cross-platform scripting language. Although Tcl can be used for a variety of programming tasks, it is most commonly used in conjunction with its graphical toolkit, Tk, for developing cross-platform GUI applications. This combination of Tcl and Tk is known as Tcl/Tk (pronounced *tickle-tee-kay*).

TIP Although Tcl/Tk are typically used on UNIX-based platforms, they are available for a number of platforms and are freely available from `http://www.tcl.tk`. TickleSharp is available from `http://forge.novell.com/modules/xfmod/project/?ticklesharp`.

As shown in Figure 5-15, TickleSharp consists of the following two files:

- The `TickleSharp.dll` assembly is the head honcho and acts a wrapper over the Tcl and the Tk shared libraries.
- The `tclwrapper` file is a shared library that allows Tcl/Tk scripts to make callbacks into managed code.

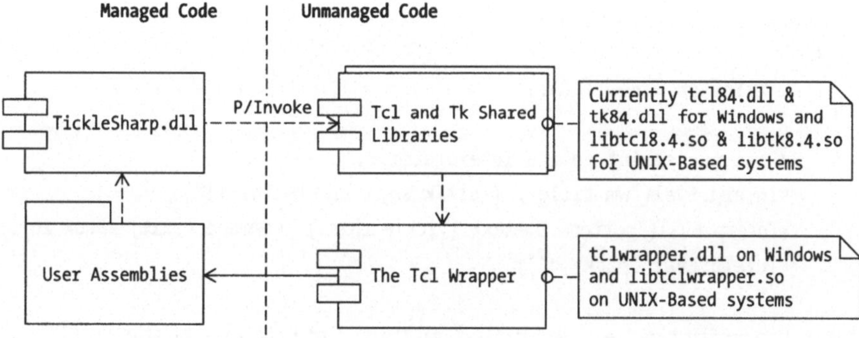

Figure 5-15. TickleSharp dependencies

Unlike the other graphical toolkits that are mentioned in this chapter, TickleSharp doesn't provide an object model that encapsulates widgets or controls, but instead it provides a number of types that wrap the Tcl/Tk interpreter. While this means that Tcl/Tk widgets cannot truly benefit from the facilities that are offered by the Common Type System, it makes it particularly simple to migrate existing Tcl/Tk scripts to work with TickleSharp.

Even without an object model, it's pretty easy to get started with Tcl/Tk, especially if you have prior Tcl/Tk knowledge. To demonstrate, we create a basic program, TickleThis, which creates a single window that contains a solitary button.

NOTE The code for this example can be found in the `Chapter_05/TickleThis` directory at `http://www.cross-platform.net` and `http://www.apress.com`.

The program's `Main()` method starts by creating an instance of `Tk` and then proceeds to pass three lines of a Tcl/Tk script to the interpreter using the `Eval()` method. While you might not be familiar with the syntax of the Tcl language, it's nevertheless relatively straightforward to understand. The code is as follows:

```
//Filename: TickleThis.cs
using System;
using TickleSharp;

namespace Crossplatform.NET.Chapter05
{
    public class TickleThis
    {
        public static void Main()
        {
          Tk tkInterp = new Tk();

          //Pass the script to the interpreter...
          tkInterp.Eval("wm title . {Tcl/Tk says Tickle This!}");
          tkInterp.Eval("button .b -text {Tickle this!} -command {exit} -padx 20");
          tkInterp.Eval("pack .b");
```

When the script has been evaluated, all that's left is to invoke the Tcl/Tk interpreter. This can be done by calling the `Run()` method, as follows:

```
          //...and run the script
          tkInterp.Run();
        }
    }
}
```

TIP To get this example working, you must first install a working version of Tcl/Tk and TickleSharp. The installation instructions for Tcl/Tk vary depending on the target platform, but you can either download and build the source code or you can download a binary for the platform(s) of your choice. To get TickleSharp installed, download the source code and follow the build instructions that are included with the download.

The final step is to compile and run the program in your favorite CLI. To get the program compiled and running using Mono on GNU/Linux, enter the following commands, which should produce an output similar to that shown in Figure 5-16:

```
mono@linux:~ % mcs TickleThis.cs /r:TickleSharp.dll
Compilation succeeded
mono@linux:~ % mono TickleThis.exe
```

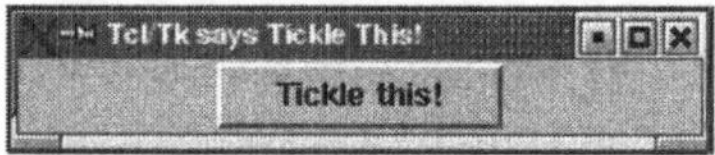

Figure 5-16. TickleThis on GNU/Linux

To contrast the difference in graphical styling that's produced when running the program on a different platform, compile and execute the program on Windows, as follows (see Figure 5-17):

```
C:\MS.NET> csc TickleThis.cs /r:TickleSharp.dll
Microsoft (R) Visual C# .NET Compiler version 7.10.3052.4
for Microsoft (R) .NET Framework version 1.1.4322
Copyright (C) Microsoft Corporation 2001-2002. All rights reserved.
C:\MS.NET> TickleThis
```

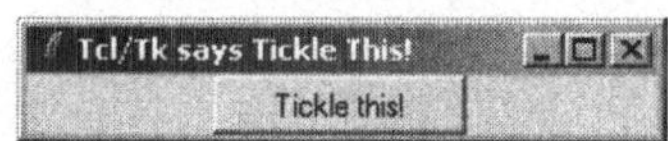

Figure 5-17. TickleThis on Windows

While the lack of an extensive object model means that using TickleSharp requires learning Tcl/Tk, because the underlying technology has been around for so long, Tcl/Tk acts as a highly stable foundation on which to build cross-platform GUI applications.

Because Tcl/Tk has also been used to create graphical interfaces for a multitude of open source applications, a lot of example Tcl/Tk code is also available. This is not only useful for the budding GUI developer, but it also makes it easy to migrate a number of existing applications to .NET.

#WT

The Sharp Widget Toolkit (SharpWT or #WT) is a C# port of Java's Standard Widget Toolkit (SWT), which aims to couple portability and performance with the native look and feel of the host platform.

The Java SWT was developed as part of the IBM-sponsored Eclipse integrated development environment (IDE) project, and #WT was originally ported from Java as part of the open source SharpDevelop IDE project. Although #WT was intended to migrate SharpDevelop from being Windows-only into being a full-fledged cross-platform IDE, because SharpDevelop has already been migrated to Gtk#—in the form of MonoDevelop—it remains to be seen whether a #WT version will ever appear.

TIP #WT can be found at `http://www.sharpwt.net`.

#WT provides a common set of GUI features through the SWT namespace, relying on different back-end implementations for different platforms. #WT currently includes a Windows and a GTK+ implementation, as shown in Figure 5-18. The original SWT also has implementations for Motif and Mac OS X Carbon, and in time, further implementations might be added to #WT.

At the time of this writing, #WT is far from complete, which makes it an impractical choice for cross-platform development. However, with its heritage firmly rooted in the Java community, when #WT is completed, it should be particularly useful for porting SWT-based Java applications and should be the ideal toolkit for developers who are using Java and .NET and who want to share knowledge between the two development platforms.

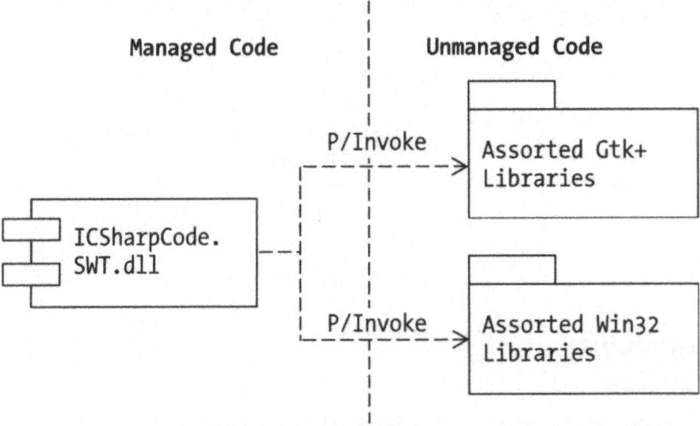

Figure 5-18. The #WT architecture

wx.NET

The wx.NET project provides .NET support for wxWidgets, which is a widely used and mature open source cross-platform toolkit of some 11 years standing; it was formerly known as wxWindows.

The focus of wxWidgets is predominantly to provide a cross-platform GUI toolkit, although it also includes a number of additional features, such as a clipboard, networking, database access, and HTML rendering.

TIP wx.NET can be found at `http://wxnet.sourceforge.net`. You can find out more about wxWidgets at the excellent Web site `http://www.wxwidgets.org`.

To simplify the dependencies and deployment of wx.NET, the project's designers elected to statically link the wxWidgets libraries into a single C shared library, `wx-C`. Not only does this mean that wxWidgets does not need to be installed, but it also ensures that a complete wx.NET installation only requires two files—the `wx.NET.dll` assembly and the `wx-c` shared library, as illustrated in Figure 5-19.

TIP Although wx.NET doesn't require a wxWidgets installation to run, if you plan to build wx.NET from source code, you need to install wxWidgets to allow wx.NET to statically link to the wxWidgets libraries.

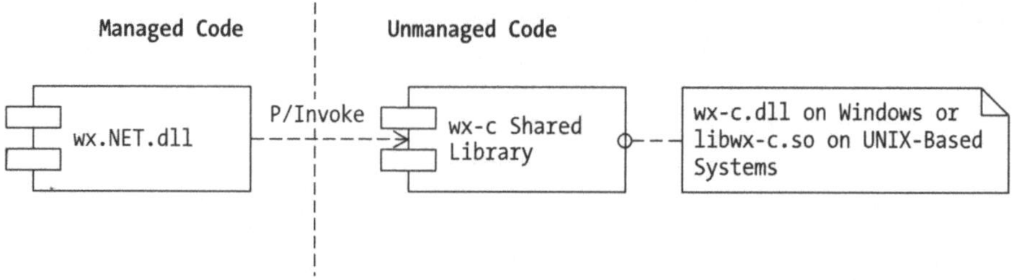

Figure 5-19. The wx.NET components

Although wx.NET is still in development, it currently supports Mac OS X, GNU/Linux, and Windows and runs under Microsoft .NET, Mono, and Portable.NET. Figure 5-20 shows a sample screen shot of wx.NET running with Portable.NET on Mac OS X.

In addition to providing source code, binary files, and documentation, wx.NET includes a number of sample applications. An excellent step-by-step tutorial also introduces a variety of wx.NET concepts and culminates in the production of an image-viewing program, `ImageView`, which is shown in Figure 5-21.

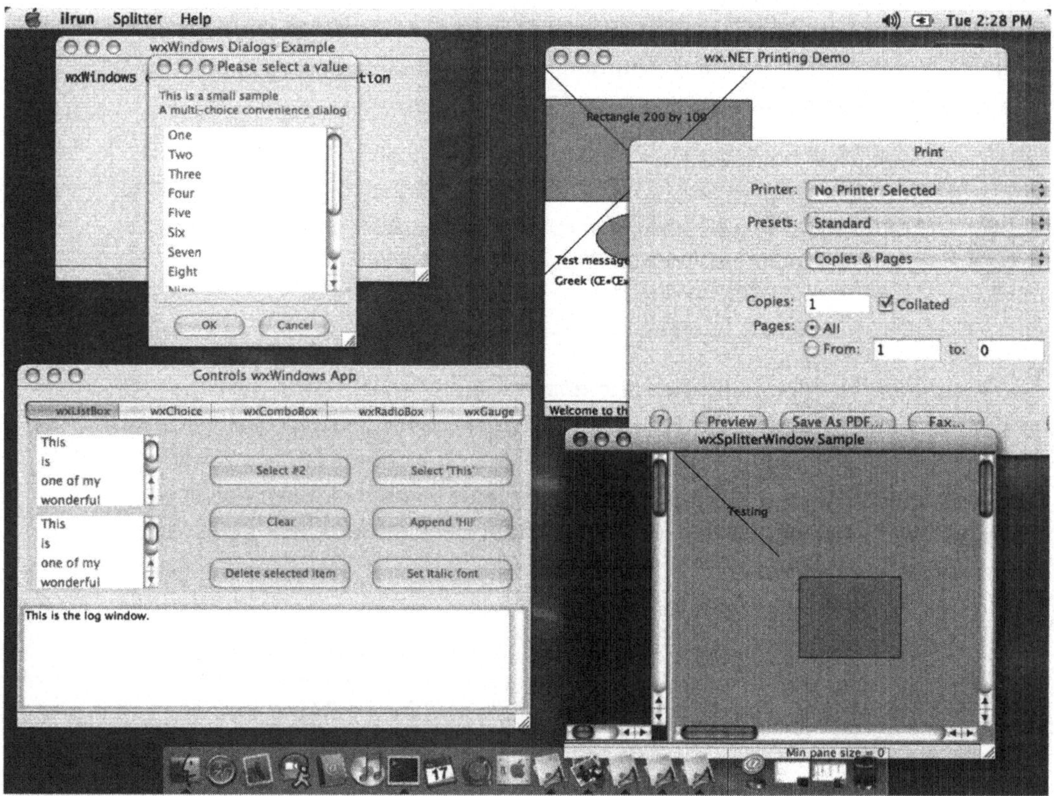

Figure 5-20. wx.NET on Mac OS X

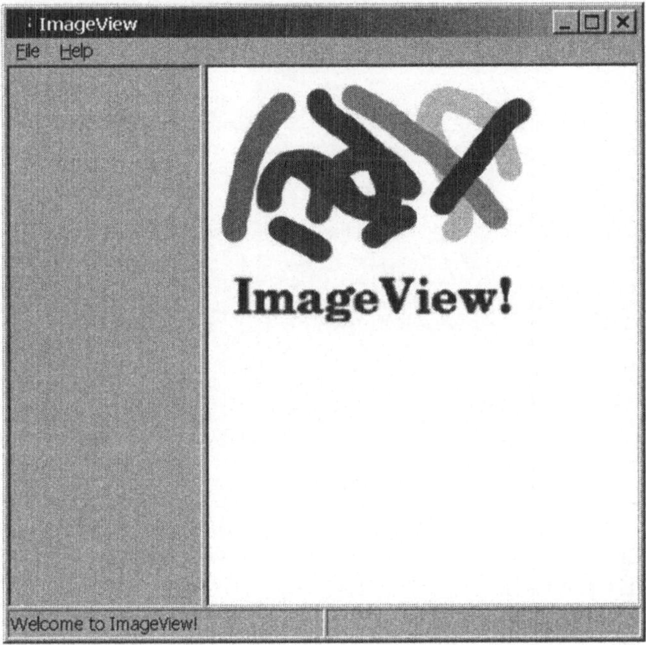

Figure 5-21. ImageView on Windows

Given that wx.NET is founded on a mature and well-documented product and it produces a native look and feel on its host platform, it's likely to gather its own loyal following, just as wxWidgets has done.

Because the wx.NET classes closely follow the wxWidgets class hierarchy, wx.NET not only makes it relatively easy to port existing wxWidgets projects, but it's also ideal for transferring wxWidgets skills and will be the de facto .NET toolkit for developers from a wxWidgets background.

Factoring in its integration with wxDesigner, a commercial GUI designer for wxWidgets, wx.NET comes across as a polished toolkit that's set to become highly popular for cross-platform .NET development.

TIP Details about wxDesigner are available from `http://www.roebling.de`.

Comparing the GUI Toolkits

You have several factors to consider when choosing the right GUI toolkit from the array of candidates. Deciding on the right toolkit is a potentially mind-boggling task, and settling on the right toolkit is as likely to be directed by personal choice as it is by technical requirements. Table 5-2 allows you to compare various toolkits that are available.

Table 5-2. A Comparison of Toolkits

Toolkit	Platforms	Dependencies	License	Design-Time Support	Look and Feel	Data Binding	Subclass Controls
Gtk#	All	GTK+	GNU LGPL	Glade#	Theme-based	In development	Yes
System.Windows.Forms	All, though treat as "work in progress"	Win32 API for Windows. Mono requires Winelib or Gtk# for non-Windows systems. PNET requires X Windows for non-Windows systems.	Depends on CLI implementation	Visual Studio .NET and SharpDevelop for Windows	Windows for MS.NET, PNET, and Mono running under Windows or Winelib. See Gtk# for Mono on other platforms.	Yes	Yes
TickleSharp	All	Tcl/Tk	GNU LGPL	Numerous designers available, such as Komodo or Visual Tcl	Native	No	No

Table 5-2. A Comparison of Toolkits (Continued)

Toolkit	Platforms	Dependencies	License	Design-Time Support	Look and Feel	Data Binding	Subclass Controls
Qt	Windows	ActiveQt and Qt	Qt is available under GPL, and ActiveQt is available under a commercial license.	Qt Designer	Theme-based	Yes	Yes
Qt#	Any platform running X Windows	Qt for X Windows	GNU GPL	No	Theme-based	No	Yes
#WT	Windows or any platform running GTK+	Win32 API for Windows; otherwise GTK+	GNU LGPL	No	Native	No	Yes
wx.NET	All	--	wxWidgets	wxDesigner	Native	Yes	Yes

Of course, some features can't be captured in Table 5-2. For example, System.Windows.Forms is the only GUI toolkit that comes with PNET, Mono, and Microsoft .NET. Because this toolkit is the one that most Windows developers are familiar with, it's likely to be used in many projects without a second thought.

Meanwhile, Qt# and Gtk# both have strong support from the open source community, but because their underlying toolkits are the basis for competing desktop managers—GNOME and KDE—a certain amount of enmity exists between their supporters.

NOTE Remember that all the toolkits are in different states of completion. To avoid tears at bedtime, the choice of toolkit should balance a toolkit's feature set with its state of progress.

While using a single toolkit is certainly the least costly approach, if you prefer to go whole hog and create an application that uses different toolkits on different platforms, you can take advantage of any toolkits that you fancy. This is a topic that's well worth delving into.

Supporting Multiple GUIs

In Chapter 4, we examined how the bridge pattern could be used in situations where different solutions were needed to solve a single problem on different platforms: taking an abstract view of a problem and encapsulating it in a class that then handles all calls from client code and forwards them to a real solution.

As we saw earlier in this chapter, this is the approach that is used in Portable.NET's implementation of `System.Windows.Forms`, with the real solution depending on the host platform; Win32 is used on Windows, and X Windows is used on other operating systems.

However, another well-known pattern promotes reuse and flexibility in GUI applications. This pattern is known as the *Model-View-Controller (MVC)* pattern.

In a nutshell, MVC helps promote code reuse and enables application flexibility by allowing one GUI toolkit to be substituted for another with relative ease. Naturally, this means that if you need to target multiple platforms with differing GUI toolkits or you decide to change your mind halfway through a project and use a *different* toolkit, MVC can help make life considerably easier. Sounds too good to be true, doesn't it?

The Model-View-Controller Pattern

To make sure that we're all singing from the same figurative song sheet, we take a detailed look at this pattern. In essence, MVC converts the user's "screen that does stuff" into the following distinct concepts, as shown in Figure 5-22:

- **Model:** Contains the functionality that handles the core logic and data. At the conceptual level, this can be thought of as a class. At the implementation level, it may be a bunch of classes masquerading as a single class via a wrapper.

- **View:** Displays those elements of the model that impart information to the user, which are essentially the public properties of the model. This is often a form or window that contains a number of controls or widgets. Of course, other types of view media exist, such as a printed sheet.

- **Controller:** Allows the user to manipulate the model by calling its publicly exposed methods or properties. A controller may either be a physical device, such as a keyboard or a mouse, or a software entity, such as a menu or a set of widgets—or a combination of both.

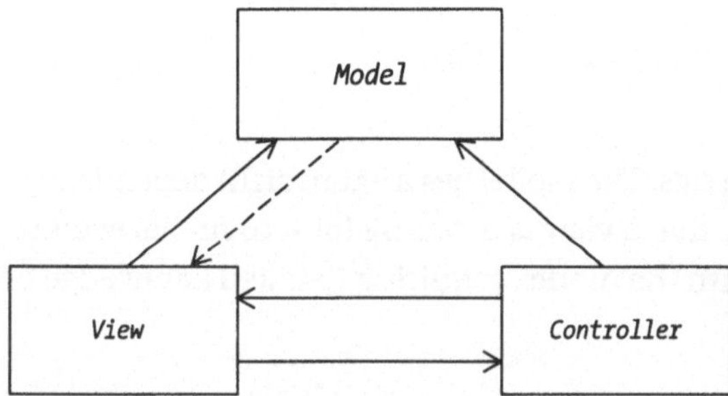

Figure 5-22. The Model-View-Controller pattern

Now that the pattern has been described from a high level, it makes sense to break the pattern down in accordance with the relationships between its constituent parts.

The Model and View Relationship

When the model changes, the view needs to be updated. Given that the controller can change the model, the controller could take responsibility for telling the view to refresh. This would be adequate if it weren't for the fact that the model may change through other, devious means that are unknown to the controller: *"Pass the serial port, Geoffrey."*

It's clear then that a more efficient mechanism is required to keep the view in line with the model. Historically, the model would store a register of references to views that need to be informed when a change is made. In C#, however, this has been superseded by the event/subscriber model. The model raises events when its state changes, and any interested views listen for these events and then refresh themselves. The concept is the same as it ever was but now takes place "under the hood," as a feature of the language. Figure 5-23 shows the relationship between the Model and View duo.

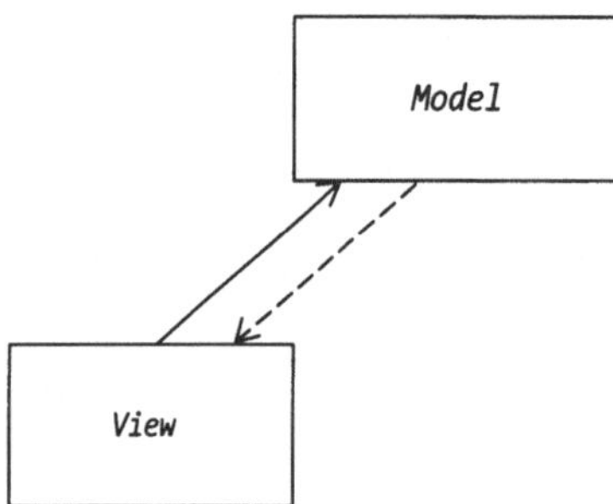

Figure 5-23. The relationship between Model and View

The relationship boils down to this: The model has a lightweight dependency on the view, needing to know only that a view is listening for it to fire its events; the view has a solid association with the model, requiring detailed knowledge of the model's `public` members.

The Model and Controller Relationship

A user manipulates the model through the controller, and the controller therefore needs explicit knowledge of the model's `public` interface. Strictly speaking, the model does not need to know anything about the controller. At this point, it's time to remember that patterns are a starting point and a communication medium; their raison d'être is not to have purists tearing their hair out when an implementation differs slightly from the prescribed template, as entertaining as that would be. More bald puritans can only be a good thing.

A subtle refinement of the relationship between model and controller is to allow the model to have a light reference to the controller. In the .NET Framework, this means that the controller can subscribe to events—such as error notification—that may be raised by the model. If this upsets your applecart, this refinement could be circumvented by using the relationship between the model and the view and the view and the controller. Figure 5-24 illustrates both the strict relationship between model and controller and the refined relationship.

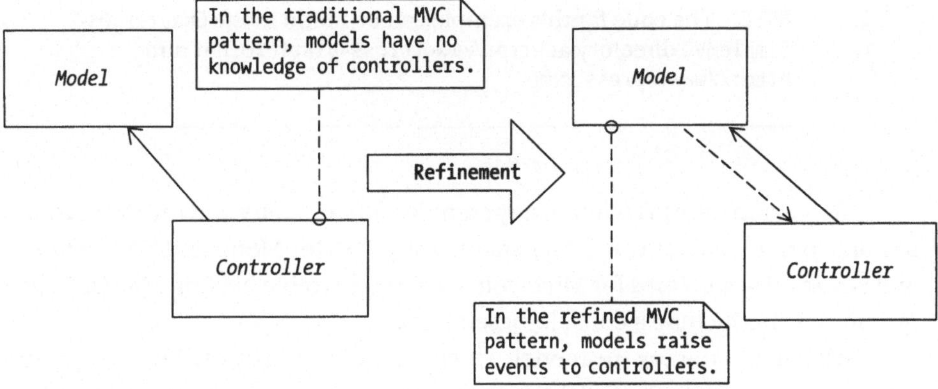

Figure 5-24. Relationships between Models and Controllers

The Controller and View Relationship

As the user manipulates the model using the controller, the controller will likely need to manipulate the view in accordance with the user's actions—for example, making a changed value a different color.

A view may require several controllers, either all available at the same time or dynamically swappable. The controller and view both need to have a reference to each other, rather than just subscribing to each other's events, as seen in Figure 5-25. This is particularly apparent when elements of the controller are displayed as part of the view (for example, a menu or a text box).

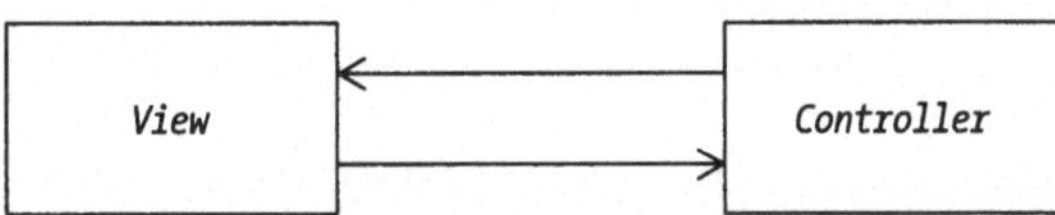

Figure 5-25. Relationship between View and Controller

An MVC Example

To illustrate the MVC pattern in action, we now run through a simple example that shows the relationships that were defined earlier and that demonstrates how to swap between different GUI toolkits.

NOTE The code for this example can be found in the `Chapter_05/SimpleMVC` directory at `http://www.cross-platform.net` and `http://www.apress.com`.

The program doesn't contain any complex functionality and revolves around a simple model that represents a person, using `Gtk#` for Mono and GNU/Linux and `System.Windows.Forms` for Microsoft .NET and Portable.NET on Mac OS X. Just for fun, we also include a console-based view.

We begin by creating the model, which is represented by the `Person` class and simply declares some private fields to store data, a simple overloaded constructor that initializes the fields. The code is as follows:

```
//Filename: Person.cs
using System;

namespace Crossplatform.NET.Chapter05
{
    public class Person
    {
        private string socialSecurityNumber;
        private string firstname;
        private string surname;
        private string email;

        public Person(string first, string surname, string ssn, string email)
        {
            this.firstname = first;
            this.surname = surname;
            this.socialSecurityNumber = ssn;
            this.email = email;
        }
    }
}
```

So far, Person is a particularly simple class, but as you will see in a moment, the complexity begins to develop as you open the class to the outside world.

The Model–View Relationship

Casting your mind back, remember that the model must notify a view when it changes, and to achieve this, we use .NET's event-handling mechanism.

The .NET convention for event handlers requires a delegate with two parameters: The first contains a reference to the object that raised the event, and the second contains an object that inherits from EventArgs and can be used to pass additional information about the event. Because we don't pass extra information to the view, we can use the EventHandler delegate to define PersonChangedEvent, as follows:

```
public event EventHandler PersonChangedEvent;
```

When raising the event, we first need to check whether any objects are subscribing to the event that is handled by the RaisePersonChangedEvent() method. We use the following code:

```
protected void RaisePersonChangedEvent(EventArgs e)
{
    //To ensure thread-safety cache PersonChangedEvent so a
    //NullReferenceException isn't generated if PersonChangedEvent changes
    //between null check and invocation.
    EventHandler handler = this.PersonChangedEvent;
    if (handler != null)
        handler (this, e);
}
```

Now that we have a method for raising the PersonChangedEvent event, we need to adjust Person to call the method whenever its fields are changed. Because the fields are private, we add some properties that enable the fields to be set and retrieved, and because set is almost identical for each property, we wrap its functionality in the SetValue() method, as follows:

```
public string Email
{
    get{ return email; }
    set{ SetValue(ref this.email, value); }
}
```

```
public string Firstname
{
    get{ return firstname; }
    set{ SetValue(ref this.firstName, value); }
}

public string SocialSecurityNumber
{
    get{return socialSecurityNumber;}
    set{ SetValue(ref this.socialSecurityNumber, value); }
}

public string Surname
{
    get{ return surname; }
    set{ SetValue(ref this.surname, value); }
}

private void SetValue(ref string field, string value)
{
    if(field != value)
    {
        field = value;
        RaisePersonChangedEvent(EventArgs.Empty);
    }
}
```

The `Person` class is now ready for the outside world, with some `private` fields and some public properties that raise the `PersonChangedEvent` when the values change. As a quick recap, the whole class's implementation is now as follows:

```
//Filename: Person.cs
using System;

namespace Crossplatform.NET.Chapter05
{
    public class Person
    {
        public event EventHandler PersonChangedEvent;
```

```
private string socialSecurityNumber;
private string firstname;
private string surname;
private string email;

public Person(string first, string surname, string ssn, string email)
{
    this.firstname = first;
    this.surname = surname;
    this.socialSecurityNumber = ssn;
    this.email = email;
}

protected void RaisePersonChangedEvent(EventArgs e)
{
    //To ensure thread-safety cache PersonChangedEvent so a
    //NullReferenceException isn't generated if PersonChangedEvent changes
    //between null check and invocation.
    EventHandler handler = this.PersonChangedEvent;
    if (handler != null)
        handler (this, e);
}

public string Email
{
    get{ return email; }
    set{ SetValue(ref this.email, value); }
}

public string Firstname
{
    get{ return firstname; }
    set{ SetValue(ref this.firstname, value); }
}

public string SocialSecurityNumber
{
    get{return socialSecurityNumber;}
    set{ SetValue(ref this.socialSecurityNumber, value); }
}
```

```
        public string Surname
        {
            get{ return surname; }
            set{ SetValue(ref this.surname, value); }
        }

        //the various properties' set implementation
        private void SetValue(ref string field, string value)
        {
            if(field != value)
            {
                field = value;
                RaisePersonChangedEvent(EventArgs.Empty);
            }
        }
    }
}
```

The View

Now that we have a complete model, we're in a position to create an `abstract` class, `View`, which we use as the base class for all the application's views.

Because all the application's display logic is necessarily implemented in `View`'s concrete subclasses, `View` is a simple class. It starts with two protected fields to store references to the model and to a controller, and then has a `public` overloaded constructor that has one parameter for the model and one for the controller. The code is as follows:

```
// Filename: View.cs
using System;

namespace Crossplatform.NET.Chapter05
{
    public abstract class View
    {
        protected Person person;
        protected Controller controller;
```

```
        public View(Person person, Controller controller)
        {
            this.person = person;
            this.controller = controller;

            this.person.PersonChangedEvent += new EventHandler(Person_Changed);
        }
```

The `public` constructor stores the passed-in model and controller before subscribing to the model's `PersonChangedEvent` by attaching its `Person_Changed()` method, as follows:

```
        protected virtual void Person_Changed (object sender, EventArgs e)
        {
             UpdateDisplay();
        }
```

The `View` class finishes with the `abstract` `UpdateDisplay()` method, which must be implemented by subclasses and is called whenever the `PersonChangedEvent` event is received from the model. The code is as follows:

```
        protected abstract void UpdateDisplay();
    }
}
```

The Model–Controller Relationship

The controller has two purposes in life: to manipulate a model and to control one or more views. In this section, we concentrate on the controller's interaction with the model.

The controller class begins with a couple of `private` fields to store references to the model and view, and then has an overloaded constructor that allows a model instance to be passed in, as follows:

```
//Filename: Controller.cs
using System;

namespace Crossplatform.NET.Chapter05
{
    public class Controller
    {
        private View view;
        private Person person;
```

```
        private Controller(){}

        public Controller(Person person)
        {
            this.person = person;
        }

        public View View
        {
            get{ return this.view; }
            set{ this.view = value; }
        }
```

As mentioned earlier in the chapter, a controller needs to have explicit knowledge of the model, and this is reflected in the `Change()` methods, each of which is responsible for changing one of the model's properties, as follows:

```
        public void ChangeFirstname(string newFirstname)
        {
            this.person.Firstname = newFirstname;
        }

        public void ChangeSurname(string newSurname)
        {
            this.person.Surname = newSurname;
        }

        public void ChangeEmail(string newEmail)
        {
            this.person.Email = newEmail;
        }

        public void ChangeSSN(string newSSN)
        {
            this.person.SocialSecurityNumber = newSSN;
        }
    }
}
```

The simplicity of the controller reflects the basic nature of this example, and many developers would be content to do without a controller class, placing the payload of methods, such as `ChangeSurname()`, directly into a view's event handlers, such as the event handler for a button click.

While avoiding controllers is acceptable for prototypes or trivial applications with only one view and a simple model, for applications with more complex models or multiple views, using a controller is the best way to show respect for the application's complexity.

The Controller–View Relationship

The MVC pattern describes the controller–view relationship as being explicit in both directions: The controller has a reference to the view, and the view has a reference to the controller.

While this example's views don't explicitly interact with the controller and the controller doesn't have any methods for instructing the view, it would be easy to add such functionality if required.

Putting It All Together: The SimpleMVC Application

Now that the basic structure of the MVC pattern has been implemented, we need to create an application to demonstrate it in use and some subclass of `View` for each of our target platforms.

To keep the application as simple as possible, we don't do anything particularly useful. We simply create an instance of the `Person` class and alter its properties a few times to see how the views respond, as follows:

```
//Filename: SimpleMVC.cs
using System;

namespace Crossplatform.NET.Chapter05
{
    public class SimpleMVC
    {
        public static void Main()
        {
            //Set up all objects and their relationships
            Person timmy = new Person("Timothy",
                                      "Ring",
                                      "000-111",
                                      "Timothy.Ring@Crossplatform.net");

            Controller controlTim = new Controller(timmy);
```

```
            View watchTim = new ConsoleView(timmy, controlTim);

            controlTim.View = watchTim;
            ChangeDetails(controlTim);
        }

        private static void ChangeDetails(Controller controller)
        {
            controller.ChangeFirstname("Tim");
            controller.ChangeSurname("King");
            controller.ChangeEmail("Tim.King@crossplatform.net");
        }
    }
}
```

The `Main()` method starts by giving birth to Timothy Ring, and it sets up a controller for manipulating him and an instance of `ConsoleView` for watching what happens to him.

As shown in the bridge example in Chapter 4, various techniques could be used to decide which subclass of `View` to create, but for the purpose of this example, we settle for manually changing the line that instantiates the `View` as required.

The program finally calls three of the controller's `Change()` methods, which should subsequently be reflected in the view.

The Console View

The `ConsoleView` is the simplest subclass of `View` and is useful for demonstrating how the MVC pattern can be used to create a nongraphical user interface.

The class contains a constructor that passes the model and controller to its base constructor. `ConsoleView` overrides the `abstract UpdateDisplay()` method, which is called when the model changes, as follows:

```
//Filename: ConsoleView.cs
using System;

namespace Crossplatform.NET.Chapter05
{
    public class ConsoleView : View
    {
        public ConsoleView(Person person, Controller controller)
                        :base(person, controller){}
```

```
        protected override void UpdateDisplay()
        {
            Console.WriteLine("*** Person has been updated ***");
            Console.WriteLine("Name is {0} {1}", person.Firstname, person.Surname);
            Console.WriteLine("SSN is {0}", person.SocialSecurityNumber);
            Console.WriteLine("Email is {0}\n", person.Email);
        }
    }
}
```

We compile and run the relevant files under Portable.NET and Mac OS X, which can be carried out with the following commands:

```
pnet@macosx:~ % cscc /out:SimpleMVC.exe SimpleMVC.cs Controller.cs Person.cs\
> View.cs ConsoleView.cs
pnet@macosx:~ % ilrun SimpleMVC.exe
*** Person has been updated ***
Name is Tim Ring
SSN is 000-111
Email is Timothy.Ring@Crossplatform.net

*** Person has been updated ***
Name is Tim King
SSN is 000-111
Email is Timothy.Ring@Crossplatform.net

*** Person has been updated ***
Name is Tim King
SSN is 000-111
Email is Tim.King@Crossplatform.net

pnet@macosx:~ %
```

Although the output is quick and dirty, it should illustrate that the pattern and application work, without getting bogged down in GUI coding. That particular delight is yet to come.

The System.Windows.Forms View

As you would expect, the `WindowsView` class is a slightly more complex subclass of `View`.

Because WindowsView needs a Form to display the Person details, the class has a single private field, form, which is declared as type WindowsViewForm and is instantiated in the class's constructor, as follows:

```
//Filename: WindowsView.cs
using System;
using System.Windows.Forms;

namespace Crossplatform.NET.Chapter05
{
    public class WindowsView : View
    {
        private WindowsViewForm form;

        public WindowsView(Person person, Controller ctrl) : base(person, ctrl)
        {
            this.form = new WindowsViewForm();
        }
```

The UpdateDisplay() method displays details of the Person instance on-screen by retrieving values form the Person's properties and writing them to Label controls on the form. The method finishes by calling the ShowDialog() method, which ensures that the from is displayed as a modal dialog. The code is as follows:

```
protected override void UpdateDisplay()
{
   this.form.firstnameLabel.Text = "First Name: " + this.person.Firstname;
   this.form.surnameLabel.Text = "Surname: " + this.person.Surname;
   this.form.socialSecurityLabel.Text = "SSN: " + this.person.SocialSecurityNumber;
   this.form.emailLabel.Text = "Email: " + this.person.Email;
   this.form.ShowDialog();
}
```

The code for the WindowsViewForm class is pretty mundane. It consists of four public fields for referencing the Label controls and a constructor, which instantiates the Labels, sets them up, and then adds them to the Form. The code is as follows:

```
//A basic nested class to act as a modal form
    private class WindowsViewForm : Form
    {
        public Label firstnameLabel;
        public Label surnameLabel;
        public Label socialSecurityLabel;
        public Label emailLabel;

        public WindowsViewForm()
        {
            //Create the label controls
            this.firstnameLabel = new Label();
            this.surnameLabel = new Label();
            this.socialSecurityLabel = new Label();
            this.emailLabel = new Label();

            SuspendLayout();

            //Set up the label's properties
            this.firstnameLabel.AutoSize = true;
            this.firstnameLabel.Location = new System.Drawing.Point(40, 40);

            this.surnameLabel.AutoSize = true;
            this.surnameLabel.Location = new System.Drawing.Point(40, 80);

            this.socialSecurityLabel.AutoSize = true;
            this.socialSecurityLabel.Location = new System.Drawing.Point(40, 120);

            this.emailLabel.AutoSize = true;
            this.emailLabel.Location = new System.Drawing.Point(40, 160);

            //Set Form properties
            this.AutoScaleBaseSize = new System.Drawing.Size(6, 20);
            this.ClientSize = new System.Drawing.Size(292, 268);
            this.Controls.AddRange(
                new System.Windows.Forms.Control[] {this.emailLabel,
                                                    this.socialSecurityLabel,
                                                    this.surnameLabel,
                                                    this.firstnameLabel});
            this.Text = "The MVC Form";

            ResumeLayout(false);
        }
    }
  }
}
```

When you run the program in a moment, you'll notice that each time the model changes, the `WindowsView` spawns a new modal form, which must be closed manually before the next change occurs. While this is by no means a paragon of good GUI design, it suffices for the needs of this example, and it helps us avoid getting bogged down with coding reams of `System.Windows.Forms` code.

Before compiling the program on Windows, remember to edit `SimpleMVCApp.cs` so that `WindowsView` is used instead of `ConsoleView`, as follows:

```
View watchTim = new WindowsView(timmy, controlTim);
```

You can now compile the program on Microsoft .NET using the following command:

```
C:\MS.NET> csc /out:mvcApp.exe person.cs viewbase.cs controller.cs WindowsView.cs
 mvcapp.cs /r:System.Windows.Forms /r:System.Drawing
```

Running the resulting program should result in a series of screens that are similar to the one shown in Figure 5-26.

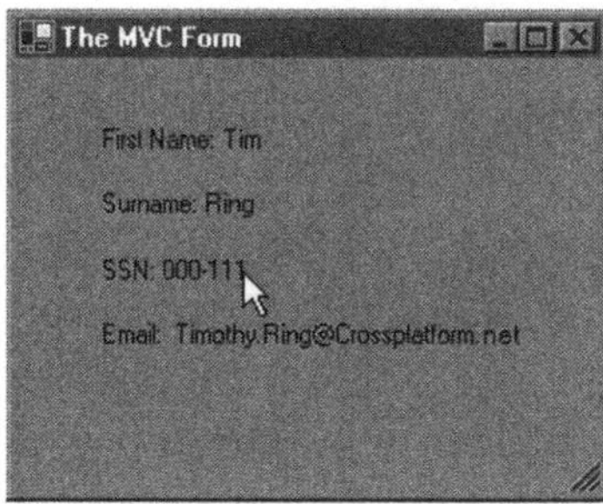

Figure 5-26. A window into the busy world of Tim King

The Gtk# View

Having now seen two different concrete implementations of the `View` class, you should have a good idea of what's coming next.

Once again, `GtkView` defines its own nested class, `GtkViewWindow`, which inherits from Gtk#'s `Dialog` class. Because the `Dialog` constructor requires a parent window to be passed in, rather than creating a parent window each time we need the dialog, the `GtkView` class creates a dummy window. The class stores the dummy window in a field and passes it into `GtkViewWindow`'s constructor in the `UpdateDetails()` method, as follows:

```
//Filename: GtkView.cs
using System;
using Gtk;

namespace Crossplatform.NET.Chapter05
{
    public class GtkView : View
    {
        private Window dummyParent;

        public GtkView(Person person, Controller controller)
                   : base(person, controller)
        {
            Application.Init();
            this.dummyParent = new Gtk.Window("Dummy");
        }

        protected override void UpdateDisplay()
        {
            GtkViewWindow form = new GtkViewWindow ("Person changed:",
                                                 this.dummyParent,
                                                 DialogFlags.DestroyWithParent,
                                                 this.person);

            form.Run();
            form.Destroy();
        }

        private class GtkViewWindow : Dialog
        {
            private Person person;

            public GtkViewWindow (string title, Window parentWindow,
                                 DialogFlags flags, Person person)
            : base(title, parentWindow, flags)
            {
                this.person = person;

                Label nameLabel = new Label(this.person.Firstname + " " +
                                          this.person.Surname);
                Label ssnLabel = new Label(this.person.SocialSecurityNumber);
                Label emailLabel = new Label(this.person.Email);
```

```
                this.VBox.PackStart(nameLabel, true, true, 0);
                this.VBox.PackStart(ssnLabel, true, true, 0);
                this.VBox.PackStart(emailLabel, true, true, 0);
                this.VBox.ShowAll();
                AddButton("OK", 0);
            }
        }
    }
}
```

Because this chapter has already looked at two Gtk# examples in depth, we won't comment on the implementation of the GtkViewWindow class, other than to say that it closely mimics the functionality of the WindowsViewForm class.

Once again, before compiling the program, remember to edit SimpleMVC.cs so that it creates an instance of GtkView, instead of ConsoleView or WindowsView.

The program can then be compiled and executed using the following commands, which should produce a screen that's similar to the one shown in Figure 5-27:

```
mono@linux:~ % mcs /out:SimpleMVC.exe SimpleMVC.cs Controller.cs Person.cs\ >
View.cs GtkView.cs -pkg:gtk-sharp
mono@linux:~ % mono SimpleMVC.exe
```

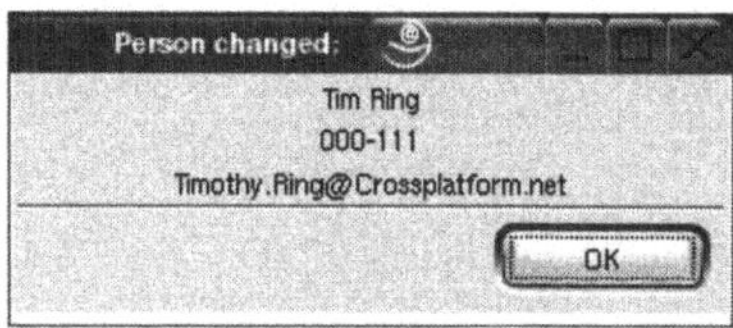

Figure 5-27. Tim King strutting his stuff courtesy of ViewGtk

And there you have it—an example of the MVC pattern using three different views, with a design that lends itself nicely to adding further GUI systems as and when required. By factoring out controller behavior into its own class, a lot of code has been made reusable, and the view class's only real responsibility is to display data to the user.

TIP One aspect of modern GUI systems that creates confusion when considering the MVC pattern is the use of forms and controls as both views and controllers. While the use of widgets that act as both view and controller can impede separating the view and controller functionality into separate classes, as we've done in this chapter, knowledge of the MVC pattern can still be used to help factor the code into a sensible and readily maintainable fashion.

Having pushed the MVC as a good pattern to follow when building applications that target more than one GUI toolkit, it also represents a reasonable design for applications that only target a single GUI toolkit. Nonetheless, if building GUIs is your thing, a number of alternative patterns are available for GUI design, including the Document View, Model View Presenter, and Presentation Abstraction Control patterns. Investigating these patterns is an excellent way to hone your cross-platform GUI skills.

Summary

Having read this chapter, you should feel reasonably prepared to tackle the expanse of GUI decisions that have unfurled in front of you.

The chapter began by discussing how a GUI system might be implemented in the ideal managed world, before investigating how Microsoft .NET, Mono, and PNET handle the thorny issue. The chapter then investigated some alternative toolkits before demonstrating how the MVC pattern can be applied to produce flexible applications that are only loosely coupled to a GUI system.

With the numerous GUI toolkits being in various states if readiness, it looks like *variety* is going to be the best word to describe cross-platform .NET GUI development for the foreseeable future. And while Microsoft's impending Avalon technology is set to surpass `System.Windows.Forms` in 2006, in all likelihood, `System.Windows.Forms` will prevail as the dominant GUI technology, purely for its wide acceptance on Windows platform.

Whether the non-Microsoft CLI implementations will embrace Avalon remains to be seen, but it looks like GUI development will continue at a frantic pace. It goes without saying that cross-platform GUI development is perfectly suited for developers who enjoy nothing more than playing with different technologies and making software beautiful for their users.

CHAPTER 6

Developing Distributed Applications

"The future is here. It's just not widely distributed yet."

—William Gibson, prophet

WITH THE VAST ARRAY of GUI libraries discussed in the previous chapter, .NET is an excellent tool for developing desktop programs, many of which can run on a single computer without a care about the external world—a perfect example of digital agoraphobia. Nonetheless, .NET also contains a broad set of classes that makes it excellent for developing applications that have their logical intestines spread across a network, and it is this class of application that we discuss in this chapter.

When the World Wide Web came to power in the 1990s, it was seen as an excellent cross-platform medium, but as the Web drew in the commercial world, the browser wars showed that not all browsers were created equal. Even though browsers have progressed far since then, it can still be difficult to create Web sites that appear uniformly across different platforms. The popularity of the Internet has not only turned Web applications into a consumer phenomenon, but it has also familiarized consumers with using numerous Internet protocols, such as SMTP, POP3, and FTP, regardless of whether they have any thought for the underlying plumbing. If we then consider the steadily increasing breadth of consumer mobile and digital TV applications, and the corporate rush to package functionality as subscriber Web services, it would be difficult to deny that we are in the tumultuous technical age of distributed applications.

Before we arrive at some of the more interesting things that you can do with two computers and a bit of wire, we start by discussing the stalwart foundation of almost all distributed applications, the venerable and highly respected mainstay of many an enterprise: the relational database.

Dealing with Databases

The most common and well understood type of server is, unsurprisingly, the Relational Database Management System, or RDBMS, which was introduced in 1970 by IBM's Edgar F. Codd. Since E.F. Codd first described relational databases as the means to facilitate—"The independence of application programs . . . from growth in data types and changes in data representation"[1]—relational databases have become the ubiquitous mechanism for storing data, and their lack of real competition has seen their servers become colloquially known as *database servers*.

.NET provides access to relational databases through numerous classes in numerous namespaces, all of which focus on the `System.Data.dll` assembly and which are collectively, and somewhat informally, known as ADO.NET. Apart from containing some highly flexible utility types—like the disconnected, relational data store, the `DataSet`—ADO.NET defines a number of interfaces that embody the concept of a .NET managed data provider, or managed provider, that are implemented as concrete sets of classes providing access to a particular type of database server or, in the .NET parlance, data source.

.NET Managed Providers

All .NET managed providers contain four main types in a simple object model that is designed to allow fast data manipulation and is based on the following four standard interfaces:

- An `IDbConnection` object enables connectivity to a data source.
- An `IDbCommand` object represents a database command that returns or modifies data.
- The `IDataReader` provides forward-only, read-only access to data.
- The `IDbDataAdapter` provides a two-way bridge between a generic `DataSet` object and a data source.

Figure 6-1 shows how these interfaces are conceptually implemented by managed providers, to provide a consistent mechanism for accessing different types of data sources.

1. E.F. Codd, *A Relational Model of Data for Large Shared Data Banks* (Association for Computing Machinery, 1970).

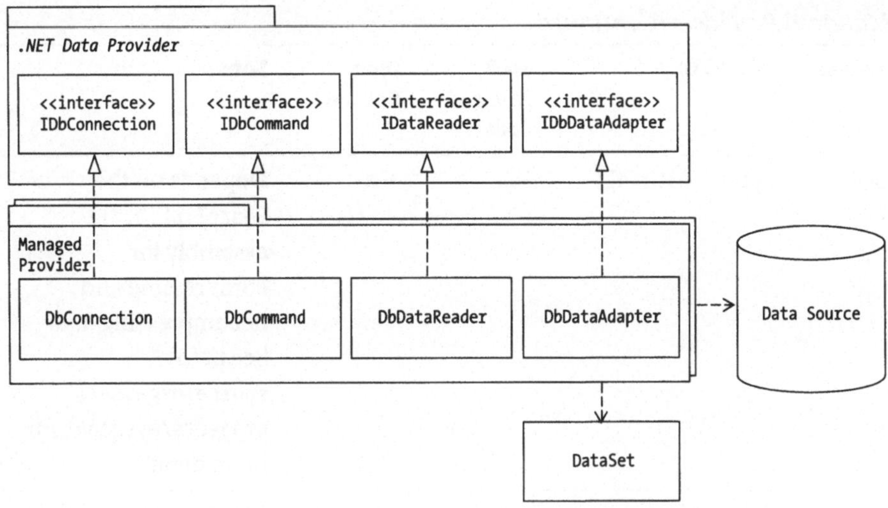

Figure 6-1. A conceptual diagram of .NET managed providers

Although Microsoft .NET only contains a limited number of managed providers, an ever-growing number of commercial and open source data providers are available from a variety of sources, many of which are also available with Mono and which are shown in Table 6-1.

Table 6-1. .NET Managed Providers

Provider	Databases	Assembly	100% Managed Code	Open Source	Notes
DB2	DB2	`IBM.Data.DB2.dll`	No	Yes	Requires the DB2 Call Level Interface shared library.
DB2Client	DB2	`Mono.Data.DB2Client.dll`	No	Yes	Requires the DB2 Call Level Interface shared library. This has been deprecated in favor of the DB2 provider.
Firebird	Firebird/ Interbase	`FirebirdSql.Data.Firebird.dll`	Yes	Yes	See `http://firebird.sourceforge.net` for more details.

Table 6-1. .NET Managed Providers (Continued)

Provider	**Databases**	**Assembly**	**100% Managed Code**	**Open Source**	**Notes**
MySqlNet	MySQL	`ByteFx.Data.dll`	Yes	Yes	Depends on the `SharpZipLib.dll` assembly for compressing and decompressing data. See `http://sourceforge.net/projects/mysqlnet` for more details.
dbProvider	MySQL	`dbProvider.dll`	Yes	No	See `http://www.einfodesigns.com` for more details.
Npgsql	Postgres	`Npgsql.dll`	Yes	Yes	See `http://gborg.postgresql.org/project/npgsql` for more details.
ODBC	RDBMS with an ODBC driver	`System.Data.dll`	No	Yes/No	
OLEDB	RDBMS with an OLE DB provider	`System.Data.dll`	No	Yes/No	
Oracle	Oracle	Mono's `System.Data.OracleClient.dll`	No	Yes/No	
SqlClient	Microsoft SQL Server 7/2000	`System.Data.dll`	Yes	Yes/No	Depends on the `Mono.Data.Tds.dll` assembly. Mono's implementation is open source, and Microsoft .NET's implementation is not.

Table 6-1. .NET Managed Providers (Continued)

Provider	Databases	Assembly	100% Managed Code	Open Source	Notes
SQLLite	SQL Lite	`Mono.Data.SqlliteClient.dll`	No	Yes	
SybaseClient	Sybase SQL Server	`Mono.Data.SybaseClient.dll`	Yes	Yes	Depends on the `Mono.Data.Tds.dll` assembly.
TdsClient	Older Sybase and MS SQL Servers	`Mono.Data.TdsClient.dll`	Yes	Yes	Depends on the `Mono.Data.Tds.dll` assembly.

The majority of the managed providers target a specific type of database server, and because they are not encumbered with the overheads of generic code, these targeted providers provide the best performance to their particular database server. A few of the providers, notably the `OLEDB`, `ODBC`, and `TdsClient` providers, are not designed to communicate with a specific type of database server but rather a generic database access API. While this allows them to be used with more than one type of database server, they generally do not perform as well as the targeted providers, and they also require an unmanaged driver for each type of RDBMS to which they are connected.

The generic providers should generally be used when the database server does not have a native provider or, in some cases, when the application must work with various types of database servers. Nonetheless, it is still preferable to avoid using the generic providers whenever possible. In the case of applications that must work with a variety of database servers, it is considered better practice to write provider-agnostic code, as explained later in the chapter. Not only does this provide the best performance, but it also avoids creating a dependency on an RDBMS from a particular vendor.

As indicated in Table 6-1, not all the managed providers are written purely in managed code; a significant portion of the providers rely on shared libraries to access their particular data source(s). Calling unmanaged shared libraries is not covered in depth until the next chapter, but, essentially, the libraries must be installed on the computer that is running .NET. Most of the shared libraries that are mentioned in the table are available for a variety of platforms. This means that the providers can generally be used for cross-platform development, although you should check that a particular library works on a particular platform before betting your next $1 million project on it.

Despite having to step carefully through a minefield of managed and unmanaged .NET providers, the breadth of native and generic providers ensures that all of the most popular and some of the most uncommon data sources can all be accessed from .NET. This ample booty enables your .NET projects to integrate with your existing database servers or, in the case of new projects, choose the perfect database server to suit your platform, performance, and cost requirements.

The ODBC Managed Provider

Open DataBase Connectivity, or ODBC, is a Microsoft API that was based on the SQL Access Group's portable database API and is widely regarded as the industry-standard database connectivity API. As shown in Table 6-1, ODBC is implemented in Windows by `odbc32.dll`, and for non-Windows systems, it is implemented by iODBC and unixODBC's implementations of `libodbc.so`.

Apart from requiring an unmanaged implementation of the ODBC API, when using ODBC, a further complication is that before it can be connected to a particular type of data source, it requires an unmanaged driver, as shown in Figure 6-2.

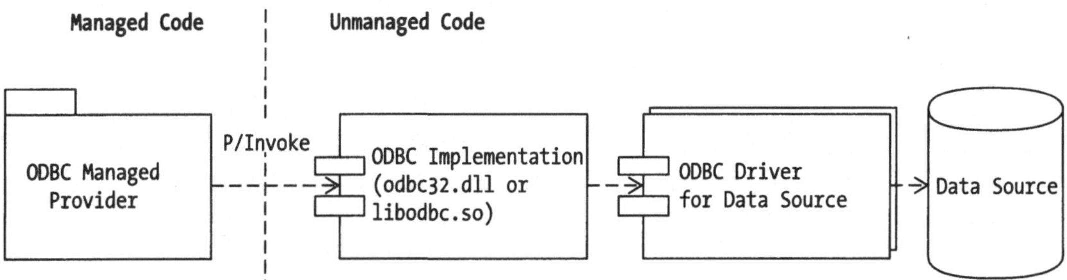

Figure 6-2. The ODBC managed provider

Nonetheless, a broad range of open source and commercial drivers are available for a number of different platforms and data sources, including Oracle, MySQL, Postgres, IBM DB2, SQL Server. and MS Access. This means that using the ODBC .NET provider is eminently suitable for cross-platform development.

TIP For a thorough list of available ODBC drivers, go to `http://www.unixodbc.org/drivers.html`.

The OLE DB Managed Provider

Following the early success of ODBC, Microsoft released OLE DB as a COM-based database connectivity layer. Providing an object model and some advanced features that are not available in ODBC, OLE DB relies heavily on COM and is for all intents and purposes a Windows-only technology.

In a similar vein to ODBC's drivers, before OLE DB can be connected to a particular type of data source, it requires an unmanaged OLE DB provider, as shown in Figure 6-3.

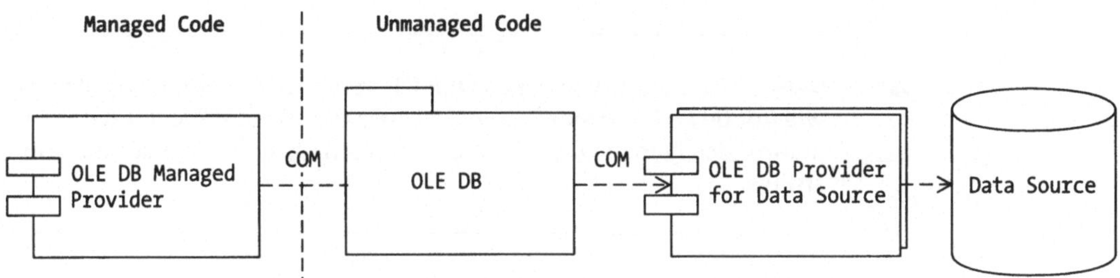

Figure 6-3. Microsoft's OLE DB managed provider

Not only are there OLE DB providers for many popular types of data source, but there's also an OLE DB provider available for ODBC. This OLE DB provider for ODBC acts as an adapter and provides access to data sources that have an ODBC driver but do not have their own OLE DB provider.

While Mono's implementation of the OLE DB managed provider is externally identical to the .NET Framework implementation, Mono's implementation uses the open source libGDA data access API for its internal implementation. In essence, Mono's OLE DB implementation is a `libGDA` managed provider that masquerades as an OLE DB managed provider, as illustrated in Figure 6-4. This means that it can be used with any data source, as long as a libGDA provider is available for that data source.

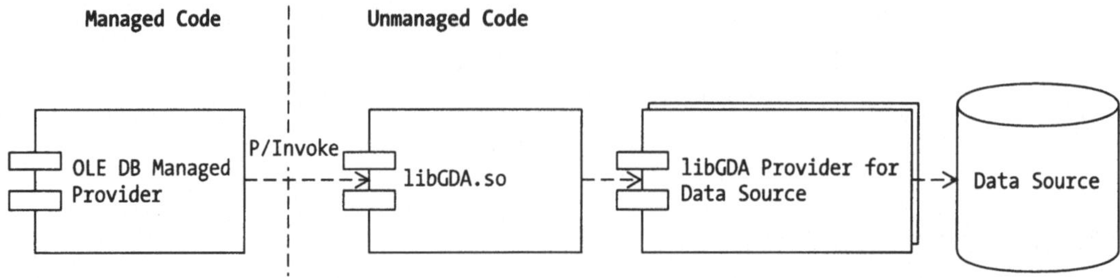

Figure 6-4. Mono's OLE DB managed provider

Although Mono's implementation cleverly allows non-Windows programs to appear as though they are using OLE DB, it raises two issues. First, a disparity exists between libGDA connection strings and OLE DB connection strings. This means that a cross-platform program using OLE DB would have to use different connection strings depending on which CLI implementation it was run on.

NOTE The disparity between OLE DB and libGDA connection strings will not be an issue indefinitely, because the Mono project intends to automatically map OLE DB connection strings to libGDA connection strings.

Second, although libGDA providers are available for a number of popular types of data source, the list is not exactly the same as for OLE DB providers. This means that some applications that work on Microsoft .NET might not work on Mono, and vice versa.

Writing Provider-Agnostic Code

When working with .NET data access code, one frequent requirement is the ability to write code that is not tightly coupled to a particular data source. The simplest approach is to use either the `ODBC` or `OLE DB` provider, both of which work with various types of database server but require unmanaged drivers for each type of database that they are connected to.

Some developers, however, prefer not to use a generic provider due to the slight performance overhead that is incurred. They instead prefer to write code that uses ADO.NET's common interfaces: `IDbConnection`, `IDbCommand`, `IDbDataAdapter`, and `IDataReader`.

Rather than declaring the dataSource parameter and the deleteEverything variable using concrete types, the following method uses the common interfaces for the declarations:

```
public int DeleteWork(IDbConnection dataSource)
{
    IDbCommand deleteEverything = dataSource.CreateCommand();
    deleteEverything.CommandText = "DELETE FROM MessageStore";

    int recordsDeleted = deleteEverything.ExecuteNonQuery();
    return recordsDeleted;
}
```

While this approach works well to ensure that the provider can be easily changed, it makes sense to ensure that all connection and data adapter objects are instantiated in one place.

A useful technique for simplifying the instantiation of connection and data adapter objects—and for that matter all data provider objects—is to use an *Abstract Factory* pattern[2] for managing the instantiation of concrete classes. One such implementation is the ProviderFactory class in the Mono.Data.dll assembly. Another alternative is the DataFacade class in the NUtility.Data.dll assembly, which builds Mono's ProviderFactory and is part of the open source NUtility class library. This library is available at http://www.blinksoftware.co.uk/nutility.

The Comment Application

To demonstrate a database application in action, we develop a completely cross-platform application by hosting a database on the open source MySQL database server and then create a simple command-line application to access the database.

The application provides a basic interface for storing and retrieving comments, and while it is not a particularly complex application, it is a good example of how a simple program can be created for sharing data over a local area network (LAN).

2. Gamma, Helm, Johnson, and Vlissides, *Design Patterns: Elements of Reusable Object-Oriented Software* (Reading, MA: Addison-Wesley, 1995).

NOTE You can download MySQL as a tarball or as binary packages for a number of platforms from `http://www.mysql.com`. The build process on UNIX-based systems is similar to the installation processes for Mono and PNET that were described in Chapter 2, so we let you decide which installation process is best for you.

Application Design

With middle-tier servers being increasingly seen as a cost-effective way to improve application performance, a popular myth has arisen that client–server applications have been resolutely superseded by *n*-tier applications. While *n*-tier applications can undoubtedly offer performance benefits, client–server applications still remain cheaper and easier to build than multitier applications. To appease both design camps without making the example overly complicated let's develop a simple *n*-tier application, where *n* happens to be 2, as illustrated in Figure 6-5.

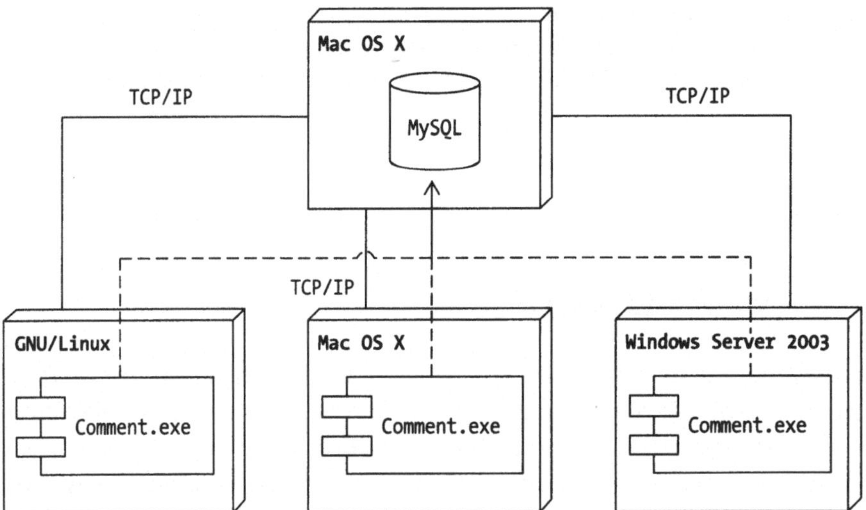

Figure 6-5. Deployment of the two-tier Comment application

As shown in Figure 6-5, we will host MySQL on a Mac OS X machine, but because it is available for most platforms, you can install it on the platform of your choice.

NOTE If you would prefer to use a database server other than MySQL, most of the SQL commands that we use are ANSI-92 SQL compliant, and the SQL scripts should be usable on most modern database servers with minimal modification.

Developing the Database

To keep the example as simple as possible, we use a data model with a single table for storing all our data. Although this is by no means the ideal podium for showing off good relational database design skills, it is the easiest way of demonstrating a cross-platform database application without getting lost in reams of SQL commands, primary and foreign keys, and assorted database paraphernalia.

NOTE The source code samples for this chapter can be found in the Downloads section of this book's Web site (`http://www.cross-platform.net`) and the Apress Web site (`http://www.apress.com`). The scripts for the database and the code for the `MessageStore.dll` assembly are in the `Chapter_06/MessageStore` directory.

We start by creating a text file that contains the SQL Data Definition Language (DDL) commands that we will use to create the database. After creating the database with a `CREATE DATABASE` command, the file contains a `CREATE TABLE` command to create a solitary table that can store the data. Finally, the script grants access permissions to the database with a username and password that can subsequently be used by the client application. The code is as follows:

```
--create_database.sql
--Run drop_database.sql to delete this database

CREATE DATABASE MessageStore;
USE MessageStore;

CREATE TABLE Message (
    MessageId INT(4) NOT NULL AUTO_INCREMENT,
    Name VARCHAR(32) NOT NULL,
    Comments VARCHAR(255) NOT NULL,
    LoggedDate DATETIME NOT NULL,
    PRIMARY KEY(MessageId)
);

GRANT ALL ON MessageStore.* TO MessageStoreUser IDENTIFIED BY 'password';
FLUSH PRIVILEGES;
```

To run this script on the MySQL server, you can pipe the contents of the file into the `mysql` program, as follows:

```
pnet@macosx:~ % mysql < create_database.sql
pnet@macosx:~ %
```

While the `mysql` program is always careful to return details of any errors to the console, it does not return any notification of success—which can be a little disconcerting. To check that the database and table have been created, run the `mysql` program in interactive mode. This allows you to query the server and run SQL commands to your heart's content. Use the following code:

```
pnet@macosx:~ % mysql
Welcome to the MySQL monitor.  Commands end with ; or \g.
Your MySQL connection id is 15 to server version: 4.0.14-standard

Type 'help' or '\h' for help. Type '\c' to clear the buffer.
mysql>
```

We can now check that the database has been created, as follows:

```
mysql> SHOW DATABASES;
+--------------+
| Database     |
+--------------+
| MessageStore |
| mysql        |
| test         |
+--------------+
3 rows in set (0.00 sec)
```

Knowing that the database now exists, you can check that the table has been created by switching to the `MessageStore` database and running the `SHOW TABLES` command, as follows:

```
mysql> USE MessageStore;
Database changed
mysql> SHOW TABLES;
+------------------------+
| Tables_in_messagestore |
+------------------------+
| Message                |
+------------------------+
1 row in set (0.00 sec)
```

Now that we have determined that the database and table have been created, all that is left to do is to create a client application. Before we leave `mysql`'s interactive mode, the following code reminds you of the table's schema:

```
mysql> DESCRIBE Message;
+------------+-------------- -+------+-----+------------+----------------+
| Field      | Type          | Null | Key | Default    | Extra          |
+------------+-------------- -+------+-----+------------+----------------+
| MessageId  | int(4)        |      | PRI | NULL       | auto_increment |
| Name       | varchar(32)   |      |     |            |                |
| Comments   | varchar(255)  |      |     |            |                |
| LoggedDate | datetime      |      |     | 0000-00-00 |                |
+------------+---------------+------+-----+------------+----------------+
4 rows in set (0.30 sec)
```

To insert a record into the `Message` table, use a standard SQL `INSERT` command, as follows:

```
mysql> INSERT INTO Message (Name, Comments, LoggedDate)
    -> VALUES('TEST', 'This is a very quick test', '2003-08-25 09:00:00');
Query OK, 1 row affected (0.00 sec)
```

The response from `mysql` indicates that one row was affected. This is exactly what we would expect, but if you would prefer to visually confirm that the record was created, run an SQL `SELECT` command against the table. To leave `mysql`'s interactive mode, simply enter the following command:

```
mysql> \q
pnet@macosx:~ %
```

Expanding the Database Toolset

Although MySQL only comes with a command-line interface by default, you can download a variety of GUIs from the MySQL Web site, each of which provides features to manage your MySQL server in the graphical splendor to which you are accustomed.

If, however, you are not using MySQL, or you would prefer to use a truly generic tool, the Mono project has created the following tools that can simplify the process of manually interacting with a database:

- **SQL# CLI:** This is a command-line tool that allows interactive execution of SQL queries and the batch execution of SQL commands from a file. SQL# CLI is distributed with Mono and currently works with a number of managed providers.

- **SQL# GUI:** This is a graphical version of the SQL# CLI program and consists of a GUI interface that uses the Gtk# toolkit, which was described in depth in Chapter 5. SQL# GUI is distributed with Mono and currently works with a number of managed providers.

Building the Client Application

Now that we have a database for storing application data, it is time to create an application that uses the database's storage services. Before we start coding, however, we must decide which provider to use for accessing the MySQL server. You can choose from the following five managed providers:

- **ByteFX.Data:** This provider is open source and is written purely in C# and therefore does not require an unmanaged driver.

- **dbProvider:** This provider is written entirely in managed code but requires a commercial license.

- **Mono.Data.MySql:** This provider relies on the unmanaged MySQL client shared library but is deprecated in favor of ByteFX.Data.

- **ODBC:** This provider requires an unmanaged MySQL ODBC driver.

- **OLEDB:** This provider requires the unmanaged `MyOLEDB` provider for Microsoft .NET or the unmanaged MySQL libGDA provider for non-Windows operating systems.

Because the ByteFX.Data provider is written explicitly for MySQL, consists entirely of managed code, and is freely available, we use it in our example. However, any of the competing managed providers might be preferable in different circumstances.

NOTE The `ByteFX.Data.dll` assembly can be used to directly access MySQL and depends on the `SharpZipLib.dll` assembly for compressing and decompressing data. Although both assemblies are included with Mono, `ByteFX.Data.dll` can also be downloaded from `http://www.sourceforge.net/projects/mysqlnet`, and `SharpZipLib.dll` can be downloaded from `http://www.icsharpcode.net/OpenSource/SharpZipLib`.

Although this is a two-tier application, it makes sense to separate the data access logic from the rather limited business logic. While separating business logic and data logic is frequently done at the class level, because we intend to reuse the `MessageStore` database in some of the later examples in this chapter, the data access code is stored in a separate assembly from the `Comment` application's business logic, as shown in Figure 6-6.

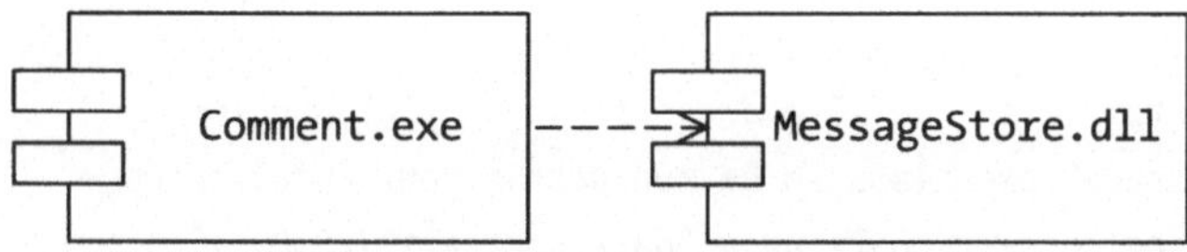

Figure 6-6. The `Comment` *package diagram*

Not only does this design help simplify maintenance for more complex applications, but it also allows the type of database server to be changed without disturbing the program's business logic.

The MessageStore Assembly

The `MessageStore` assembly contains a single class, `MessageStore`, which is responsible for connecting to the database and retrieving and manipulating data from the `Message` table. The `MessageStore` class and its members are shown in Figure 6-7.

MessageStore
+GetMessages(): DataSet +SaveMessage(name: string, comments: string) -FormatDate(data: DateTime): string

Figure 6-7. The `MessageStore` *class*

The class definition starts with a constant declaration for the connection string to the MySQL database, and contains details of the host server's IP address, the database's name, and the username and password that were specified in the `create_database.sql` file.

Because the following code uses the loopback address for the data source, you must remember to substitute in your own computer's IP address if you want the `MessageStore.dll` assembly to work across your local area network.

```
//Filename: MessageStore.cs
using System;
using System.Data;
using ByteFX.Data.MySqlClient;

namespace Crossplatform.NET.Chapter6.Data
{
    public class MessageStore
    {
        //Remember to substitute in the IP address of your MySQL machine
        //to allow the MessageStore class to be run across your local network
        private const string connectionString = "data source=127.0.0.1;" +
                "user id=MessageStore;pwd=password;database=MessageStore";
```

TIP Because storing an inline connection string is not very flexible and requires recompilation of the assembly to change the data source, a popular alternative is to store the connection string in a configuration file. Because configuration files are application specific and we intend to use the `MessageStore` assembly with a number of example applications in this chapter, it makes sense to define the connection string in one place, which in this example is within the assembly. Should you want to separate the connection string from the assembly, it would be straightforward to alter the constructor to include an additional string parameter, or you could read in a string from a resource file.

After the connection string is an instance field for storing a `MySqlConnection` object, which we instantiate in the class's constructor, passing in the previously defined connection string, as follows:

```
private readonly MySqlConnection conn;

public MessageStore()
{
    conn = new MySqlConnection(connectionString);
}
```

Now that the `MessageStore` class has the means to connect to a database, it needs a mechanism for retrieving records from the database. When designing a .NET database application, you must decide which of ADO.NET's two competing data-retrieval mechanisms should be used: `DataReaders` or `DataSets`. On the one hand, `DataReaders` provide the fastest way to read data, require an open connection to the database, and allow forward-only, read-only access until they are disconnected. On the other hand, `DataSets` provide a flexible, serializable data store that acts as a relational Data Transfer Object,[3] which is ideal for moving data between different and potentially distributed layers of an application. Having retrieved data through an open connection, a `DataSet` can still provide access to the data after its connection has been closed. Coupled with its ability to handle schematic and relational information, this makes the `DataSet` ideal for applications that need to carry out more complex data manipulations.

3. Fowler, Martin, *Patterns of Enterprise Application Architecture* (Reading, MA: Addison-Wesley, 1995).

Although the MessageStore class could use either data-retrieval mechanism—and the simplicity of the Comment application might suggest that a DataReader would be preferable—because we're going to reuse the MessageStore assembly in some applications later in the chapter, the added flexibility offered by the DataSet makes it the ideal choice to deal with the unknown requirements of the later programs. Now that we have decided on the data-retrieval mechanism to use, we can implement the GetMessages() method, as follows:

```
//Retrieve the records from the DB
public DataSet GetMessages()
{
    const string sqlCmd = "SELECT * FROM Message " +
                          "ORDER BY LoggedDate DESC";
    MySqlDataAdapter adapter = new MySqlDataAdapter(sqlCmd, conn);

    conn.Open();
    DataSet records = new DataSet();
    adapter.Fill(records, "Message");
    conn.Close();

    return records;
}
```

The GetMessages() method is a perfect example of how simple retrieving data using an ADO.NET DataSet can be. After opening the connection, it passes a DataSet to adapter's Fill() method, which internally calls the SELECT command to populate the DataSet. The method finishes by doing some housekeeping and closing the connection before returning the newly filled DataSet.

With the class now having the capability to retrieve data, it needs a mechanism for adding messages to the database, so mimicking the simplicity of the GetMessages() method, we add the SaveMessage() method, as follows:

```
//Insert the message into the DB...
public void SaveMessage(string name, string comments)
{
    string sqlCmd = "INSERT INTO Message(Name,Comments,LoggedDate)" +
                    "VALUES('{0}','{1}','{2}')";

    sqlCmd  = String.Format(sqlCmd,
                            PrepareString(name),
                            PrepareString(comments),
                            FormatDate(DateTime.Now));
```

```
        MySqlCommand insertCommand = new MySqlCommand(sqlCmd, conn);

        conn.Open();
        insertCommand.ExecuteNonQuery();
        conn.Close();
    }

    //Double-up single quotes to stop strings from
    //being inadvertently delimited in SQL queries.
    private string PrepareString(string value)
    {
        return value.Replace("'", "''");
    }
```

The method starts by declaring a string that contains a template `INSERT` command, which is populated by calling `String.Format` to insert the relevant values into the template's placeholders.

Because we're using strings that have been entered by the user, it's essential to ensure that any single quotes in the `name` and `comments` parameters are doubled up. This ensures that the SQL query isn't inadvertently delimited by a stray single quote, which could result in a malformed SQL query, or purposefully delimited in an attempt by the user to piggyback his own SQL commands into being executed.

Because we need to insert a `DateTime`, the class must ensure that the value is in the correct format for MySQL, which is handled by the `FormatDate` method that we will look at shortly.

When the text for the `INSERT` command has been created, the method instantiates a `MySqlCommand` by passing in the SQL command string and the class's connection instance. The connection is then opened and the `MySqlCommand`'s `ExecuteNonQuery` method is called before the connection is closed. By ensuring that the connection is only held open for the minimum time necessary, it reduces the overhead that's associated with an open connection on the database server. This is a useful technique for reducing the load on the server and enhancing the application's scalability.

The only missing piece of the puzzle is the `FormatDate()` method that simply formats a `DateTime` so that it is in the correct format for MySQL. The following code shows the `FormatDate()` method:

```
        private string FormatDate(DateTime date)
        {
            return date.Year + "-" +
                   date.Month + "-" +
                   date.Day + " " +
                   date.Hour + ":" +
                   date.Minute + ":" +
                   date.Second;
        }
    } /* class MessageStore */
} /* namespace Crossplatform.NET.Chapter6.Data */
```

We now have a complete class that can be used for retrieving records from and adding records to the MessageStore database. By using a number of the ADO.NET classes, as shown in Figure 6-8, the classes' code is kept simple, proving how easy it is to use ADO.NET when writing data access code.

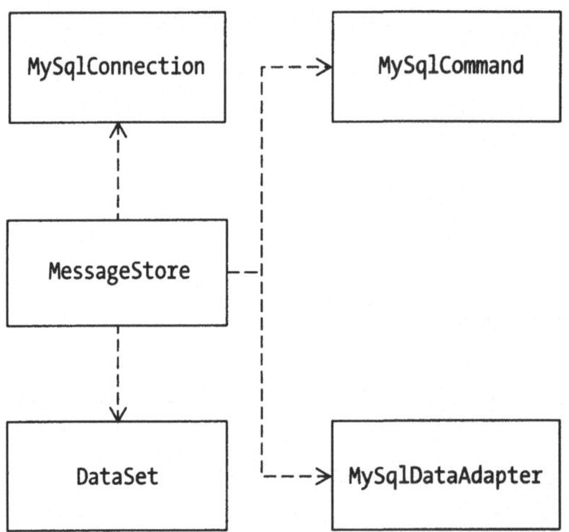

Figure 6-8. The MessageStore *classes' dependencies*

Before we attempt to compile the assembly on Windows, GNU/Linux, or Mac OS X, we should take into consideration the assembly's dependencies, as shown in Figure 6-9.

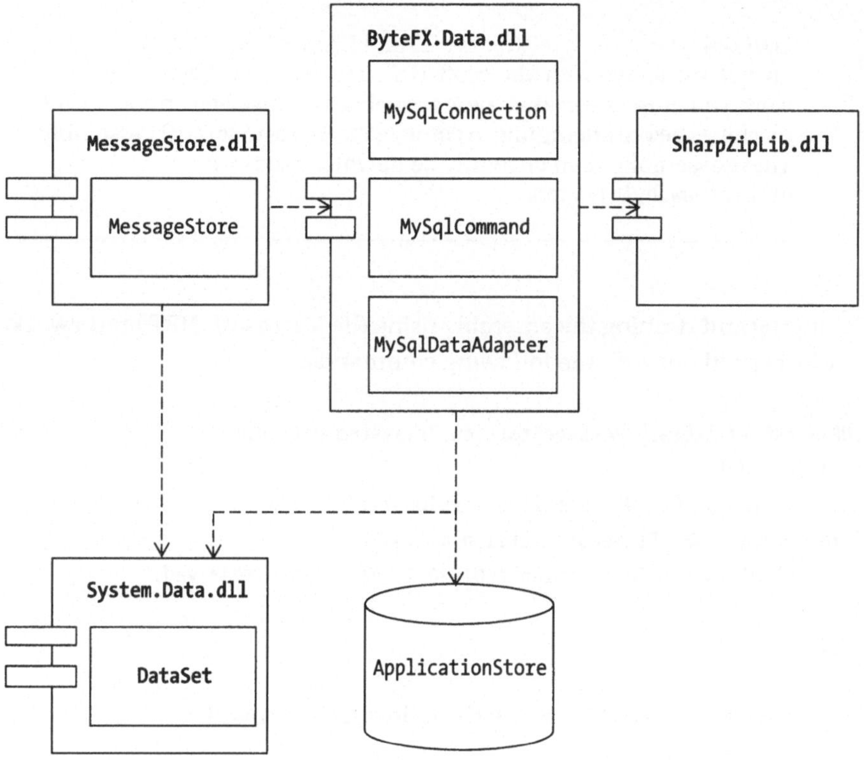

Figure 6-9. The `MessageStore.dll` *assembly dependencies*

A Remembrance of Projects Past

JK Hey MJ, this UML diagramming is great stuff, eh?

MJ Well they do say a picture's worth 1,000 words.

JK I dig the way the classes can be shown in relation to the DLLs. I can't imagine how much time I could have regained from reducing the written documentation on my past projects.

MJ As a technical snob, I have to admit favoring working with those developers who use diagrams to document their software—it's certainly better than working with developers who bring you an apple every day.

JK So, you could say "Some UML diagrams a day keep the apple-wielding developers at bay."

CAUTION Because ByteFX.Data.dll and ICSharpCode.SharpZipLib.dll are not distributed with Microsoft .NET, if you're using the .NET Framework, you must ensure that these assemblies are installed on your client machines before attempting to compile the MessageStore.dll assembly. These assemblies can currently be downloaded from http://www.bytefx.com.

Compiling and running the assembly using the Microsoft .NET Framework can now be carried out with the following commands:

```
C:\MS.NET> csc /t:library MessageStore.cs /r:System.Data.dll
/r:ByteFX.Data.dll
Microsoft (R) Visual C# .NET Compiler version 7.10.3052.4
for Microsoft (R) .NET Framework version 1.1.4322
Copyright (C) Microsoft Corporation 2001-2002. All rights reserved.

C:\MS.NET>
```

For Mono under GNU/Linux, use the following commands:

```
mono@linux:~ % mcs /t:library MessageStore.cs /r:System.Data.dll \
> /r:ByteFX.Data.dll
Compilation succeeded
mono@linux:~ %
```

And finally, for Portable.NET on Mac OS X, use the following commands:

```
pnet@macosx:~ % cscc /t:library MessageStore.cs /r:System.Data.dll \
> /r:ByteFX.Data.dll /out:MessageStore.dll
pnet@macosx:~ %
```

We now have a basic assembly that handles our data access needs, but before putting it through its paces, we need to build a client assembly that requires its services.

The Comment Program

To complete the application, we need a simple program with two functions: The first one retrieves records from the database; the second one adds an entry into the database.

NOTE The code for the Comment program is in the `Chapter_06/Comment` directory at this book's Web site (`http://www.cross-platform.net`) and the Apress Web site (`http://www.apress.com`).

Because the program is so simple, all the code will be placed in the `Main()` method of the `Comment.cs` file, as follows:

```
//Filename: Comment.cs
using System;
using System.Data;
using Crossplatform.NET.Chapter6.Data;

namespace Crossplatform.NET.Chapter6
{
    class Comment
    {
        private const string errorMsg = "error '{0}' was raised from '{1}'";

        static void Main(string[] args)
        {
            try
            {
                if(args.Length == 1)
                {
                        MessageStore store = new MessageStore();
                        store.SaveMessage(Environment.UserName + "@" +
                                          Environment.MachineName,
                                          args[0]);
                }
                else if(args.Length == 0)
                {
                    MessageStore store = new MessageStore();
                    DataSet messages = store.GetMessages();

                    foreach(DataRow record in messages.Tables[0].Rows){
                        string line = String.Format("On {0} {1} said '{2}'",
                                        ((DateTime)record["LoggedDate"]),
                                        record["Name"],
                                        record["Comments"]);
                        Console.WriteLine(line);
                    }
                }
```

```
                else
                {
                    Console.Error.WriteLine("Usage: Comment.exe comments");
                }
            }
            catch (Exception ex)
            {
                Console.Error.WriteLine(errorMsg, e.Message, e.Source);
            }
        }
    }
}
```

The Main() method starts by counting the number of arguments in the program to determine whether it should display entries, add an entry, or display some usage instructions on the console. Because the method only expects a single argument when adding an entry, any comments that contain white space must be delimited with double quotes on the command line.

If the program is passed one argument, it instantiates the MessageStore class and calls the SaveMessage() method, passing in a string that contains the current username and hostname and the contents of the command-line argument. If the program is passed no arguments, it instantiates the MessageStore class and calls the GetMessages() method, storing the results in a DataSet. After a DataSet has been retrieved, it iterates through each of the DataRows in the Rows collection, using the field values to populate a string template that is then written to the console.

Figure 6-10 shows the dependencies that are required to compile the Comment.exe assembly.

Compiling the program using the .NET Framework can then be carried out with the following commands:

```
C:\MS.NET> csc Comment.cs /r:MessageStore.dll /r:System.Data.dll
Microsoft (R) Visual C# .NET Compiler version 7.10.3052.4
for Microsoft (R) .NET Framework version 1.1.4322
Copyright (C) Microsoft Corporation 2001-2002. All rights reserved.

C:\MS.NET>
```

For Mono under GNU/Linux, use the following commands:

```
mono@linux:~ % mcs Comment.cs /r:MessageStore.dll /r:System.Data.dll
Compilation succeeded
mono@linux:~ %
```

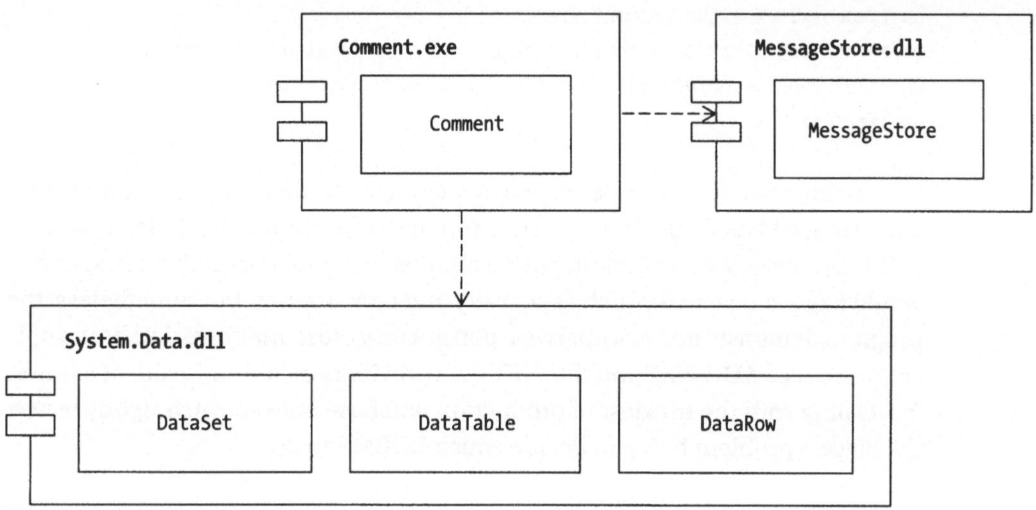

Figure 6-10. The `Comment.exe` *assembly dependencies*

And finally, for Portable.NET on Mac OS X, use the following commands:

```
pnet@macosx:~ % cscc Comment.cs /r:MessageStore.dll /r:System.Data.dll \
> /out:MessageStore.dll
pnet@macosx:~ %
```

If you now run the program on Windows with no command-line arguments, you should retrieve one comment, which is the comment that was manually added to the database earlier:

```
C:\MS.NET> Comment.exe
On 25/08/2003 09:00:00 TEST said 'This is a very quick test'
C:\MS.NET>
```

To check that the functionality to add an entry works, we can run it on GNU/Linux with the following command-line argument:

```
mono@linux:~ % mono Comment.exe 'And this is also a quick test'
mono@linux:~ %
```

We can then check that it worked by running the program on Portable.NET with no arguments, as follows:

```
pnet@macosx:~ % ilrun Comment.exe
On 25/08/2003 12:13:04 mono@linux said 'And this is also a quick test'
On 25/08/2003 09:00:00 TEST said 'This is a very quick test'
pnet@macosx:~ %
```

So there you have it: a basic, two-tier application that can retrieve and store data using a MySQL database and can run under Microsoft .NET, Mono, and PNET. Of course, we have sidestepped a number of issues that production systems would have to deal with, such as security and concurrency, but nonetheless, the program demonstrated an otherwise perfunctory cross-platform database application. In fact, ADO.NET and the .NET data providers include a wealth of features for dealing with the trickiest of production database issues, which rightly leaves the biggest problem being to decide which RDBMS to use.

The Tangled Wide Web

Although database applications are by far the most common type of distributed application, the word *database* has never managed to lose its zeitgeist role as the bastion of boring corporate processes. In comparison, Web applications have received quite amazing press in the last decade and, after computer games, were the first software to be accepted in their own right as mass consumer products. Not only did the word *Web* become synonymous with the underlying Internet, but it also brought with it a wealth of phrases, such as *Web site*, *homepage*, and *URL*, and it heralded the beginning of the age of connectivity.

Apart from turning the Internet into a triumphant consumer phenomenon, the Web also infiltrated the business world in the form of intranets and has also proved invaluable in the business-to-business and business-to-consumer marketplaces in the form of extranets. While the Web's public success is invariably due to the mixture of garish colors, branding, and, occasionally, ingenious coding that bedecks Web pages, a very good technical reason exists for the Web's success. This reason is the ease of deployment and maintenance that is offered by targeting a Web browser instead of the more traditional desktop.

If Web sites are the public face of the Internet, the Web server is the skull beneath the face. Along with the benefits of simplified design, deployment, and maintenance that are inherent in Web applications comes a heavy reliance on the capabilities of the underlying Web server. While uptime, scalability, and performance can all be handled to a certain degree by carefully designing an application's architecture, without the use of a solid Web server, a Web-based application will invariably slip, and the resulting farce will be in drastic need of a facelift.

.NET rightly contains an expansive array of classes for handling Web functionality. These classes reside in the various `System.Web` namespaces and are informally known as ASP.NET. Being the modern technology that it is, .NET changes the balance somewhat. While the Web server still maintains logistical importance as the underlying powerhouse behind Web applications, ASP.NET carries out a number of services that traditionally belonged in the domain of the Web server itself—such as request filtering and access control—by implementing a pipelined system of response and request preprocessing and post-processing. By bringing a slew of advanced functionality within ASP.NET itself, it is conceptually simpler to use with different Web servers, because ASP.NET reduces its reliance on the Web server implementing certain functionality.

This section demonstrates how ASP.NET can be used for Web-enabling cross-platform programs, but before we examine some applications that demonstrate the inherent power of ASP.NET, we take a quick detour and examine how the different CLI implementations implement ASP.NET.

Microsoft .NET Framework

Although the .NET Framework's implementation of ASP.NET is designed to be portable across different Web servers, the version of ASP.NET that ships with the Microsoft .NET Framework 1.0 and 1.1 only works with Microsoft's IIS server 4, 5, and 6. Despite an egregious reputation brought about by continued attacks from the black hat community, the IIS Web server is predictably popular with Windows shops and lies behind many a successful Web site and Windows DNA application.

The Wonderful Wizard of OS

JK When you say *black hat community*, you honestly expect me to believe that the witches have it in for IIS?

MJ Indeed. Haven't you seen all the flying monkeys around here? Wake up man, and don't smell . . . those . . . popp . . . ezzzz . . . .

JK Ooh, my head.

MJ Hah, and what about your feet? You look like a right Billyboy with these ridiculous ruby slippers on.

WWOS* I'll get you Billyboy—and your server too!

JK & MJ There's no place like Redmond; there's no place like Redmond . . .

*Wicked Witch of Open Source

While IIS's success is invariably due to its being packaged with Windows, its extensibility API, ISAPI, has ensured that IIS moves with the times and has allowed IIS to serve first CGI, then ASP, and now ASP.NET programs. A simplification of the ISAPI architecture is depicted in Figure 6-11.

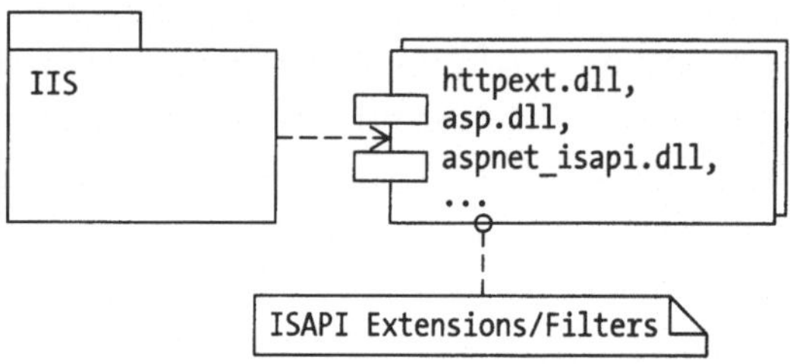

Figure 6-11. The IIS extension architecture

ASP.NET's compatibility with IIS relies on the aspnet_isapi.dll ISAPI extension, which acts as a go-between for IIS and ASP.NET by forwarding HTTP requests to managed code and fielding HTTP responses, as shown in Figure 6-12.

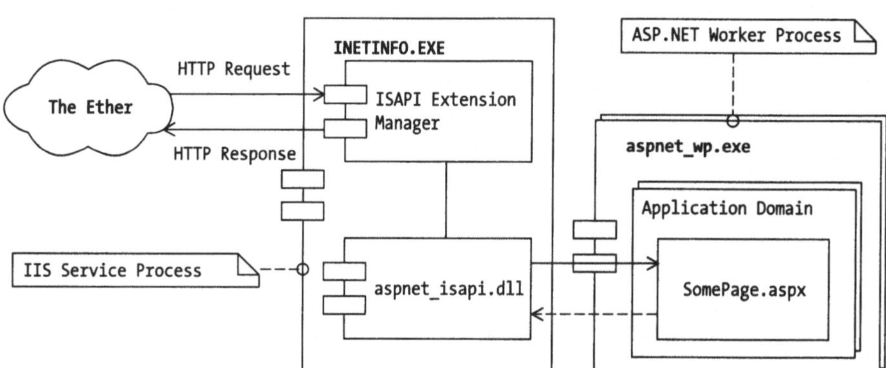

Figure 6-12. ASP.NET running on Windows/IIS

Unlike most command-line and GUI programs, which rely on ephemeral operating system processes to host their application domains, Web applications are generally accessed sporadically, and because creating Windows processes incurs a substantial computational overhead, Web applications require their application domains to be hosted in long-lived processes. IIS can therefore be configured to use a number of ASP.NET worker processes, each of which can host a number of application domains, and therefore a number of ASP.NET applications, while providing the responsiveness that is required to satisfy a throng of insatiable Web users.

Windows 2000 and Windows XP Installation

Installing ASP.NET on a computer that is running Windows 2000 or Windows XP Professional is simply a matter of ensuring that IIS is installed before installing Visual Studio .NET or the .NET Framework SDK.

To install IIS on a Windows 2000 or Windows XP Professional computer, follow these steps:

1. Open the Add/Remove Programs dialog box from the Control Panel.
2. Click the Add/Remove Windows Components button.
3. Select the Internet Information Services (IIS) check box in the Components list, and then click the Next button to complete the wizard.

You can then install ASP.NET by installing the .NET Framework SDK or Visual Studio .NET on the computer.

Windows Server 2003 Installation

Installing ASP.NET on a computer that is running Windows Server 2003 can either be done by using the Manage Your Server wizard or by using the Add/Remove Programs dialog box.

To install ASP.NET using the Manage Your Server wizard, follow these steps:

1. Click the Add or Remove a Role button, and move through the wizard until you see the Server Role screen.
2. Select Application server (IIS, ASP.NET) from the Server Role list, and click the Next button.
3. In the Web Application Server Options screen, select the Enable ASP.NET check box, and then click the Next button to complete the wizard.

To install ASP.NET using the Add/Remove Programs dialog box, follow these steps:

1. Open the Add/Remove Programs dialog box from the Control Panel.
2. Click the Add/Remove Windows Components button.
3. Select the Application Server check box in the Components list, and then click the Next button to complete the wizard.

Mono

Mono currently supports ASP.NET on two different Web servers: XSP and Apache. XSP is a small Web server that was written by the Mono team in C# and is used by the Mono developers for testing ASP.NET applications. Apache is frequently touted as the world's most popular Web server, running more Web sites than any other type of Web server, and like most open source software, it is available on a wide variety of platforms.

XSP

Written in C# and running entirely in managed code, XSP is undoubtedly the easiest way of getting up and running with ASP.NET. The simple design of XSP is shown in Figure 6-13.

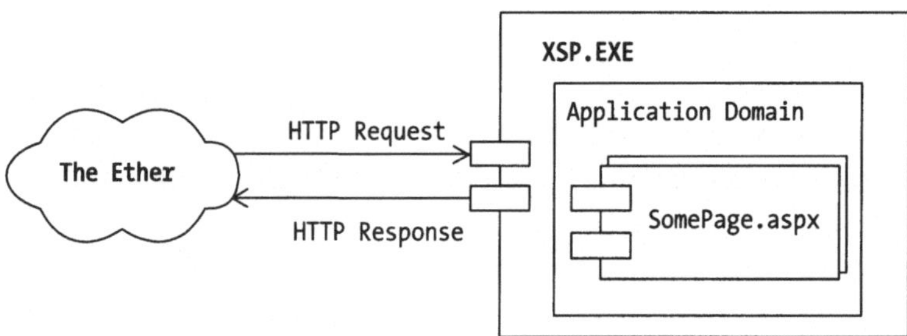

Figure 6-13. ASP.NET running under XSP

While XSP does not have many of the advanced options that are associated with most modern, production-quality Web servers, it is nonetheless perfectly suited for testing ASP.NET code on different platforms and is an excellent Web server for prototyping ASP.NET applications.

Because of its very limited functionality, XSP serves as living proof that ASP.NET's pipelined architecture reduces ASP.NET's dependency on using specific Web server services.

Installing XSP on GNU/Linux

NOTE XSP can be downloaded from the Mono channel in Red Carpet or from the Downloads page on the Mono Web site at `http://www.go-mono.com`.

Building XSP simply involves running the following commands:

```
mono@linux:~ % tar -xzvf xsp*.tar.gz
mono@linux:~ % cd xsp*
mono@linux:~ % ./configure --prefix=/usr
mono@linux:~ % make
...
mono@linux:~ % make install
...
```

After building XSP, the `xsp.exe` program should have been copied to the `/usr/bin` directory, and a number of test files should have been copied to the `/usr/share/doc/xsp/test` directory.

You can now run XSP by executing the following commands:

```
mono@linux:~ % cd /usr/share/doc/xsp/test
mono@linux:~ % mono /usr/bin/xsp.exe
Listening on port: 8080
Listening on address: 0.0.0.0
Root Directory: /usr/share/doc/xsp/test
Virtual directory: /
```

To confirm that XSP is running correctly, aim your favorite browser at `http://127.0.0.1:8080`. This should bring up the `index.aspx` page, with a list of demonstration ASP.NET pages, as shown in Figure 6-14.

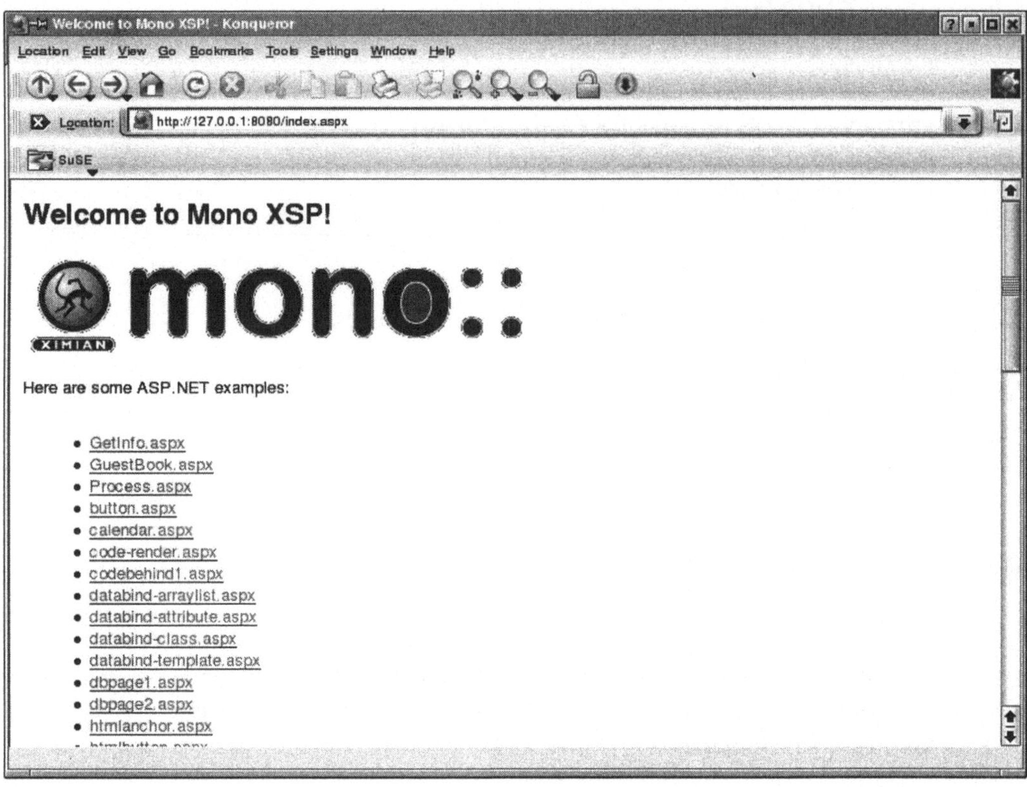

Figure 6-14. The XSP home page as seen by the Konqueror Web browser

Apache

The Apache Web server is the open source community's poster-child application. It is the application that first put the *server* in *Web server* and the application that proves that not-for-profit software can compete with the very best commercial software.

Apache originated as a slew of patches for the National Center for Supercomputing Applications (NCSA) HTTP server. This gained it a reputation for being a *patchy* server, but despite its humble beginnings, Apache has been crafted into a powerful and highly flexible server that can accommodate a variety of platforms and environments through its modular design, which is shown in Figure 6-15.

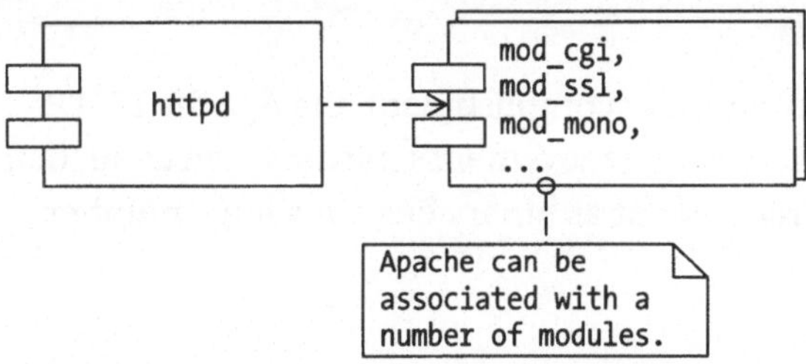

Figure 6-15. The Apache module architecture

With only a minimal amount of functionality contained within the `httpd` program, the bulk of Apache's functionality is encapsulated in a number of modules. This allows an administrator to configure the server to meet his exact requirements. Although Apache's module architecture is philosophically similar to the IIS extension API, ISAPI, in practical terms, Apache also uses modules to encompass a number of the core features that are implemented internally within IIS.

To run ASP.NET applications, Apache requires the addition of the `mod_mono` module, and while Apache modules are generally not compatible with both the 2.0.*x* and 1.3.*x* versions of Apache, `mod_mono` is, thankfully, an exception to this rule.

When the Apache server receives an HTTP request, if it determines that the request is for an ASP.NET resource, it passes the request to the `mod_mono` module, which subsequently forwards the request via a socket to the `mod-mono-server.exe` assembly . The `mod-mono-server.exe` assembly, which is hosted within an instance of the Mono runtime, is responsible for hosting the user applications and is therefore where the bulk of the ASP.NET processing occurs. The interaction between Apache, the `mod_mono` module, and `mod-mono-server.exe` is shown in Figure 6-16.

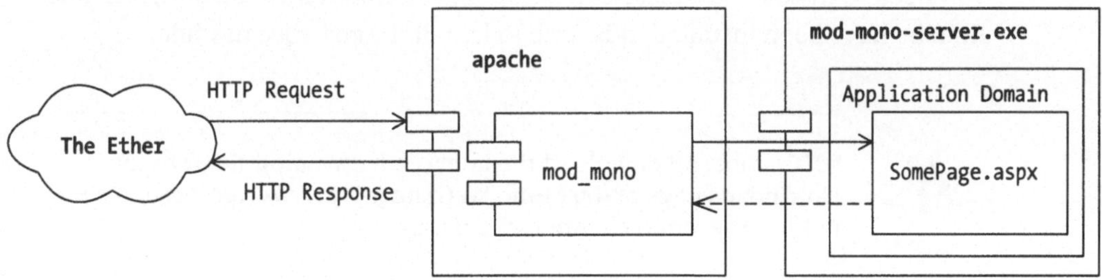

Figure 6-16. ASP.NET running under apache and `mod_mono`

Installing Apache on GNU/Linux

As the veracious pinnacle of open source accomplishment, the Apache HTTP server follows a number of the open source movement's maxims, and as such, it can either be downloaded as source code or as binary files for a large number of platforms.

NOTE The Apache Web server can be freely downloaded from the HTTP Server project page on the Apache Software Foundation's Web site at `http://www.apache.org`.

Because the binary installation process differs for each platform and the source code installation process is similar to the installation process for Mono and PNET that was described in Chapter 2, we install Apache from source code, as follows:

```
mono@linux:~ % tar -xzvf httpd-2.*.tar.gz
mono@linux:~ % cd httpd-2.*
mono@linux:~ % ./configure --prefix=/usr --enable-so
...
mono@linux:~ % make
...
mono@linux:~ % make install
...
```

After Apache has been installed, and if you have not already installed XSP, you need to install it, as described earlier in the chapter. When both XSP and Apache have been installed, it is time to install the `mod_mono` module.

NOTE You can download the latest `mod_mono` module from the Downloads page of the Mono Web site (`http://www.go-mono.com`) or from the Mono channel of Red Carpet.

The `mod_mono` module can be installed using the following commands:

```
mono@linux:~ % tar -zxvf mod_mono*.tgz
mono@linux:~ % cd mod_mono*
mono@linux:~ % ./configure --prefix=/usr
...
mono@linux:~ % make
...
mono@linux:~ % make install
...
```

TIP If you have Apache installed in a nonstandard directory, the installation process might complain about not finding apxs. In this case, you need to use the `--with-apxs` argument when calling `configure`, as follows:

```
./configure --prefix=/usr --with-apxs=/home/user/httpd/bin/apxs
```

If you are using Apache 2.0.*x* and get a compilation error stating the `apr.h` header cannot be found, you need to specify the `--with-apr-config` option, providing the full path to `apr-config`, as follows:

```
./configure --prefix=/usr --with-apr-config=/usr/bin/apr-config
```

Now that all the binary files are in place, all that is left is to edit Apache's configuration file, `httpd.conf`, and ensure that the `mod_mono` module is loaded when Apache starts.

The `httpd.conf` file can be found in the `/usr/httpd/conf/` directory and should have already been modified during the installation process to include the following line:

```
LoadModule mono_module modules/libmod_mono.so
```

You should now add the following two lines to the configuration file. These two lines redirect all requests for `/demo` to the `/usr/share/doc/xsp/test` directory and register both paths as mono application paths.

```
Alias /demo "/usr/share/doc/xsp/test"
MonoApplications "/demo:/usr/share/doc/xsp/test"
```

Finally, add the following lines to the file, which configure mono to be the program to handle the /demo path.

```
<Location /demo>
    SetHandler mono
</Location>
```

When you've saved these changes to the configuration file, it's time to run the Apache server, which can be done by executing the following command:

```
mono@linux:~ % /usr/local/apache2/bin/apachectl start
```

TIP If you now point your Web browser at your Apache server (for example, http://127.0.0.1/demo/index.aspx), you should be greeted by the index page, which contains links to a number of sample ASP.NET pages. If index.aspx doesn't display properly, you can find a number of installation hints and tips in the INSTALL file that comes with mod_mono.

Portable.NET

At the time of writing, Portable.NET does not support ASP.NET, but the project team is planning to imminently port Mono's implementation of ASP.NET, which should mean that PNET will eventually support both XSP and Apache.

You should find that getting ASP.NET working with Portable.NET is almost identical to the process that was outlined for Mono. We recommend that you check Portable.NET's Web site (http://www.southern-storm.com.au/portable_net.html) for the status of PNET's ASP.NET support.

What's in a Name: GNU/Linux

When Linus Torvalds failed to give the kernel that he had written an adequate name, Ari Lemmke, the administrator of the first FTP site to host Linux, took Linus's name and followed the sporadic habit of naming UNIX-style operating systems with a word that ends with the letter *X*. And Linux was born.

Nonetheless, a kernel maketh not an operating system. When the Linux kernel had been released, it would probably have been consigned to the annals of history if not for a number of farsighted hackers who decided to bundle it with the wealth of applications and tools from the free software organization GNU (meaning "GNU's Not UNIX").

With the broad range of GNU tools containing far more lines of code than the Linux kernel, it's fair to say that the phenomenon that people frequently refer to as Linux is actually more GNU than Linux, and while the name Linux is undoubtedly more consumer friendly, the people at GNU appreciate the use of the operating system's full name. This is why we do our best to honor GNU in this book by referring to the operating system as GNU/Linux.

Introducing ASP.NET

While to the average layperson a Web application suggests a Web site, applications that run on Web servers are not tied to a single delivery channel and can target a variety of devices, including traditional browsers, PDAs, cell phones, and digital TV, each of which tends to require a specific type of markup language. This ever-increasing consortium of target platforms and markup languages raises the question "What exactly is a Web application?" Is it a complex XHTML site that is viewed on a PC, a WML application that is displayed on WAP cell phone, a cHTML site on a Japanese i-mode phone, or a basic HTML application for a handheld computer or PDA?

Rather than worrying about using the term *Web* to refer to potentially non-Web client applications, we define a Web application to be an application that is hosted on a Web server and that is responsible for responding to client requests by serving markup language that can subsequently be rendered as a user interface (UI) on the client machine. An ASP.NET application can then be described as a Web application that is created with ASP.NET. Although such semantic quibbling might seem unimportant, ASP.NET was consciously designed to cope with a mixture of delivery channels, and although this book uses examples that target traditional browsers, ASP.NET can easily be used to work with any markup language that takes your fancy.

ASP.NET's core functionality is implemented in the `System.Web` namespace, with the main classes that deal with creating Web applications—in contrast to those that deal with Web services that we discuss later in the chapter—being implemented in the `System.Web.UI` namespace. For Web applications, the primary class of interest is the `Page` class, which represents an ASPX file, and is also known as a *Web Forms page*. The `Page` class contains methods and properties that allow programs to access various facets of ASP.NET and is event driven, allowing code to programmatically interact with various stages of the request-handling and response-generating process.

ASP.NET also provides a variety of control classes, with each set of controls being designed for specific delivery channels. All ASP.NET controls, including the actual `Page` class, inherit from the `System.Web.UI.Control` class. Currently, the following two sets of controls exist for generating HTML-based user interfaces:

- `System.Web.HtmlControls`: Can be used for simple, high-performance HTML interfaces
- `System.Web.WebControls`: Can be used to simplify the construction of highly functional HTML interfaces

TIP With the release of .NET Framework 1.1, support for targeting mobile devices was made available in the `System.Web.Mobile` and `System.Web.UI.MobileControls` namespaces. Both these namespaces are currently in development for Mono and should soon be available for use in cross-platform projects.

A Single-File ASP.NET Application

So now that we have gotten through some preliminary banter and hopefully have at least one Web server at our beck and call, we delve into ASP.NET, starting with a simple Web forms page that recalls the `GetInfo` program from Chapter 2.

NOTE The code for this example is in the `Chapter_06/GetInfo` directory at this book's Web site (`http://www.cross-platform.net`) and the Apress Web site (`http://www.apress.com`).

Because this is a warm-up application, we create the most basic kind of ASP.NET application, which requires a single ASPX file that contains a mixture of HTML and C# code, as follows:

```
<%@ Page language="c#"%>
<!-- Filename: GetInfo.aspx -->

<html>
 <head>
  <title>Cross-platform .NET: GetInfo</title>
  <link href="_css/getinfo.css" type="text/css" rel="STYLESHEET"></link>
 </head>
 <body>
  <h1>ASP.NET does GetInfo</h1>
   <table border="1" width="300">
    <tr><td>Operating system: </td>
     <td><%= System.Environment.OSVersion.Platform.ToString() %></td></tr>
    <tr><td>OS Version: </td>
     <td><%= System.Environment.OSVersion.Version.ToString() %></td></tr>
    <tr><td>Todays date is: </td>
     <td><%= System.DateTime.Today.ToString() %></td></tr>
   </table>
 </body>
</html>
```

Although the majority of the file is pure HTML, the first line contains an ASP.NET `@ Page` directive, which can be used for configuring a number of properties. But in this case, it just stipulates that the page uses C#.

The only other non-HTML code in the file is the contents of the three table cells, which are delimited between pairs of `<%` and `%>` symbols. These delimiters should be familiar to the users of various Web-scripting technologies, such as ASP and JSP, and they are used to declare some inline code, which is run by the Web server before the page is sent to a Web browser.

In the `GetInfo.aspx` file, the inline code carries out very little work, retrieving a few values from the `System.Environment` and `System.DateTime` classes that are written to the browser by declaring the opening delimiters with equal signs.

Also, because raw HTML is generally bland, the file also contains an HTML `<link>` element that references a *Cascading Style Sheet* file, `getinfo.css`, which has the following contents:

```
H1
{
    font-size: large;
    font-weight: bold;
}
BODY
{
    color: #000000;
    font-size: small;
    font-family: Arial, sans-serif;
    background-color: #FFFFFF;
}
TABLE
{
    cellspacing: 0px;
    cellpadding: 0px;
    border-width: 1px;
    border-style: solid;
    border-color: Gray;
}
TR
{
    valign: top;
    border-style:none;
}
TH
{
    width: 50%;
    background-color: #CCCCCC;
    text-align: left;
    border-style:none;
}
TD
{
    border-style:none;
    background-color: #66CCFF;
}
```

Single-File Application Deployment

Now that we have our ASPX page, it is time to deploy the page. This brings us to an interesting ASP.NET phenomenon: Unlike with all the previous examples, we do not need to manually compile our code, because ASP.NET handles the compilation for us. This is because when the ASPX file is first requested, ASP.NET compiles it into a temporary assembly that is used to respond to all subsequent requests until the ASPX file changes, at which point ASP.NET automatically recompiles the file.

Although this leads to a slight performance hit as the code is compiled when a page is first requested, it not only keeps the deployment of ASPX pages simple, but it is also a dramatic improvement over the performance of traditional ASP pages, which were not compiled.

TIP Microsoft's implementation of ASP.NET stores the temporary assemblies in the `%SYSTEMROOT%\Microsoft.NET\Framework\vx.x\Temporary ASP.NET` directory, where `vx.x` is the version of the .NET Framework. Mono's implementation of ASP.NET stores the temporary assemblies in the `/tmp` directory for UNIX operating systems and in the Windows `temporary` directory for Windows.

Because ASP.NET can compile the page for us, we can therefore ignore the usual command-line shenanigans and browse straight to the `GetInfo.aspx` file in the Web browser of our choice, as shown in Figure 6-17.

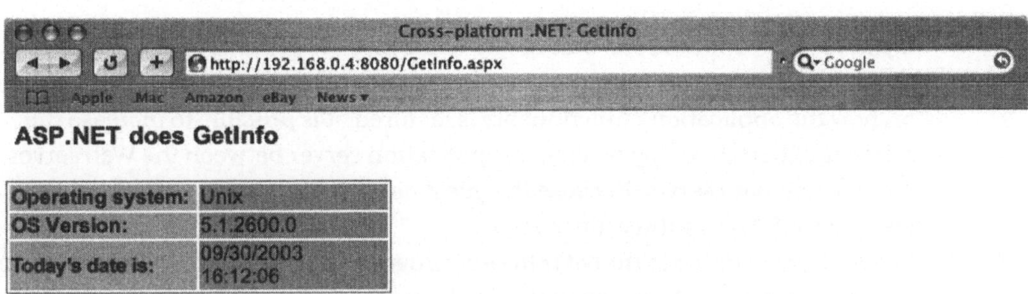

Figure 6-17. Hosting `GetInfo.aspx` on XSP and GNU/Linux

Although `GetInfo.aspx` demonstrates how easy it can be to create ASP.NET applications, a couple of points need to be addressed. First, inviting visitors to see which operating system a Web server is running is an administrator's nightmare and a cracker's wet dream. Second, although using inline code is ridiculously simple, it is generally considered to be a bad coding practice that should be shunned for all but the smallest presentation-related programming tasks. Of course, ASP.NET, being the advanced Web-development toolset that it is, not only supports inline code but also supports an assortment of features that allow you to factor a Web application's code to befit the requirements, as we see in the next example.

The Guest Book Web Application

ASP.NET has many advanced features that it would take many pages to cover in any real breadth, including a sophisticated caching mechanism, a thorough security framework, and a variety of classes for storing page, session, and application state.

To give a general overview of some of the standard features, we now revisit the Comment application from earlier in this chapter, and we use ASP.NET to create a Web-based interface that allows Internet users to leave their comments and e-mail addresses in a guest book.

NOTE The code for the guest book example is in the `Chapter_06/GuestBook` directory at this book's Web site (`http://www.cross-platform.net`) and the Apress Web site (`http://www.apress.com`).

Application Design

Dynamic Web applications that access databases are generally split over at least three tiers: the Web browser, the Web server, and the database server. Depending on how the application's functionality is factored, it is possible to increase the number of tiers, often by placing an application server between the Web server and the database server. Because the guest book application is not particularly complex, it follows a three-tier design.

As demonstrated in the `GetInfo.aspx` program, ASP.NET applications contain a mixture of markup language and code. Because `GuestBook.aspx` is more complex than `GetInfo.aspx`, we use a feature of ASP.NET, known as *codebehind*. This feature allows the program's logic to be separated from its markup code by storing code and markup language in different files. By enforcing the separation of UI elements from UI logic, codebehind makes it easier to maintain ASP.NET applications and allows Web designers and programmers to work on applications together. Figure 6-18 shows how `GuestBook.aspx`'s use of codebehind maps to the traditional 3-layers used in n-tier applications.

As shown in the figure, because we already have already created an assembly that can read and write from the MySQL `MessageStore` database, the codebehind file reuses the `MessageStore.dll` assembly to save and retrieve entries from the guest book.

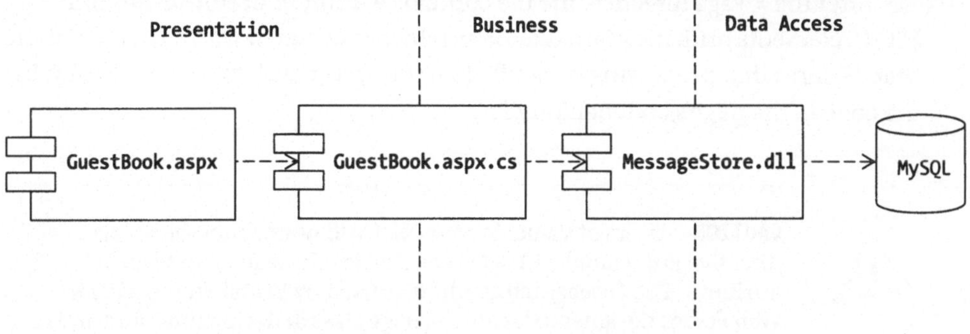

Figure 6-18. The 3-layers of the GuestBook.aspx *application*

The GuestBook.aspx Page

While similar to the GetInfo.aspx file, the GuestBook.aspx file does not contain C# code. The GuestBook.aspx file consists of an @ Page directive, and some HTML and some ASP.NET markup elements, which the ASP.NET page processor uses when processing the codebehind file.

Once again, the file begins with an @ Page directive, but rather than declaring a language as we did in the previous example, it instead stipulates that the page is related to a source code, or codebehind file, GuestBook.aspx.cs, and that the page inherits from the Crossplatform.NET.GuestBook.GuestBookPage class. The code is as follows:

```
<%@ Page Src="GuestBook.aspx.cs" AutoEventWireup="false"
        Inherits="Crossplatform.NET.GuestBook.GuestBookPage" %>
<!--GuestBook.aspx -->

<html>
 <head>
  <title>Cross-platform.NET - Guestbook</title>
  <link href="_css/guestbook.css" type="text/css" rel="STYLESHEET"></link>
 </head>

 <body>
  <h1>Cross-platform.NET Guestbook</h1>

  <p>Please enter your criticism and platitudes below.</p>
  <form runat="server">
```

After the @ Page directive, the file contains a number of run-of-the-mill HTML elements until the <form> element, which is declared with a runat attribute that declares that processing is handled on the server and, more specifically, by the code in the page's codebehind file.

CAUTION Users of Visual Studio .NET will notice that the @ Page directive is declared with a Codebehind attribute instead of an Src attribute. The Codebehind attribute is used by Visual Studio .NET's Web Forms designer to locate the page class at design time, and an Src attribute is not required because the codebehind file is compiled at design time. To ensure that your ASP.NET pages are cross-platform, you must use the Src attribute or you should precompile your code-behind assemblies.

As mentioned earlier in the chapter, ASP.NET provides two different sets of controls for producing for HTML: HtmlControls and WebControls. HtmlControls are directly related to HTML elements, and as such, their object model reflects the underlying HTML syntax. WebControls do not directly relate to HTML elements and provide a rich object model that, in some cases, implements functionality that would be particularly arduous to implement using HtmlControls. Because of the expressive power of WebControls, we use them exclusively in this chapter to the detriment of HtmlControls.

TIP If you have UI elements that don't require processing on the server, you can reduce their performance overhead by removing the runat="server" attribute and thereby converting them into plain HTML elements.

After the <form> element, we have an <asp:customvalidator> element, which marks the presence of an ASP.NET CustomerValidator Web Control.

```
<asp:customvalidator id="FormValidator" runat="server"
OnServerValidate="ValidateForm" EnableClientScript="False"
ErrorMessage="Please enter a valid Email address and your thoughts in the
            Comments field."></asp:customvalidator>
</asp:customvalidator>
```

The CustomerValidator control is one of ASP.NET's validation controls and is used to check some validation criteria, displaying an error message in place of the <asp:customvalidator> element if the validation criteria are not met.

After the CustomerValidator, the file contains an HTML table, which contains two TextBox Web Controls. After processing by ASP.NET's page processor, these Web Controls generate HTML tags for storing the user's name and comments, as follows:

```
<table>
 <tr>
  <th>Name:</th>
  <td><asp:textbox id="Email" runat="server" size=""></asp:textbox></td>
 </tr>

 <tr valign="top">
  <th>Comment:</th>
  <td>
   <asp:textbox id="Comments" runat="server"
              TextMode="Multiline" columns="50" rows="10" wrap="true">
   </asp:textbox>
  </td>
 </tr>
```

Finally, the page finishes with some HTML that contains a Button Web Control, which generates an HTML submit button to allow the contents of the form to be submitted to the server. Although the submit button is declared with an onclick attribute, because the runat attribute is set to server, the form does not attempt to call a client-side routine but instead calls the GuestBookPage class's SaveEntry() method, which we declare in the following codebehind file:

```
 <tr>
  <td colSpan="2">
   <asp:button id="Submit" onclick="SaveEntry"
             runat="server" Text="Submit">
   </asp:button></td>
 </tr>

</table>
 </form>
 </body>
</html>
```

The GuestBook.aspx.cs File

Like any other C# source code file, the codebehind file `GuestBook.aspx.cs` starts by declaring the namespaces that it uses, before declaring the `Crossplatform.NET.GuestBook` namespace and the `GuestBookPage` class. The `GuestBookPage` class then declares `protected` field declarations for each of the Web controls in the `GuestBook.aspx` file and a `private` field for storing an instance of the `MessageStore` class, as follows:

```
using System;
using System.Web;
using System.Web.UI;
using System.Web.UI.WebControls;
using System.Text.RegularExpressions;
using Crossplatform.NET.Chapter6.Data;

namespace Crossplatform.NET.GuestBook
{
    public class GuestBookPage : System.Web.UI.Page
    {
        protected TextBox Email;
        protected TextBox Comments;
        protected CustomValidator FormValidator;
        protected Button Submit;

        private MessageStore dataStore;
```

The relationship between the `GuestBookPage` class and these instance fields is shown in Figure 6-19.

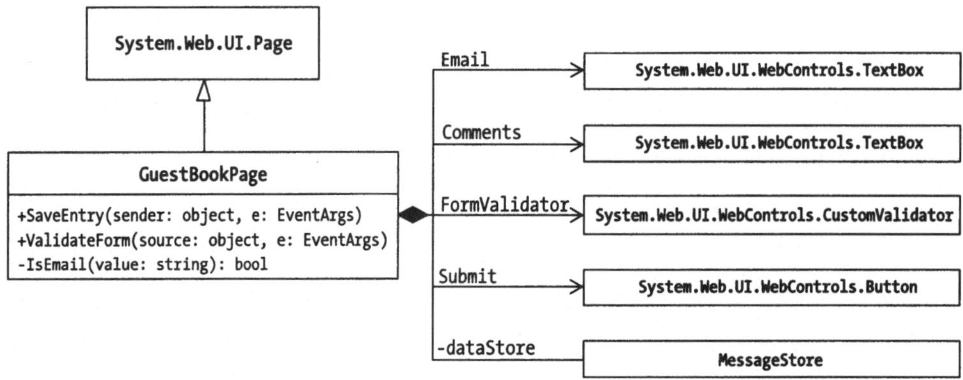

Figure 6-19. The `GuestBookPage` *class*

The class then contains a default constructor, which is used to instantiate the `MessageStore` class, as follows:

```
public GuestBookPage()
{
    dataStore = new MessageStore();
}
```

After the constructor, the class contains the `SaveEntry()` method, which is called in response to the `GuestBook.aspx` page's submit button being clicked. The method starts by calling the base class's `IsValid()` method, which attempts to validate all the page's `Validator` controls by calling the methods that are specified in each control's `OnServerValidate` property.

If the call to `IsValid()` returns `true`, the contents of the `Name` and `Comments` `TextBoxes` are passed to the `MessageStore`'s `SaveMessage()` method and the contents of the `Name` and `Comments` `TextBoxes` are emptied. If the call to `IsValid()` returns `false`, the method does nothing further, as demonstrated by the following code:

```
public void SaveEntry(object sender, EventArgs e)
{
    if(Page.IsValid)
    {
        dataStore.SaveMessage(Email.Text, Comments.Text);

        // Clear the field values
        Email.Text = String.Empty;
        Comments.Text = String.Empty;
    }
}
```

The last two methods that we need to complete the class are the `ValidateForm()` method, which was specified in the `OnServerValidate` property of the `CustomValidator` control, and the `IsEmail()` method, which uses .NET's `Regex` class to determine whether a string contains a valid e-mail address. The code is as follows:

```
public void ValidateForm(object source, ServerValidateEventArgs args)
{
    args.IsValid= (IsEmail(Email.Text) &
                   Comments.Text != String.Empty);
}
```

```
            private bool IsEmail(string value)
            {
                string emailExpr = @"^([a-zA-Z0-9_\-\.]+)@((\[[0-9]{1,3}\.[0-9]"+
                                   @"{1,3}\.[0-9]{1,3}\.)|(([a-zA-Z0-9\-]+\.)+)"+
                                   @")([a-zA-Z]{2,4}|[0-9]{1,3})(\]?)$";

                return (new Regex(emailExpr).IsMatch(value));
            }
        }
    }
```

Multiple-File Application Deployment

As mentioned earlier in this chapter, ASP.NET can automatically compile code. This is as true for applications that use codebehind as it is for single-file applications.

For applications that need to be linked against precompiled assemblies, the assemblies must either be installed in the .NET's shared assembly location—which is the GAC for Microsoft .NET or the standard assembly directory for PNET and Mono—or the assemblies can be placed in a `bin` subdirectory under the application's directory. In the latter case, ASP.NET automatically links the application against them.

CAUTION Be aware that unlike the usual .NET rule of installing support libraries in the same directory as an application, ASP.NET requires support assemblies to be placed in a `bin` subdirectory.

In the case of the `GuestBook.aspx` application, you should copy the `MessageStore.dll`, `ByteFX.dll`, and `SharpZipLin.dll` assemblies into the `bin` subdirectory under the `xsp` directory.

If you now aim your browser at the `GuestBook.aspx` page on the server, you should see a fairly minimalistic form with fields for a name and comments. If you fill in the form without entering values for both the `Name` and `Comment` fields, the `FormValidator` control will fail its validation, causing an error message to be displayed in the middle of the page, as shown in Figure 6-20.

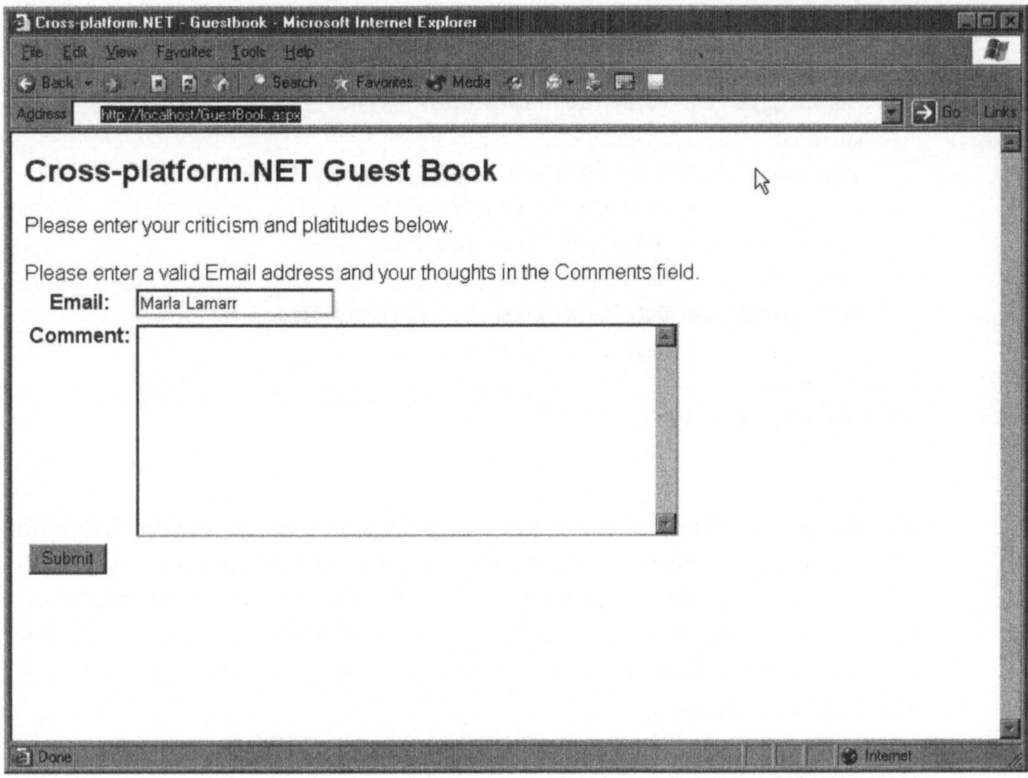

Figure 6-20. The `GuestBook.aspx` *application*

Displaying Previously Saved Messages

While the `GuestBook.aspx` application allows users to add entries to the guest book, it currently lacks a way of displaying previous entries. Because the `MessageStore` class has the `GetMessage()` method, which returns a `DataSet` that contains the previous messages, all that is needed is to add some plumbing to call the method and show the contents of the `DataSet` on-screen. For the sake of simplicity, and to showcase how ASP.NET handles *data binding*, we display the messages in a `DataGrid` Web Control.

We start by inserting a `DataGrid` Web Control into the `GuestBook.aspx` file by adding the following lines to the `GuestBook.aspx` file, after the closing `</table>` tag but before the closing `</form>` tag:

```
<p>
<asp:DataGrid id="MessageGrid" runat="server" AutoGenerateColumns="False">
 <AlternatingItemStyle BackColor="Silver"/>
 <HeaderStyle Font-Bold="True" BackColor="#3399FF"/>
 <Columns>
  <asp:BoundColumn DataField="LoggedDate" ReadOnly="True"
                   HeaderText="Date:"/>
  <asp:BoundColumn DataField="Name" ReadOnly="True"
                   HeaderText="Email:"/>
  <asp:BoundColumn DataField="Comments" ReadOnly="True"
                   HeaderText="Comments:"/>
 </Columns>
</asp:DataGrid>
</p>
```

This declares the DataGrid and sets some rudimentary properties that define which columns are bound to the DataGrid and how the columns are styled.

Now all that's left is to update the codebehind file so that it binds the DataSet to the DataGrid. The first modification to make to the GuestBook.aspx.cs file is to add a declaration of the MessageGrid field for storing a reference to the DataGrid Web Control, as follows:

```
protected DataGrid MessageGrid;
```

We then add an OnPreRender() method to handle the page's PreRender event. As its name suggests, the PreRender event is fired just before the page is rendered. By carrying out data binding during the prerendering stage of processing, we can ensure that the DataGrid is bound after the rest of the page's processing has occurred. This means that if the form has just been submitted, the new message will have been saved before the messages are retrieved from the database. The OnPreRender() method is as follows:

```
private void OnPreRender(object sender, System.EventArgs e)
{
    //Retrieve DataSet and bind to datagrid control...
    this.MessageGrid.DataSource = dataStore.GetMessages();
    this.MessageGrid.DataBind();
}
```

The Page Class's Event Model

As mentioned earlier in this chapter, the ASP.NET `Page` class defines an event model that allows code to be written that hooks into a number of stages in the page's processing lifetime. The events defined for the `Page` class are as follows:

- `Init` Event: The page has been initialized.
- `Load` Event: The page has been loaded and all the page's controls have been fully initialized.
- `PreRender` Event: The page processing is about to complete.
- `Unload` Event: The page processing has completed.
- `Error` Event: An unhandled exception has occurred.
- `AbortTransaction` Event: The transaction that the page was participating in has been aborted.
- `CommitTransaction` Event: The transaction that the page was participating in has been committed.
- `DataBinding` Event: The page has been data-bound.
- `Disposed` Event: The page has been disposed.

Finally, we modify the default constructor by associating the class's `PreRender` event with the `OnPreRender()` method. This ensures that the method is called before the page is sent to a browser. The code is as follows:

```
public GuestBookPage()
{
    this.PreRender += new System.EventHandler(this.OnPreRender);
    dataStore = new MessageStore();
}
```

Saving both the files and browsing to the application's URL again, you should now have a data-bound application that displays all the contents of the `MessageStore` database, as shown in Figure 6-21.

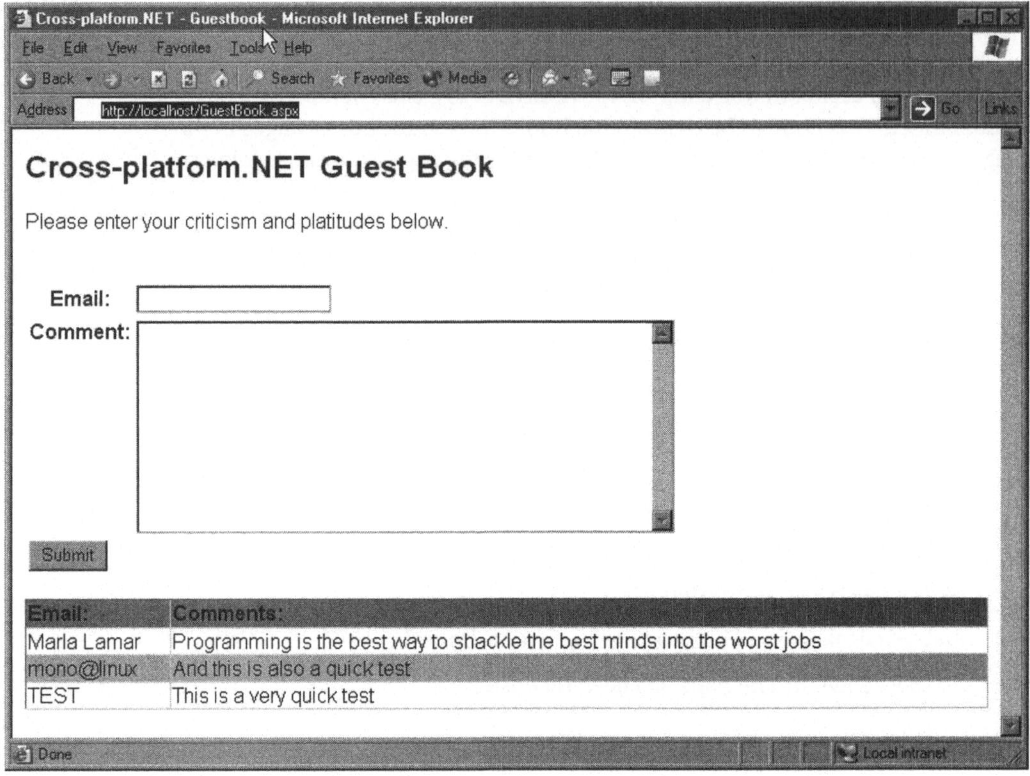

Figure 6-21. ASP.NET does data binding

So there you have it: a simple Web application that provides Web site users with a guest book.

Using the Model-View-Controller Pattern with ASP.NET

While ASP.NET's codebehind facility deftly splits a Web page's layout from its presentation logic, it does not suggest a particular design for the underlying classes that handle the user interface.

As mentioned in Chapter 5, the most popular design pattern for user interfaces is the Model-View-Controller (MVC) pattern, which separates the logic into three elements: the *controller*, which responds to user requests; the *model*, which implements application logic; and the *view*, which generates a display for the user.

Using the MVC pattern for Web applications can not only help to decrease code duplication and simplify maintenance, but it can also make it easier to test the application, because the handling of a request can be tested separately from the generation of a response.

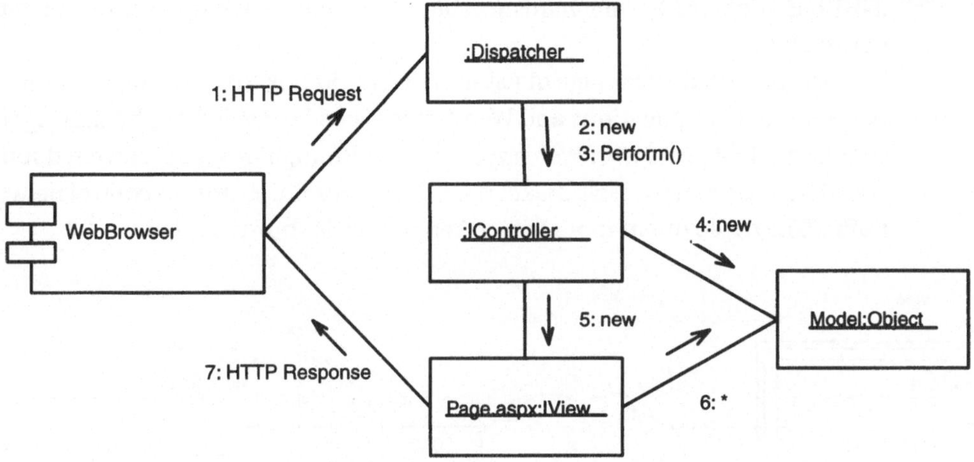

Although you can develop ASP.NET applications using your own implementation of the MVC pattern, the popular Java MVC framework—Maverick—has been ported to .NET and is an excellent way of creating cross-platform ASP.NET applications using the MVC pattern.

To read more details about Maverick.NET or to download the framework, go to the Maverick.NET Web site at `http://mavnet.sourceforge.net`.

Web Services

With all the praise that has been lauded on the Web, it is little wonder that all manner of *next big things* have also attempted to jump onto the connectivity wagon. From multimedia refrigerators that connect to the Internet to light bulbs with IP addresses, the connectivity arena has not only encouraged technical innovation but also its fair share of lunacy. Whether pinging the lights or letting the groceries download the latest Britney Spears pictures will ever truly catch on, only time will tell, but in the meantime, the *next big thing* is much more modest, is unlikely to make consumers drool, and is something that is already helping to make developers' lives easier. Welcome to the humble world of the *Web service*!

Like Web applications, Web services are generally hosted on HTTP servers, but unlike Web applications, they are not intended for user consumption, but rather for programmer consumption. Instead of using HTML to create a user interface, Web services rely on the XML-based Simple Object Access Protocol (SOAP), which allows client applications to send requests to access remote objects that are hosted on the Web server. Such remote invocation methods are generically known as *remote procedure calls*, or RPCs. Apart from Web services,

.NET has another RPC mechanism called *Remoting*, which is described in detail in Chapter 9.

One potential advantage of using HTTP for RPC is that communication between client applications and Web services can be carried out by sharing the standard HTTP ports with Web applications, although this is somewhat double-edged because it conversely makes it harder for administrators to control network traffic. The deployment model for a Web service is shown in Figure 6-22.

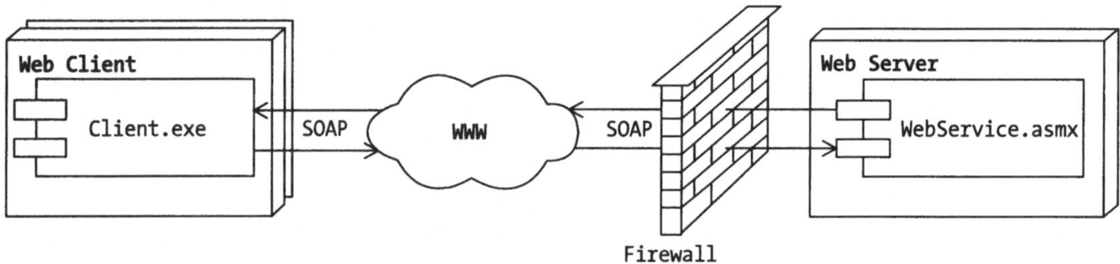

Figure 6-22. Web service deployment

Of course, a number of other RPC technologies, such as CORBA, DCOM, and RMI, can also be configured to use different TCP/IP ports, but because each of them relies on its own binary message format, they can only be consumed by client applications that understand their particular message format. Because Web services only require that clients have the ability to process XML, they are frequently touted as an excellent interoperability mechanism for cross-platform development.

NOTE Web services are not technically tied to HTTP and can theoretically use other Internet transport protocols, such as FTP or SMTP. Because HTTP is by far the most common protocol for Web services, we only discuss HTTP-based Web services in this chapter, and we leave the consideration of alternative transport protocols to the reader's discretion.

In general, Web services are the ideal tool to use when creating a distributed application that can service a number of unknown client applications, which might be written in any number of odd technologies. However, before deciding that Web services are the ideal RPC technology to use in every situation, note that SOAP is a verbose protocol. If performance is at a premium and you only have a controlled set of client applications, .NET Binary Remoting is generally a much more suitable technology to use than Web services.

ASP.NET Web Services

In similar vein to Web applications, ASP.NET Web services are created by placing a scripting file in a directory that is being served by the Web server. These files are also compiled on first use and support the codebehind model. Web service script files can be distinguished from Web application files by their `asmx` file extensions.

Web services are implemented in ASP.NET by the `System.Web.Services` namespaces, with subsidiary functionality in the `System.Web.Configuration`, `System.Web.Description`, `System.Web.Discovery`, and `System.Web.Protocols` namespaces. A class that implements a Web service can optionally inherit from the `WebService` class, which provides access to some of the common ASP.NET objects, such as HTTP context and the application and session state.

To demonstrate a cross-platform Web service, we revisit the `Comment` application and implement a simplified version that only retrieves existing comments, but it uses a Web service and can be run on any machine that has an Internet connection.

The Web Comment Application Design

Like the guest book application, the Web Comment application follows a three-tier design, but due to the need to marshal calls to the Web service across the Internet, the application requires a number of extra classes, as shown in Figure 6-23.

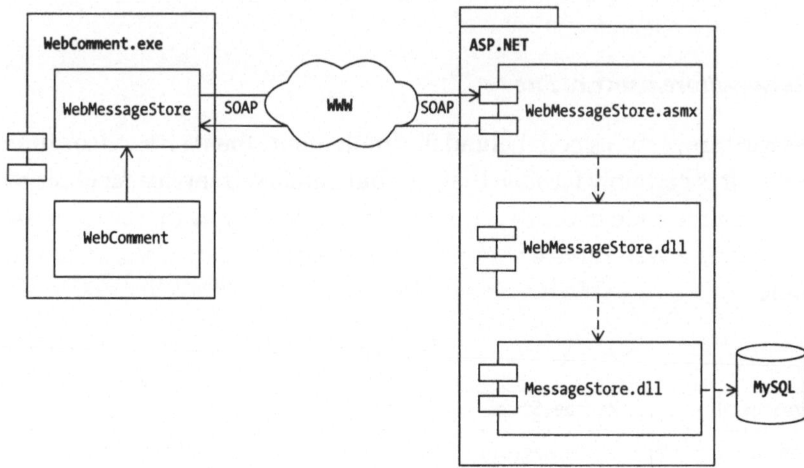

Figure 6-23. The Web Comment application

NOTE The code for the Web Comment program is available from the `Chapter_06/WebComment` directory at this book's Web site (`http://www.cross-platform.net`) and the Apress Web site (`http://www.apress.com`).

The WebMessageStore.asmx File

Unlike ASPX files, ASMX files do not start with an `@Page` directive, but rather with an `@ WebService` directive. While ASMX files support inline code, we will take advantage of codebehind. This means that the `WebMessageStore.asmx` file is rather anaemic and only contains the following lines:

```
<%@ WebService
Class="Crossplatform.NET.Chapter6.WebMessageStore, WebMessageStore.asmx"
%>
```

Note that unlike the `@ Page` directive, the `@ WebService` directive doesn't have an `Inherits` attribute; instead, it relies on the `Class` attribute to declare the name of the type that implements the Web service's logic.

TIP As shown in the previous code, the `Class` attribute can support full type names in the format *type, assembly.* While including the assembly name is optional, if it is excluded, on the first call to the Web service, ASP.NET will query all the assemblies in the `bin` directory to find the type; this incurs a slight performance overhead.

The WebMessageStore.asmx.cs File

The `WebMessageStore.asmx.cs` codebehind file implements the Web service's functionality. While it is certainly feasible that we could add Web service facilities by modifying the source code in the `MessageStore.cs` file, we follow the less invasive practice of creating a Web service wrapper for the `MesssageStore` class, as shown in Figure 6-24.

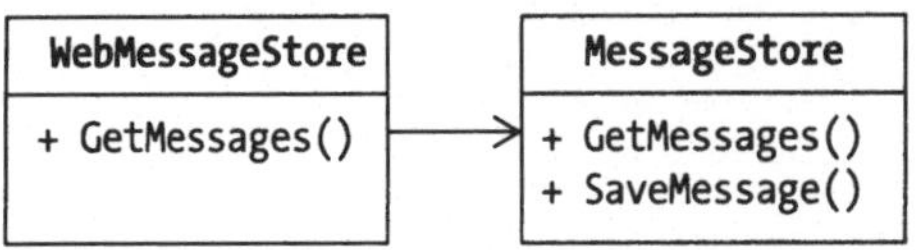

Figure 6-24. The Web service wrapper

Although creating the new WebMessageStore class to act as the Web service adds an extra layer to the application, it is a good practice to follow, because it allows the Web service to be modified separately from the application's business logic.

Because the WebMessageStore class only has to act as a light wrapper for the MessageStore class, it only requires a minimal amount of code, as follows:

```
//Filename: WebMessageStore.asmx.cs
using System;
using System.Data;
using System.Web;
using System.Web.Services;
using Crossplatform.NET.Chapter6.Data;

namespace Crossplatform.NET.Chapter6
{
    [WebService(Namespace="http://www.cross-platform.net/GuestBook/",
               Description="Provides access to the Guest Book entries")]
    public class WebMessageStore : WebService
    {
        [WebMethod(Description="Retrieves all Guest Book entries")]
        public DataSet GetMessages()
        {
            return new MessageStore().GetMessages();
        }
    }
}
```

Apart from namespace references, the main points worth focusing on are that the WebMessageStore class and the GetMessages() method are both declared as public and that they are respectively declared with WebService and WebMethod attributes. The WebService attribute is optional and can be used to add more information about the Web service. In this case, the attribute adds both a *description* and a *namespace*, where the namespace has nothing to do with .NET namespaces but instead acts as a unique identifier for the Web service. The WebMethod attribute must be declared for any methods that are to be made available as part of the Web service; the attribute also allows certain properties to be set.

TIP Although using the WebService attribute is not required, it is a good idea to always use it so that the namespace property can be given a unique *Uniform Resource Indicator (URI)* that is controlled by your organization.

Because the @ WebService directive that is used in the ASMX file does not support an Src attribute, the file must now be manually compiled into an assembly.

The assembly can be compiled using Mono under GNU/Linux as follows:

```
mono@linux:~ % mcs /t:library /out:WebMessageStore.dll WebMessageStore.asmx.cs\
> /r:MessageStore.dll /r:System.Data.dll /r:System.Web.Services.dll
Compilation succeeded
mono@linux:~ %
```

The compilation using Microsoft .NET is as follows:

```
C:\MS.NET> csc /t:Library /out:WebMessageStore.dll WebMessageStore.asmx.cs\
r:MessageStore.dll /r:System.Data.dll /r:System.Web.Services.dll
Microsoft (R) Visual C# .NET Compiler version 7.10.3052.4
for Microsoft (R) .NET Framework version 1.1.4322
Copyright (C) Microsoft Corporation 2001-2002. All rights reserved.

C:\MS.NET>
```

Now that the assembly has been compiled, you should move the WebMessageStore.dll file into the bin subdirectory.

Web Service Proxy

Now that the service has an ASMX file and a codebehind assembly, it is time to concentrate on a client application. Although the server is ready to be called, the client program needs a mechanism to call the Web service. Since the Web service talks in XML, the client program needs to generate correctly formatted XML messages to call the Web service, and the client program needs to understand the XML responses that it gets. Although it is technically possible to use the System.Xml namespace to manually create and convert Web service messages, it would involve a lot of dull coding, and because .NET provides something to do the job for us, we may as well use it.

The mechanism for converting the XML into something meaningful is a *remote proxy*, which is shown in Figure 6-25.

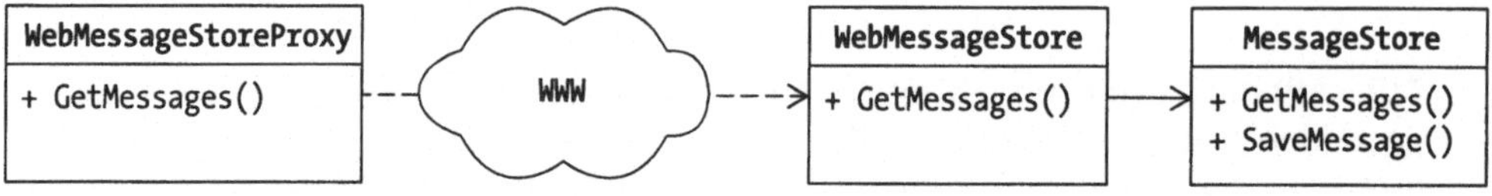

Figure 6-25. The Web service proxy

The remote proxy implements the same public interface as the Web service class, but it contains the plumbing to connect to the Web service and to relay requests and responses between the client program and the Web service.

TIP Proxy classes are a mechanism for providing surrogate objects that can stand in for real objects by implementing the same public interface as the objects that they represent. Remote proxies acts as ambassadors, allowing the client to have a local object reference while the actual implementation is situated on a remote machine.

Despite the proxy code's esoteric nature—indeed, a lot of the details will only appeal to developers with a thing for protocols—the class is spectacularly compact and is definitely worth a quick look:

```
//Filename: WebMessageStoreProxy.cs
using System;
using System.Web.Services;
using System.Web.Services.Protocols;
using System.Xml.Serialization;

[System.Web.Services.WebServiceBinding(Name="WebMessageStoreSoap")]
public class WebMessageStoreProxy :
System.Web.Services.Protocols.SoapHttpClientProtocol
{
    public WebMessageStoreProxy()
    {
        this.Url = "http://127.0.0.1:8080/WebMessageStore.asmx";
    }
```

The class declaration begins with a `WebServiceBinding` attribute, which is used to specify details of how the proxy will bind to the Web service. The class inherits from `SoapHttpClientProtocol`, which allows the proxy to communicate using SOAP. The class then implements a default constructor that is responsible for setting the URL of the Web service.

The `GetMessages()` method is declared with a `SoapDocumentMethod` attribute that determines how the SOAP request messages will be formatted. The method's payload is particularly light and is only responsible for packaging parameters for the Web method, invoking the request to the Web method, and unpacking any return value and casting it to the expected type. The code is as follows:

```
    [System.Web.Services.Protocols.SoapDocumentMethod(
        "http://www.cross-platform.net/GuestBook/GetMessages",
        RequestNamespace="http://www.cross-platform.net/GuestBook/",
        ResponseNamespace="http://www.cross-platform.net/GuestBook/")]
    public System.Data.DataSet GetMessages()
    {
        object[] results = this.Invoke("GetMessages", new object[0]);
        return ((System.Data.DataSet)(results[0]));
    }
}
```

As we mentioned before, the code in the proxy class is unlikely to be of much interest to the average developer.

However, with a ridiculous consortium of options available, such as the ability to declare asynchronous Web methods, for those with a bent for control freakery, proxies can give precise control over how the client application communicates with the Web service.

Building Better Proxy Classes

For developers who are more interested in the broader scope of application development than the intricacies of Web service plumbing, it is possible to automatically generate the proxy code using Microsoft .NET or Mono's cunning Web Service Description Language (WSDL) tools.

The WSDL is an XML language that, unsurprisingly, describes Web services. WSDL lists the methods that are implemented by the Web service and includes a variety of details, such as the number and type of parameters, that are required by client programs to call the methods.

Microsoft's and Mono's implementations of ASP.NET automatically generate a WSDL file for a Web service file when a client accesses the URL of the Web service with a `?WSDL` suffix. When a WSDL file has been produced, you can parse the file and use code-generation techniques to create a proxy class for interacting with the Web service; Microsoft .NET and Mono include a tool, `WSDL.exe`, which does exactly this.

When `WSDL.exe` is called with the URL of a Web service's WSDL file, it generates the proxy code to access the Web service and saves the code in a file with the default name that is equal to the Web service name with a `.cs` extension.

For example, running the following command on the .NET Framework generates a proxy class in a file called `WebMessageStore.cs`:

```
C:\MS.NET> Wsdl.exe http://127.0.0.1:8080/WebMessageStore.asmx?wsdl
C:\MS.NET>
```

After you have generated proxy code, you can either include the code directly in your client applications or you can modify the code to tweak certain elements of the plumbing.

Client Application

Now that we have created the Web service and the proxy to call the Web service, all that is needed is an application to make use of the Web service. The role of client application will be handled by the `WebComment.cs` class, and is essentially a slimmer version of the `Comment.cs` file, as follows:

```
//Filename: WebComment.cs
using System;
using System.Data;
using Crossplatform.NET.Chapter6.Data;

namespace Crossplatform.NET.Chapter6
{
    class WebComment
    {
        private const string errorMsg = "error '{0}' was raised from '{1}'";

        static void Main(string[] args)
        {
            try
            {
                WebMessageStoreProxy store = new WebMessageStoreProxy();
                DataSet messages = store.GetMessages();

                foreach(DataRow record in messages.Tables[0].Rows){
                    string line = String.Format("On {0} {1} said '{2}'",
                                 ((DateTime)record["LoggedDate"]).ToString(),
                                 record["Name"],
                                 record["Comments"]);
                    Console.WriteLine(line);
                }
            }
```

```
            catch (Exception e) {
                Console.Error.WriteLine(errorMsg, e.Message, e.Source);
            }
        }
    }
}
```

Apart from missing the SaveMessage() method, the only real change is that the references to the MessageStore class have been replaced with references to the WebMessageStoreProxy class.

A Better Comment Program

If we were to extend the WebComment application by also implementing the SaveMessages() method, both the Comment.exe and WebComment.exe programs would have the same external functionality, but they would use different mechanisms to access the data store. A better solution would be to have one Comment.exe program that could be configured to use a local or Web-based storage mechanism at runtime.

This could be done by defining an IMessageStore interface, which would be implemented by both the MessageStore and IMessageStoreProxy classes. The Comment.exe program could then be changed to use the IMessageStore interface, with the actual concrete type to use being defined within the program's configuration file.

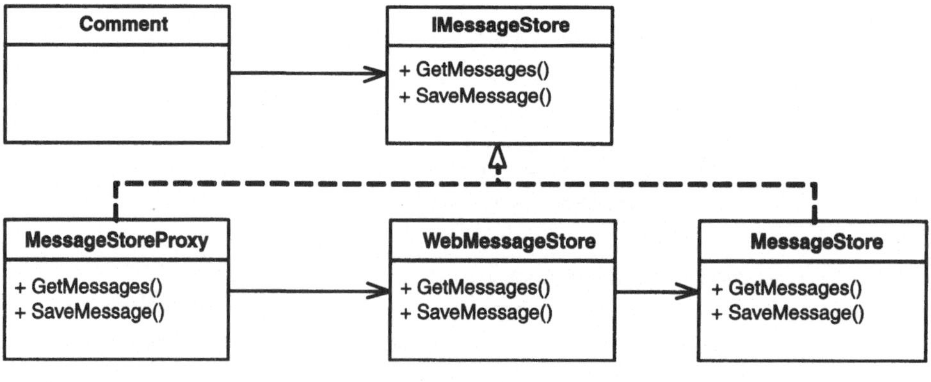

When developing Web service client applications, consider whether the details of the Web service are likely to change during the lifetime of the application. If the details are likely to change in a limited and predictable manner, such as the URL changing occasionally, the proxy code can be modified to select the URL at runtime, and the application classes can be compiled into the same assembly. If more thorough plumbing details might change—for example, different suppliers might offer similar Web services—it is preferable to compile the proxy into its own assembly. This allows the Web service to be swapped without recompiling the application.

Because the `WebMessageStore` is unlikely to change, we can compile the proxy into the same assembly as the `WebComment` class, which can be carried out using Mono under GNU/Linux as follows:

```
mono@linux:~ % mcs /t:exe /out:WebComment.exe WebComment.cs \
> WebMessageStoreProxy.cs /r:System.Data.dll /r:System.Data.dll \
> /r:System.Web.Services.dll /r:MessageStore.dll
Compilation succeeded
mono@linux:~ %
```

Similarly, for Microsoft .NET, use the following commands:

```
C:\MS.NET> csc /t:exe /out:WebComment.exe WebComment.cs WebMessageStoreProxy.cs
/r:System.Data.dll /r:System.Web.Services.dll /r:MessageStore.dll
Microsoft (R) Visual C# .NET Compiler version 7.10.3052.4
for Microsoft (R) .NET Framework version 1.1.4322
Copyright (C) Microsoft Corporation 2001-2002. All rights reserved.

C:\MS.NET>
```

Now that the Web service is working and we have built the client application, the client application can be run under the .NET Framework using the following commands:

```
C:\MS.NET> WebComment.exe
On 26/08/2003 16:22:16 Marla Lamar said 'Programming is the best way to
 shackle the best minds into the worst jobs'
On 26/08/2003 16:20:47 mono@linux said 'And this is also a quick test'
On 26/08/2003 16:20:18 TEST said 'This is a very quick test'
C:\MS.NET>
```

The client application can be run using Mono under GNU/Linux with the following commands:

```
mono@linux:~ % mono WebComment.exe
On 26/08/2003 16:22:16 Marla Lamar said 'Programming is the best way to
 shackle the best minds into the worst jobs'
On 26/08/2003 16:20:47 mono@linux said 'And this is also a quick test'
On 26/08/2003 16:20:18 TEST said 'This is a very quick test'
mono@linux:~ %
```

So there you have it: a working Web service that allows users to access the `MessageStore` database over the Internet. Not only is this an excellent way to allow functionality to be called across the Internet, but it is also ideal for facilitating interoperability with non-.NET client applications.

ASP.NET Cross-Platform Issues

While ASP.NET was designed with Web server portability firmly in mind and is innately cross-platform, as mentioned in Chapter 4, cross-platform developers should be aware of a couple of issues.

First, the `System.Web.Security` namespace contains some classes that provide authentication against Windows/IIS and Microsoft Passport, and neither of these mechanisms is currently implemented in Mono. Because Passport is Microsoft's implementation of a single sign-on authentication service—with the goal of allowing Internet users to carry out all their online activities under a single identity—and considering that it is surrounded by an ongoing monopolization controversy, it is fairly unlikely that Mono will ever provide support for Passport. While Windows authentication is certainly less controversial, and might one day be implemented by Mono, because it relies on the underlying security model of Windows, it is unlikely to be of much use in the cross-platform arena.

Second, ASP.NET provides a number of facilities for maintaining state during the lifetime of a client session; these facilities are implemented in the `System.Web.SessionState` namespace. Microsoft .NET allows session state to be disabled or stored in a variety of different ways, including within the ASP.NET process, in an SQL Server database, or in a Windows State Server Service. Mono currently only supports the disabling of session state or the storing of in-process session state.

Summary

Whether you simply need to access a database, build a flashy-looking Web site, or develop a truly distributed application with Web services, we hope that this chapter has helped demonstrate that .NET is an excellent tool for building distributed, cross-platform applications. With an assortment of namespaces providing a wide variety of functionality, .NET can certainly help developers build distributed applications with minimal effort. However, a couple of issues have evoked widespread industry commentary.

One of the most hotly debated issues is ADO.NET's lack of a functionally complete mechanism for writing provider-agnostic code. Although, as described earlier in this chapter, a number of interfaces go some of the way in helping write provider-agnostic code, a few oddities in the ADO.NET object model mean that it can be decidedly nontrivial to write code that works with a variety of managed providers. Although using one of the generic providers, such as the OLE DB or ODBC managed provider, can solve this problem, as can using one of the open source products mentioned previously, Microsoft looks set to try and tackle this problem in the next release of the .NET Framework, .NET 2.0. Although this is little consolation at the moment, it at least shows that Microsoft is committed to responding to the community, and you can be certain that the other CLI implementations will closely follow suit.

Discussing all the intricacies of distributed cross-platform applications could take an entire book in its own right, and we have only scratched the surface in this chapter. While we will revisit distributed applications in Chapter 8, where we discuss Remoting and touch on application servers, we have not even mentioned the powerful networking classes of the `System.Net` namespace and the low-level classes of the `System.Net.Sockets` namespace. Not only do these namespaces make it possible to interact with known networking protocols, but they also provide an excellent toolset for writing custom protocols.

To finish the chapter, and as a last, light-hearted example of a distributed application, we finish the implementation of our very own, creatively named HTML browser. While its lack of ability to render HTML into a human-readable fashion precludes us from calling it a Web browser, if you consider that the browser wars of the 1990s were largely driven by a corporate desire for platform supremacy, we think that this HTML browser indicates that .NET is an ideal cross-platform tool for distributing the future:

```
//Filename: HtmlBrowser.cs
using System;
using System.Net;
using System.IO;
namespace Crossplatform.NET.Chapter6
{
    class HtmlBrowser
    {
        static void Main(string[] args)
        {
            if (args.Length != 1)
            {
                Console.Error.WriteLine("Please supply a URL to browse.");
                return;
            }
            try
            {
                WebResponse response;
                response = WebRequest.Create(args[0]).GetResponse();

                StreamReader reader;
                reader = new StreamReader(response.GetResponseStream());
                Console.WriteLine(reader.ReadToEnd());

                reader.Close();
                response.Close();
            }
            catch(Exception e)
            {
                Console.Error.WriteLine(e.Message);
            }
        }
    }
}
```

CHAPTER 7

Using Native Code

"Use your enemy's hand to catch a snake."

—Persian proverb

WHILE THE BRUNT of this book describes how .NET can be used to develop software that runs on a variety of platforms, this chapter is something of a black sheep in that it investigates the converse issue of how .NET can be used to access platform-specific, native code. Although this chapter might grate against the honed sensibilities of this book's more puritanical readership, the ability to call native code is an essential feature that allows .NET applications to take advantage of underlying platform features, in exactly the same way that the Java Native Interface affords Java developers the ability to call native code.

Although applications that call native code are a potential headache for cross-platform developers, they can nonetheless access features that would otherwise be unavailable and, if the native code is from a cross-platform library, the overall application can still be used across different platforms.

This chapter discusses .NET's native interoperability mechanism, *Platform Invoke (P/Invoke)*, and shows how it can be used on different platforms and how its sensible use can minimize platform dependencies. Before we delve into the depths of using P/Invoke in application code, we try to soothe the bitter pill of using native code by starting with a quick exposition of how the various CLI implementations themselves rely on native code.

Native Code Reliance

It's easy to imagine a technically ideal world where programmers would be revered like rock stars, laptops would be powered by epidermal friction, and all CLI implementations would be implemented in pure managed code. Of course, this book would be little more than a pamphlet, groupies would be continually disappointed by their heroes' inability to communicate, and programmers would have a tendency of rubbing their laptops against their groins for that little bit more power. And that's not mentioning .NET's performance, which would be decidedly more ooze than oomph.

While managed code invariably has a number of advantages over unmanaged code, the different CLI implementations rely on native code to different extents, either for improved performance or simply to take advantage of existing functionality that is available from within native code. Although it might be philosophically preferable for the CLI implementations to be entirely written in managed code, it would nonetheless be impractical for the CLIs to be completely written in managed code. For exactly the same reasons, situations also occur when it is preferable for you to use native code for your own .NET solutions.

Platform Invoke vs. Internal Calls

Having already mentioned that the CLI's mechanism for calling native code is called Platform Invoke, it's time to confess that it's actually only a part of the story. While Platform Invoke is a useful mechanism for application programming, the CLI also provides an internal mechanism for calling native code; any method that directly makes use of this internal mechanism is appropriately known as an *internal call*.

In comparison to P/Invoke, which is used for calling functions in external, shared libraries, internal calls are more insidious because they call directly into the CLI runtime.

While internal calls provide a high-performance method to access native code, because they are directly dependent on the internal facilities of the CLI runtime, only a single runtime is likely to implement them. This effectively means that any assembly that uses internal calls is tightly coupled to its associated runtime, and for this reason, assemblies such as `System.dll` are not interchangeable between the different CLI implementations.

CLI Reliance on Native Code

In comparison to Chapter 4, which dissected the .NET Framework assemblies depending on whether they relied on platform-specific architectural features, this section covers the cleaner concept of which assemblies rely on native code. Although this section is obviously related to architectural dependence, its existence is justifiable because there is no reason for an assembly that relies on native code to also rely on a platform's architectural features.

A good example of the separation between architectural dependence and native code dependence is Microsoft .NET 1.1's `System.Data.dll` assembly. Although the assembly relies on a number of native libraries, including two of Windows' core API libraries, `kernel32.dll` and `advapi32.dll`, the actual assembly doesn't rely on architectural features of the Windows operating system but instead uses native code to reduce the complexity of the managed implementation.

By investigating how the different CLIs rely on native code, we can arrive at a coarse analysis of how innately cross-platform each of the CLI implementations is.

Microsoft .NET Framework

When Microsoft released its shared-source Rotor for a number of operating systems, as mentioned in Chapter 1, one might hope that the majority of the .NET Framework's assemblies would have been written in pure managed code. However, because Microsoft's commercial implementation of .NET is only available for Windows, it's perhaps unsurprising that, in fact, a significant proportion of its assemblies rely on native Windows code, as shown in Table 7-1.

Table 7-1. Microsoft .NET Framework's Use of Unmanaged Code

Calls Unmanaged Code	Pure Managed Code
cscompmgd.dll	Accessibility.dll
IEHost.dll	CustomMarshalers.dll
Microsoft.VisualBasic.dll	EnvDTE.dll
mscorcfg.dll	IEExecRemote.dll
Regcode.dll	IIEHost.dll
System.dll	IsymWrapper.dll
System.Configuration.Install.dll	Microsoft.JScript.dll
System.Data.dll	Microsoft.VisualBasic.Vsa.dll
System.Design.dll	Microsoft.VisualC.dll
System.DirectoryServices.dll	Microsoft.Vsa.dll
System.Drawing.dll	Microsoft.Vsa.Vb.CodeDOMProcessor.dll
System.Drawing.Design.dll	Microsoft_VsaVb.dll
System.EnterpriseServices.dll	Office.dll
System.Management.dll	stdole.dll
System.Messaging.dll	System.Runtime.Remoting.dll
System.ServiceProcess.dll	System.Runtime.Serialization.Formatters.Soap.dll
System.Web.dll	System.Security.dll

Table 7-1. Microsoft .NET Framework's Use of Unmanaged Code (Continued)

Calls Unmanaged Code	Pure Managed Code
`System.Web.Mobile.dll`	`System.Web.RegularExpressions.dll`
`System.Web.Services.dll`	`System.Xml.dll`
`System.Windows.Forms.dll`	
`mscorlib.dll`	

As you can see, in terms of quantity, it is pretty much an even match on both sides of the table. While the managed code enthusiasts might long to say "libraries on the left please leave the arena," this would leave little to play with and would prove especially catastrophic if you consider that Microsoft .NET's core library, `mscorlib.dll`, relies on native code.

While the sheer number of Microsoft .NET libraries that rely on native code might seem shocking at first—after all, .NET is meant to be Microsoft's investment in the future and not a cheap veneer on the past—the main reason that over half of Microsoft's assemblies rely on native code is that it reduces the effort needed to reimplement functionality that's already available in the Windows API. In effect, this helped Microsoft to get .NET to the market much earlier than would have otherwise been possible.

While performance and architectural dependencies mean that a number of the assemblies will undoubtedly retain their reliance on native code, Microsoft has made a firm commitment to porting as many of the libraries as feasible to managed code, and when .NET 2.0 is released, a number of the assemblies in Table 7-1—including the previously singled out `System.Data.dll`—will consist entirely of managed code.

Mono

In comparison to Microsoft's CLI implementation, Mono relies on native code in only a handful of assemblies, as shown in Table 7-2.

Table 7-2. Mono's Use of Unmanaged Code

Calls Unmanaged Code	Pure Managed Code
ByteFX.Data.dll	Accessibility.dll
Mono.Cairo.dll	Commons.Xml.Relaxng.dll
Mono.Data.DB2Client.dll	Cscompmgd.dll
Mono.Data.MySql.dll	I18N.CJK.dll
Mono.Data.PostgreSqlClient.dll	I18N.dll
Mono.Data.SqliteClient.dll	I18N.MidEast.dll
Mono.Directory.LDAP.dll	I18N.Other.dll
Mono.Posix.dll	I18N.Rare.dll
Mono.Security.Win32.dll	I18N.West.dll
Mscorlib.dll	ICSharpCode.SharpZipLib.dll
System.dll	Microsoft.VisualBasic.dll
System.Data.dll	Microsoft.VisualC.dll
System.Data.OracleClient.dll	Microsoft.Vsa.dll
System.Drawing.dll	Mono.CSharp.Debugger.dll
System.Windows.Forms.dll	Mono.Data.SybaseClient.dll
System.Web.dll	Mono.Data.Tds.dll
System.Xml.dll	Mono.Data.TdsClient.dll
	Mono.GetOptions.dll
	Mono.Http.dll
	Mono.PEToolkit.dll
	Mono.Security.dll
	Npgsql.dll

Table 7-2. Mono's Use of Unmanaged Code (Continued)

Calls Unmanaged Code	Pure Managed Code
	NUnit.Framework.dll
	NUnit.Util.dll
--	PEAPI.dll
	System.Configuration.Install.dll
	System.Design.dll
	System.DirectoryServices.dll
	System.Drawing.Design.dll
	System.EnterpriseServices.dll
	System.Management.dll
	System.Messaging.dll
	System.Runtime.Remoting.dll
	System.Runtime.Serialization.Formatters.Soap.dll
	System.Security.dll
	System.ServiceProcess.dll
	System.Web.Services.dll

By the clever use of existing cross-platform native libraries, Mono is fundamentally written in managed code, which bodes well for its portability.

PNET

With the DotGNU project's goal for Portable.NET being a highly portable CLI implementation, it is unsurprising that PNET's assemblies have a minimal reliance on native code, as demonstrated by Table 7-3.

Ironically, with the understandable exception of PNET's fundamental assemblies, such as `mscorlib.dll` and `System.dll`, most of Portable.NET's reliance on native code is due to the project team's policy of using Mono assemblies to bulk out the core PNET assemblies.

Table 7-3. Portable.NET's Use of Unmanaged Code

Calls Unmanaged Code	**Pure Managed Code**
DotGNU.SSL.dll	Accessibility.dll
Mono.Data.DB2Client.dll	cscompmgd.dll
Mono.Data.MySql.dll	cstest.dll
Mono.Data.PostgreSqlClient.dll	Custommarshalers.dll
Mono.Directory.LDAP.dll	DotGNU.Images.dll
Mono.Posix.dll	DotGNU.SSL.dll
mscorlib.dll	I18N.dll
OpenSystem.C.dll	I18N.CJK.dll
System.dll	I18N.MidEast.dll
System.Data.dll	I18N.Other.dll
System.Data.OracleClient.dll	I18N.Rare.dll
System.Drawing.Win32.dll	I18N.West.dll
Xsharp.dll	ICSharpCode.SharpZipLib.dll
	ISymWrapper.dll
	Microsoft.JScript.dll
	Microsoft.VisualBasic.dll
	Microsoft.VisualC.dll
	Microsoft.Vsa.dll
	Mono.Data.Tds.dll
	Mono.GetOptions.dll
	Npgsql.dll
	PEAPI.dll
	System.Configuration.Install.dll
	System.Drawing.dll
	System.Drawing.Postscript.dll
	System.Drawing.Xsharp.dll

Table 7-3. Portable.NET's Use of Unmanaged Code (Continued)

Calls Unmanaged Code	Pure Managed Code
	System.EnterpriseServices.dll
	System.Management.dll
	System.Messaging.dll
	System.Net.IrDA.dll
	System.Runtime.Serialization.Formatters.Soap.dll
	System.ServiceProcess.dll
	System.Windows.Forms.dll
	System.Xml.dll

The NativeProbe Tool

Analyzing the different approaches that the CLI implementers have taken to resolve the issue of managed versus native code, it's interesting to consider that if a CLI's level of progress is judged by its proportion of managed code rather than the breadth of its feature set, the tables are truly turned on their head, with PNET and Mono in the lead and Microsoft trailing somewhere beyond the curve of the horizon.

While it's certainly fun to look at the progress of the CLIs from a different perspective, for the majority of developers, the most pressing concern that's raised by .NET's ability to call native code is how it affects their own cross-platform endeavors. While we shortly arrive at the topic of using native code in your cross-platform projects, we first tackle the problem of determining whether a third-party assembly relies on native code.

Of course, just because an assembly relies on a native library, that does not mean it will work in a cross-platform scenario—which is, after all, the complex issue that this book attempts to deal with—but any assembly that relies on native code should certainly set off the warning lights. If assemblies were road signs, assemblies that invoke native code would all read "Proceed with Caution."

The tool that we prefer to use when weeding out potentially dangerous assemblies is the excellent `NativeProbe.exe` tool, which analyzes assemblies using a mixture of reflection and binary analysis of the assembly's underlying Portable Executable (PE) file.

NOTE The source code samples for this chapter can be found in the Downloads section of this book's Web site (`http://www.cross-platform.net`) and the Apress Web site (`http://www.apress.com`). NativeProbe is available in the `Chapter_07/NativeProbe` directory.

As you would expect, `NativeProbe` is itself a cross-platform tool, and it works with the different CLIs on the various platforms that they support. To display its usage instructions, run the executable file with no command-line arguments, as demonstrated on Mono and GNU/Linux as follows:

```
mono@linux:~ % mono NativeProbe.exe
Probes assemblies to determine their use of native code

Usage: PIProbe.exe [/X] [/T] [/M] [/P] [/G] [/N] [/H] [/?] [filenames]
/X        Produces XML output
/T        Probes type details
/M        Probes method details
/P        Show details of P/Invoke calls
/G        Only show purely managed results
/N        Only show native dependent results
/H | /?   Show these program details
filenames A list of filenames or directories to probe

mono@linux:~ %
```

While we use `NativeProbe` with our own native dependent assemblies later in the chapter, you can see it in action by targeting the `System.Data.dll` assembly. Because Portable.NET relies on Mono's implementation of ADO.NET, the assembly is the same for Mono and PNET, which somewhat simplifies the probing. Starting with PNET, `NativeProbe.exe` can be run as follows:

```
pnet@macosx:~ % ilrun NativeProbe.exe System.Data.dll
System.Data.dll uses PInvoke.

pnet@macosx:~ %
```

While it's all right to determine that an assembly invokes native code, we can take things further, and by specifying the `/T` switch, we can request details about which of the assembly's types invoke native code.

CAUTION Before you try to use the /T switch, be warned that the System.Data.dll assembly contains a lot of types (over 250 for Mono or PNET). To make things more manageable, you can specify the /N switch, which reduces the output to show only types that invoke native code.

Running on Mono and GNU/Linux, we can see that two of the assembly's internal types rely on native code, as follows:

```
mono@linux:~ % mono NativeProbe.exe System.Data.dll /T /N
System.Data.dll uses PInvoke.
- libgda uses PInvoke.
 - libodbc uses PInvoke.

mono@linux:~ %
```

To see how Microsoft's implementation fares, we can finally run the tool on the .NET Framework's System.Data.dll assembly, but to spice things up a little, we request the output in XML by adding the /X switch, as follows:

```
C:\MS.NET> NativeProbe.exe System.Data.dll /T /N /X
<PIProbe timestamp="18/12/2003 16:23:21">
  <Assembly name="System.Data.dll" pinvoke="True" internalcall="False">
    <Type name="NativeMethods" pinvoke="True" internalcall="False"/>
    <Type name="SafeNativeMethods" pinvoke="True" internalcall="False"/>
    <Type name="UnsafeNativeMethods" pinvoke="True" internalcall="False"/>
    <Type name="Odbc32" pinvoke="True" internalcall="False"/>
    <Type name="Dbnetlib" pinvoke="True" internalcall="False"/>
    <Type name="Advapi32" pinvoke="True" internalcall="False"/>
  </Assembly>
</PIProbe>

C:\MS.NET>
```

So there you have it. You've seen how NativeProbe makes it easy to analyze whether an assembly is dependent on native code without having to resort to that well-known developer's anathema, the manual.

Of course, it's worth remembering that just because an assembly doesn't rely on native code, it won't necessarily run on all CLI implementations or on all platforms. However, carrying out a quick analysis of an assembly's native code dependencies is the first step in determining whether an assembly is likely to cause problems in a cross-platform scenario.

Alternatives to `NativeProbe`

While `NativeProbe.exe` is definitely our preferred way of determining whether an assembly relies on native code, you might find that its nuances don't agree with your own sensibilities. The good news is that `NativeProbe` is only the tip of the figurative iceberg, and a number of free tools are available that can also provide details of an assembly's native code dependencies.

For those who prefer GUI applications to command-line tools, check out Anakrino (`http://www.saurik.com/net/exemplar/`) or Reflector (`http://www.aisto.com/roeder/dotnet/`), both of which also serve as decompilers but lack the ability to save output to a file or quickly analyze multiple assemblies.

As a final option, Portable.NET comes with the `ilnative.exe` tool. This is an unmanaged command-line tool that is similar to `NativeProbe.exe`, but it can't provide XML output and doesn't have as many options for filtering the output.

Calling Native Code: Platform Invoke

Having seen that native code plays a vital part within the CLI implementations, it is time to have a look at how you can use native code from within your own cross-platform projects. While a good rule is to steer clear of native code whenever possible, it's important to understand the issues that relate to calling native code to ensure that, when required, you can leverage the underlying features of the platforms that your applications are running on.

As you may already be aware, the mechanism that provides interoperability between managed and unmanaged code in .NET is known as Platform Invoke, or P/Invoke, and is illustrated in Figure 7-1.

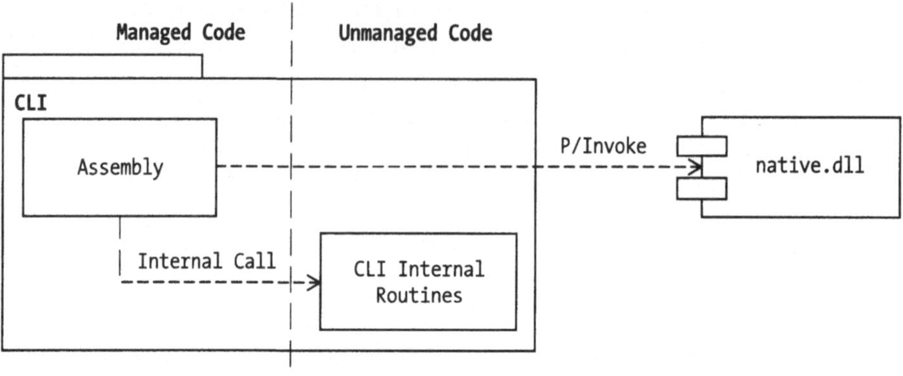

Figure 7-1. Calling native code

By acting as a bridge between .NET and native code, P/Invoke allows functions that are stored within unmanaged dynamic link libraries, such as those in the Win32 API, to be easily called from managed code.

Nonetheless, interoperability is a broad subject, with numerous twists and turns covering everything from marshaling data across the P/Invoke boundary to handling the disparity of services between the managed and unmanaged worlds. Indeed, this section barely scratches the surface but instead gives broad coverage of the interoperability issues that are most likely of interest in cross-platform development.

The most conspicuous part of P/Invoke is undoubtedly the `DllImport` attribute, which is used to declare that a method is implemented in an external, unmanaged library.

For example, the following declaration declares a method that, when called in managed code, can invoke the `GetCurrentProcessId()` Win32 API function, which is in the `kernel32.dll` library:

```
[DllImport("kernel32.dll")]
private unsafe static extern uint GetCurrentProcessId ();
```

Developers from a Visual Basic background and steeped in the ways of the Win32 API will notice that `DllImport` is used in much the same way as VB's `Declare` statement. The VB6 equivalent of the previous declaration is as follows:

```
Declare Function GetCurrentProcessId Lib "kernel32"
                Alias "GetCurrentProcessId" () As Long
```

P/Invoke Security

One key difference between assemblies that call unmanaged code and those that don't is that by calling unmanaged code, an assembly can instigate operations that aren't subject to the CLI's security framework.

Because calling unmanaged code potentially allows an assembly to bypass its permissions, the ECMA standards define the `SecurityPermissionFlag.UnmanagedCode` security flag, which must be granted before an assembly is allowed to call native code.

For Microsoft's .NET Framework, the permission to call unmanaged code can be granted or taken away from assemblies using the .NET Framework configuration tool or by editing the underlying `security.config`, `enterprise.config`, and `machine.config` configuration files.

Unfortunately, at the time of this writing, neither PNET nor Mono offers a complete implementation of .NET's security infrastructure; it is therefore currently impossible to restrict an assembly from calling unmanaged code across all the CLI implementations. However, both projects are actively working on their security infrastructures, and it won't be long before all the CLI implementations allow assemblies to be restricted from calling native code without the due authority.

Apart from declaring the name of the dynamic library that contains the function and the entry point to call, `DllImport` can be used to specify a number of other settings, as shown in Table 7-4.

Table 7-4. The `DllImport` *Attribute's Fields*

Field	**Purpose**
`BestFitMapping`	Determines whether unmappable Unicode characters should be mapped to similar ANSI characters when marshaling Unicode strings to ANSI. This field was added in .NET 1.1.
`CallingConvention`	Determines the calling convention to use when calling a native method, which specifies the underlying stack semantics of the call.
`CharSet`	Determines how managed strings should be marshaled to unmanaged code.
`EntryPoint`	Specifies the function name or ordinal position of the native function to be called.

Table 7-4. The `DllImport` *Attribute's Fields (Continued)*

Field	Purpose
`ExactSpelling`	Specifies whether the entry point should be modified to correspond to the configured character set, which can be useful when calling functions in the Win32 API.
`PreserveSig`	Specifies whether the function signature should be preserved exactly and is used to control return types when interoperating with COM libraries on Windows.
`SetLastError`	Specifies whether error information will be made available through the static `Marshal.GetLastWin32Error()` method when running on Windows.
`ThrowInUnmappableChar`	Specifies whether an exception should be thrown when an attempt is made to marshal an unmappable character from a Unicode to an ANSI string. This field was added in .NET 1.1.

Like the majority of .NET's interoperability functionality, the `DllImport` attribute resides within the `System.Runtime.InteropServices` namespace, which is a treasure trove of all things related to marshaling and interoperability. Before we get too entrenched in the finer points of marshaling data across the P/Invoke bridge, we take a look at a working example that demonstrates how simple things can be when we're not burdened with managing any troublesome parameters.

P/Invoke Made Easy: Retrieving a Process ID

For this example, we create a bijou command-line program that determines the process identifier for the process that it is running in and displays the result to the console before promptly exiting.

NOTE The code for this example is available from the `Chapter_07/GetProcessId` directory at this book's Web site (`http://www.cross-platform.net`) and the Apress Web site (`http://www.apress.com`).

Apart from some bog-standard C# code, the `GetProcessId.cs` file contains a couple of salient points for our native code endeavors. First, the file code references the `System.Runtime.InteropServices` namespace with a `using` declaration, and second, it uses a `DllImport` attribute to declare a single native method, `getProcessId()`, which is similar to the example that we saw earlier. The code is as follows:

```
//GetProcessId.cs
using System;
using System.Runtime.InteropServices;

namespace Crossplatform.NET.Chapter07.PInvokeTest
{
    public class GetProcessId
    {
        [DllImport("libc", EntryPoint="getpid")]
        private static extern int getProcessId();

        //Kick things off...
        public static void Main()
        {
            Console.WriteLine("Process ID: {0}", getProcessId());
        }
    }
}
```

Unlike the previous example, the code doesn't use the external function's name, `getpid()`, for the internal method name, but instead it specifies an internal name of `getProcessId()`, and it uses the `DllImport` attribute's `EntryPoint` field to declare the external function's name.

You might also have noticed that rather than referencing the Win32 API's `kernel32.dll` library, the code instead references `libc`, which is the standard C library.

Without worrying about these slight modifications, we get things rolling by compiling the code on Mono and GNU/Linux, as follows:

```
mono@linux:~ % mcs GetProcessId.cs
Compilation Succeeded
mono@linux:~ %
```

For PNET on Mac OS X, use the following command:

```
pnet@macosx:~ % cscc GetProcessId.cs
Compilation Succeeded
pnet@macosx:~ % %
```

Finally, on Microsoft .NET, use the following command:

```
C:\MS.NET> csc GetProcessId.cs
Microsoft (R) Visual C# .NET Compiler version 7.10.3052.4
for Microsoft (R) .NET Framework version 1.1.4322
Copyright (C) Microsoft Corporation 2001-2002. All rights reserved.

C:\MS.NET>
```

Once you have the program compiled, it's time to put P/Invoke to the test.

To get this pinnacle of P/Invoke usage running on Mono and GNU/Linux, use the following command:

```
mono@linux:~ % mono GetProcessId.exe
Process ID: 1291
mono@linux:~ %
```

On PNET and Mac OS X, use the following command:

```
pnet@macosx:~ % ilrun GetProcessId.exe
Process ID: 494
pnet@macosx:~ %
```

And finally, for Microsoft .NET, use the following command:

```
C:\MS.NET> GetProcessId.exe
Unhandled Exception: System.DllNotFoundException: Unable to load DLL (libc).
   at Crossplatform.NET.Chapter07.PInvokeTest.GetProcessId.getProcessId()
   at Crossplatform.NET.Chapter07.PInvokeTest.GetProcessId.Main()
C:\MS.NET>
```

As you can see, while everything runs as expected on GNU/Linux and Mac OS X, things are not so rosy on Windows.

Of course, this is exactly what was expected. If you recall, the `DllImport` attribute referenced the `libc` library, and while `libc` is the standard C library on non-Windows platforms, it's not readily available on Windows. It is therefore perfectly reasonable that the .NET Framework complained that it was unable to load the DLL.

TIP While `libc` is not commonly installed on Windows, various implementations are available for Windows; this means that it's technically possible to use P/Invoke and `libc` in cross-platform projects. One implementation of `libc` is available with Microsoft's UNIX Services for Windows. Also, the open source GNUWin32 project contains a partial implementation that can be found at `http://gnuwin32.sourceforge.net`.

To fix this problem, we create a new source code file, `WinGetProcessId.cs`. This is essentially the same as `GetProcessId.cs`, although we change the `DllImport` attribute to reference the original Win32 API function, as follows:

```
[DllImport("kernel32.dll", EntryPoint="GetCurrentProcessId")]
```

This new file in its entirety then becomes the following:

```
//WinGetProcessId.cs
using System;
using System.Runtime.InteropServices;

namespace Crossplatform.NET.Chapter07.PInvokeTest
{
    public class WinGetProcessId
    {
        [DllImport("kernel32", EntryPoint="GetCurrentProcessId")]
        private static extern int getProcessId();

        //Kick things off...
        public static void Main()
        {
            Console.WriteLine("Process ID: {0}", getProcessId());
        }
    }
}
```

Finally, we compile and run it on Microsoft .NET using the following commands:

```
C:\MS.NET> csc WinGetProcessId.cs
Microsoft (R) Visual C# .NET Compiler version 7.10.3052.4
for Microsoft (R) .NET Framework version 1.1.4322
Copyright (C) Microsoft Corporation 2001-2002. All rights reserved.

C:\MS.NET> WinGetProcessId.exe
Process ID: 3112
C:\MS.NET>
```

So there you have it: an assembly that works on Windows and performs the same task as `GetProcessId.exe` running on GNU/Linux or Mac OS X. If you're a stickler for detail, you might want to try running `WinGetProcessId.exe` on Mac OS X or GNU/Linux, in which case you should be greeted with a `DllNotFoundException`.

TIP Although retrieving the current process's ID is perfect material for a simple P/Invoke example, in a real .NET application, you don't have to rely on either POSIX's `getpid()` or Win32's `GetCurrentProcessId()` function, because the .NET Framework provides its own way to achieve the same result: `System.Diagnostics.Process.GetCurrentProcess().Id`.

To put some icing on the cake and corroborate everything that we've said in this section, run `NativeProbe.exe /E` on either of the programs, as shown here on Mono running under GNU/Linux:

```
mono@linux:~ % mono NativeProbe.exe GetProcessId.exe /M /N /E
getprocessid.exe uses PInvoke.
 - GetProcessId uses PInvoke.
  - getProcessId() uses PInvoke (DLL: libc - Function: getpid)

mono@linux:~ %
```

Factoring Platform-Dependent Code

Now that we've seen a simple program that uses P/Invoke, it has raised an interesting issue: To get our `GetProcessId` program to run on different platforms, we've had to create two separate source code files. This has resulted in two different assemblies, neither of which is cross-platform. This situation is summed up in Figure 7-2.

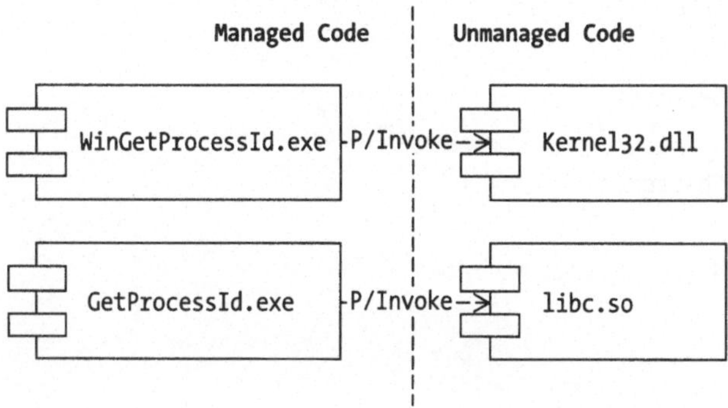

Figure 7-2. The dualistic nature of cross-platform reality

While this approach has allowed us to get the job done on three different operating systems, it is by no means an elegant solution, and it would certainly prove impractical in all but the simplest cross-platform projects. Therefore, before we progress to how P/Invoke can be used to call more complex native functions, we now have a look at how code that uses P/Invoke can be factored in a number of different ways to suit a variety of different project requirements.

Cross-Platform Source Code

While the first version of `GetProcessId` required two different source files, we can improve on this by placing all the code in one source file. This results in some cross-platform source code that needs to be compiled differently depending on which platform it is intended to run.

The trick to creating cross-platform source code is to use conditional compilation directives so that the source code is compiled based on the conditional symbol definitions that are used at compile time.

NOTE The code for this improved example is in the `Chapter_07/GetProcessId2` directory at this book's Web site (`http://www.cross-platform.net`) and the Apress Web site (`http://www.apress.com`).

To demonstrate this, we can modify the `GetProcess.cs` file to include both the `DllImport` declarations for Windows and for UNIX platforms, as follows:

```
//GetProcessId2.cs
using System;
using System.Runtime.InteropServices;

namespace Crossplatform.NET.Chapter07
{
    public class GetProcessId
    {

#if WINDOWS
        [DllImport("kernel32.dll", EntryPoint="GetCurrentProcessId")]
#else
        [DllImport("libc", EntryPoint="getpid")]
#endif
        private static extern int getProcessId();

        //Kick things off...
        public static void Main()
        {
            Console.WriteLine("Process ID: {0}", getProcessId());
        }
    }
}
```

As you can see, the Windows declaration follows a `#if WINDOWS` directive, which means that it can only be compiled if the `WINDOWS` conditional compilation symbol is defined. Similarly, the UNIX declaration follows a `#else` directive, which means that it can only be compiled if the `WINDOWS` conditional compilation symbol is not defined.

So, to compile this program using Microsoft .NET under Windows, pass the `/D:WINDOWS` switch to the C# compiler, as follows:

```
C:\MS.NET> csc GetProcessId2.cs /D:WINDOWS
Microsoft (R) Visual C# .NET Compiler version 7.10.3052.4
for Microsoft (R) .NET Framework version 1.1.4322
Copyright (C) Microsoft Corporation 2001-2002. All rights reserved.

C:\MS.NET>
```

The generated assembly, `GetProcessId2.exe`, can then be run as follows:

```
C:\MS.NET> GetProcessId2.exe
Process ID: 2929
C:\MS.NET>
```

To build an assembly that can work on Mac OS X and GNU/Linux, you then need to compile the program as before, without the /D switch.

To compile and run the program on Mono and GNU/Linux, use the following commands:

```
mono@linux:~ % mcs GetProcessId2.cs
Compilation Succeeded
mono@linux:~ % mono GetProcessId2.exe
Process ID: 1477
mono@linux:~ %
```

Or, if you prefer to see things running on PNET and Mac OS X, use the following commands:

```
pnet@macosx:~ % cscc GetProcessId2.cs
Compilation Succeeded
pnet@macosx:~ % ilrun GetProcessId2.exe
Process ID: 524
pnet@macosx:~ %
```

So there you have it—a single source code file that can be compiled to work on different platforms.

Of course, if you're going to follow the path that's offered by cross-platform source code, you need to be careful not to mix up your assemblies that are compiled for different platforms. Indeed, the one problem with this approach is that you either have to supply source code to be compiled on your users' machines or you have to supply prebuilt binaries for the different platforms that your application runs on.

In fact, as you probably have noticed in a number of the preceding chapters, this is the standard approach that is used by the open source community and is suitably used in both PNET and Mono. One benefit that cross-platform source code offers over other approaches is that because the choice of which native function to call is made at compilation time, at runtime, there is no performance hit of deciding which library to call.

Cross-Platform Binary Implementation

Having now seen two approaches for calling different native functions on different platforms, it's time to look at one last approach that can allow our program to be packaged as a cross-platform binary file and therefore be capable of running on any of the platforms under the microscope.

The key to creating a cross-platform binary implementation is to factor the platform-dependent code into separate classes and then to decide which type of object to instantiate at runtime. Because the platform-dependent classes simply package different implementations of the same functionality, it makes sense that they inherit from the same class, which we will call `Platform`, as shown in Figure 7-3.

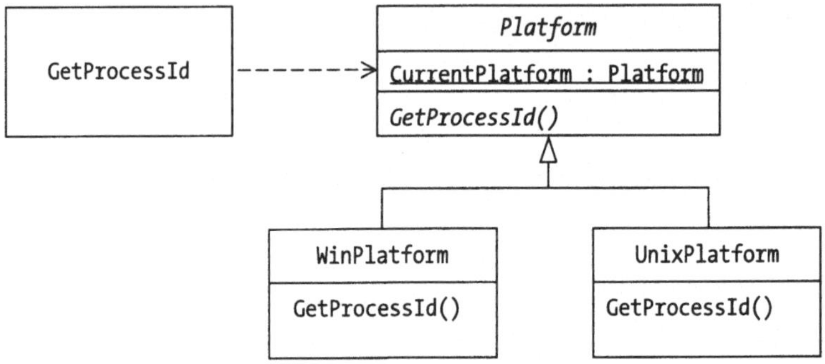

Figure 7-3. An object-oriented approach to P/Invoke

The `WinPlatform` and `UnixPlatfrom` concrete classes serve as wrappers to the native code. This means that neither the `GetProcessID` or `Platform` class needs to know that the concrete implementations are using native code, which adheres to the object-oriented idiom of making a class's implementation opaque.

NOTE The code for this improved example is in the `Chapter_07/GetProcessId3` directory at this book's Web site (`http://www.cross-platform.net`) and the Apress Web site (`http://www.apress.com`).

The implementation of the `UnixPlatform` class is particularly simple and essentially only contains the external declaration and a wrapper method, `GetProcessId()`, as follows:

```
//UnixPlatform.cs
using System;
using System.Runtime.InteropServices;

namespace Crossplatform.NET.Chapter07
{
    public class UnixPlatform : Platform
```

```
    {
        [DllImport("libc", EntryPoint="getpid")]
        private static extern int getpid();

        public override int GetProcessId()
        {
            return getpid();
        }
    }
}
```

The WinPlatform implementation is then practically identical, with the obvious exception that instead of referring to the UNIX getpid() function, it refers to the Windows GetCurrentProcessId() function, as follows:

```
//WinPlatform.cs
using System;
using System.Runtime.InteropServices;

namespace Crossplatform.NET.Chapter07
{
    public class WinPlatform : Platform
    {
        [DllImport("kernel32", EntryPoint="GetCurrentProcessId")]
        private static extern int GetCurrentProcessId();

        public override int GetProcessId()
        {
            return GetCurrentProcessId();
        }
    }
}
```

Now, while the main purpose of the Platform class is to act as a superclass for the concrete UnixPlatform and WinPlatform classes, it's also the ideal place to provide a mechanism to decide which concrete class should be used, depending on the underlying operating system.

The class therefore contains a static field called currentPlatform, which is instantiated in the class's type initializer according to whether the code is running on Windows. The operating system the code is running under is determined by the IsWindows() method, which makes its judgment based on the value of the Environment.OSVersion.Platform property.

The implementation of Platform.cs is then as follows:

```
//Platform.cs
using System;

namespace Crossplatform.NET.Chapter07
{
    public abstract class Platform
    {
        private Platform currentPlatform;

        static Platform()
        {
            if (IsWindows())
                currentPlatform = new WinPlatform();
            else
                currentPlatform = new UnixPlatform();
        }

        protected Platform(){}

        public static Platform CurrentPlatform
        {
           get { return currentPlatform; }
        }

        public abstract int GetProcessId();

        //Provide a cheap way of seeing if we're on Windows
        private static bool IsWindows()
        {
            PlatformID platform = Environment.OSVersion.Platform;

          return (platform == PlatformID.Win32NT || platform == PlatformID.Win32S
                   || platform == PlatformID.Win32Windows
                   || platform == PlatformID.WinCE);
        }
    }
}
```

Now that we have the platform-dependent code, the final piece of the puzzle is the actual program file, `GetProcessId3.cs`. This file uses the `Platform.CurrentPlatform` property to retrieve a concrete `Platform` instance and then instantly calls the `GetProcessID()` method, which calls the correct native function, as follows:

```
//GetProcessId3.cs
using System;

namespace Crossplatform.NET.Chapter07
{
    public class GetProcessId3
    {
        //Kick things off...
        public static void Main()
        {
            Console.WriteLine("Process ID: {0}",
                             Platform.CurrentPlatform.GetProcessId());
        }
    }
}
```

As you can see, the program's `Main()` method is now much tidier than the first two implementations, and although there is the added complexity of having a number of different class files, we have a firm foundation on which to add further platform-dependent functionality when and as required.

Although we discuss binary packaging options at the end of this section, we first check that everything works by compiling all our source code into single assembly, as shown in Figure 7-4.

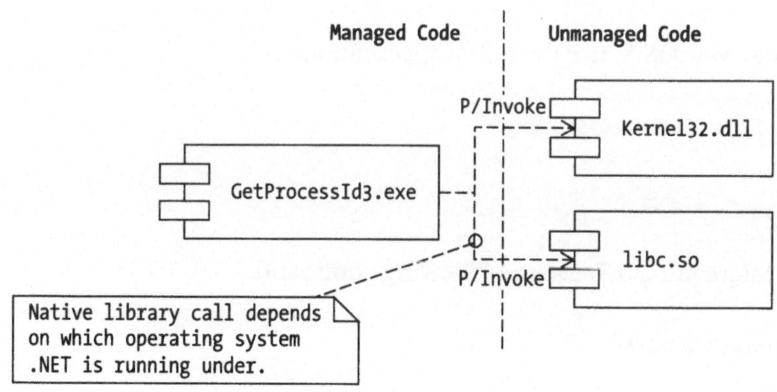

Figure 7-4. Deploying `GetProcessId3.exe` *as a single assembly*

To compile `GetProcessId3` on the Microsoft .NET Framework under Windows, use the following command:

```
C:\MS.NET> csc GetProcessId3.cs *Platfrom.cs
Microsoft (R) Visual C# .NET Compiler version 7.10.3052.4
for Microsoft (R) .NET Framework version 1.1.4322
Copyright (C) Microsoft Corporation 2001-2002. All rights reserved.

C:\MS.NET>
```

On Mac OS X and GNU/Linux, use the following command:

```
mono@linux:~ % mcs GetProcessId3.cs *Platfrom.cs
Compilation Succeeded
mono@linux:~ %
```

And for PNET on Mac OS X, use the following command:

```
pnet@macosx:~ % cscc GetProcessId3.cs *Platfrom.cs
Compilation Succeeded
pnet@macosx:~ %
```

Running the `GetProcessId3.exe` assembly on Mono and GNU/Linux, use the following command:

```
mono@linux:~ % mono GetProcessId.exe
Process ID: 997
mono@linux:~ %
```

On PNET and Mac OS X, use the following command:

```
pnet@macosx:~ % ilrun GetProcessId.exe
Process ID: 199
pnet@macosx:~ %
```

Finally, on Microsoft .NET, use the following command:

```
C:\MS.NET> GetProcessId3.exe
Process ID: 3013
C:\MS.NET>
```

Voilà! You now have a binary solution that works on all platforms.

Refined Binary Deployment

While the `GetProcessId3.exe` program aptly demonstrated a cross-platform binary solution to the problem of calling native code, in a real-world scenario, the solution's solitary assembly would unfortunately need recompiling whenever you wanted to change either of the native code wrappers, `UnixPlatform` and `WinPlatform`, or if you decided to add more functionality to the `Platform` class.

A refinement to the packaging involves compiling each of the classes into their own assembly, as demonstrated in Figure 7-5.

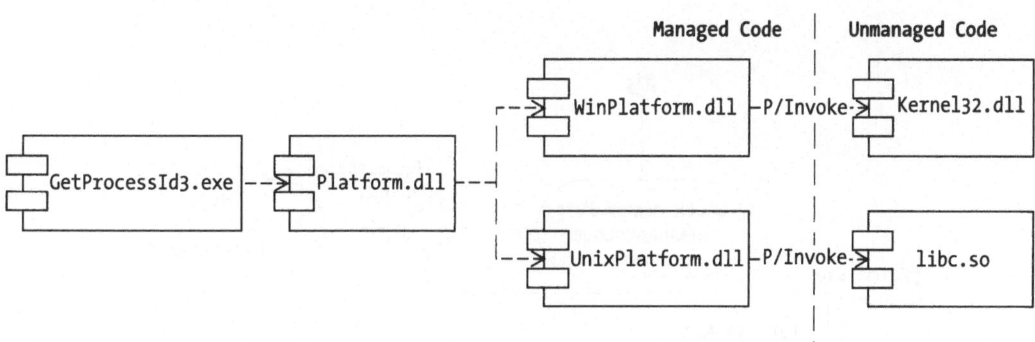

Figure 7-5. Deploying cross-platform functionality in different assemblies

Not only does this allow the `Platform` class to be extended as required without modifying the executable file, but it also allows the individual platform wrappers to be changed independently of everything else.

For example, if you discovered that Microsoft's Visual C library, `msvcrt.dll`, contained a function called `_getpid()`, you might decide to change the `WinPlatform` class to call it instead of `kernel32.dll`, which would simply involve changing the external declaration in `WinPlatform.cs` to the following:

```
[DllImport("msvcrt.dll", EntryPoint="_getpid")]
private unsafe static extern int GetCurrentProcessId();
```

Apart from the slight performance overhead of determining the native function call at runtime, the main problem with this approach is that in complex projects, the calls to native code might have no functional relationship to each other. In effect, the `Platform.dll`, `WinPlatform.dll`, and `UnixPlatform.dll` assemblies would be used as central repositories for methods that bore no relationship to each other, other than having underlying implementations in native code.

Advanced Platform Invoke

Having seen how easy it can be to call native code from managed code, it's time to delve a little further into the mysteries of Platform Invoke and see what happens under the covers. After all, the CLI does a fair bit of work translating even the simplest DllImport declaration into a real native call, and by understanding how the Platform Invoke mechanism works, you can start using native code to carry out more complex and therefore more interesting things.

When Platform Invoke calls an unmanaged function, it basically performs a sequence of activities, as shown by the activity diagram in Figure 7-6.

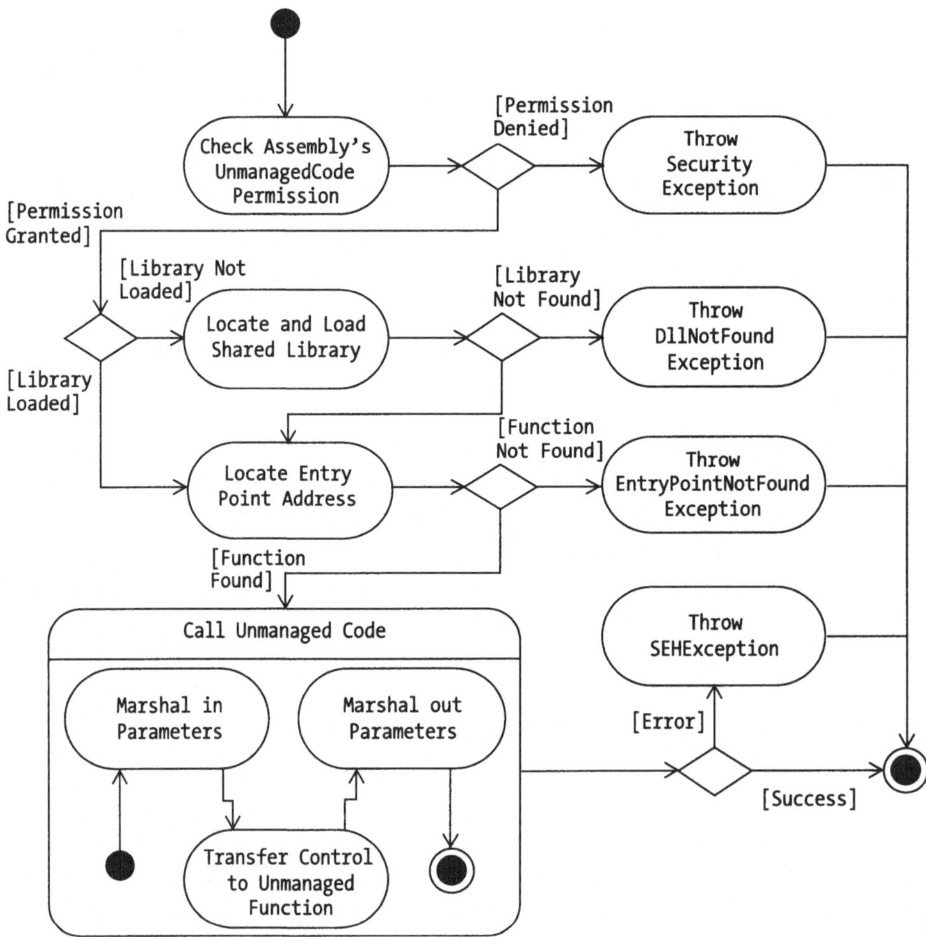

Figure 7-6. P/Invoke unplugged

If the library hasn't been loaded, the CLI locates and loads the library, after which it locates the address of the function, or entry point, to call. When the CLI has determined the address of the function to call, it pushes the function's address onto the stack, marshals any parameters, and pushes them on the stack before transferring control to the function. Finally, when the external function returns, the CLI ensures that any out parameters from the unmanaged function are marshaled.

Because each of those steps has its own foibles, it makes sense to investigate each step in more depth, after which you should have an excellent idea of just how many machinations are hidden behind a single, innocent `DllImport` declaration.

Locating Shared Libraries

While our discussion on calling native shared libraries has so far assumed that different operating systems can have different libraries for carrying out the same purpose, in a number of situations, the same shared library is available for a number of different operating systems.

Although these cross-platform shared libraries can have significantly different filenames for each operating system, it is not uncommon for the shared libraries to have similar base names, with Windows libraries using the `.DLL` (or `.dll`) extension, GNU/Linux using the `.so` extension, and Mac OS X using the `.dylib` extension. Additionally, it's a common convention for UNIX-based systems to prefix library names with `lib`, and because both GNU/Linux and Mac OS X are UNIX-based, their libraries generally follow this convention.

To simplify calling the same library on different operating systems, you don't need to specify the actual filename extension or `lib` prefix when declaring the `DllImport` attribute, because the CLI implementation can automatically detect and use the correct prefix and extension, depending on the underlying operating system.

As an example, we mentioned in Chapter 6 that Mono's `System.Data.OracleClient.dll` assembly implements a managed provider that gives access to Oracle databases and relies on the unmanaged Oracle Call Interface (OCI) library.

If you were to delve into Mono's source code, you would notice that the `OciCalls.cs` file declares a number of external functions that specify *oci* as the library name, as shown here:

```
[DllImport ("oci")]
internal static extern int OCITransCommit (IntPtr svchp,
                                           IntPtr errhp,
                                           uint flags);
```

As you would expect, the OCI on Windows is called `oci.dll`, but on GNU/Linux, it's called `libclntsh.so` rather than `liboci.so`. So what's going on, and why does the code work on GNU/Linux?

Mono's Library-Mapping Mechanism

Apart from the simple library name mapping already described, Mono also provides a configurable library-mapping mechanism that can be used to map virtual library names into actual library names. It is this configurable mapping mechanism that allows Mono to find the Oracle Call Interface on GNU/Linux, even though the code declares a number of imports from a library called `oci`.

To create a library mapping for an assembly, a configuration file needs to be created for the assembly and stored in the same directory, with the configuration file containing a `<dllmap/>` entry, as follows:

```
<configuration>
    <dllmap dll="oci" target="clntsh" />
</configuration>
```

Although the target can specify the full library name, as shown in the previous code, you can also omit the prefix and filename extension, because Mono's simple mapping system takes account of missing prefixes and extensions.

Mono also provides a second way to create library mappings at a global level rather than on a per-assembly basis. However, it is generally preferable to use the per-assembly mechanism, because it allows different assemblies to map to different versions of shared libraries.

To create a global mapping, a `<dllmap/>` element simply needs to be added to the `/etc/mono/config` configuration file. In fact, Mono's default configuration file comes with a number of predefined entries.

Shared Library Search Paths

One important disparity to be wary of when calling native code on different operating systems is that each operating system has its own policy for determining where to find shared libraries. While this shouldn't interfere with your cross-platform projects if you're using the preinstalled libraries that came with your operating systems, you will invariably find that you have more than one version of a library on an operating system. In this case, understanding how the operating system, and therefore .NET, can locate the library can be essential to the correct functioning of your program.

Windows Library Search Paths

In the wonderful world of Windows, the order in which Platform Invoke attempts to load a shared library is determined by the Windows `LoadLibrary()` API function, which searches for libraries depending on a couple of factors.

First, it depends on whether the version of Windows is based on the Windows NT kernel (Windows NT, XP, and Server 2003) or the Windows 95 kernel (Windows 95, 98, and Me).

Second, for versions of Windows later than Windows XP, Microsoft includes an added security feature called the `SafeDllSearchMode`. When this feature is turned on, Windows ensures that the current directory is searched after the `System` and `Windows` directories. This helps ensure that malicious code cannot redirect calls into system libraries by changing the current directory.

TIP The `SafeDllSearchMode` is controlled in the registry and is turned on when the `HKEY_LOCAL_MACHINE\System\CurrentControlSet\Control\Session Manager\SafeDllSearchMode` key is 1. For Windows XP SP1 and Windows Server 2003, `SafeDllSearchMode` is enabled by default and must be explicitly turned off by setting the registry key's value to 0.

As you can see from the activity diagram in Figure 7-7, when .NET attempts to call a native function, it doesn't lightly throw a `DllNotFoundException`.

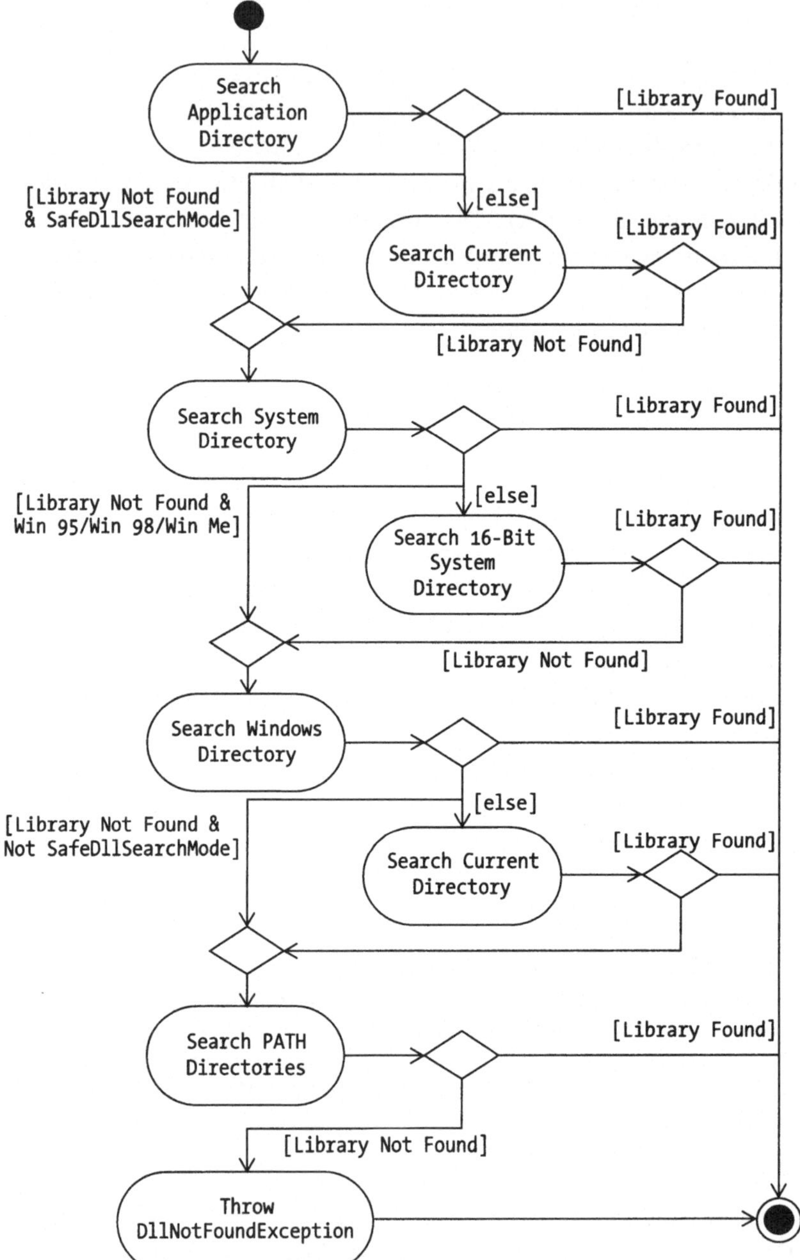

Figure 7-7. The Windows DLL search order

TIP If UML activity diagrams aren't a staple part of your development diet, you might want to brush up on your UML skills by taking a quick detour to Appendix A.

GNU/Linux Library Search Paths

Unlike the Windows search process, on GNU/Linux, the loading of shared libraries is the epitome of simplicity and is handled by the `dlopen(3)` function, which searches for libraries, as shown in Figure 7-8.

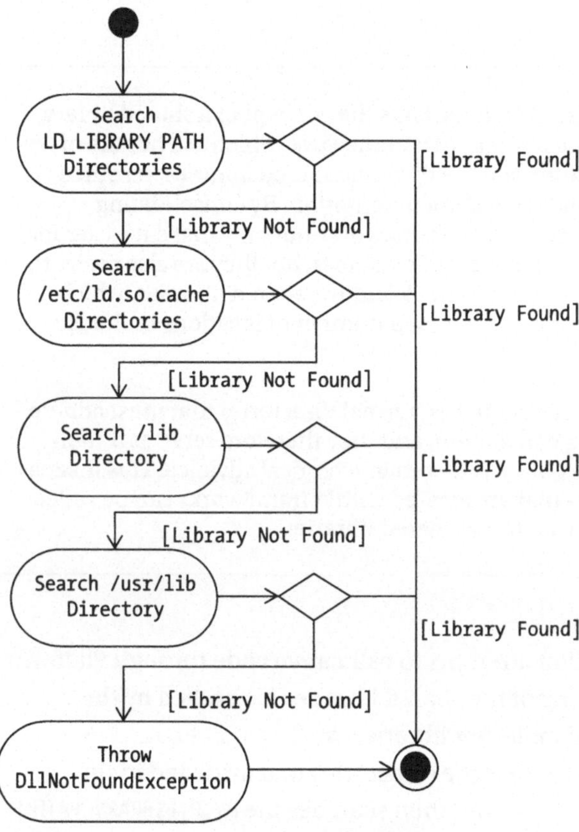

Figure 7-8. The GNU/Linux shared library search order

Although P/Invoke can search the directories that are listed in the user's `LD_LIBRARY_PATH` environment variable first if `/lib` and `/usr/lib` don't suffice, it is generally considered better security practice to use the `/etc/ld.so.cache` instead of `LD_LIBRARY_PATH`.

To modify the `/etc/ld.so.cache`, log in with root access and edit the `/etc/ld.co.config` file, which contains a list of directories to search. Then run the `ldconfig(8)` program.

Mac OS X Library Search Paths

With Mac OS X having its heritage in UNIX, it is unsurprising that the mechanism it uses for locating shared libraries is conceptually very similar to that used in GNU/Linux.

NOTE Although Mac OS X maintains the concept of a shared library, it also introduces the concept of a framework, which is a bundle of files packaged together, such as dynamic shared libraries, resource files, header files, and related documentation. By consolidating related files in a single bundle, frameworks not only make it easier for shared code to locate the relevant resources, but they are also easier to deploy than traditional UNIX and Windows shared libraries, which often involves strewing files across a number of locations in the file system.

Frameworks are implemented as normal directories that must adhere to a specific naming convention, and they therefore serve as a standardized packaging policy, rather than technical advance. This means that shared libraries that are located within frameworks can be called in the same way as traditional shared libraries.

When a CLI implementation attempts to call native code through Platform Invoke on Mac OS X, the loading of the shared libraries is handled by the dynamic linker, `dyld`, which searches for libraries, as shown in Figure 7-9.

The dynamic linker first searches the directories that are listed in the `DYLD_FRAMEWORK_PATH` for frameworks and then searches the `DYLD_LIBRARY_PATH` environment variable for libraries. If a shared library is not found according to the directories that are listed in either variable, the directories that are listed in the `DYLD_FALLBACK_FRAMEWORK_PATH` and `DYLD_FALLBACK_LIBRARY_PATH` environment variables are checked.

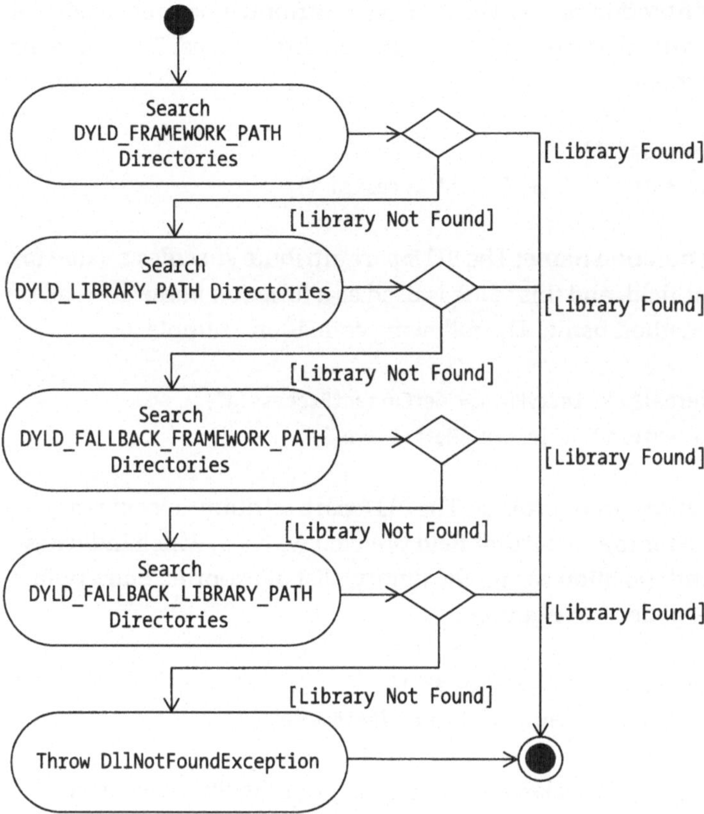

Figure 7-9. The Mac OS X shared library search order

By default, the `DYLD_FALLBACK_FRAMEWORK_PATH` variable contains a number of directories, including `~/Library/Frameworks`, `/Library/Frameworks`, `/Network/Library/Frameworks`, and `/System/Library/Frameworks`. The `DYLD_FALLBACK_LIBRARY_PATH` variable contains a number of usual suspects from the UNIX world, such as `~/lib`, `/usr/local/lib`, `/lib`, and `/usr/lib`.

This invariably boils down to the fact that as long as a shared library is installed in one of the standard locations, a CLI implementation shouldn't have a problem locating the binary file.

Locating Entry Points

After .NET has located the correct shared library to load, it must locate the address of the function's code within the library, the so-called the entry point.

P/Invoke allows entry points to be specified in the following three ways:

- **Implicitly by function name:** The DllImport attribute does not specify an entry point; instead, the name of the .NET method is used. The following code is an example:

```
[DllImport("kernel32")]
private static extern int GetCurrentProcessId ();
```

- **Explicitly by function name:** The DllImport attribute specifies a value for the EntryPoint field, and this value is used as a function name, instead of the internal method name. The following code is an example:

```
[DllImport("kernel32", EntryPoint="GetCurrentProcessId")]
private static extern int InternalMethodName();
```

- **Explicitly by entry point ordinal:** The DllImport attribute specifies a numeric value for the EntryPoint field prefixed with a #, which indicates the entry point's position within the library's list of exported entry points. The following code is an example:

```
[DllImport("kernel32", EntryPoint="#3")]
private unsafe static extern int InternalMethodName();
```

If the CLI has found the declared shared library but the library does not contain the specified entry point, an EntryPointNotFoundException is thrown, in much the same way as a DllNotFoundException is thrown if the actual shared library cannot be found.

Windows Entry Points

To complicate matters further, on Windows, theWin32 API functions that handle strings come in two different variants: those that expect strings encoded using the local codepage and those that expect them encoded in Unicode.

NOTE The code for this section is available in the Chapter_07/WinEntryPoint directory at this book's Web site (http://www.cross-platform.net) and the Apress Web site (http://www.apress.com).

For example, to display a Windows message box, there is not only an entry point for the local codepage function, MessageBoxA, but also an entry point for the

Unicode version of the function, `MessageBoxW`. The following rules for translating between entry point versions are simple:

- An *A* suffix indicates the local code page, where *A* stands for ANSI.
- A *W* suffix indicates Unicode, where *W* stands for wide characters.

CAUTION *ANSI* doesn't really mean ANSI, but rather it means the *local code page*. While it might well be ANSI/ASCII, it could equally well be a *double-byte character set (DBCS)* that is used for encoding non-Latin characters, such as Japanese or Korean.

In practice, this means that you must be doubly careful when using Win32 API functions that manipulate strings, because calling the wrong entry point invariably translates your strings into gibberish.

Because the default `CharSet` field for the `DllImport` attribute is `CharSet.Ansi`, the simplest way to specify an ANSI function is to avoid using the suffix, as follows:

```
[DllImport("user32.dll")]
static extern int MessageBox(IntPtr handle, string msg,
                             string caption, int type);
```

If you get the urge to be explicit, you can specify the ANSI variant explicitly by targeting the ANSI variant, `MessageBoxA`, as follows:

```
[DllImport("user32.dll" EntryPoint = "MessageBoxA")]
static extern int MessageBox(IntPtr handle, string msg, string caption, int type);
```

If you prefer to call the Unicode variant, you have to explicitly set the `CharSet` field in the `DllImport` attribute to a value of `CharSet.Unicode`, as follows:

```
[DllImport("user32.dll", CharSet = CharSet.Unicode)]
static extern int MessageBox(IntPtr handle, string msg,
                             string caption, int type);
```

`System.Byte (byte)`, `System.SByte (sbyte)`, `System.Int16 (short)`, `System.UInt16 (ushort)`, `System.Int32 (int)`, `System.UInt32 (uint)`, `System.Int64 (long)`, `System.UInt64 (ulong)`, `System.IntPtr`, `System.UIntPtr`, single-dimensional arrays of blittable types, and value types that only contain blittable fields.

For all other data types, P/Invoke has a set of default marshaling rules that dictate how the data type is transformed, whether the external function can change data that is passed to it, and how to optimize the marshaling of the data type. Nonetheless, these nonblittable types can have ambiguous representations in managed or unmanaged code. In this case, you must explicitly define how P/Invoke marshals the data type.

For example, managed strings can be represented in unmanaged code in a number of ways, including the ANSI and Unicode representations that we saw earlier.

TIP For a thorough treatment of cross-platform marshaling, read Jonathan Pryor's article "Everything you never wanted to know about marshaling," which is available at `http://www.cross-platform.net/interop.html`.

Calling Conventions

Although marshaling is the crux of the complexity that is associated with Platform Invoke, you must also ensure that the correct calling conventions are specified for all imported functions. A calling convention essentially dictates how parameters are moved to and from the stack for a function call, and while understanding the low-level stack gymnastics of the different calling conventions is not necessary for the majority of .NET programmers, specifying the correct calling convention is vital.

In practice, different libraries use different calling conventions, and while each operating system usually has a preferred calling convention, you cannot assume that one calling convention will suffice for all the libraries on one platform or even for the same library on different operating systems.

To set the calling convention to use for a native function, the `DllImport` attribute's `CallingConvention` field can be specified with one of the following values from the `CallingConvention` enumeration:

- `Winapi`: Uses the platform's default calling convention.
- `Cdecl`: Uses the standard C calling convention. Allows variable arguments; caller cleans the stack.

- `StdCall`: Uses the Pascal calling convention. Requires a fixed number of arguments; callee cleans the stack.
- `ThisCall`: The `this` pointer is stored in a register, and other parameters go on the stack. Used by some C++ compilers.
- `FastCall`: Places more arguments in registers instead of the stack. This calling convention is not currently supported by .NET.

For example, the OpenAL 3D sound library uses the `Cdecl` calling convention on all operating systems, and the declaration for the `alcMakeContextCurrent` function could be as follows:

```
[DllImport("OpenAL32.dll", CallingConvention= CallingConvention.Cdecl)]
public static extern int alcMakeContextCurrent(IntPtr context);
```

If the `CallingConvention` field is not explicitly given a value, the calling convention is set to the default calling convention for the operating system. This default is `StdCall` for Windows and `Cdecl` for UNIX-based operating systems.

Declaring Parameter Directions

So far, none of the function declarations have explicitly declared the direction of their parameters, which means that their parameters default to being *In* parameters. You can explicitly declare the direction of a parameter in the following three ways:

- An `[In]` parameter implies that the parameter's managed data is copied into unmanaged memory but is not copied back again. As previously stated, this is the default behavior when no direction is explicitly declared.
- An `[Out]` parameter implies that the parameter does not require managed memory to be copied into unmanaged memory, but on the function's return, the parameter's unmanaged representation is copied into managed memory.

  An example of a function that uses an `[Out]` parameter is the Win32 API's `GetSystemDirectory()` function. However, because `StringBuilder` parameters are implicitly `[Out]` parameters, it could equally be declared without specifying `[Out]`, as follows:

```
[DllImport("kernel32")]
public static extern int GetSystemDirectory([Out] StringBuilder buffer, int
                                            size);
```

- An `[In, Out]` parameter implies that the parameter requires its managed memory representation to be copied into unmanaged memory, and on the function's return, the parameter's unmanaged representation is then copied into managed memory.

Invoking C++ Code from .NET

While the preponderance of C code makes it the de facto standard for system and application APIs on the vast majority of platforms, a significant proportion of business software was written in C++ to take advantage of its object-oriented features.

Given that .NET's main scope is within the business arena and that C# itself is an evolutionary step from C++, it would be handy if C++ code could be called from .NET.

While Microsoft provides a solution to this problem, in the form of Managed Extensions for C++, it does so by adding a number of unsightly and nonstandard modifications to the C++ language. This, in turn, makes it inherently platform dependent and is unsuitable for cross-platform development. While ECMA is going through the process of standardizing a C++ binding for .NET, called C++/CLI, it's likely to be some time before C++/CLI becomes a viable option.

Fortunately, all is not lost. A great open source tool, called the Simplified Wrapper and Interface Generator (SWIG), is available, which makes calling C++ code from .NET—and a number of other languages—a real possibility. SWIG is essentially a compiler that takes C or C++ declarations and uses them to create the wrappers that are necessary to access those declarations from other languages.

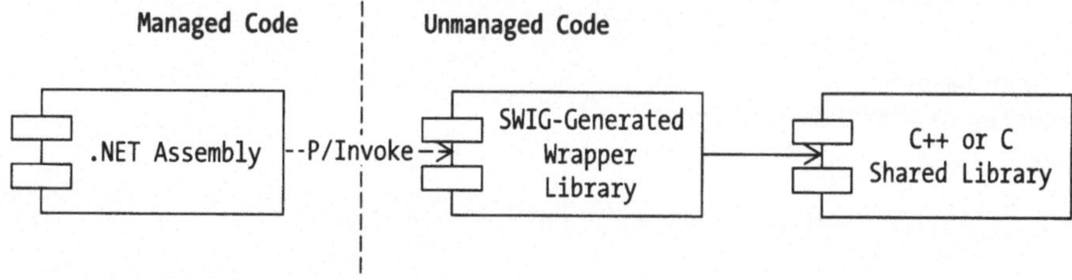

While a whole book could probably be written on the intricacies of SWIG, a thorough manual is available with the latest version of the software, which can both be downloaded from `http://www.swig.org`.

NOTE If you decide to be clever and explicitly name the Unicode entry point, you still have to set the `CharSet` field, because if you don't, it will default to `CharSet.Ansi`. This means that .NET will still attempt to translate your strings into Unicode, resulting in unreadable strings.

A simple program that could be used to call any of these functions is as follows:

```
//WinEntryPoints.cs
using System;
using System.Runtime.InteropServices;

class PlatformInvokeTest
{
    //Place your chosen DllImport decalration here...

    public static int Main()
    {
        return MessageBox(IntPtr.Zero, "Hello from the Win32 API!",
                          "A Win32 Message Box!", 0);
    }
}
```

Marshaling

Having just seen how strings can be passed into native unmanaged functions, it's time to discuss the broader issue of how data is passed between managed and unmanaged code.

Because unmanaged functions need to be able to receive data in the form of parameters and to return data in the form of a return value or out parameters, P/Invoke provides facilities to copy data between managed and unmanaged memory. In some circumstances, P/Invoke can pin variables in managed memory and thereby avoid the performance hit of a data copy. Because the representation of a particular data type might be different in managed and unmanaged code, P/Invoke also provides the facility to convert the managed representation of a data type into an unmanaged representation, and vice versa, in a process known as *marshaling*.

Unfortunately, marshaling carries with it an associated performance hit, but because many data types share a common representation in both managed and unmanaged memory, P/Invoke can directly copy these data types with no conversion; this is known as *blitting*. The list of blittable .NET types includes

An Advanced P/Invoke Example: Cross-Platform Audio

To cap off our adventures with P/Invoke, we create an example that calls the OpenAL library, which is an industry-standard, cross-platform library for generating 3D sound. Although OpenAL provides a number of advanced facilities, such as calculating Doppler shifts, we simply use it to play a short WAV file.

Because even playing a short WAV file requires a large number of native calls, rather than wrapping up the OpenAL library ourselves, we cheat a little and use the open source Tao.OpenAL library. This allows us to concentrate on the important issue of creating some cross-platform sound to frighten the neighbors with.

Installing OpenAL

To get Tao.OpenAL working, you first need to install an OpenAL shared library. The OpenAL Web site (`http://www.openal.org`) contains links to binary installers for both Windows and Mac OSs.

If you need to install OpenAL on GNU/Linux and it isn't already installed with your GNU/Linux distribution, you need to download the source code from the Internet and manually build it.

To download the source code, you need access to Creative's open source CVS repository. You can do this by running the following commands on the command line, using a password of *guest* when prompted:

```
cvs -d:pserver:guest@opensource.creative.com:/usr/local/cvs-repository login
cvs -d:pserver:guest@opensource.creative.com:/usr/local/cvs-repository co openal
```

After the second command has completed, you should have a directory called `openal` below the current working directory. You can then navigate into the `openal/linux` directory and, as long as you have `autotools` installed, you can run the following commands to build and install the library:

```
sh ./autogen.sh
./configure --prefix=/usr/local
make
make install
```

Installing Tao.OpenAl.dll

To install Tao.OpenAl, you need to download the complete TAO library, which, apart from wrapping OpenAL, also wraps a number of other cross-platform libraries, such as the OpenGL 3D library, the DevIL image-manipulation library, and the SDL multimedia library.

NOTE TAO can be downloaded from `http://www.randyridge.com/Tao`, although it has recently merged with the Mono project and will be available with Mono in due course.

For Windows, binary versions of TAO are available directly from the Web site, but for all other platforms, you must download the source code and build it using your favorite C# compiler or the Nant build tool, which is discussed in Chapter 9.

Because the name of the OpenAL library is platform dependent, Tao uses conditional compilation to allow its source code to be built for different operating systems. This is handled by declarations in the `Al.cs` and `Alc.cs` files, which are similar to those that follow:

```
#if WIN32
    public const string AL_NATIVE_LIBRARY = "OpenAL32.dll";
#elif UNIX
    public const string AL_NATIVE_LIBRARY = "libopenal.so";
#elif MACOS
    public const string AL_NATIVE_LIBRARY = "OpenAL";
#endif
```

This allows all the external function declarations to be declared with the `AL_NATIVE_LIBRARY` constant, as demonstrated in the following `alGetError()` function, which retrieves the last error number to occur within OpenAL:

```
[DllImport(AL_NATIVE_LIBRARY, CallingConvention=CALLING_CONVENTION)]
public static extern int alGetError();
```

This means that to compile `Tao.OpenAl.dll` for a specific platform, you need to define a compilation symbol on the command line. The following examples show how Microsoft's `csc` compiler could be used to compile an assembly for Mac OS X and then other UNIX-based operating systems:

```
csc Al.cs Alc.cs Alut.cs /D:MACOS
csc Al.cs Alc.cs Alut.cs /D:UNIX
```

Under the Covers of TAO.OpenAL

Tao.OpenAL contains three main classes, Al, Alc, and Alut, which closely map to sets of related OpenAL functions and are illustrated in Figure 7-10. In fact, the Alut class and the associated native functions are not strictly part of the OpenAL specifications but are rather a toolkit of useful functions that is built on top of the lower-level OpenAL functions.

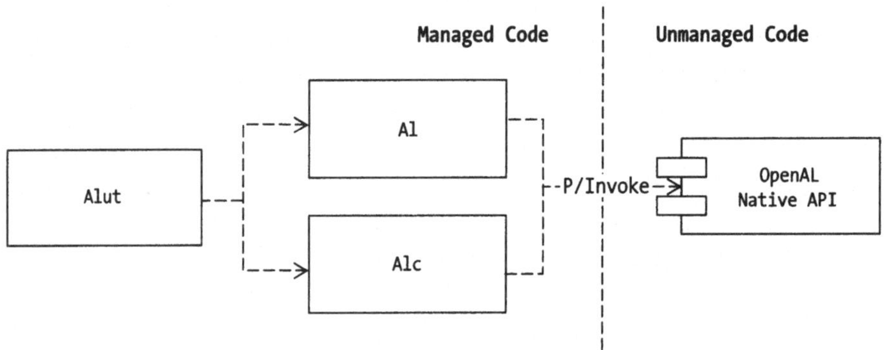

Figure 7-10. The class dependencies in Tao.OpenAL

Because Alut is not technically a part of the core OpenAL shared library, the Tao implementation of Alut cannot rely on any Alut functions being available in any particular implementation of the OpenAL shared library. Therefore, Tao implements Alut as pure managed code that uses the Al and Alc classes to handle all OpenAL calls.

A simple example of an Alut method is the alutInit() method, which retrieves a pointer to a sound device and then creates a context for the device, as follows:

```
//Initializes OpenAL device and context.
public coid alutInit()
{
    IntPtr device = Alc.alcOpenDevice(String.Empty);
    IntPtr context = Alc.alcCreateContext(device, IntPtr.Zero);
    Alc.alcMakeContextCurrent(context);
}
```

Before looking at the declarations for the three Alc methods, we should point out that because the OpenAL library uses the Cdecl calling convention across all operating systems, each of the Tao source files also declares the following CALLING_CONVENTION constant:

```
private const CallingConvention CALLING_CONVENTION = CallingConvention.Cdecl;
```

This constant is then used in each of the DllImport declarations to ensure that the correct calling convention is used. The declarations for the alcOpenDevice, alcCreateContext, and alcMakeContextCurrent functions, as called by the alutInit() method, are then as follows:

```
 [DllImport(ALC_NATIVE_LIBRARY, CallingConvention=CALLING_CONVENTION,
          CharSet=CharSet.Ansi)]
public static extern IntPtr alcOpenDevice(string deviceName);

[DllImport(ALC_NATIVE_LIBRARY, CallingConvention=CALLING_CONVENTION)]
public static extern IntPtr alcCreateContext([In] IntPtr device,
                                             [In] ref int attribute);

[DllImport(ALC_NATIVE_LIBRARY, CallingConvention=CALLING_CONVENTION)]
public static extern int alcMakeContextCurrent([In] IntPtr context);
```

Note that the declarations extensively use the IntPtr type, which is a value type that can be used to hold a pointer or a handle and is frequently used when calling native functions.

The WavPlayer Program

Now that we've had a quick tour through how Tao.OpenAL calls the underlying native OpenAL library, it's time to put it to the test and build a simple application—and make some noise.

Although the WavPlayer program will be very simple, its dependency on Tao.OpenAL means it will be indirectly dependent on different native libraries according to the underlying operating system, as illustrated in Figure 7-11.

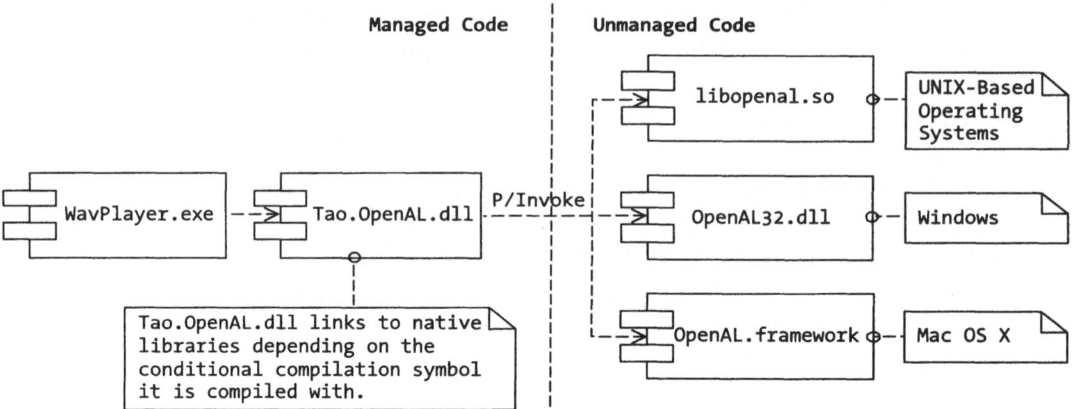

Figure 7-11. The Tao.OpenAL *architecture*

NOTE The code for this the WavPlayer program is available in the Chapter_07/WavPlayer directory at this book's Web site (http://www.cross-platform.net) and the Apress Web site (http://www.apress.com). Precompiled binary files of Tao.OpenAl.dll are available in the Chapter_07/Tao.OpenAl directory for Windows, GNU/Linux, and Mac OS X.

As you might have guessed from Figure 7-11, the program's source code is placed in a single file, WavPlayer.cs, which starts by declaring a few private fields that we use to store data in between method calls. The code is as follows:

```
//Filename: WavPlayer.cs
using System;
using Tao.OpenAl;

namespace Crossplatform.NET.Chapter7
{
    class WavPlayer : IDisposable
    {
        private int buffer;                          //Buffer to hold sound data.
        private int source;                          //The sound source
        private float pitch = 0.3F;                  //The pitch
        private string fileName;                     //The file to play
```

The class's constructor takes a filename that is stored in the instance's `fileName` field. The class then initializes OpenAL by calling the `alutInit()` method that we saw earlier and then loads the WAV file into memory by calling the `LoadData()` method, which we will come to in a moment. The code is as follows:

```
//Initialize the player
public WavPlayer(string fileName)
{
    this.fileName = fileName;
    Alut.alutInit();
    LoadALData();
}

public void Dispose()
{
    //Do some housecleaning
    Al.alDeleteBuffers(1, ref this.buffer);
    Al.alDeleteSources(1, ref this.source);
    Alut.alutExit();
}
```

Following directly after the constructor, the `Dispose()` method allows the caller to carry out some basic housekeeping by deleting the buffer source and then cleanly exits from OpenAL by calling the `alutExit()` method.

Managing Handle References

A common way of handling unmanaged resources in .NET is to embody the resource in a wrapper class. This reduces the need to directly deal with handles to unmanaged resources.

For example, the following class allows managed code to carry out an operation on an unmanaged resource by calling the `DoSomething()` method:

```
public class UnmanagedResourceWrapper
{
    public readonly IntPtr Handle;

    public UnmanagedResourceWrapper ()
    {
        handle = OpenUnmanagedResource();
    }
```

```
    ~UnmanagedResourceWrapper ()
    {
        CloseUnmanagedResource (Handle);
    }

    public void DoSomething()
    {
        DoUnmanagedThing(Handle);
    }
}
```

If the unmanaged resource needs to be passed to a native call using Platform Invoke, the naive approach would be to pass in the handle to the unmanaged resource, as follows:

```
Public void NaiveMethod()
{
    UnmanagedResourceWrapper wrapper = new UnmanagedResourceWrapper ();
    CallPlatformInvoke(wrapper.Handle);
}
```

Although the code looks fairly innocuous, a problem is lurking, because the wrapper object technically becomes eligible for garbage collection before the native call returns. Because the garbage collector runs on its own thread and the class implements a finalizer, `~UnmanagedResourceWrapper()`, the garbage collector could call the finalizer and therefore close the resource before `DoUnmanagedThing()` returns. This introduces an undesirable race condition between the garbage collector's call to the finalizer and `DoUnmanagedThing()`.

.NET's solution to this problem is the `HandleRef` class. This class can be implicitly converted into an `IntPtr` and ensures that the managed object isn't garbage-collected before the native call returns, as demonstrated in the following method:

```
Public void BetterMethod()
{
    UnmanagedResourceWrapper wrapper = new UnmanagedResourceWrapper();
    HandleRef hr = new HandleRef(wrapper, wrapper.Handle);
    CallPlatformInvoke(hr);
}
```

However, a better approach, which absolves client code from worrying about such irksome issues, is to implement the wrapper class to more intelligently *handle* the handle, as follows:

```
public class UnmanagedResourceWrapper : IDisposable
{
    private HandleRef handle;

    public UnmanagedResourceWrapper ()
    {
        IntPtr h = OpenUnmanagedResource();
        handle = new HandleRef (this, h);
    }

    public HandleRef Handle
    {
        get{ return handle; }
    }

    public void Dispose()
    {
        Close();
        System.GC.SuppressFinalize (this);
    }

    private void Close ()
    {
        CloseUnmanagedResource (Handle);
        handle = new HandleRef (this, IntPtr.Zero);
    }

    ~UnmanagedResourceWrapper()
    {
        Close();
    }
}
```

This improvement not only implements the `IDispose` interface, whose `Dipose()` method is the preferred way for clients to drop resources, but it also removes the race condition by using `HandleRef` instead of `IntPtr`. Additionally, the class's finalizer guarantees that the unmanaged resource will be closed, even if `Dispose()` isn't called.

This improved wrapper class allows the naive method that was first mentioned to be used without worrying about the race condition, as follows:

```
Public void NaiveButBuglessMethod()
{
    UnmanagedResourceWrapper wrapper = new UnmanagedResourceWrapper();
    CallPlatformInvoke(wrapper.Handle);
}
```

The LoadALData() method, which is called in the constructor, starts by loading the WAV file into a buffer that is referenced by the class's buffer field. After the file has been loaded into the buffer, it is bound to a sound source, which subsequently allows the source to play the WAV file. The code is as follows:

```
//Load the data for playing
private void LoadALData()
{
    byte[] data;
    int format, frequency, loop, size;

    //Load the wav data into a buffer.
    Al.alGenBuffers(1, out this.buffer);
    Alut.alutLoadWAVFile(this.fileName, out format, out data,
                         out size, out frequency, out loop);
    Al.alBufferData(this.buffer, format, data, size, frequency);
    Alut.alutUnloadWAV(format, out data, size, frequency);

    //Bind the buffer with the source.
    Al.alGenSources(1, out this.source);
    Al.alSourcei(this.source, Al.AL_BUFFER, this.buffer);
    Al.alSourcef(this.source, Al.AL_PITCH, this.pitch);
}
```

The Play() method is extremely lightweight and merely acts as a wrapper to the alSourcePlay() method of the Al class, as follows:

```
//Play the WAV file...
public void Play()
{
    Al.alSourcePlay(this.source);
}
```

The program's missing piece is the Main() method, which instantiates the WavPlayer class and calls the Play() method, specifying a WAV file to play. Because

OpenAL creates its own thread for playing the WAV file, we include a call to `Console.ReadLine()` so that the program doesn't inadvertently exit before the WAV file has had a chance to play. We use the following code:

```
        //The program's entry point
        static void Main(string[] args)
        {
                //Play the wav file.
                new WavPlayer("ding.wav").Play();

                Console.WriteLine("Press enter to exit...");
                Console.ReadLine();
        }
    }
}
```

So now that we have our program, it's time to compile it on each of our CLI implementations. Then perhaps we can see which one sings the loudest.

TIP Remember that the `Tao.OpenAL.dll` assembly only works on the operating system that it was compiled for. To facilitate this example, we have included three different copies of the `Tao.OpenAL.dll` library in the `Chapter07/Tao.OpenAL` directory, which is available at this book's Web site (`http://www.cross-platform.net`) and the Apress Web site (`http://www.apress.com`).

To compile the program on Microsoft .NET, use the following command, assuming that `Tao.OpenAL.dll` is in the same directory as `WavPlayer.cs` and that you have correctly installed OpenAL on your computer:

```
C:\MS.NET> csc /t:exe WavPlayer.cs /r:Tao.OpenAl.dll
Microsoft (R) Visual C# .NET Compiler version 7.10.3052.4
for Microsoft (R) .NET Framework version 1.1.4322
Copyright (C) Microsoft Corporation 2001-2002. All rights reserved.

C:\MS.NET>
```

On Mono and GNU/Linux, use the following command:

```
mono@linux:~ % mcs /t:exe WavPlayer.cs /r:Tao.OpenAl.dll
Compilation Succeeded
mono@linux:~ %
```

For PNET on Mac OS X, use the following command:

```
pnet@macosx:~ % cscc /t:exe WavPlayer.cs /r:Tao.OpenAl.dll /out:WavPlayer.exe
Compilation Succeeded
pnet@macosx:~ %
```

Running the `GetProcessId3.exe` assembly on Mono and GNU/Linux, use the following command:

```
mono@linux:~ % mono WavPlayer.exe
Press enter to exit...

mono@linux:~ %
```

For PNET and Mac OS X, use the following command:

```
pnet@macosx:~ % ilrun WavPlayer.exe
Press enter to exit...

pnet@macosx:~ %
```

Finally, for Microsoft .NET, use the following command:

```
C:\MS.NET> WavPlayer.exe
Press enter to exit...

C:\MS.NET>
```

So there you have it: a sound solution that works on all platforms. Of course, we've only explored the bare minimum of functionality in this section, but it's easy to see how the program could be enhanced by allowing a filename to be passed into the program, with other arguments controlling the pitch, volume, and some added niceties like a variable Doppler effect.

Summary

Having started this chapter by analyzing how each CLI implementation relies on native code by using the `NativeProbe.exe` tool, we then looked at how to use Platform Invoke in our own programs before finally looking at a practical example of how P/Invoke can be useful in a cross-platform application.

While calling native code is somewhat at odds with the philosophy behind managed code, the ability to use a platform's native features is an essential trick that can reduce development time, allow the reuse of legacy code, and sometimes provide performance that would be hard to match in purely managed code. In all likelihood, this means that managed and unmanaged code will continue to have an important partnership that will help bring many cross-platform .NET projects successfully to the market.

Because C has been a highly popular language since the 1970s, it's not surprising that a wealth of native code is written in C, but despite C's august heritage, the language inevitably comes with a lot of baggage. Not only can unmanaged libraries introduce errors and security holes that would otherwise be banished by the CLI, but they also serve to decrease an application's potential portability. Used shrewdly, .NET's ability to call native code is an indispensable tool; used crudely, it's the bane of a cross-platform developer and is liable to send many good developers into desperate fits of laptop groin rubbing.

CHAPTER 8

Remoting, Components, and Interoperability

"If they introduce interoperability without a deal with us, it's a hack, and it doesn't really work."

—Barry Schuler, president of AOL Interactive Services

AS THE BACKWASH of technical progress is sucked from the shoreline, it leaves hundreds of little rock pools, each teaming with technologies that are destined to dry out unless habitually supervised by support teams. While writing well-factored, object-oriented code can go a long way to reducing future maintenance costs, the reality is that development shortcuts are often made to reduce initial project costs. This, in effect, saddles an unavoidable burden of debt on system maintenance. Coupling these issues with the personnel factor—the older a system becomes, the harder it is to find staff who are able or willing to work with the technologies of yesteryear—it's easy to understand why industry analysts suggest that keeping these rock pools filled with water can be significantly more expensive than developing new technologies. And if supporting mature systems wasn't enough, the need to modernize aging but functional systems, integrate systems from different vendors running on different operating systems, and show at least an inkling of interest in the latest technical fashion are frequently the straws that not only break IT managers' backs but also rupture their dreams, constipate their sanity, and induce their early retirement.

While many software vendors attempt to guarantee future business by locking clients into their products, such an approach is at odds with a common enterprise application operational requirement: the ability to reliably integrate and interoperate with existing systems, many of which were written many years previously, using technologies that have long since seen their halcyon days. Although the IT industry has been conspicuously aware of the issues surrounding integration and interoperability since the 1970s, the fact that *interoperability* is used more frequently as a marketing buzzword than as a word from the technical lexicon might help explain why many vendors feel that interoperability is of little consequence to the technical success of their products.

When Microsoft added AOL compatibility to Windows Messenger without AOL's blessing, even though Barry Schuler was keen to disparage Microsoft, it was a wonderful example of interoperability and an even better example of the corporate misappropriation of polysyllabic words.

An interesting sentiment championed by Julio Silva[1] is that there are two different concepts often lumped together under the interoperability umbrella: the integration of disparate systems, or *intra-operability*, and the interaction of incongruent systems, or *interoperability*. Where intra-operability involves merging distinct systems into an inseparable whole system, interoperability deals with ensuring that separate systems can communicate with each other while maintaining their independence. Because .NET provides mechanisms to facilitate both concepts, we clearly distinguish between them in this chapter.

This chapter therefore illustrates how .NET can be used as a cross-platform, pain-killing tool for implementing intra-operability and interoperability between systems. Where the previous chapter discussed the use of Platform Invoke for calling C APIs, this chapter focuses on demonstrating code intra-operability and interoperability using components, and finishes by showing how .NET Remoting underlies and backs up these concepts.

Code Integration: Intra-operability

Before looking at how .NET eases the implementation of interoperable systems, we need to look at the related but distinct matter of how the Common Language Infrastructure (CLI) architecture allows code that is written in different languages to be integrated into a consistent system, in the process known as intra-operability.

Following the standardization of ANSI C and POSIX in the 1980s, the IT industry looked set to reap the benefits of compatibility that was offered by the dual pillars of commonality and standardization. Nonetheless, the desire to solve particular problems with finesse promoted a continual proliferation of languages, and with many of these languages sharing little parity, difficulties have continued as developers have struggled to integrate square code into a round hole. While many languages have bindings that allow them to call C libraries—indeed, the CLI's C binding mechanism, Platform Invoke, was discussed thoroughly in the previous chapter—it's still highly desirable to be able to integrate with code that is written in other languages, especially as users of different platforms have their own pet languages.

1. J.C. Silva, "Technical Agnosticism: The New Techno-religion," *.NET Developers Journal*, April 2003.

The Common Language System

Since the lure of component architectures first promised real language independence, it was the subsequent rise of the Virtual Machine (VM) that heralded in the real era of intra-operability. After Microsoft acquired Omniware (which was a system for producing and executing mobile code[2]) in 1996, its foray into intra-operable VM technology began in earnest, and the CLI was born. While the CLI was being designed it made sense to create a language to take advantage of the CLI's features and that language was C#, which has an august ancestry, as illustrated in Figure 8-1.

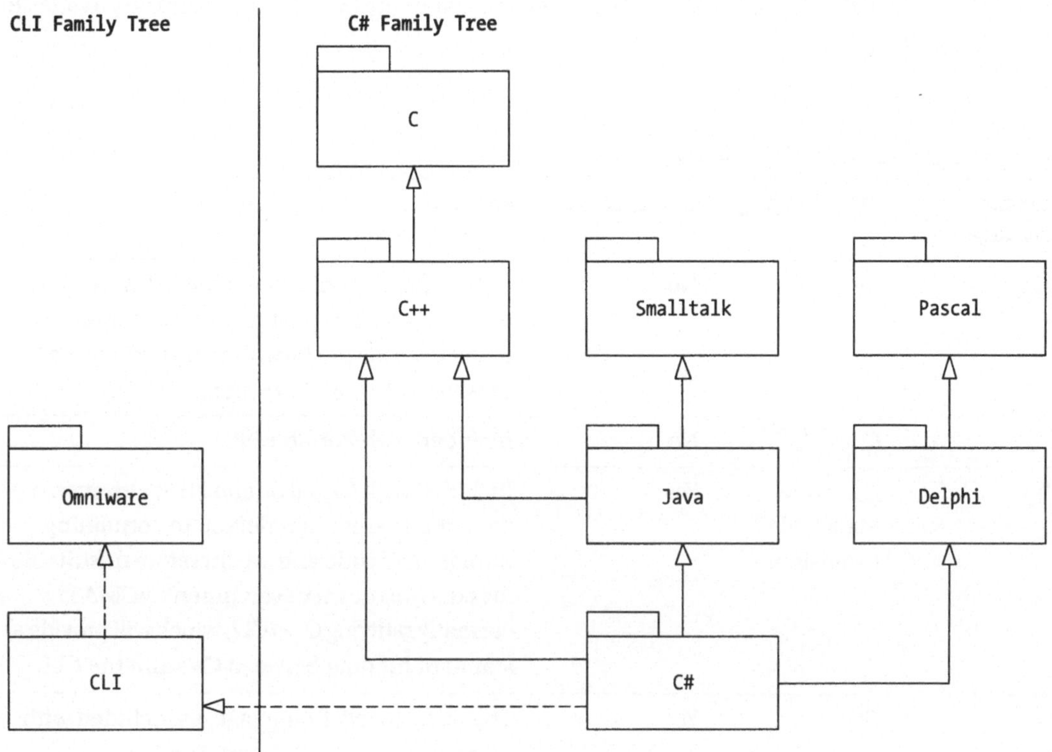

Figure 8-1. The history of C#

While the CLI is explicitly designed to confer language intra-operability, it does not guarantee that all the code written in one .NET language will be usable from another .NET language. Although the Common Type System provides a

2. Lucco, Sharp, and Wahbe, *Omniware: A Universal Substrate for Web Programming*, 1995, `http://www.w3.org/Conferences/WWW4/Papers/165/`.

framework that defines how types are managed in the runtime and as such it is vitally important for cross-language integration, the CLI also defines a set of intra-operability rules called the *Common Language Specification (CLS)*. Any .NET library assembly that adheres to the CLS rules can be called a *CLS-compliant framework* and is guaranteed to be usable by any other language that has a .NET compiler. Such libraries can advertise their CLS compliance by declaring the `CLSCompliant` attribute with the attribute's solitary parameter set to `true`.

A language or compiler that can use CLS-compliant frameworks is called a *CLS consumer*, which means that all .NET languages can be considered CLS consumers. In contrast, a language or compiler that has the ability to create CLS-compliant frameworks is called a *CLS extender*, and therefore not all .NET languages are guaranteed to be CLS extenders. Although it is by no means a complete list, Table 8-1 shows the most popular compilers that are currently available for .NET.

Table 8-1. Available .NET Languages

Standard Language	.NET Language	CLS Extender	Notes
Ada	A#	No	A .NET implementation of the software engineer's language of choice. For more details, see `http://www.usafa.af.mil/dfcs/bios/mcc_html/a_sharp.html`.
C	C	No	Included with Portable.NET.
C++	C++ with Managed Extensions	Yes	Included with Visual Studio.NET, although generated assemblies default to containing unmanaged code and are therefore unsuitable for cross-platform development. ECMA is currently ratifying C++/CLI, which will provide a standard binding between C++ and the CLI.
C#	C#	Yes	The de facto .NET language, as included with Mono, Microsoft .NET, and PNET.
COBOL	NetCOBOL	Yes	For more details, see `http://www.netcobol.com`.
Delphi	Delphi	Yes	For more information, see `http://www.borland.com`.
Eiffel	Eiffel for .NET	Yes	For more information, see `http://www.eiffel.com`.
Forth	Delta Forth for .NET	Yes	For more information, see `http://www.dataman.ro/dforth`.

Table 8-1. Available .NET Languages (Continued)

Standard Language	.NET Language	CLS Extender	Notes
Fortran	Salford Fortran for .NET	Yes	For more information, see `http://www.salfordsoftware.co.uk`.
Java	Java	Yes	Included with Portable.NET (as part of cscc) and with Visual Studio .NET (Visual J#), and implemented with the IKVM Java-to-.NET bridge (`http://weblog.ikvm.net`).
JavaScript	JavaScript	Yes	Included with Visual Studio .NET.
Nemerle	Nemerle	No	A hybrid, functional, object-oriented and imperative language that was developed especially for the CLI. For more information, go to `http://www.nemerle.org`.
Pascal	Pascal	Yes	For more information, see `http://www.tmt.com`.
Perl	PerlNET	No	A commercial binding that allows assemblies to access Perl code running within the traditional Perl interpreter. For more information, see `http://www.activestate.com/.NET`.
Perl	Perl for .NET	Yes	A research project that demonstrates the ability to compile Perl code into IL, Perl for .NET does not provide production-enabling performance. For more information, see `http://www.activestate.com/.NET`.
PHP	PHP	Yes	For more information, see `http://www.akbkhome.com/Projects/PHP_Sharp`.
PHP	PHP Mono Extensions	No	For more information, see `http://www.php.net/~sterling/mono/`.
Prolog	P#	Yes	Instead of using a compiler, P# uses a translator that produces C#, which can then be compiled with a standard C# compiler. For more information, see `http://www.dcs.ed.ac.uk/home/jjc`.
Python	IronPython	No	For more information, see `http://ironpython.com/`.

Table 8-1. Available .NET Languages (Continued)

Standard Language	.NET Language	CLS Extender	Notes
Python	PythonNET	No	For more information, see `http://www.zope.org/Members/Brian/PythonNet/index_html`.
Python	Python for .NET	Yes	A research project that demonstrates the ability to compile Python code into IL, Python for .NET does not provide production-enabling performance. For more information, see `http://www.activestate.com/.NET`.
RPG	AVR RPG	Yes	For more information, see `http://www.asna.com`.
Smalltalk	S#	Yes	For more information, see `http://www.smallscript.org`.
Visual Basic	VB.NET	Yes	Included with Visual Studio.NET, Mono, and PNET.

Not all of these compilers run on all platforms, but because they mostly generate managed code, the compilers can be hosted on a supported platform to compile code into assemblies, which can subsequently be run on a platform of choice.

CAUTION Because .NET contains some features that have no direct equivalent in certain languages, some of the compilers rely on modified versions of their language to allow them to can act as CLS consumers. Before attempting to compile source code into managed code, you should therefore check the specific details of the language to determine whether any modifications need to be made to the source code.

To demonstrate the power of .NET's intra-operability features, we look at an example that highlights how versatile .NET is as an integration tool by seeing how .NET code can be integrated with its biggest rival: Java.

Java and .NET Intra-operability

While the rivalry between Java and .NET and their respective champions, Sun and Microsoft, is well documented, when the two technologies are compared objectively, the similarities between them suggest that they are highly suitable partners for a bit of tête-à-tête intra-operability.

The Java Platform

While this is not the place to discuss Java in any real depth, we think it's worthwhile to give a brief précis for those readers who have been living under a rock. Although Java is often considered foremost as a language, it is much more than that. It includes a virtual machine, an extensive class library, and a veritable swath of design guidelines. Taking these facts together with Java's mantra of "Write once, run anywhere," it does not take much insight to see why Java is sometimes referred to as a platform in its own right.

While the Java language bears more than a passing resemblance to C#, it's not only the languages' syntax that are similar, but a striking correspondence also exists between Java's class libraries and the .NET Framework Class Library. In practice, this means that Java experience is easily transferable to .NET and vice versa.

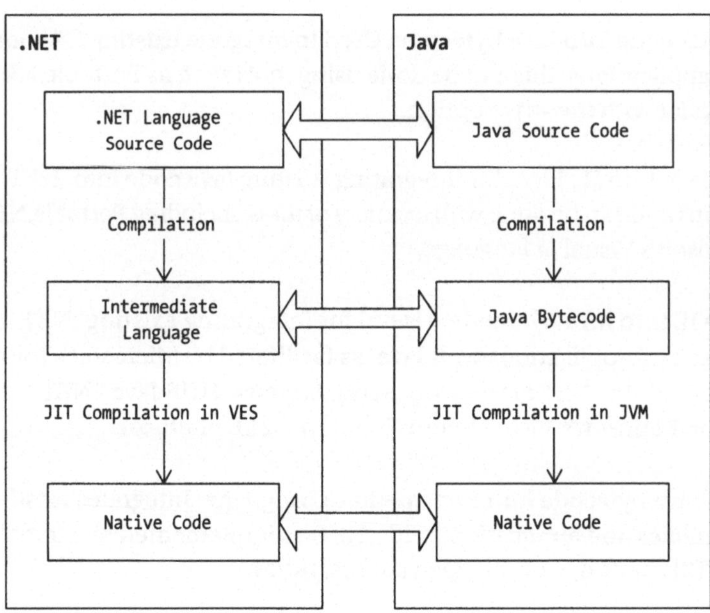

If we compare Java to .NET, we can safely say the following:

- The Java language is equivalent to a .NET language.
- The Java bytecode is equivalent to the Intermediate Language (IL).
- The Java Virtual Machine, or JVM, is equivalent to the Virtual Execution System.

The Java language, which is commonly stored in `.java` files, is compiled by a Java compiler into Java bytecode. The bytecode is stored in `.class` files, which can then be run on any Java Virtual Machine.

While it wasn't explicitly designed for the purpose of intra-operability, the JVM has been targeted by a multitude of languages. This means that like .NET, the Java platform facilitates intra-operability, but because it was not designed for that purpose, Java's intra-operability features are not as clearly supported as .NET is by the Common Language System and Common Type System.

With .NET and Java being as close to each other as any pair of siblings born a decade apart, the number of options for intra-operability between Java and .NET are multitudinous. This broad range of options allows .NET and Java intra-operability to be tailored for a wide range of development strategies. The main intra-operability options available today are as follows:

- **Compile C# code into Java bytecode:** Used to integrate existing C# code into Java applications, this can be done using tools such as Portable.NET's `cscc` compiler with the `-mjvm` option.

- **Compile Java into IL:** Ideal for integrating existing Java code into .NET applications and can be done with a variety of tools, including Portable.NET and Microsoft's Visual J# language.

- **Translate IL into Java bytecode:** Useful for integrating existing .NET assemblies and applications with Java, as facilitated by Microsoft's Jbimp, (available with the .NET Framework SDK), Stryon's iHUB Java 2NET Bridge, and Mainsoft's Visual MainWin for the J2EE platform.

- **Translate Java bytecode into Intermediate Language:** Integrates existing Java assemblies and applications with .NET, as implemented by Stryon's iHUB NET2Java Bridge or the open source, IKVM.

- **Translate Java into C#:** Useful for porting Java source code into C# and can be carried out with Microsoft's Java Language Conversion Assistant, which can also convert JavaServer Pages (JSPs) and servlets into ASP.NET.

- **Translate .NET Assemblies into Java:** Can be used to port existing .NET assemblies and applications to Java and can be done by using tools such as Stryon's iNET IL2java.

Because Java and .NET are so intra-operable, the burning issue of "Mine is better than yours," which is so popular with technology fundamentalists, is largely irrelevant and decidedly a damp squib. We're not saying that Java and .NET do not have notable differences, but where Java is like skinning a cat, .NET is like decanting a cat skin.

Bridging Java to .NET: IKVM

To demonstrate some live Java and .NET intra-operability, we use the open source IKVM, which is a Java Virtual Machine written in .NET and which currently runs under Microsoft .NET and Mono.

TIP You can download binary files and source code for IKVM from `http://weblog.ikvm.net`.

IKVM works by translating Java bytecode into the equivalent Intermediate Language at runtime. This requires mapping elements of the Java object model to the .NET object model and handling calls to the Java class libraries with a .NET assembly that implements the Java class library.

The main components of IKVM, shown in Figure 8-2, are as follows:

- The `ikvm.exe` loader, which loads the IKVM runtime and instigates program execution.

- The `ikvmstub.exe` stub generator, which can be run against a .NET assembly to create stub classes so that Java programs can be compiled against .NET types.

- The VM runtime, `IKVM.Runtime.dll`, which carries out Just-In-Time (JIT) compilation and verification of Java bytecode to IL, remaps common Java objects to their equivalent .NET objects, and executes the resulting code.

- The `IKVM.GNU.Classpath.dll` assembly, which contains a managed version of the Java class library. The classpath assembly is not part of IKVM but is a version of GNU Classpath that has been compiled into an assembly. See `http://www.gnu.org/software/classpath/` for more details on GNU Classpath.

- The optional `IKVM.JNI.CLR-Win32.dll` assembly, which implements the Java Native Interface for Microsoft .NET and is not compatible with other CLI implementations.
- The optional `IKVM.JNI.Mono.dll` assembly, which implements the Java Native Interface for Mono and is not compatible with other CLI implementations.

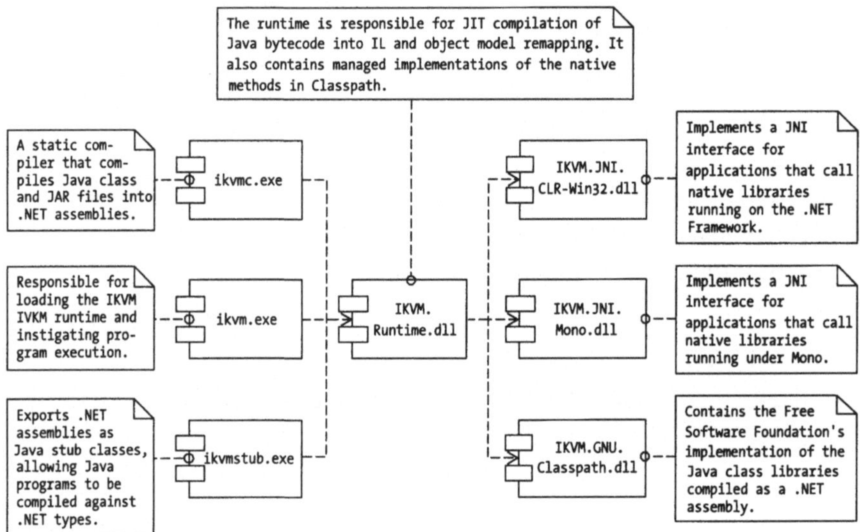

Figure 8-2. The IKVM runtime environment

Although the idea of getting Java integrated with .NET might seem tricky to follow at first, a few simple examples can demonstrate how easy it actually is.

A Simple Example

To demonstrate IKVM in action, we start with the simplest Java program imaginable, which we save in the file `Hello.java`. Even if you have no Java experience, it should not be overly taxing to work out what the program can do.

NOTE The source code samples for this chapter can be found in the Downloads section of this book's Web site (`http://www.cross-platform.net`) and the Apress Web site (`http://www.apress.com`). The code for this example can be found in the `Chapter_08/HelloJava` directory. Because IKVM does not currently work with Portable.NET version 0.6.6, we do not demonstrate the examples in this section on Portable.NET. However, this situation is likely to change with one of the future releases of Portable.NET.

The Java program's code is as follows:

```
//Hello.java
public class Hello
{
  public static void main(String args[])
  {
    System.out.println("Hello from Java!");
  }
}
```

Once you have saved the file, the `Hello.java` file can be compiled into the `Hello.class` file with the following command, as demonstrated here on Windows using Sun's `javac` compiler:

```
C:\MS.NET> javac Hello.java
```

NOTE You can download a variety of different Java compilers, virtual machines, and environments from a multitude of suppliers. The choice includes everything from Sun's full-blown Enterprise Edition, J2EE, to open source implementations. For this example, we settled on Sun's J2SE Software Development Kit, which is available from `http://java.sun.com`, although any Java environment should be sufficient for these examples.

To check that the `Hello.class` program works as well in IKVM as it does in a standard JVM, we first test it with Sun's `java` loader and then run it with `ikvm`, as follows:

```
C:\MS.NET> java Hello
Hello from Java!
C:\MS.NET> ikvm Hello
Hello from Java!
C:\MS.NET>
```

You can see that for our simple example, IKVM is no different than Sun's JVM, which is what we would expect. If you stop to think that you have just run a Java class file inside the Microsoft .NET CLR, it's still pretty neat though. Nonetheless, this section is not about running Java programs but rather about intra-operability, so we modify the code slightly and try something a little different, as follows:

```
//Hello2.java
public class Hello2
{
  public static void main(String args[])
  {
    System.out.println("Hello from Java!");
    cli.System.Console.WriteLine("Hello from .NET!");
  }
}
```

Although this is essentially the same as before, we have updated the file and class name and added a rather familiar call to `System.Console.WriteLine`, with the one peculiarity being the use of the `cli` prefix. IKVM requires that all .NET namespaces are prefixed with `cli`. This avoids clashes between .NET namespaces and Java package names.

To compile the `Hello2.java` file, we now need to reference the .NET `System` namespace, which raises an interesting issue: The Java compiler needs to reference an assembly, but it has no idea what a .NET assembly is. IKVM gets around this by supplying a variety of stub classes that are stored in Java JAR files—or compressed packages. These stub classes only contain declarations of the .NET Framework classes, but they fool the compiler into thinking that it has an implementation for the .NET classes and therefore allows compilation to succeed. When the IKVM runtime comes across a reference to a stub class, the runtime connects the reference to the real .NET implementation.

If you downloaded IKVM's source code, the classpath directory will contain some prebuilt JAR files for some of the main assemblies in the Microsoft .NET Framework. To run IKVM against a different CLI implementation, you need to create your own stub classes using the `ikvmstub.exe` program.

For this example, we only need access types in the `mscorlib.dll` assembly. This means that we only need to run `ikvmstub.exe` against the `mscorlib.dll` assembly for our chosen CLI implementation.

On Mono and GNU/Linux, creating a JAR file for `mscorlib.dll` can be done with the following command, which creates `mscorlib.jar` in the current working directory:

```
mono@linux:~ % mono ikvmstub.exe /usr/local/lib/mscorlib.dll
```

Once we've created the stub classes, we can compile the `Hello2.java` program by referencing the `mscorlib.jar` file, as demonstrated on GNU/Linux as follows:

```
mono@linux:~ % javac Hello2.java -classpath ./mscorlib.jar
```

The Hello2 program can now be tested by executing the following command, which, unlike IKVM for Windows, uses a colon instead of a semicolon to separate the classpath entries:

```
mono@linux:~ % mono ikvm.exe -cp .:./mscorlib.jar Hello2
Hello from Java!
Hello from .NET!
mono@linux:~ %
```

So there you have it! The Hello2 program has now generated output not only from Java's System.out class but also from .NET's System.Console class. Apart from touching on the underlying power of Java and .NET intra-operability, this also demonstrates that both class libraries can live together amicably in the same program.

Intra-operable Oddities

One noteworthy side effect of the Java class library being implemented in the IKVM.GNU.Classpath.dll assembly is that the Java class library becomes available to all .NET consumers, as demonstrated by the call to the Math.random method in the following C# program:

```
//Filename: Perversion.cs
using java.lang;

//Fear to tread where nonsense prevails...
class Perversion
{
    static void Main()
    {
        System.Console.WriteLine(Math.random());
    }
}
```

While such techniques might interest developers with a strong Java background, repeated indulgence in the Java class libraries is a sure sign of language insecurity and should probably be dealt with by a cathartic cup of coffee.

To finish off this discussion of intra-operability, we consider a fictional, but potentially realistic, business situation.

Using .NET to Integrate VB6 with Java

The highly successful Caffeine Corporation has just brought troubled software manufacturer Gatessoft and needs to integrate bits of its software into Caffeine's own products. While Gatessoft was a devout Windows shop and has reams of VB6 code, Caffeine Corp. is a religious advocate of GNU/Linux, with all of its software written in Java.

While one option would have been for Caffeine Corp. to run the legacy VB6 code on Windows and use .NET Remoting to communicate with the VB objects by using COM interoperability, Caffeine Corp. strategically decided to integrate various bits of Gatessoft's code by using .NET to glue VB code to its Java code.

The legacy VB code is first converted into VB.NET code before it is compiled into .NET assemblies. Because the Caffeine Corp. employees have their work cut out for them, we focus on how they might reuse a simple Soundex algorithm, which produces a phonetic encoding of a word and can be used to hash surnames for database lookups.

NOTE The code for this example can be found in the `Chapter_08/Soundex` directory at this book's Web site (`http://www.cross-platform.net`) and the Apress Web site (`http://www.apress.com`).

The VB Phoneticator Assembly

Although Visual Basic .NET is not backward compatible with Visual Basic 6, it is similar enough to allow VB6 code to be ported with a certain amount of shoehorning. See Figure 8-3.

Soundex
+Soundex(strInput: string): string

Figure 8-3. The `Soundex` *class*

In our case, the VB6 code consists of is a single file, `Soundex.cls`, which implements a VB6 class with a single function, `Soundex`, as follows:

```
'Soundex.cls
Public Function Soundex(ByVal strInput As String) As String

    Const ENCODING_LENGTH = 4

    Dim strChar As String
    Dim intCharValue As Integer
    Dim intOutputLength As Integer
    Dim intLastCharValue As Integer
    Dim intLoopVar As Integer

    Dim intInputLength As Integer : intInputLength = Len(strInput)

    'Ensure we are dealing with uppercase
    strInput = UCase(strInput)

    'Grab the first letter
    Soundex = Left$(strInput, 1)
    intOutputLength = 1

    'Encode the remaining letters as numbers
    For intLoopVar = 2 To intInputLength
        strChar = Mid(strInput, intLoopVar, 1)

        Select Case strChar
            Case "B", "P", "F", "V"
                intCharValue = 1
            Case "C", "S", "G", "J", "K", "Q", "X", "Z"
                intCharValue = 2
            Case "D", "T"
                intCharValue = 3
            Case "L"
                intCharValue = 4
            Case "M", "N"
                intCharValue = 5
            Case "R"
                intCharValue = 6
        End Select
```

```
        If (intCharValue And (intCharValue <> intLastCharValue)) Then
            Soundex = Soundex & CStr(intCharValue)
            intOutputLength = intOutputLength + 1
            If (intOutputLength = ENCODING_LENGTH) Then Exit For
        End If

        intLastCharValue = intCharValue : intCharValue = 0
    Next

    'Add zeroes if the encoding is short
    If (intOutputLength < ENCODING_LENGTH) Then
        Soundex = Soundex & String(ENCODING_LENGTH - intInputLength, "0")
    End If

End Function
```

While an in-depth explanation of the code falls outside this chapter's scope, the function takes a single `String` parameter and returns the Soundex encoding of that string, which consists of the first letter of the input string followed by three digits. If the input string is not long enough to produce a four-character encoding, the encoding is padded with zeroes.

The Soundex Algorithm

The Soundex algorithm is a method for hashing English words—and typically surnames—into a small code space based on pronunciation rather than spelling. The traditional algorithm was first used during the 1880 U.S. census. The algorithm approximates the sound of the word by reducing each word into a string of four characters, with the first character being an uppercase letter and the remaining characters being digits that represent the word's initial consonants.

For example, when the name *Ashcraft* is encoded, the algorithm returns a value of A226. Although this might not look particularly spectacular in its own right, if we consider the name *Ashcroft* or *Ashkraft*, both encoded values are A226. This makes Soundex very useful for indexing English surnames.

While better phonetic encoding algorithms exist (such as Metaphone), Soundex includes a number of variants that offer slightly different phonetic accuracies, and due to the low computational overhead for encoding Soundex, it has seen widespread use to the detriment of the more phonetically accurate algorithms.

Porting VB6 code to VB.NET can be fraught with difficulties, depending on exactly which VB6 features the code was originally implemented with, but luckily for us, the `Soundex` code is a particularly clean sample.

We first need to copy the code into a new file, `Phoneticator.vb`. We then modify the file to import the `Microsoft.Visualbasic` namespace, which implements the majority of the old VB6 functions. Then we declare the file's CLS compliance and wrap the `Soundex` function within the `Phoneticator` namespace and `Phoneticator` class declaration, as follows:

```
'Phoneticator.vb
Imports Microsoft.VisualBasic

'Guarantee CLS compliance
<Assembly: CLSCompliant(True)>

Namespace Phoneticator
    Public Class Phoneticator
        Public Function Soundex  (ByVal strInput As String) As String
            'Implementation left out for brevity...
        End Function
    End Class
End Namespace
```

Because we have imported the `Microsoft.VisualBasic` namespace, the rest of the code is almost entirely compatible with VB.NET, apart from the third-to-last line, which uses the VB6 `String` function and clashes with the .NET `String` type:

```
Soundex = Soundex & String(ENCODING_LENGTH - intInputLength, "0")
```

This can be easily fixed by replacing the call to `String` to the `StrDup()` method, which takes the same parameters and only differs in name, as follows:

```
Soundex = Soundex & StrDup(ENCODING_LENGTH - intInputLength, "0")
```

After we have made the changes, we can compile the `Soundex.dll` assembly by using one of the VB.NET compilers. Because Mono's `mbas` compiler is heavily under development at the time of this writing, we focus on the .NET Framework's `vbc.exe` compiler, which can be used as follows:

```
C:\MS.NET> vbc /t:library Soundex.vb /r:Microsoft.VisualBasic.dll
Microsoft (R) Visual C# .NET Compiler version 7.10.3052.4
for Microsoft (R) .NET Framework version 1.1.4322
Copyright (C) Microsoft Corporation 2001-2002. All rights reserved.

C:\MS.NET>
```

Now that we have compiled our VB assembly, we need to test that it fulfils its role. This involves writing a simple Java program to put the VB.NET Soundex assembly through its paces.

Calling VB from Java

The Java program consists of a single `Soundex.java` file, which contains minimal logic, as follows:

```
//Soundex.java

//All .NET namespaces begin with cli.
import cli.Phoneticator.*;

public class Soundex
{
    //Display the program's output
    private static void printResults(String name, String encoding)
    {
      System.out.println("The soundex encoding of " + name + " is " + encoding);
    }

    public static void main(String args[])
    {
        //The name to encode should be the only argument
        if (args.length != 1)
        {
            System.out.println("Please pass in a surname to encode.");
        }
        else
        {
            String surname = args[0];
            printResults(surname, Phoneticator.Soundex(surname));
        }
    }
}
```

Before we do anything else with the `Soundex.java` file, Java needs stub classes for the `Phoneticator.dll` assembly, which we can create by using the `ikvmstub.exe` program again, as follows:

```
C:\MS.NET> ikvmstub Phoneticator.dll
Warning: Assembly loaded from c:\MS.NET\phoneticator.dll instead
C:\MS.NET>
```

After the program has completed running, a new file called `Phoneticator.jar` is created in the current working directory. We can now use this file as a reference when compiling `Soundex.java`.

TIP You can also access .NET classes from Java without creating stub classes, by using Java's `Class.forName()` method and Java Reflection.

The `Soundex.java` file can be compiled by using the following command:

```
C:\MS.NET> javac -classpath Phoneticator.jar Soundex.java
C:\MS.NET>
```

We can now run the program with IKVM like this:

```
C:\MS.NET> ikvm -classpath .;Phoneticator.jar Soundex Ashcraft
The Soundex of Ashcraft is A226
C:\MS.NET>
```

This is excellent proof that Java and .NET can intra-operate seamlessly. The example that you just saw might be a mite elemental, but it nonetheless shows the underlying power of .NET's architecture and illustrates how .NET can be used to merge functionality that is developed in different languages and for different platforms.

While the critics might choose to waste their time throwing bricks at either technology, the truth is that they both work well together and can undoubtedly be two of the most important tools in any developer's toolkit for many years to come. Although we have only focused on one tool, if the ever-increasing number of .NET and Java intra-operability products is anything to go by, in all likelihood, Java and .NET will get closer together in the future. The critics might eventually be silenced as the boundaries between Java and .NET gradually become amorphous.

What's in a Name: Windows

Back in the days when MS-DOS advocates disparagingly referred to Mac OSs as having a Windows, Icons, Mice and Pointers, or WIMP interface, Microsoft's dream of an advanced GUI-based operating system was quickly taking shape. By the time the new operating system was ready to be rolled out, it was Microsoft's marketing whiz, Rowland Hanson, who sealed the company's fate by convincing Bill Gates that *Windows* wasn't a feeble name but instead a stroke of marketing genius. Just imagine how the world would be different today if Mr. Gates had stuck to his preferred moniker, the exciting, guaranteed-to-sell-a-million-copies *Interface Manager*.

Interoperability

Interoperability can be defined as the capability of two or more systems to operate effectively together, via the exchange of information or by the provision and consumption of services. In the context of .NET, interoperability relates to the ability of .NET programs to communicate with other programs, which may or may not be running within a .NET CLI and are potentially running on different operating systems and hardware platforms. While the discussion on distributed applications in Chapter 6 covered some specific types of interoperable programs, we now take a broader look at the issue of making interoperable software.

The basis of making any system interoperable involves either using a predefined communication mechanism or implementing and clearly defining your own communication mechanism. This could theoretically be anything from a shared file format or a binary interface to a full-blown network protocol. Of course, the trick to maximizing a system's potential interoperability is not to roll out your own mechanism but rather to use one of the existing mechanisms. For .NET, this means one of the following choices:

- **Web services:** As mentioned in Chapter 6, Web services are touted as a strong contender for the interoperability crown, and they provide a common communication mechanism for the widest variety of technologies and platforms. Although Web services cannot match the performance of alternate technologies, they are ideal for servicing unknown client applications or applications on the other side of a firewall.

- **Component-based architecture:** By building a system with a common component architecture, the system can duly communicate with other systems that use the same component architecture. Although .NET does not define a component architecture in the traditional sense of the Component Object Model (COM) or the Common Object Request Broker Architecture (CORBA), it is nonetheless a suitable option for integrating with existing systems and is discussed in depth, later in the chapter.

- **.NET Remoting:** The generally proscribed solution for ensuring interoperability between .NET systems is .NET's Remoting infrastructure, which is a highly configurable mechanism for remotely accessing objects. Although Remoting is generally touted as providing interoperability between .NET implementations, the Remoting.Corba project demonstrates that Remoting can also be used for interoperability with systems not running under .NET.

- **Network protocols:** Because a number of well-defined network protocols adroitly perform specific purposes, it makes sense to use an existing protocol that implements the required services. For example, a system that deals with the storage and retrieval of files could use the File Transfer Protocol (FTP), and a system that sends instant messages could use Internet Relay Chat (IRC) or Jabber. Although implementing a full-blown network protocol from scratch is an arduous task, a growing number of .NET assemblies implement various network protocols and are an ideal basis for making specific types of interoperable systems.

- **Common data format:** The simplest way for two systems to interoperate is for them to share data in a predefined format. Because eXtensible Markup Language (XML) is now the de facto format for data exchange and .NET contains a broad range of classes for handling XML files, the simplest way to make a system interoperable is to produce or consume XML files that adhere to a defined schema.

With this wide variety of mechanisms to choose from, .NET unquestionably allows you to select the right interoperability mechanism to suit the exact requirements for an application. Because we have already demonstrated Web services, common data formats speaks for themselves, and network protocols are a complex topic that falls outside of our mandate, we focus on .NET's two most important interoperability mechanisms for the rest of the chapter: *Remoting* and *Components.*

.NET Remoting

.NET Remoting—or, as the cognoscenti call it, *Remoting*—is the mechanism that lets objects that are running in different application domains to communicate with each other. In practice, this means that it allows objects to correspond with each other, whether they're running in different application domains in a single process, in different processes on the same computer, or in processes running on any number of computers that are connected over network. Figure 8-4 illustrates the different circumstances under which Remoting is used.

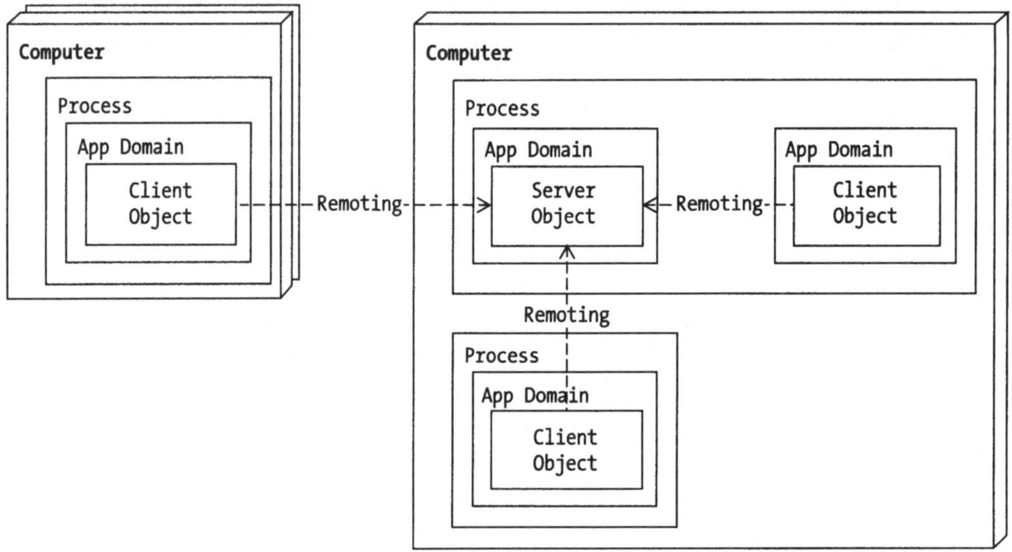

Figure 8-4. .NET Remoting boundaries

The good news for the cross-platform developer is that because Remoting is a fundamental part of the CLI infrastructure, Microsoft .NET, Mono, and Portable.NET all contain highly compatible Remoting implementations. These implementations can be accessed programmatically through the `System.Runtime.Remoting` namespace and a number of ancillary namespaces.

TIP For thorough coverage of Remoting, read Ingo Rammer's excellent book *Advanced .NET Remoting* (Apress, 2002), which sensibly comes in both C# and VB.NET flavors.

One of the nicest features of Remoting, which has put a tear in the eye of many a developer on first sight, is that it carefully abstracts interprocess communication, providing an easily customizable infrastructure with great flexibility, without requiring any low-level knowledge about encoding or communication protocols.

Of course, sometimes an application requires special treatment, and the Remoting object model provides plenty of scope to override default behaviors. The object model does anything from overriding the interception and lifetime of remote objects to the implementation of new communication channels and message formatters. We don't even dare to contemplate the breadth of Remoting in this section, but instead, we scratch the surface and show enough detail to open the discussion on interoperability and the relevance that it holds for cross-platform development.

Application Domain Contexts

Although Remoting is generally only considered in the context of distributed applications, it is actually the tip of .NET's advanced interception mechanism, which allows custom services to be hooked on method calls. As programming legend Don Box puts it: "The CLR provides a rich architecture for modelling method invocation as an exchange of messages."[3]

While it's certainly true to say that the application domain is the most common Remoting boundary, there is another Remoting boundary, called a .NET *context*. Every application domain can potentially be subdivided into a number of contexts, with the communication between different contexts being subsequently handled by Remoting. An application domain's objects can then be described as *context-agile* or *context-bound*, where all objects are explicitly context-agile unless their class derives directly or indirectly from `ContextBoundObject`. As a rule, context-bound objects are created in the same context as their creator, unless they have context attributes that require a differently configured context.

A detailed discussion of contexts is beyond the scope of book. However, note that contexts allow Remoting's message-passing infrastructure to be used within an application domain.

Marshaling Objects

Before an object can be used across a Remoting boundary it must be prepared for cross-boundary communication in is a process known as *marshaling*. Depending on the implementation details of an object's underlying class, it can be marshaled in one of three different ways: unmarshallable, marshal-by-value, and marshal-by-reference.

The simplest case of marshaling—which is technically not a type of marshaling—is for an object not to be marshaled and is shown in Figure 8-5.

---

3. Don Box and Chris Sells, *Essential .NET Volume 1: The Common Language Runtime* (Reading, MA: Addison-Wesley, 2003).

This means that it cannot be used across a Remoting boundary. Objects that are unmarshallable are fairly irrelevant to our current discussion, but it's worth pointing out that by default, all .NET classes cannot be marshaled.

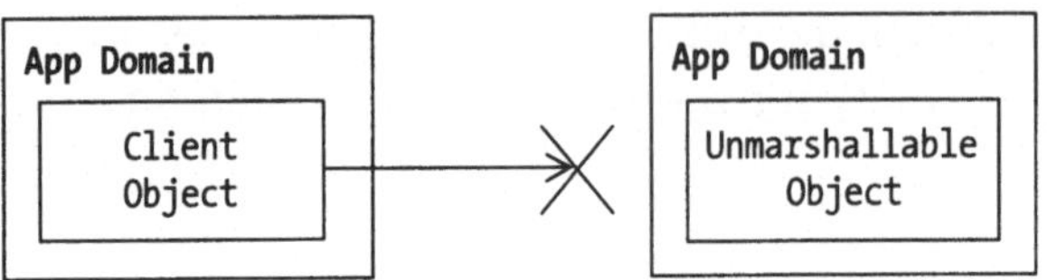

Figure 8-5. Unmarshallable objects

For marshal-by-value objects, a physical copy of the object is constructed for passing across the Remoting boundary, as shown in Figure 8-6. In this way, marshal-by-value objects are conceptually the same as value parameters, which are parameters that are declared without the `ref` or `out` keywords. To specify that a class should create objects that are marshaled by value, the class can either be declared with the `Serializable` attribute, in which case all the public and private fields are serialized with the object, or it should implement the `ISerialize` interface, in which case the object's serialization can be customized.

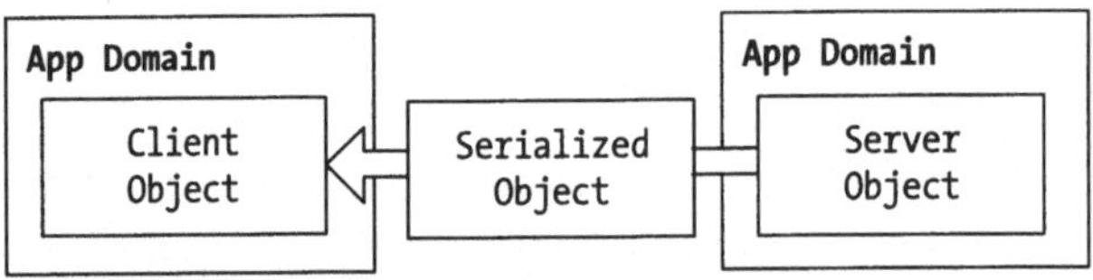

Figure 8-6. Marshaling objects by value

The final marshaling option is for objects to be marshal-by-reference, which is illustrated in Figure 8-7. This means that the object physically remains in the application domain in which it was instantiated, and any objects that want to access it from external application domains must communicate by using a proxy object. The client object interacts with the proxy as though it were the server object, and the proxy object deals with handling the call across the Remoting boundary. For an object to be marshaled by reference, it must be instantiated from a class that inherits directly or indirectly from the `MarshalByRefObject` class.

To clarify the different types of marshaling, it makes sense to mention the relationship between the different types. All parameters and return values that are declared on the methods of a marshal-by-reference object must be either marshallable by value or by reference.

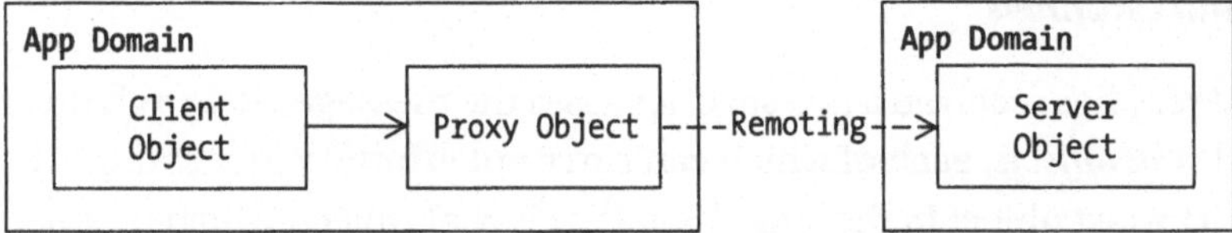

Figure 8-7. Marshaling objects by reference

NOTE Because marshaling is defined for objects, it is worth considering how static members work. After all, static members are not associated with a particular object, so how can they be marshaled? In fact, static members cannot be marshaled, which means that static methods are always run within the Remoting boundary in which they are called.

Before we demonstrate how the various marshaling options work in the real world, we need to dig a little deeper into the internals of the Remoting infrastructure. This gives you a good background for understanding some of the material later in the chapter.

The Remoting Architecture

As mentioned earlier, Remoting is part of .NET's interception mechanism, which allows the CLI's usual stack-based method calls to be converted into message-based calls. Before we go any further, however, we must come clean and admit that when we described marshaling by reference, we mentioned a proxy object. This object was actually a euphemism for a mob of various objects that we will now have a closer look at.

Proxies and Messages

When a client interacts with a marshal-by-reference object, it instead deals with an object called a *transparent proxy*, which is automatically generated by the CLI. When the transparent proxy receives a method call, it verifies the number and type of the call's parameters, and after checking that the parameters are valid, it packages the method call into an object that implements the `IMessage` interface. After the `IMessage` object has been created, it is passed to a `RealProxy` object, which is also automatically generated by the CLI. Unlike the transparent proxy, however, the `RealProxy`'s implementation can be overridden and provides an excellent mechanism for implementing custom Remoting solutions.

Formatters and Channels

After the RealProxy has received a message, it passes the message along a chain of objects called *sink objects*, each of which can carry out arbitrary processing on the message. The last object in the sink chain is a Channel object, which uses a Formatter object to encode the message and then transports the message using a specific protocol.

Choosing a Channel

Although the .NET Framework only comes with two channel implementations, TcpChannel and HttpChannel, due to .NET's excellent support from the development community, .NET is a bit like cable television, and it has a wealth of hearty, informative channels to choose from.

The TcpChannel formats messages with the BinaryFormatter class and provides very good performance, but because TcpChannel uses TCP/IP, it is not particularly firewall friendly. In contrast, the HttpChannel formats messages using the SoapFormatter class. This results in larger packets than the TcpChannel, but it is considerably easier to route through firewalls.

As if choosing between two channels wasn't hard enough, the steadily growing number of channels can make choosing the right channel a real headache. You have the following choices:

- **Genuine Channels:** A commercial package of channels, including a bidirectional TCP channel, an enhanced HTTP channel, a UDP channel, and a shared memory channel
- **Jabber Channel:** An open source channel that relies on the increasingly popular Jabber XML protocol
- **MSMQ Channel:** An open source channel that uses Microsoft Message Queue Server
- **Named Pipes Channel:** An open source channel that uses named pipes
- **Secure TCP Channel:** An open source TCP channel that uses RSA to encrypt the channel's contents
- **SMTP Channel:** An open source channel that uses e-mail
- **TCPEx Channel:** An open source bidirectional TCP channel

For more information on the currently available channels, go to Brian Ritchie's .NET Remoting Central, which can be found at http://www.dotnetpowered.com/remoting.aspx.

When a message arrives in the application domain, it is received by a `Channel` object, unformatted with a `Formatter`, and then passed up through a sink chain. The final object in the sink chain is a `StackBuilder`, which unpacks the `IMessage` and then invokes the real method on the server object. The relationships between these various objects are shown in Figure 8-8.

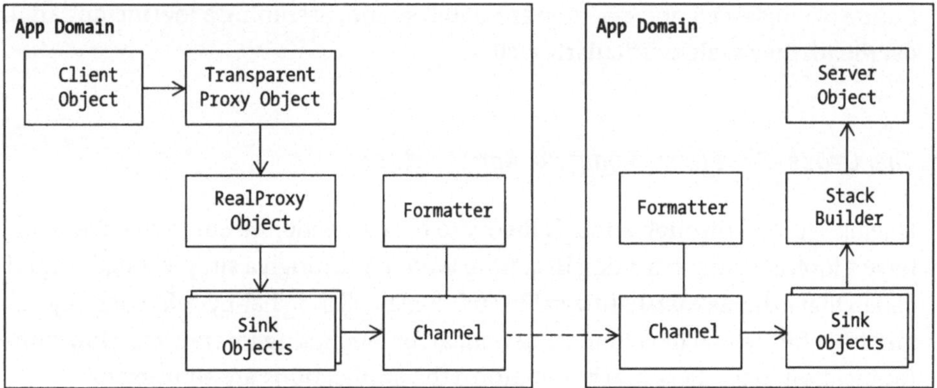

Figure 8-8. Calling a remote object

If the method being called has any `ref` or `out` parameters, or a return value, after the method call has completed, the process is reversed, and the results are sent back to the client in a new message object.

Activation Choices

The final point that we need to make about .NET Remoting is that marshal-by-reference objects come in two varieties: *client-activated* objects and *well-known* objects.

Client-activated objects are created on the server as soon as the client calls `new` and in that regard are similar to objects that are created within the client's application domain. A client-activated object can only service a single client application, and if the client application instantiates two client-activated objects of the same type, two instances are created within the remote application domain.

Well-known objects are created on the server when a client makes a method call on the object rather than when the client calls `new`, which in effect saves a network round-trip. Because their instantiation cannot be separated from a method call, unlike client-activated objects, well-known objects can only be created with a default constructor.

Just to confuse things further, two different types of well-known objects exist: *singleton* objects and *single-call* objects. A singleton object implies that only one instance of the class can exist within an application domain at one time. This means that no matter how many clients communicate with a singleton object in an application domain, they are all serviced by the same object. In contrast, single-call objects are created when a message is received from a client, and they are destroyed as soon as the message has been processed. Because of the transient nature of single-call objects, they are stateless and, assuming a low instantiation overhead, they scale particularly well.

The Cross-Platform Logging Application

Having scuttled through enough theory to bore a beetle, we cut to the chase and have a look at some Remoting in action. We work through a simple logging application that exhibits marshal-by-value and single-call marshal-by-reference objects, and hopefully show how Remoting is ideal for facilitating interapplication communication, regardless of what platform the applications are running on.

Unlike a real-world application, our application implements a minimal payload, with both the client and server programs logging details of the machines that they form connections with. The client initiates all communication by passing its details of its host computer to a method on a remote, marshal-by-reference object, which in turn returns details of the computer on which it is being hosted. Although either the client or server program could store the logged details in some kind of data repository, for the purposes of this demonstration, we output logged details to the console.

The application is formed from three different assemblies: a client program, `SimpleClient.exe`; a server program, `SimpleServer.exe`; and an assembly that contains the implementation of the remote objects, `RemoteObjects.dll`.

TIP Because PNET doesn't currently contain the main Remoting assembly, `System.Runtime.Remoting.dll`, and it only contains a partial implementation of `System.Runtime.Serialization.Soap.dll`, you must copy these two libraries from Mono to get this example working. This process of hybridization was discussed in Chapter 3 and simply requires the two assemblies to be copied into PNET's `/lib/cscc/lib` directory.

As shown in Figure 8-9, the `RemoteObjects.dll` assembly is present on both the client and server computers.

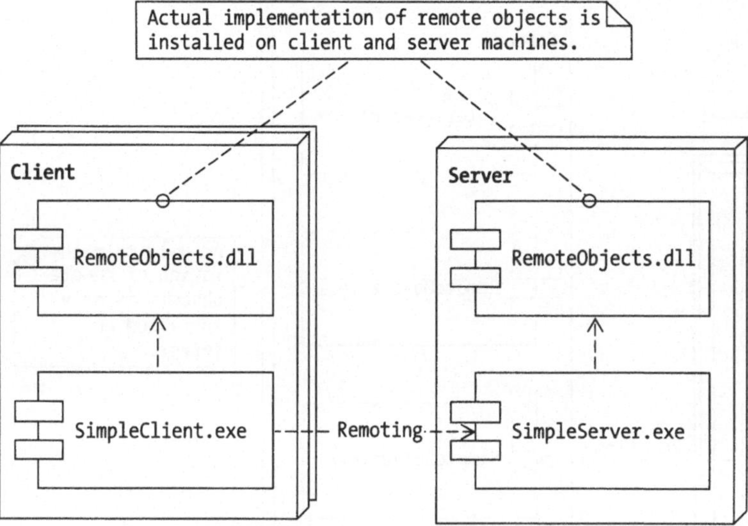

Figure 8-9. Simple remote application deployment

In many situations, it would be preferable not to require the presence of the remote objects on the client computer. The two most frequently cited reasons are as follows:

- The need to secure application logic (by stopping interested parties from peeking through the code)
- The need to simplify client installation

Installing the remote objects on the client computer can be avoided by careful use of interfaces. The remote objects are made to implement interfaces, and the client program is programmed against the interfaces rather than the concrete types.

An assembly that contains the interface definitions is then installed on the client computer, as shown in Figure 8-10, but the actual implementation of the remote objects is kept safely in an assembly on the server computer. As long as the remote objects still conform to the interface definitions, their implementation can change without having to recompile the client program. This not only helps with maintenance, but it also allows sensitive code to be kept off the client computers.

Because we are installing both the client and server programs on our computers in the current example, we have no reason to use interfaces, but it is a good practice to follow for applications where the server and client programs will not be run on the same computers.

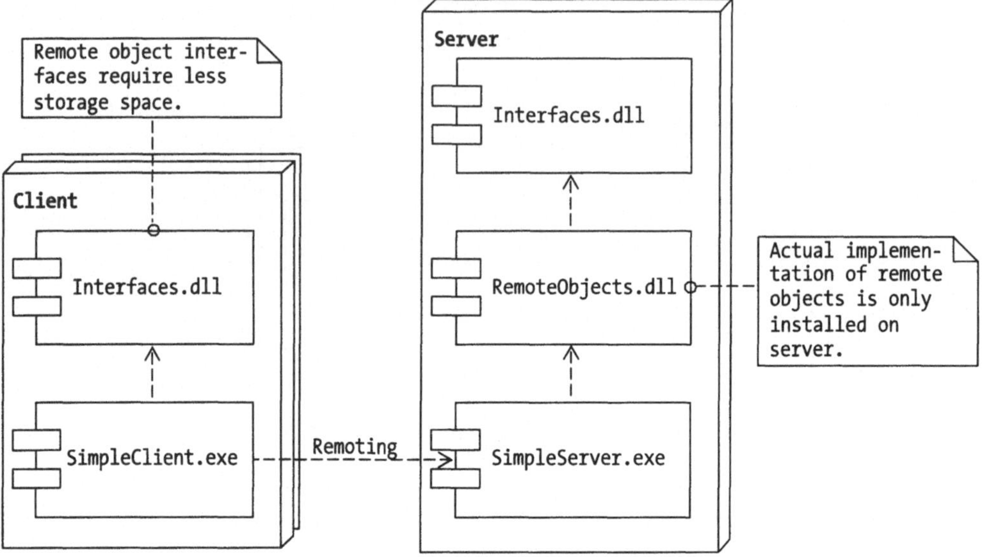

Figure 8-10. Remote application deployment using interfaces

NOTE The code for this example can be found in the `Chapter_08/RemoteObjects` directory at this book's Web site (`http://www.cross-platform.net`) and the Apress Web site (`http://www.apress.com`).

The RemoteObjects.dll Assembly

The application's communication is carried out through the interaction of two classes, `HostDetails` and `RemoteLog`, which we implement in the `RemoteObjects.dll` assembly, as shown in Figure 8-11.

HostDetails
+UserName: string +OperatingSystem: string +TimeStamp: DateTime
+LogAccess(HostDetails, TextWriter)

Figure 8-11. The `HostDetails` *class*

The HostDetails class is used to transport the data across the Remoting boundary and therefore needs to be implemented as a marshal-by-value object. Because this example is just a demonstration, we settle for passing some data that should be familiar from earlier chapters, although in practice, you could pass any data that took your fancy. As mentioned earlier, marshal-by-value objects must either be declared with the Serializable attribute or they must implement the ISerialize interface. Because the default serialization is adequate for our needs, we settle for using a Serializable attribute, as follows:

```
//Filename: RemoteObjects.cs
using System;
using System.IO;

namespace Crossplatform.NET.Chapter8
{
    [Serializable]
    public class HostDetails
    {
        private string userName;
        private string operatingSystem;
        private DateTime timeStamp;

        //Provide a default constructor
        public HostDetails()
        {
            this.userName = Environment.UserName + "@" + Environment.MachineName;
            this.operatingSystem = Environment.OSVersion.Platform.ToString();
            this.timeStamp = DateTime.Now;
        }

        public string UserName
        {
            get { return this.userName; }
        }

        public string OperatingSystem
        {
            get { return this.operatingSystem; }
        }

        public DateTime TimeStamp
        {
            get { return this.timeStamp; }
        }
```

Apart from some private fields that are used for storing the actual data, the HostDetails class is extremely lightweight and contains a read-only property for each of the private fields. To finish the class, we add the static LogAccess() method that can be used to write data from a HostDetails object to a TextWriter. The method is called by the client and server programs when logging details, and is as follows:

```
        public static void LogAccess(HostDetails clientDetails, TextWriter
logWriter)
        {
            //Bow to simplicity and log in to the console...
            logWriter.WriteLine("Connection at {0} to user {1} (running {2})",
                                clientDetails.TimeStamp.ToString(),
                                clientDetails.UserName,
                                clientDetails.OperatingSystem);
        }
    }
```

In contrast to the HostDetails class, the second class, RemoteLog, is marshaled by reference and therefore needs to derive from MarshalByRefObject, as illustrated in Figure 8-12.

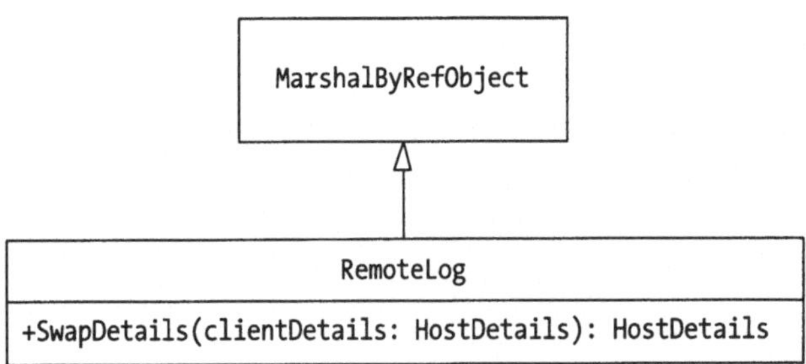

Figure 8-12. The RemoteLog *class*

RemoteLog contains one method, SwapDetails(), which takes a single HostDetails parameter that it writes to the log before returning a HostDetails object for the computer that it executed on, as follows:

```
    public class RemoteLog : MarshalByRefObject
    {
        public HostDetails SwapDetails(HostDetails clientDetails)
        {
            HostDetails.LogAccess(clientDetails, System.Console.Out);
            return new HostDetails();
        }
    }
}
```

To compile the `RemoteObjects.dll` assembly on Microsoft .NET, run the following command:

```
C:\MS.NET> csc /t:library RemoteObjects.cs
Microsoft (R) Visual C# .NET Compiler version 7.10.3052.4
for Microsoft (R) .NET Framework version 1.1.4322
Copyright (C) Microsoft Corporation 2001-2002. All rights reserved.

C:\MS.NET>
```

For Mono running under GNU/Linux, use the following command:

```
mono@linux:~ % mcs /t:library RemoteObjects.cs
Compilation Succeeded
mono@linux:~ %
```

Finally, for Portable.NET on Mac OS X, use the following command:

```
pnet@macosx:~ % cscc /t:library RemoteObjects.cs /out:RemoteObjects.dll
pnet@macosx:~ %
```

The SimpleServer.exe Program

Now that you have an assembly that contains the remote objects, you need a program to host the `RemoteLog` objects on your server. We look at advanced hosting options later in this chapter, but in the meantime, we create a simple console program to host the objects.

The program's logic is saved in a file called `SimpleServer.cs`, which implements the `SimpleServer` class and contains a single `Main()` method that acts as the program's entry point. As you can probably tell from the namespace declarations, this example uses a TCP channel for its communication, but the HTTP channel could be used instead. The `SimpleServer` program is as follows:

```
//Filename: SimpleServer.cs
using System;
using System.Runtime.Remoting;
using System.Runtime.Remoting.Channels;
using System.Runtime.Remoting.Channels.Tcp;

namespace Crossplatform.NET.Chapter8
{
    public class SimpleServer
    {
        public static void Main()
        {
            //Register a server channel
            ChannelServices.RegisterChannel(new TcpChannel(30303));
```

The `Main()` method starts by registering a `TcpChannel` with the `ChannelServices` class, which is responsible for managing Remoting channels. Because the `TcpChannel`'s constructor is called with a port number, which we arbitrarily chose as 30303, the `RegisterChannel` method can infer that it is a server channel.

TIP The TCP channel can be configured to listen on any port number from 1 to 65,535, but because the ports under 1330 are assigned to well-known protocols, it is considered polite (and sensible) to always use a port number above 1023. If politeness or common sense is not enough to convince you of using port numbers above 1023, keep in mind that on UNIX-based systems, only the `root` user can bind to ports under 1023.

After registering the channel, the `RemoteLog` type needs to be registered as a well-known object, which is carried out with a call to the `RemotingConfiguration` class's `RegisterWellKnownServiceType` method.

```
//Register the well known object
Type rt = typeof(RemoteLog);
RemotingConfiguration.RegisterWellKnownServiceType (
                      rt, "chapter8",
                      WellKnownObjectMode.SingleCall);
```

While we are on the subject, it is worth reiterating that the `ChannelServices` class is used to manage an application domain's channels and the `RemotingConfiguration` class is used to manage remote objects. These are two vitally important classes that handle Remoting logistics, and when you get the chance, it is definitely worth investigating their other members.

As you can see, when the call to RegisterWellKnownServiceType is made, the type of the object to be hosted is passed in as a parameter, as is a URI with a value of chapter8 and the well-known object activation mode of SingleCall. Because the RemoteLog class contains no instance fields, it cannot hold state between invocations and is therefore adequate as a single-call object. As we mentioned earlier, each instance of a single-call object exists solely during the period of a method call. This means that single-call objects can be more easily scaled for high-bandwidth applications than singleton objects.

After registering the RemoteType class, the Main() method ends by printing a message to the console and allowing the user to exit the program by pressing Return.

```
            //Keep serving until told otherwise
            Console.WriteLine("Press Return to exit");
            Console.ReadLine();
        }
    }
}
```

Having run through the rather lithe implementation of the server, you can now build the SimpleServer.exe assembly on Microsoft .NET using the following command:

```
C:\MS.NET> csc SimpleServer.cs /r:System.Runtime.Remoting.dll /
r:RemoteObjects.dll
Microsoft (R) Visual C# .NET Compiler version 7.10.3052.4
for Microsoft (R) .NET Framework version 1.1.4322
Copyright (C) Microsoft Corporation 2001-2002. All rights reserved.

C:\MS.NET>
```

On Mono running under GNU/Linux, use the following command:

```
mono@linux:~ % mcs SimpleServer.cs /r:RemoteObjects.dll \

> /r:System.Runtime.Remoting.dll
Compilation Succeeded
mono@linux:~ %
```

Finally, on Portable.NET running under Mac OS X, use the following command:

```
pnet@macosx:~ % cscc SimpleServer.cs /r:System.Runtime.Remoting.dll \

> /r:RemoteObjects.dll /out:SimpleServer.exe
pnet@macosx:~ %
```

While you might be raring to test your wonderful creation, you must first create a client application, as described in the next section.

The SimpleClient.exe Program

As the final piece of the Remoting puzzle, it is now time to create a client program that you can use for flooding the server with remote method requests. The `SimpleClient.exe` program takes a single command-line argument with a hostname or IP address, which it will use in an attempt to create a channel to the server. After the program has opened a channel, it calls the `RemoteLog`'s `SwapDetails()` method and ends by printing to the console the contents of the `HostDetails` that was returned from the method call.

Once again, the file starts with some namespace declarations and then declares the `SimpleClient` class with a single method, `Main()`, as follows:

```
//Filename: SimpleClient.cs
using System;
using System.Runtime.Remoting;
using System.Runtime.Remoting.Channels;
using System.Runtime.Remoting.Channels.Tcp;

namespace Crossplatform.NET.Chapter8
{
    public class SimpleClient
    {
        public static void Main(string[] args)
        {
```

The `Main()` method starts by checking whether the program was called with a single argument. If it was, the program assumes that it was a host address. Otherwise, the program uses the local machine's loopback address, `127.0.0.1`, which will prove handy when testing both the client and server on the same machine. When the host address has been decided, it is merged into a hard-coded server address, which also specifies the server's port and URI, as previously defined in the `SimpleServer.exe` program:

```
//Use the given host address or default to the loopback address
string hostAddress = (args.Length == 1) ? args[0] : "127.0.0.1";
string serverAddress = String.Format("tcp://{0}:30303/chapter8",
                                      hostAddress);
```

The code then calls the `ChannelServices.RegisterChannel()` method, which is reminiscent of the server's code, but it does not specify a port address because it only needs to register a client channel, as follows:

```
//Register a client channel
ChannelServices.RegisterChannel(new TcpChannel());
```

Now comes the crux of the remote call as the program attempts to get a reference to a `RemoteLog` object by calling the `RemotingServices.Connect()` method. Remember that because the `RemoteLog` object is a single call object, it cannot be instantiated on the server yet, but now that the client has a reference to the remote object, it can call the object's methods as though it were local. Because making remote method calls can be prone to communication errors, we wrap the calls in a `try...catch` block, as follows:

```
try
{
    //Get a reference to the object
    RemoteLog obj = (RemoteLog)
              RemotingServices.Connect(typeof(RemoteLog),
                                       serverAddress);
```

It is now simply a matter of invoking the `SwapDetails()` method with a new instance of the `HostDetails` object, and then passing the returned `HostDetails` instance to the `LogAccess()` method, as follows:

```
    //Make the call to the object and show the results
    HostDetails sd = obj.SwapDetails(new HostDetails());
    HostDetails.LogAccess(sd, System.Console.Out);
}

catch(Exception ex)
{
    //Always be prepared...
    Console.Error.WriteLine("An error occurred: {0}", ex.Message);
}
        }
    }
}
```

So there you have it: a very simple client program to communicate with a very simple server. To get the program compiled on the .NET Framework, use the following command:

```
C:\MS.NET> csc SimpleClient.cs /r:RemoteObjects.dll
Microsoft (R) Visual C# .NET Compiler version 7.10.3052.4
for Microsoft (R) .NET Framework version 1.1.4322
Copyright (C) Microsoft Corporation 2001-2002. All rights reserved.

C:\MS.NET>
```

For Mono running under GNU/Linux, use the following command:

```
mono@linux:~ % mcs SimpleClient.cs /r:RemoteObjects.dll \

> /r:System.Runtime.Remoting.dll
Compilation Succeeded
mono@linux:~ %
```

Finally, on Portable.NET running under Mac OS X, use the following command:

```
pnet@macosx:~ % cscc SimpleClient.cs /r:RemoteObjects.dll \

> /r:System.Runtime.Remoting.dll /out:SimpleClient.exe
pnet@macosx:~ %
```

Putting It All Together

Now that all the components are ready, it's time to kick things off by firing up the `SimpleServer.exe` program on Windows. Use the following command:

```
C:\MS.NET> simpleserver.exe
Press Return to exit.
```

Before we attempt to connect to the server from another platform, try opening another command prompt and then run the `SimpleClient.exe` program without any arguments, as follows:

```
C:\MS.NET> simpleclient.exe
Connection at 16/09/2003 15:43:10 to user MJEASTON@WINDOWS (running Win32NT)

C:\MS.NET>
```

As you can see, the client printed some details and then quit, as we expected. If you have another look at the server's console window, you should find that it's been updated and now contains a connection message, as follows:

```
C:\MS.NET> simpleserver.exe
Press Return to exit.
Connection at 16/09/2003 15:43:10 to user MJEASTON@WINDOWS (running Win32NT)
```

Excellent! Everything has run smoothly, and both programs have output the message that we expected. Nonetheless, however cool it may seem, we've only managed to show a .NET program calling another program on the same machine. We now take things to the next level and run the `SimpleClient.exe` program on Mono, remembering that because the client program will not be running on the same computer, we must pass in the IP address of the server, as follows:

```
mono@linux:~ % mono SimpleClient.exe 192.168.0.3
Connection at 16/09/2003 16:02:43 to user MJEASTON@WINDOWS (running Win32NT)

mono@linux:~ %
```

As you can see, we get an almost identical message to the one that we got when running the client on Windows. While we're at it, we may as well try running the program on Portable.NET, as follows:

```
pnet@macosx:~ % mono SimpleClient.exe 192.168.0.3
Connection at 16/09/2003 16:17:27 to user MJEASTON@WINDOWS (running Win32NT)

pnet@macosx:~ %
```

If you now check the server's console window, you find that the server's log has been updated twice to show the two connections that you just made from Mono and PNET.

```
C:\MS.NET> simpleserver.exe
Press Return to exit.
Connection at 16/09/2003 15:43:10 to user MJEASTON@WINDOWS (running Win32NT)
Connection at 16/09/2003 16:02:45 to user mono@linux (running 128)
Connection at 16/09/2003 16:17:29 to user pnet@macosx (running 128)
```

And there you have it: a brief but functional example of how .NET can be used to facilitate cross-platform communication. We didn't mention a number of topics that would need to be addressed in a production system—such as the use of configuration files to store channel details or how to control object lifetimes using leasing services—but you should have a good idea about how Remoting can be used. This can serve as a good background to some of the techniques that we discuss in the section "Components," later in this chapter.

Chunky vs. Chatty Interfaces

Remoting is an excellent mechanism for distributing application logic over numerous nodes, but that is not to say that it should be used without due concern during the design phase of a project. In particular, consider that each remote method call carries with it a substantial communication overhead. Because of this transport delay, it makes sense to package a number of method calls together and request a chunk of functionality in a single request, rather than sending a piecemeal flurry of method request messages.

In particular, a stateful class's properties should not be accessed remotely but should be lumped together so that a number of the properties can be set or retrieved in a single method call.

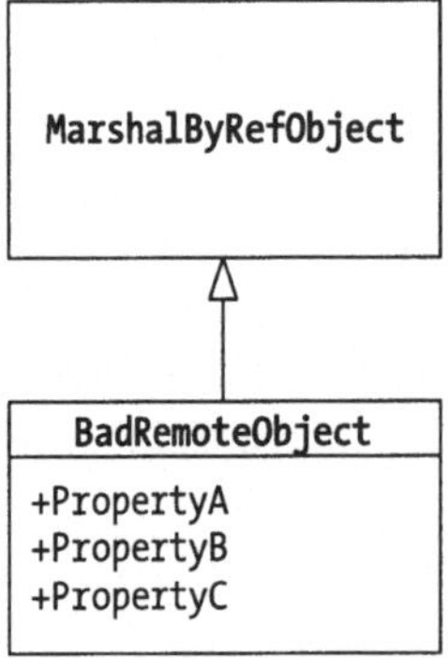

For stateful objects that do need to be accessed remotely, a popular solution is to create a class called a *remote facade*, which repackages property and method calls together, and thereby reduces the cumulative effects of network latency.

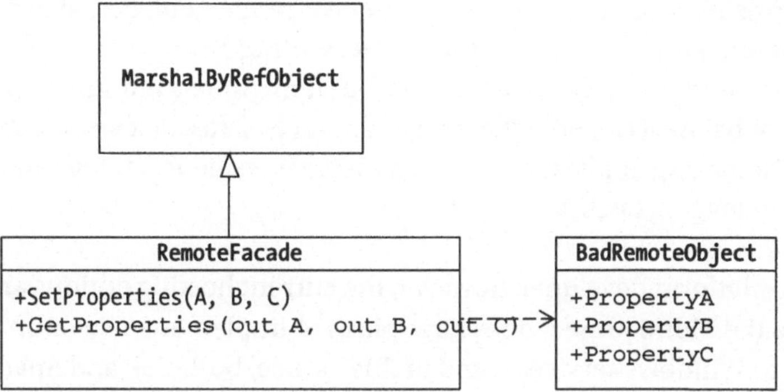

This principle not only applies to .NET Remoting but also to any other type of Remote Procedure Call (RPC) mechanism, such as Web services, and it can be reduced to the following phrase: For remote calls, chunky interfaces are preferable to chatty ones.

Hosting Remote Servers

The final Remoting issue that we need to tackle is where you should host your remote objects. In the `RemoteLog` example, we used a minimalist console program. This was fine for a quick-and-dirty example where we needed a scarcity of code, but it's not particularly worthy of a robust production system, where you're more likely to be worried by a scarcity of remote objects. You probably won't be surprised that you have three main possibilities for hosting remote objects on Windows; they are as follows:

- **An Internet Information Server (IIS):** Can be used to host remote objects that use the HTTP channel. Hosting objects in IIS is as simple as creating an IIS virtual application and then placing the relevant assemblies in the virtual application's `bin` folder, and as such, it is the simplest way to reliably host remote objects. Hosting in IIS provides the advantages that are offered by IIS's security and logging facilities, but because HTTP is slower than TCP, it is not appropriate when maximum performance is required, and neither is it appropriate when the channel might change.

- **A Windows service:** Can be used to host remote objects using any channel. Requires a host class to implement a Windows service and therefore to derive from the `ServiceBase` class. Although Windows services can be extremely reliable hosts for remote objects, a number of operational issues, such as threads, security, and logging, need to be handled by the programmer to guarantee reliability.

- **A GUI or console program:** Can be used to host remote objects using any channel. As shown in the `RemoteLog` example, writing a simple console or GUI program is ideal for demonstrations, but it might require substantial development before it can offer the infrastructural facilities that are required by serious Remoting applications, such as service resilience, integrated security, and logging facilities.

For the cross-platform developer, however, the current hosting options are a little bleak. While the Mono project does have plans to implement a daemon that's equivalent to Windows services—and in due course, both XSP and Apache can be expected to host HTTP channels—at the time of this writing, none of these are viable options.

Before you consign yourself to developing a 5,000-line console program, the good news is that you have one other option, in the form of the Mono Application Server.

The Mono Application Server

Although not officially part of the Mono project, the Mono Application Server (MAS) is designed to host various types of applications, and it can currently host Web applications using the XSP Web server, FTP applications, and remote object applications.

NOTE To find out more about the Mono Application Server or to download the latest version, go to `http://www.dotnetpowered.com/appserver.aspx`.

Apart from its attractive, Web-based administration program—seen in Figure 8-13—MAS also implements integrated security and logging and has the ability to load and unload assemblies on demand.

Because it was designed around an extensible architecture, MAS will, in all likelihood, be extended to host new application types in the future, and it is an excellent cross-platform tool for consolidating the hosting of server applications.

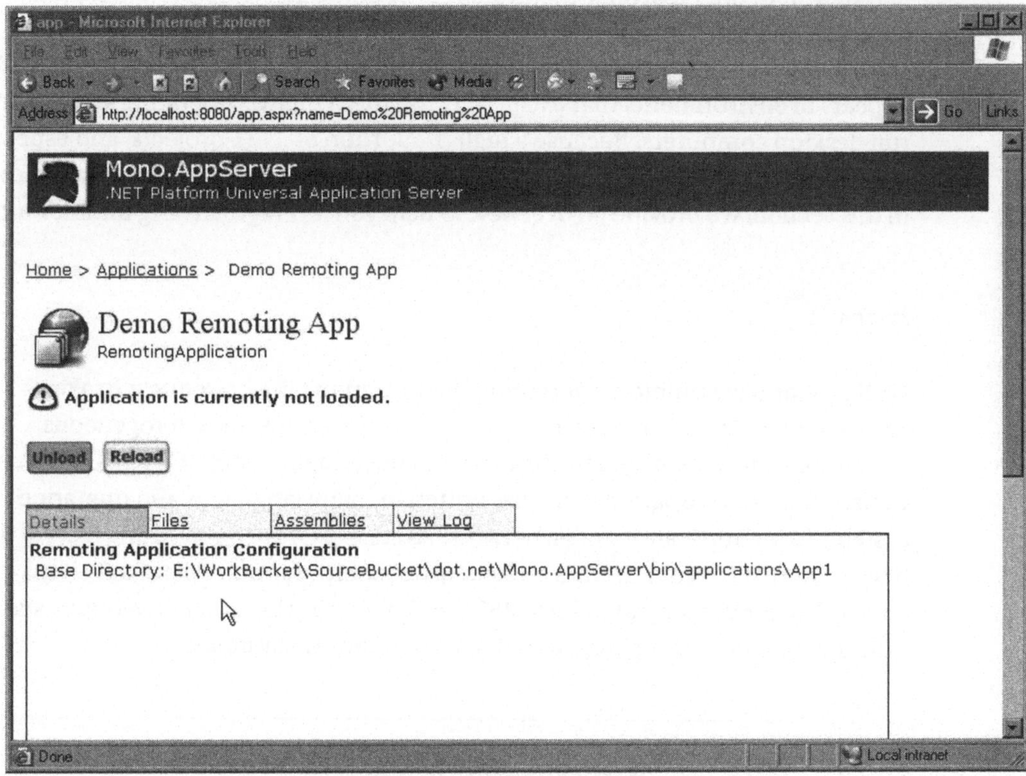

Figure 8-13. Administering the Mono Application Server

Components

After the wilderness years of the 1980s, the field of systems integration changed radically in the 1990s with the rise to power of middleware, a layer of connectivity software that provides essential services on top of legacy applications on heterogeneous platforms. Although a mixture of industry and academic organizations produced a variety of competing middleware offerings, the two that most successfully captured the world's imagination were the Object Management Group's CORBA and Microsoft's COM.

Sharing a number of similarities in their designs, CORBA and COM both provide an object-oriented approach to the systems integration conundrum and are often referred to as component-based technologies. They both allow systems to be built from different languages, they both define underlying network protocols, and they both offer a diverse assortment of application services. Nonetheless, although they are conceptually similar, they are used in quite different circumstances. CORBA is popular in completely heterogeneous environments, and COM appears in environments that exclusively use the Windows operating systems to run desktop computers. Because a high proportion of .NET projects, and especially cross-platform projects, involve integrating with component technologies, in this section, we provide an overview to help you leverage existing middleware.

CORBA

CORBA—or if we unfold its acronym, the Common Object Request Broker Architecture—is a set of open middleware specifications for heterogeneous computing and is managed by the Object Management Group (OMG). CORBA is designed to allow programs that are written in many languages and operating systems to interoperate across a network. As such, CORBA has a strong historical background as the middleware technology of choice for non-Microsoft shops and is also tightly integrated into J2EE's architecture. This makes it a highly significant technology for gluing together cross-platform systems.

NOTE For the lowdown on CORBA, go to the OMG Web site at `http://www.corba.org`.

CORBA applications consist of objects, each of which has an interface definition that is declared using the Object Management Group's Interface Definition Language (IDL). This is conceptually equivalent to the Web Service Description Language (WDSL) that is used to describe Web services. These interface definitions are syntactical contracts that declare the list of operations and parameters provided by a server object. IDL is programming language independent and has mappings to a variety of popular programming languages, which means that CORBA objects can be accessed from any language that has a mapping to OMG IDL. While no official mapping currently exists between .NET and IDL, as we will see in a short while, a number of unofficial .NET mappings are perfectly adequate for our needs.

When a client wants to invoke an operation on a CORBA object, it uses the IDL interface to specify the operation that it wants to perform and to marshal—that is, prepare—the operation's arguments. When the invocation reaches the server object, the IDL interface is used to unmarshal the arguments before the actual operation is invoked. The interface definition holds the same role when returning results to the client, marshaling the results on the server object and then unmarshaling the results when they reach the client. This is in the same concept that we introduced earlier in the explanation of .NET Remoting. To carry out the marshaling and unmarshaling, the IDL needs to be compiled into a client-side and server-side proxy. The client-side proxy is referred to as a *stub*, and the server-side proxy is referred to a *skeleton*.

As shown in Figure 8-14, the call between a stub and a skeleton is carried out by a component called an Object Request Broker (ORB). For in-process or local invocation, a single ORB can be used, and for distributed invocation, two ORBs are involved, one on the client and one on the server. The protocol that ORBs use to communicate with each other is known as the Internet Inter-ORB Protocol, or IIOP.

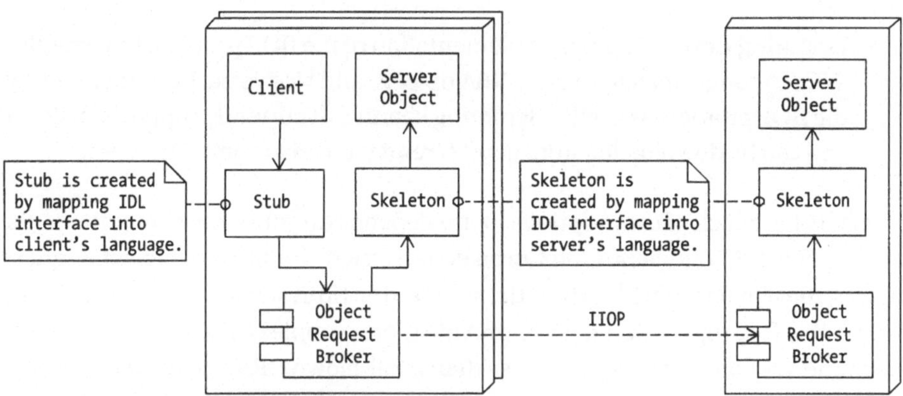

Figure 8-14. An overview of CORBA's architecture

CAUTION One criticism that is often leveled at CORBA is that although it defines a thorough set of specifications, different ORB vendors implement different subsets of the standards. This has led to certain ORBs being unable to interoperate with other ORBs. It is therefore frequently and rightly suggested that CORBA is not the paragon of interoperability that it was intended to have been. In practical terms, this means that you should always thoroughly test your .NET code with any ORBs that you intend to interoperate with—and preferably as early in the project as possible.

With CORBA being the main rival to Window's COM technology, CORBA interoperability was, for obvious reasons, not included in Microsoft's .NET Framework. However, the following three open source projects implement .NET–CORBA interoperability in a variety of ways:

- **IIOP.NET:** An implementation of the IIOP protocol that was created by the Swiss firm Elca Informatique SA and has been tested with a number of different ORBs and J2EE implementations. IIOP.NET is implemented using Remoting and is based on the CORBA 2.3.1 specifications, and it supports IIOP 1.0, 1.1, and 1.2. For more details on IIOP.NET or to download the source code or binary code, go to `http://iiop-net.sourceforge.net`.

- **The Harmless ORB:** A managed ORB implementation that is based on the openORB Java project. While Harmless has the advantage of being managed code, at the time of this writing, it does not yet implement all the CORBA 2.4.2 specifications, and it might cause problems when used in collaboration with other CORBA implementations. To download Harmless or to read a more in-depth description of its features, go to `http://harmless.sourceforge.net`.

- **Remoting.Corba:** Another implementation of the IIOP protocol that enables .NET to communicate with CORBA objects, and vice versa, by implementing the IIOP protocol as a .NET Remoting channel. It currently supports IIOP 1.0 and can be downloaded from `http://remoting-corba.sourceforge.net`.

Choosing which of these options to use depends on your project requirements. Because IIOP.NET and Remoting.Corba do not strictly implement Object Request Brokers, they do not provide any of the standard CORBA services and are probably less suitable for projects that need to provide more complex CORBA services. At the same time, they are both simpler to use than a full-blown ORB and are therefore more appropriate than Harmless when CORBA is just being used as an interoperability mechanism.

Rather than getting too involved with the intricacies of CORBA, we now look at a simple example that uses Remoting.Corba to demonstrate how easily .NET can be integrated with CORBA.

The Uptime Server

To show .NET and CORBA integration in all its glory, we now implement a highly useful `Uptime` server, which has the simple task of allowing CORBA clients to query how long the server has been running.

NOTE The code for this example can be found in the `Chapter_08/Uptime` directory at this book's Web site (`http://www.cross-platform.net`) and the Apress Web site (`http://www.apress.com`).

Because Remoting.Corba provides an `IiopServerChannel`, as shown in Figure 8-15, the server can potentially allow any type of CORBA client to connect, no matter what language the client has been written in.

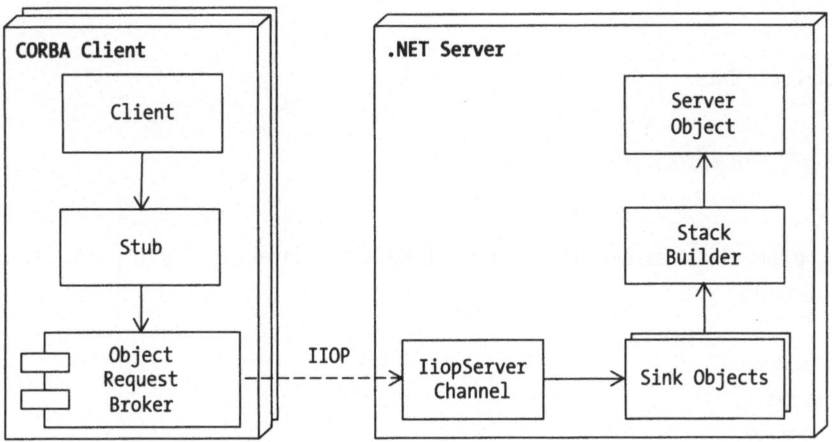

Figure 8-15. A .NET CORBA server

As mentioned earlier, the first thing that we need is an interface definition for each of the server's objects. For the Uptime server, we have the object, `Uptime`, with one method, `GetSeconds()`, which can be described with the following IDL file:

```
//Uptime.idl
interface Uptime
{
    long GetSeconds();
};
```

As you can see, the IDL interface definition is similar to a C# interface definition. The main difference is the relationship between IDL types and .NET types, as you will see shortly. Like most CORBA implementations, Remoting.Corba comes with an IDL compiler that processes IDL files and generates stub and skeleton code. Remoting.Corba's tool is called `IDL2CS`, but because the `Uptime` server is particularly simple, we dispense with the niceties that are proffered by `IDL2CS` and instead opt for manually writing the code.

The key to implementing a CORBA interface using Remoting.Corba is to create an `abstract` class that inherits from `CorbaObject` class, as shown in Figure 8-16. The `CorbaObject` class implements the basic operations required of all CORBA objects, and, because it's derived from `MarshalByRefObject`, the `CorbaObject` class can guarantee that its concrete ancestors can be accessed remotely.

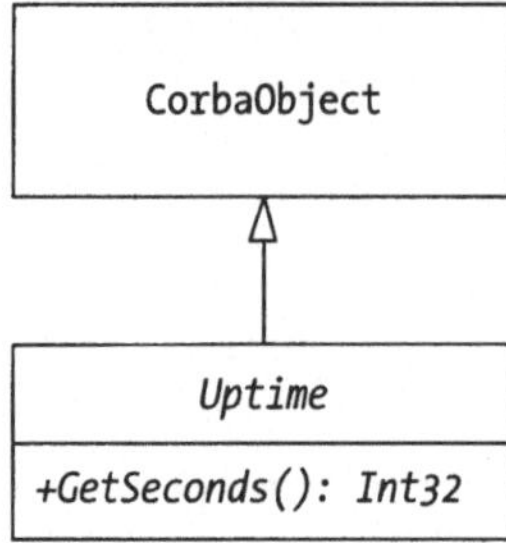

Figure 8-16. The abstract `Uptime` *class*

The `Uptime` class corresponds to the `Uptime` IDL interface and is implemented by the following code:

```
//UptimeServer.cs
using System;
using System.IO;
using System.Runtime.Remoting;
using System.Runtime.Remoting.Channels;
using Remoting.Corba;
using Remoting.Corba.Channels.Iiop;

namespace Crossplatform.NET.Chapter8
{
    [CorbaTypeId("IDL:Uptime:1.0")]
    public abstract class Uptime: CorbaObject
    {
        public abstract int GetSeconds();

        //Allows clients to query whether an object implements an interface
        public override bool is_a(string repositoryId)
        {
          return (repositoryId == CorbaServices.GetRepositoryId(typeof(Uptime)));
        }
    }
```

You may have noticed that the return value for `GetSeconds()` has been swapped from IDL's `long` to a C# `int`. As we mentioned before, IDL's types must be mapped to their equivalent .NET types, and because IDL's `long` type is a 32-bit integer, the method must use a .NET `Int32` as the return type, which is the same as a C# int.

After the `GetSeconds()` declaration is a method called `is_a()`. This method allows CORBA clients to query whether an object supports a particular CORBA interface. Because `is_a()` is declared as an `abstract` method in the `CorbaObject` class, it must be implemented in all classes that derive from `CorbaObject`.

Now that we have an abstract `Uptime` class, it's time to implement the server object, which is done by creating a concrete class that inherits from the `abstract` `Uptime` class, as illustrated in Figure 8-17.

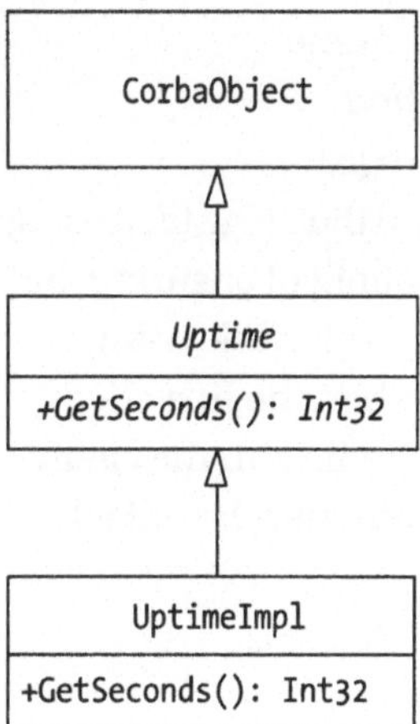

Figure 8-17. The `UptimeImpl` *class*

While this separation between the `abstract` class and the implementation is not strictly necessary, it does allow the CORBA-specific code to be kept in the `abstract` class, and makes the implementation of `UptimeImpl` particularly simple, as follows:

```
// Implementation
public class UptimeImpl: Uptime
{
    private readonly DateTime startTime = DateTime.Now;

    public override int GetSeconds()
    {
        TimeSpan time = DateTime.Now.Subtract(startTime);
        return (int)time.TotalSeconds;
    }
}
```

As you can see, the server only contains some elementary business logic, recording the time at which it is instantiated in the read-only `startTime` field and then calculating the total number of seconds that it has been running for, when GetSeconds() is invoked.

To finish the Uptime server, we need to host the UptimeImpl object, which is once again done with a simple console program. In a similar vein to the previous SimpleServer example, Main() begins by creating and registering a channel instance, although in this case, it uses the Iiop.IiopServerChannel class. Unlike the previous example, it specifies 0 for the port number in the channel's constructor to indicate that the port should be dynamically assigned at runtime.

Similarly, whereas the previous example used the method RemotingConfiguration.RegisterWellKnownServiceType() to register the object, in this case, we explicitly instantiate UptimeImpl and then register it using the RemotingServices.Marshal() method. This provides the benefit of ensuring that the UptimeImpl object is instantiated when the server is first run, while using RegisterWellKnownServiceType only instantiates the object when the first client calls the server. Because the whole purpose of the server is to inform the client how long it has been running, it is vital that the server instantiates the object when it is created, rather than waiting for a client call.

The complete code for the UptimeServer class is then as follows:

```
// Application main
class UptimeServer
{
    static void Main(string[] args)
    {
        IiopServerChannel channel = null;
        try
        {
            //Register the channel
            channel = new IiopServerChannel(0);
            ChannelServices.RegisterChannel(channel);

            //Ensure that object is instantiated immediately
            UptimeImpl uptime = new UptimeImpl();
            RemotingServices.Marshal(uptime, "Uptime");

            //Determine the IOR
            string ior = channel.GetUrlsForUri("Uptime")[0];
            Console.WriteLine(ior);
```

```
                //Write the IOR to a file for use by clients
                if ((args.Length == 1))
                {
                    using (StreamWriter file = new StreamWriter(args[0]))
                    {
                        file.Write(ior);
                    }
                }
            }
            catch (Exception e)
            {
                Console.Error.WriteLine("Error creating IOR: {0}", e.Message);
            }
            finally
            {
                //Keep serving until told otherwise
                Console.WriteLine("Press Return to exit");
                Console.ReadLine();
                ChannelServices.UnregisterChannel(channel);
            }
        }
    }
}
```

The first notable difference from the previous Remoting example is the presence of logic to obtain a URI for the channel. In the case of CORBA, this is called an Interoperable Object Reference, or IOR. The IOR is required by a CORBA client to determine how to connect to the server. If the program is called with a command-line argument, the IOR is written to the named file, which can then be used by clients to access the server, as we see in the next section.

Having finished the server code, all that's left is to build the `UptimeServer.exe` executable file, which can be done on Microsoft .NET as follows:

```
C:\MS.NET> csc UptimeServer.cs /r:Remoting.Corba.dll
Microsoft (R) Visual C# .NET Compiler version 7.10.3052.4
for Microsoft (R) .NET Framework version 1.1.4322
Copyright (C) Microsoft Corporation 2001-2002. All rights reserved.

C:\MS.NET>
```

On Portable.NET, build the program with the following command:

```
pnet@macosx:~ % cscc UptimeServer.cs /r:Remoting.Corba.dll /out:UptimeServer.exe
pnet@macosx:~ %
```

On Mono running under GNU/Linux, use the following command:

```
mono@linux:~ % mcs UptimeServer.cs /r:Remoting.Corba.dll
Compilation Succeeded
mono@linux:~ %
```

You now should be the proud owner of a brand new CORBA server—or if you're following us on all three platforms, three CORBA servers. As a preliminary test, you can try running the program by passing in an IOR filename to generate the IOR file for use by clients. While you should be able to run the server on any platform, we can test it on Mono with the following command:

```
mono@linux:~ % mono UptimeServer.exe uptime.ior
IOR:010000001d00000049444c3a6f6d672e6f72672f434f5242412f4f626a6563743a312e300000000
00100000000000000220000000101000000b000000474c454e425552474945000be0400000600000055
7074696d65
Press Return to exit
```

TIP Because the server's clients must use the IOR exactly as it's generated by the server, you should always allow the server to create the IOR file to ensure that clients can communicate with the server. Although it's tempting, copying and pasting the IOR from a terminal window can result in extraneous new line characters that can lead to hours of teeth gnashing and hair pulling.

The Uptime Client

Like a restaurant with no patrons, there's nothing more depressing than having a server with no clients. The good news is that because we already have an IDL file that contains the object's definition and an IOR file containing the connection details, very little work is required to create a client program.

If you've had enough of C# or want to create an unmanaged CORBA client, you could use an IDL compiler to generate the stub code in your language of choice. However, since Remoting.Corba helpfully provides an CORBA client channel, IiopClientChannel, and this is a .NET book, we'll settle for creating a simple client program using C#. IiopClientChannel is the kindred spirit of the IiopServerChannel class that was mentioned earlier, and its place in the scheme of things is shown in Figure 8-18.

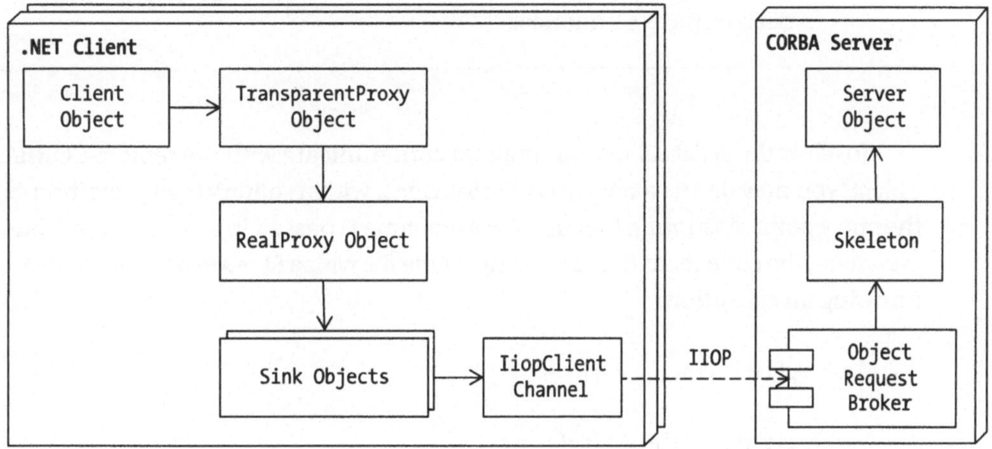

Figure 8-18. A .NET CORBA client

The client program is stored in a file called UptimeClient.cs. Unsurprisingly, this file starts with a slew of namespace definitions, which are followed by an interface definition that corresponds to the IDL interface and is the client-side equivalent to the server's abstract Uptime class, as follows:

```
//UptimeClient.cs
using System;
using System.IO;
using System.Runtime.Remoting.Channels;
using Remoting.Corba.Channels.Iiop;

namespace Crossplatform.NET.Chapter8
{
    interface Uptime
    {
        int GetSeconds();
    }
```

CAUTION The `Uptime` interface does not follow the .NET convention of preceding the interface name with a capital *I*, because the name must match the IDL interface name. Although the IDL interface could have been declared as `IUptime`, it is not an IDL convention to use a preceding *I* for interface names, and we would therefore recommend that this is one of the only times that you don't use a preceding *I* when declaring a .NET interface.

To allow the `UpdateClient` program to communicate with the remote CORBA object, you now define a new class, `CorbaClient`, with a solitary `Main()` method as the entry point. Assuming that the IOR's filename is passed in as a command-line argument, the code reads in the contents of the file with a `StreamReader`, otherwise throwing an exception.

```
class UptimeClient
{
    static void Main(string[] args)
    {
        try
        {
            //Read the IOR from the file
            if (args.Length < 1)
                throw new Exception("IOR filename not specified.");

            string ior;
            using (StreamReader iorFile = new StreamReader(args[0]))
            {
                ior = iorFile.ReadToEnd();
            }
```

Once the IOR has been retrieved, an instance of the `Iiop.IiopClientChannel` class is created and then registered with the .NET Remoting architecture with a call to the `ChannelServices.RegisterChannel()` method.

```
            //Register IIOP channel with Remoting
            ChannelServices.RegisterChannel(new IiopClientChannel());
```

The remote object is then accessed with a call to the `Activator.GetObject()` method, which is passed in the `Uptime` interface type and the server's IOR. Finally, the `GetSeconds()` method is called on the reference to the remote object, and the result is output to the console window.

```
            //Create the remote proxy
            Uptime server = (Uptime)Activator.GetObject(typeof(Uptime), ior);

            //Invoke the method
            Console.WriteLine("The server has been running for {0} seconds.",
                              server.GetSeconds().ToString());
        }
        catch (Exception ex)
        {
            Console.Error.WriteLine("The following error occurred: {0}",
                                    ex.Message);
        }
    }
  }
}
```

As the code involves file access and making remote invocation calls over the network, the method is wrapped in a `try...catch` block to ensure that any errors are gracefully passed back to the user.

Now that you have a client program, you can test both the server and the client by opening a new console window and then building and running the client, remembering to pass in the name of the IOR file. If the server isn't still running from before, make sure that you run it first, as shown in the previous section.

You can then build and run the `UptimeClient.exe` program on Portable.NET as follows:

```
pnet@macosx:~ % cscc UptimeClient.cs /r:Remoting.Corba.dll /out:UptimeClient.exe
pnet@macosx:~ % ilrun UptimeClient.exe uptime.ior
The server has been running for 0 seconds.
pnet@macosx:~ %
```

On Mono running under GNU/Linux, use the following commands:

```
mono@linux:~ % mcs UptimeClient.cs /r:Remoting.Corba.dll
Compilation Succeeded
mono@linux:~ mono UptimeClient.exe uptime.ior
The server has been running for 3 seconds.
mono@linux:~
```

Finally, on the Microsoft .NET Framework, use the following commands:

```
C:\MS.NET> csc UptimeClient.cs /r:Remoting.Corba.dll
Microsoft (R) Visual C# .NET Compiler version 7.10.3052.4
for Microsoft (R) .NET Framework version 1.1.4322
Copyright (C) Microsoft Corporation 2001-2002. All rights reserved.

C:\MS.NET> UptimeClient.exe uptime.ior
The server has been running for 6 seconds.
C:\MS.NET>
```

As you might have expected, each time the client program is run, it reports a steadily increasing uptime count, and it continues to do so until the `UptimeServer.exe` program is shut down. In fact, the server is only stable for 68 years, after which the first client request causes the `int` return value to overflow. However, if you need your CORBA servers to run for more than 68 years, you should not only use a larger return type but also use an ORB to provide extra resilience.

Having now had a cursory look at how .NET can be used to host and access objects through CORBA, it's time to confess that we failed to mention some of the more complex issues—like asynchronous method calls or handling CORBA exceptions—but we hope that you now have a good idea of how .NET and CORBA can satisfy some of your cross-platform integration needs.

COM

While CORBA is undeniably the component technology of choice in the world of heterogeneous systems, in the world of Windows, COM is king. The Component Object Model (COM) evolved from Microsoft's Object Linking and Embedding (OLE) document-integration technology. This technology first appeared in the early 1990s as a general-purpose mechanism for integrating components.

Originally comprised of a language-neutral binary specification and some basic runtime services, COM gradually spread to include a number of enhanced features, such as remotely accessible components through Distributed COM (DCOM), reusable interface components known as ActiveX controls, and enterprise runtime services with Microsoft Transaction Server (MTS) and later COM+.

Coupling COM's successes with the ability to rapidly create COM components that was proffered by VB6 and then the ability to script COM components using VBScript, COM rapidly became the framework that underlies component reuse on Windows. As system administrators enthusiastically carried out repetitive tasks with the Windows Scripting Host and Web developers quickly developed dynamic Web applications using Active Server Pages (ASPs), it is little surprise that COM started to be considered as a development religion. In the words of the COM guru Don Box: "COM is love."

Cross-Platform COM

Despite the love affair that many Windows developers had—and in some cases still hold—with COM, it has a decidedly checkered past when it comes to platform independence. Although in many regards it is similar to CORBA—for example, every COM interface is defined using the Microsoft Interface Definition Language (MIDL)—because the binary implementation is geared around Windows, COM is very much out of its depth when removed from the haven of Windows.

Nonetheless, two products that manage to demonstrate COM working without Windows are Software AG's EntireX product, which includes an implementation of DCOM for UNIX, and Mainsoft's MainWin, which provides a Windows/COM runtime for various flavors of UNIX. Similarly, because a significant portion of Windows programs rely on COM, the Wine project that was mentioned in Chapter 5 also contains a partial implementation of COM, which is essential in helping Wine in its goal of running Windows programs on other operating systems.

Another cross-platform technology that is closely related to COM is Mozilla's XPCOM, which stands for Cross-Platform COM. XPCOM is essentially a framework for creating cross-platform, language-neutral components and shares some notable similarities with COM. Not only are XPCOM interfaces defined with a similar IDL, but XPCOM also has an almost identical interface-querying mechanism that requires every interface to derive from the same base interface (`IUnknown` for COM and `nsISupports` for XPCOM). While they are similar, however, XPCOM components are not binary compatible with COM components. This means that in the context of this book, XPCOM is most relevant as a shortcut for porting COM code to non-Windows platforms.

NOTE For more information on XPCOM, go to `http://www.mozilla.org/projects/xpcom`.

Although, in some ways, COM can be considered as a rudimentary platform-independent technology, using COM-based applications in heterogeneous environments is decidedly nontrivial. It follows that integrating cross-platform .NET applications with COM is harder than integrating with CORBA, but in the next couple of sections, we investigate how Microsoft .NET implements COM interoperability and how this affects cross-platform .NET applications.

Microsoft .NET COM Interoperability

With .NET being, in many ways, the evolutionary descendant of COM, it should come as no surprise that Microsoft .NET contains a barrage of facilities for those organizations with a heavy investment in COM, and Microsoft .NET assuages their progression from COM to .NET.

In comparison to .NET classes, which reside in assemblies, COM components are stored in COM component servers, which are generally dynamic link libraries or executable files. The metadata that is associated with COM components is stored in type libraries, which can either be packaged with the component server or stored in an external file with a `.tlb` file extension. Although COM's separation between code and metadata can be seen as a precursor to .NET's assemblies, no direct compatibility exists between COM and .NET. Microsoft's approach to .NET and COM interoperability involves using the .NET or COM metadata to create a *callable wrapper*, which acts as a proxy for the real type.

To access COM components from .NET, .NET provides the Type Library Importer tool, `tlbimp.exe`. When fed a COM type library, this tool generates an interoperability assembly, as shown in Figure 8-19.

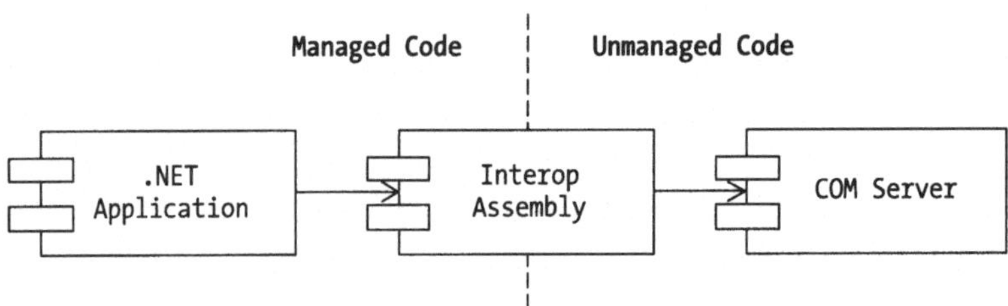

Figure 8-19. Accessing COM from .NET

These interoperability assemblies contains classes known as *Runtime Callable Wrappers*, which are responsible for marshaling all requests to the COM component server and have their lifetimes managed by the .NET garbage collector.

Conversely, to access .NET components from COM, .NET provides the Type Library Exporter tool, `tlbexp.exe`. When fed an assembly, this tool generates a COM type library for the assembly, as shown in Figure 8-20, which can then be registered on the client machine.

When a COM application attempts to instantiate objects in that type library, .NET dynamically creates an object known as a *COM Callable Wrapper*, which is responsible for marshaling all requests to the .NET assembly.

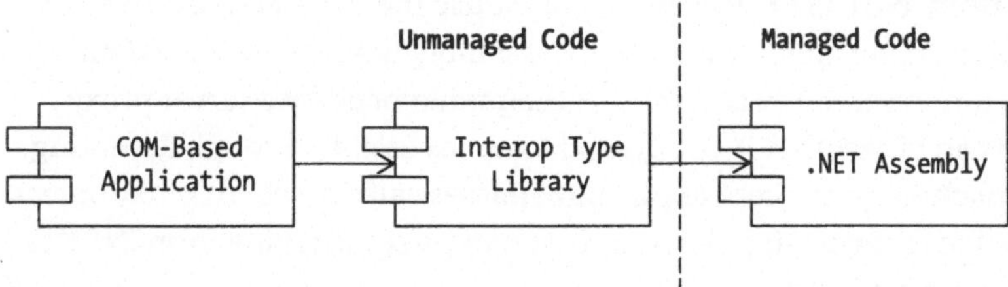

Figure 8-20. Accessing .NET from COM

Cross-Platform COM Interoperability

In comparison to Microsoft .NET, and at the time of this writing, both Mono and Portable.NET are noticeably devoid of any COM interoperability features. Indeed, with the lightest COM applications relying on the extensive COM runtime and the Windows registry for configuration, COM as a technology is comparable in complexity to .NET itself.

Although the Mono project has distant plans to implement COM interoperability on Windows and XPCOM interoperability on non-Windows systems, because COM is strongly rooted to Windows, you'll probably never be able to create fully cross-platform .NET applications that interoperate with cross-platform–hosted COM components. Nonetheless, cross-platform developers can still use a few tricks when working on systems that require COM interoperability; these tricks are as follows:

- For systems that are based on Visual Basic 6 COM components, the source code can be migrated to VB.NET. Because Visual Basic 6 hides all the underlying COM plumbing, this approach is no more complex than migrating any other VB6 project to .NET.
- For all other systems, the COM part of the system can be run on Windows computers with the .NET part of the system run on a cross-platform .NET implementation, using a technique known as .NET–COM bridging.

While the first option is certainly viable in a number of situations, the easiest and more flexible option is to use bridging, which can be implemented using .NET Remoting. Bridging be done in both directions, and because it does not involve modifying existing COM components, it does not open any opportunities to introduce errors into working parts of the system.

To bridge from .NET to COM, you must first use the .NET Framework's `tlbimp.exe` tool to create an interoperability assembly that can be hosted on Windows. The interoperability assembly is then referenced by a server proxy object, which is an object that is configured to be accessible through Remoting. On the client machines, the client application passes calls to a client proxy object that is responsible for accessing the remote server proxy. Bridging from .NET to COM is shown in Figure 8-21.

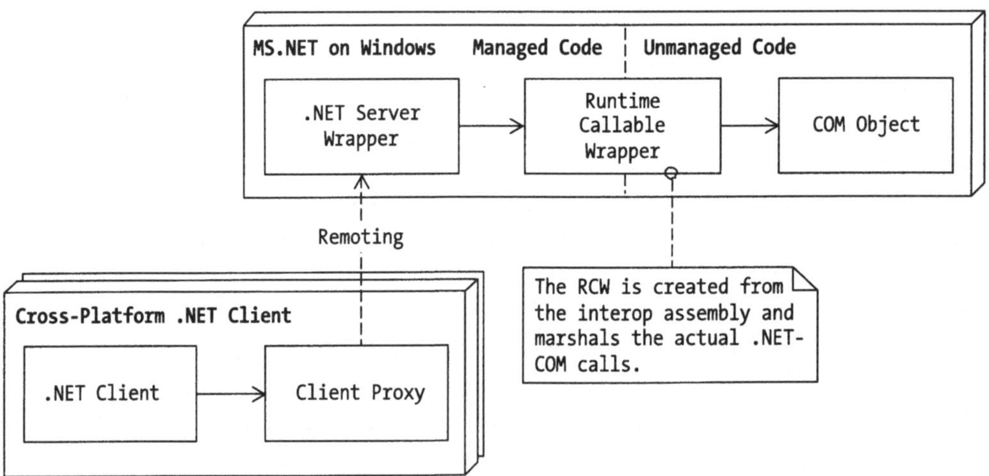

Figure 8-21. Bridging from .NET to COM

For the opposite situation, you should use Microsoft .NET's `tlbexp.exe` tool to create an interoperability type library for the *client proxy* objects that will be hosted on the Windows client machines. The client proxy objects use Remoting to access a server proxy, which then passes calls on to the actual server objects. Bridging from COM to .NET is shown in Figure 8-22.

Since we've already looked at two .NET Remoting examples in this chapter, we will not look at any of implementation details for how this bridging would be performed, although it should be fairly obvious how the earlier examples form the basis for a cross-platform COM interoperability solution.

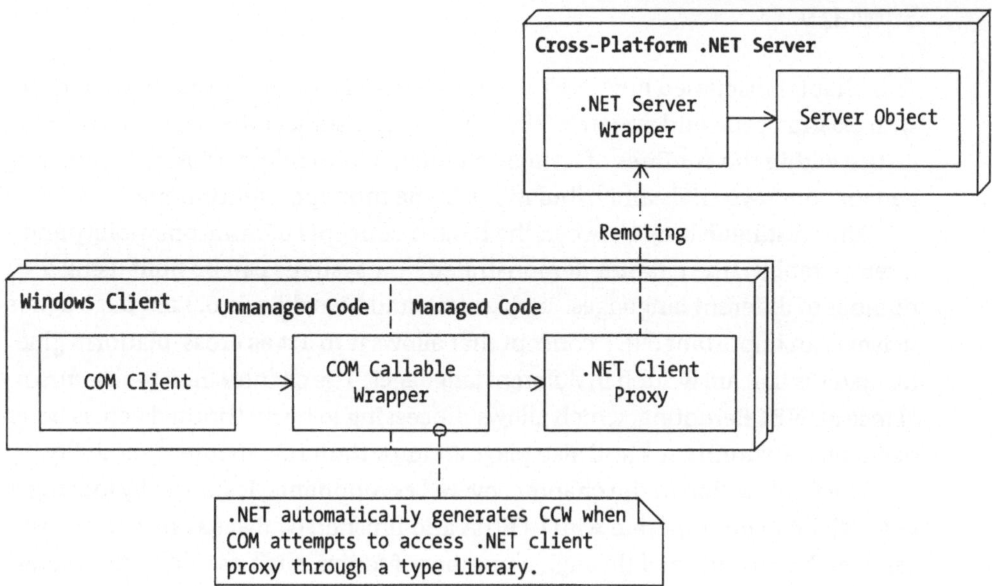

Figure 8-22. Bridging from COM to .NET

Middleware Alternatives: The Internet Communications Engine

While CORBA and COM are undoubtedly the central characters in the middleware story, a number of alternative technologies have important parts to play. The most contemporary contender for the middleware crown is probably the Internet Communications Engine, or ICE, which was created as a feature-rich, open source alternative to CORBA and COM.

Based on a robust infrastructure, ICE is available for a number of platforms and provides an impressive list of services, including a thorough security system, automatic object persistence with versioning, and a software-updating service. Because Mono includes a binding to ICE, it is an ideal middleware choice for greenfield projects that cannot rely exclusively on .NET for interoperability and require an alternative middleware technology.

For more information on the Internet Communication Engine, visit `http://www.zeroc.com`.

Summary

This chapter discussed how .NET can be used for integrating and interoperating with existing code and systems. While it's a broad subject that can't be given justice within the confines of a single chapter, it hopefully serves as a launching pad for your own trials and tribulations in the interoperability arena.

After distinguishing between the related concepts of intra-operability and interoperability, the chapter demonstrated how systems can be built using a number of different languages, such as Java and Visual Basic 6. Language agnosticism is an important .NET concept that allows it to act as cross-platform glue for systems that are written in different languages. The chapter then took a cursory glance at .NET Remoting, which allows processing to be distributed across heterogeneous environments and also plays an important role in interoperability.

The final section of the chapter covered components. It started by looking at how .NET can interoperate with CORBA and finished by discussing enterprise services, having breezed through a number of topics, such as COM interoperability, XPCOM, and the Internet Communications Engine.

While the IT industry's corporate marketing machines have recently taken it upon themselves to place interoperability squarely within the remit of Web services, the CLI's cross-platform and language-neutral features beg to disagree. As this chapter has shown, the CLI is an excellent tool for building systems that integrate with legacy applications written in a variety of languages and run on a broad range of platforms. Above all, the cross-platform capabilities of the different CLI implementations prove that Web services are not the only word in interoperability.

CHAPTER 9

Testing and Building Strategies

"... you should use a Domain Model whenever the complexity of your domain logic is greater than 7.42. The bad news is that nobody knows how to measure the complexity of domain logic."

—Martin Fowler, author

AT THIS POINT in the story of cross-platform development, if you've faithfully followed the preferred sequence of chapters—that is, in a linear fashion as opposed to dipping in and out—you should have enough knowledge to begin some serious projects. It's now time to round it all off with a bit of best practice that can help in developing cross-platform software in a coherent and consistent manner.

Given that developing software for a single platform can be a hard enough task in its own right, the added complexity of targeting a number of platforms can often catalyze a project into a splitting headache. Before you head for the pharmacist, however, relief is available in the form of some tools that can really share the burden.

These tools can reduce the maintenance overhead that is associated with a project, while boosting the quality of the finished article. Additionally, these tools can make it easier to maneuver through midproject U-turns as the conjoined evils of feature creep and feature change are exorcised and made safe. Could these tools be the magical silver bullet that slays the beast? We're going to find out—we are, of course, talking about unit testing and build tools.

Testing, Testing, 1,2,3: Using NUnit

"Oh yuck. Nobody wants to talk about testing. Testing is the ugly stepchild of software development."

—Kent Beck, *Extreme Programming Explained: Embrace Change*

There are some who say that no product is too simple for testing, and yet others have never worked on a project with any formal testing strategy. At some point in their career, especially early on, most developers will harbor guilt about testing. They step through their code when a method is completed, but they feel that if only they could just push a button to perform a test, their lives would be easier—and they wouldn't need to keep looking over their shoulder every time some code is changed.

If any of this strikes a chord in your heart, now's the time to jump on the bandwagon and make your working life easier. Whatever your own personal reality, there can be no doubt: If single-platform software requires testing, testing software for multiple platforms is unequivocally essential. In fact, it's fair to say that each deployment platform increases the developer's problem domain, because each deployment may throw up a bug that is specific to that platform. As you code around these issues every time they arise, you'll need some way to retain confidence in your code, and you must be sure that a fix for platform A does not introduce a bug for platform B, the solution to which breaks platform C—and so on.

Furthermore, providing an automated test suite can help to reduce code ownership. When a developer breaks *your* code, he will know about it as soon as he runs the tests, and he can take appropriate measures to fix the problem that he has introduced.

Types of Testing

In the context of software development, testing can be divided into the following categories:

- **Integration testing:** Here various components of a process are checked for correct interaction, say, the passing of an order from a Web site into the shipping of a product to a customer.
- **Regression testing:** Here previously fixed issues are tested to make sure that the latest changes have not undone earlier work.
- **Acceptance testing:** This is testing by a client in the real world, also known as everyday use.

In addition to these testing flavors, you have the concept of the *unit test,* which focuses on the functionality and usage of a class and its public members. To examine the public aspects and behavior of a class without caring about the internal workings of that class is known as *blackbox* testing. Figuratively, you have a black box that represents a machine, you cannot see into it or know how it works, and either it does what it is supposed to or it doesn't. Conversely, *whitebox* testing—although *transparentbox* would be more in keeping with the analogy—concerns itself with the inner workings of a class, its private fields, and methods and the interplay between them.

If you've ever stepped through your code with a debugger, you've already performed whitebox testing. Unit testing is a prime example of blackbox testing, but it can serve well in the field of regression testing, simply by keeping your tests and running them whenever a change is made to the codebase. As obvious as it may seem, a test is for life, not just for Christmas. Unit testing is also a cornerstone of the development methodology known as *Extreme Programming*.

Extreme Programming

Extreme Programming is an agile methodology, born out of the realities of moving goalposts, feature creep, and clients who haven't decided what they want. Sound familiar?

With a number of high-profile features such as pair programming, test-driven development, and intense customer interaction, Extreme Programming is generally considered to be a methodology that's rich in promise, although some schools of thought question its general applicability. A prime example of this questioning is Doug Rosenberg and Matt Stephens's book *Extreme Programming Refactored: The Case Against XP* (Apress, 2003).

Regardless of your take on Extreme Programming, a number of positive side effects are attributed to it, one of them being the family of unit testing frameworks, which includes NUnit.

As its name suggests, NUnit is a unit testing tool for .NET classes. It is a C# port and adaptation of Kent Beck and Erich Gamma's JUnit, a popular unit testing tool for the Java platform.

NOTE You can read about NUnit and download it from `http://www.nunit.org`. Its Java precursor, JUnit, is available from `http://www.junit.org`.

Installing NUnit for the .NET Framework

Installation of NUnit involves downloading and running the Windows installation package from the NUnit Web site. When the installer has completed, it will have placed shortcuts in the Start menu for two different versions of NUnit: a console version, `nunit-console.exe`, and a GUI version, `nunit-gui.exe`.

The console-based version can produce an XML file as output and is suitable for automated testing, as shown in Figure 9-1. The GUI version allows for greater user interaction and is shown in Figure 9-2.

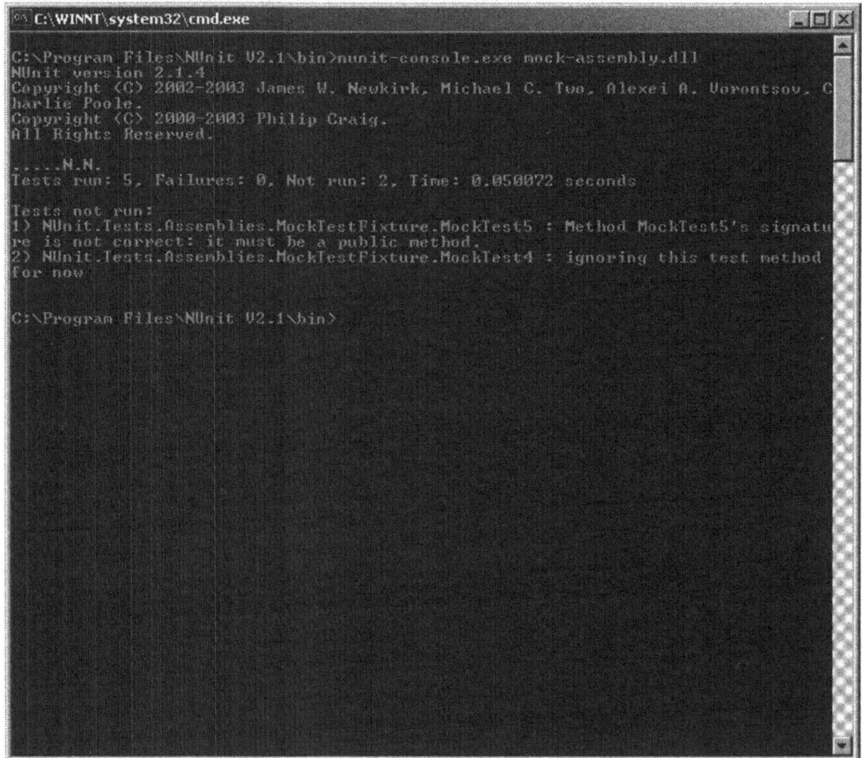

Figure 9-1. The console version of NUnit

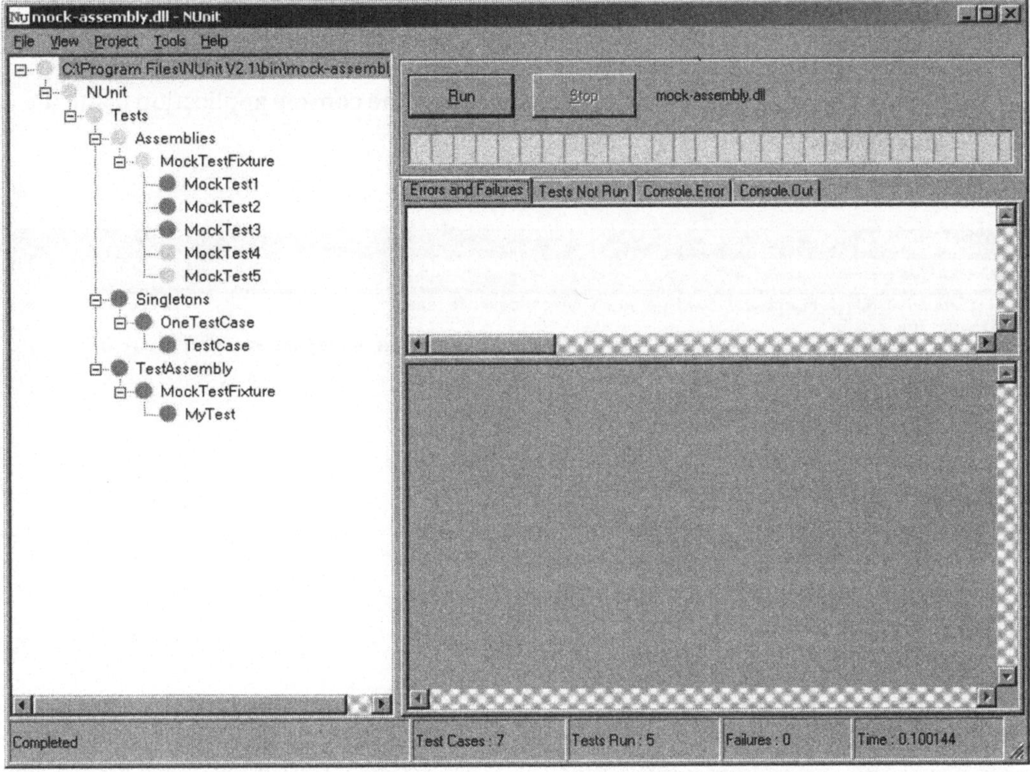

Figure 9-2. The GUI version of NUnit

The license for NUnit is based on the open source zlib/libpng license, and in effect, it means that you can use NUnit free of charge for development purposes.

TIP For more explicit detail on the particulars of the NUnit license, we recommend `http://www.nunit.org/license.html`.

Installing NUnit for Mono

When using NUnit with Mono, you currently have two choices: The NUnit project provides a separate console-only version of the source code specifically for the Mono project, and the Mono community hosts another version that has a Gtk# front end.

Installation of the console-only version involves downloading the latest ZIP file from the Web site and unpacking the ZIP file. The executable file can then be found in the /bin directory.

Figure 9-3 shows the results of running the console application using the /? flag.

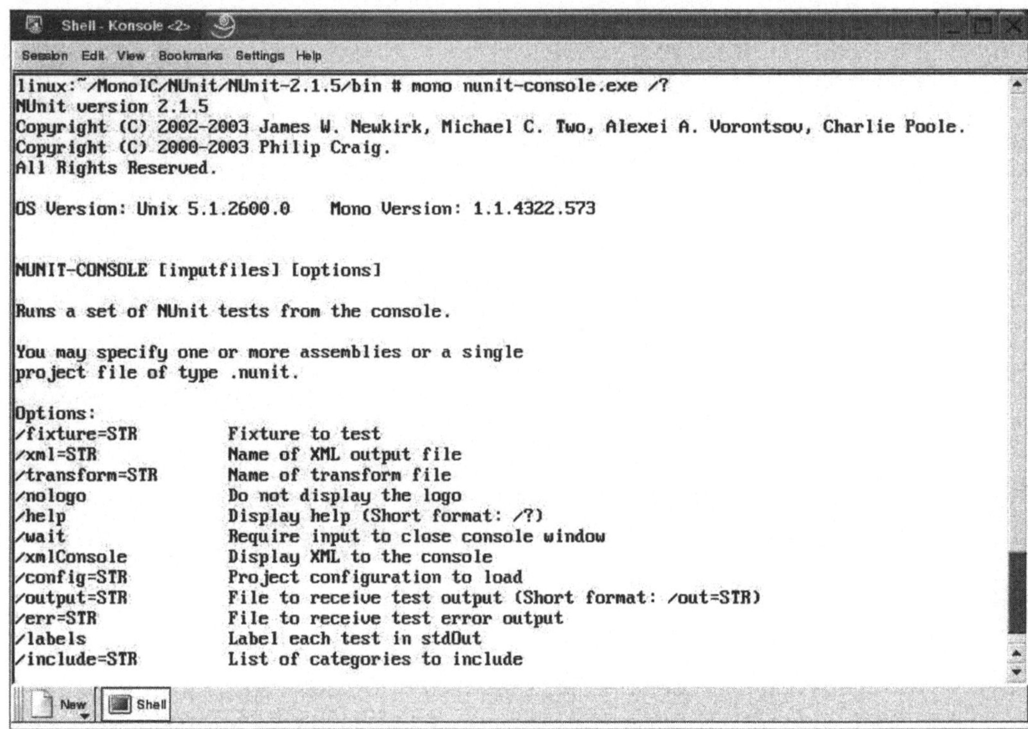

Figure 9-3. The console version of NUnit running under Mono

To install the Gtk# version of NUnit, the source code needs to be acquired from the Mono Concurrent Versions System (CVS) repositories. Unfortunately, an explanation of the use of CVS is beyond the scope of this book, but it's highly likely that it will one day be released as binary packages by some friendly souls in the Mono community.

Figure 9-4 illustrates the clean, smooth lines of the Gtk# GUI, having loaded and executed the NUnit-supplied tests in `mock-assembly.dll`.

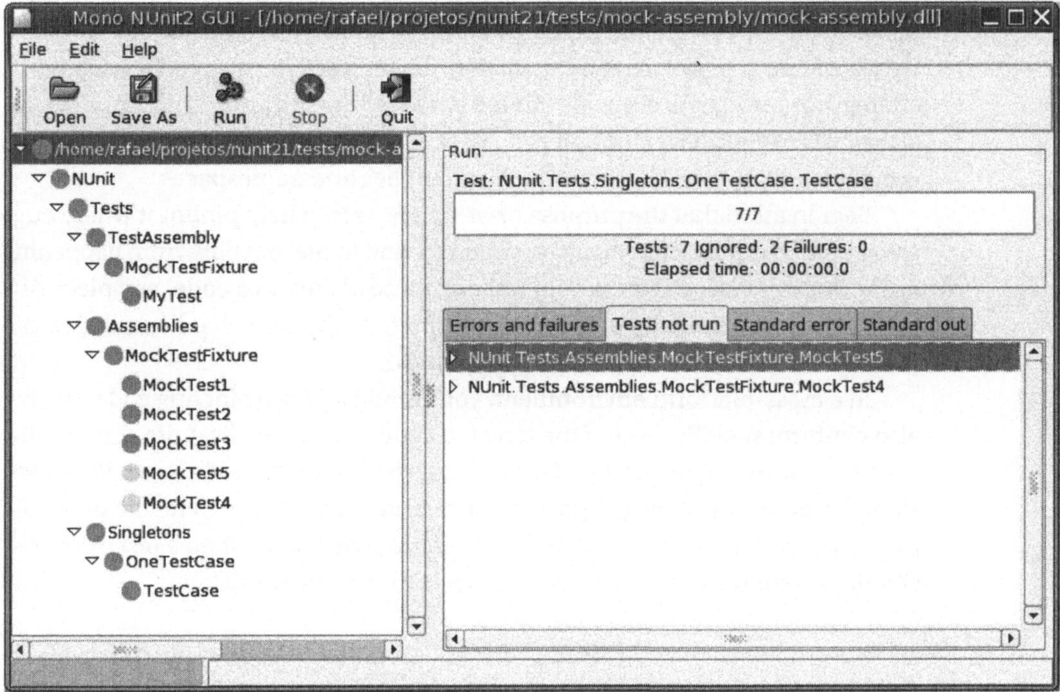

Figure 9-4. The Gtk# version of NUnit running under Mono

Unit Testing with Portable.NET

Currently, NUnit does not run under Portable.NET, but a number of interested parties are sporadically working on this omission, and it's likely that both console and GUI versions will run under Portable.NET in the near future.

Basic Unit Testing

As stated earlier, a unit test is a blackbox test whereby a class and its publicly available features are tested to ensure that the methods and data members all perform as expected.

For example, if your class is designed to add three numbers, your test will know all the inputs and the expected output without necessarily knowing the details of how it performs the calculation. To get started, you need a sensible strategy for testing. As ever, you should strive for organization and simplicity in all aspects of your development process, and for this reason, it makes sense to group your tests into sensibly named assemblies and namespaces.

Bear in mind that the purpose of writing tests is to help pinpoint where bugs may occur, to expose bugs that have occurred, and to prevent bugs from happening again. For this reason, you should test any piece of complex code, any piece of code whose functionality may be misinterpreted, any code that has failed in the past, and any code that is about to be changed.

In a cross-platform environment, you should add tests for any code that is also platform specific, even if the targeted code is intrinsically quite simple—for example, the use of library A on GNU/Linux over library B on Microsoft Windows. In such simple cases, the purpose of the test changes slightly to reflect the complexity of the source code tree, rather than the code itself. When a test exits, it should be removed only when the code it tests no longer exists.

Getting Started

What exactly is an NUnit test? It is an ordinary C# class definition that contains specially marked methods, each of which performs one or more tests. Using attributes that are defined in `NUnit.Framework`, you mark your test class with `TestFixtureAttribute` and your test methods with `TestAttribute`. All test classes must have a `public` default constructor, and all test methods must be public with no return value.

By conforming to these rules, the NUnit applications—remember, both GUI and console flavors exist—are able to load your test classes and execute the methods that are marked with the `Test` attribute.

The following example is a lightweight illustration of the NUnit attributes in action. As usual, the code begins with using statements, followed by a namespace definition. Next up, a new class is defined and is marked with the TestFixture attribute, and this allows the NUnit application to identify the class as a container for some test methods. The code is as follows:

```
using System;
using NUnit.Framework;
namespace NUnitExamples
{
    [TestFixture]
    public class AssertionMethods
    {
        // all test classes must have a public default constructor
        public AssertionMethods(){}

        [Test]
        public void Assert1()
        {
            int x = 2;
            int y = 3;

            //Since 2 is not equal to 3, this test will fail
            Assert.AreEqual(x,y);
        }
    }
}
```

Finally, a simple method is defined and marked with the Test attribute. This test checks that the value of X is equal to the value of Y by calling the Assert.AreEqual() method. Because X and Y are not equal, the test will fail. NUnit allows the user to test bool expressions, equality, object sameness, and null status.

NUnit's Assert class has a number of different methods for use in unit tests, as shown in Table 9-1.

Table 9-1. Assertion Methods

Method	Description
Assert.IsTrue(bool expression)	If expression evaluates to true, the test passes. Consider the method bool IsValidEmail(string email). As you would expect, this function returns true if the passed-in email parameter is a valid e-mail and false if email is not a usable e-mail address. To test this method, you would use Assert.IsTrue(IsValidEmail("Jason.king@crossplatform.net")). In this case, the test passes, where Assert.IsTrue(IsEmail("MJ.Easton&&crossplatform.net") should fail, provided that IsEmail() is working properly.
Assert.IsFalse(bool expression)	Same as for Assert.IsTrue, but the test passes if expression evaluates to false.
Assert.AreSame(Object Expected, Object Actual)	Checks that objects Expected and Actual refer to the same object. Note that this is not the same as being equal in value.
Assert.AreEqual(Object Expected, Object Actual)	Tests for equality of objects, using Expected.Equals(), which can, of course, be overridden in your own classes. For example, if you have a Person class with Firstname, Surname, and SocialSecurityNumber properties, you may decide that two Persons are the same if their SocialSecurityNumber is the same, regardless of the names. If Expected and Actual are both nulls, they are considered to be equal. Numerics are compared via conversion to strings, which is a neat method for dealing with different numeric types.
Assert.AreEqual(int Expected, int Actual)	Straightforward equality test for two integers.

Table 9-1. Assertion Methods (Continued)

Method	Description
`Assert.AreEqual (float Expected, float Actual, float Delta)`	Equality testing with a twist! The third parameter, `Delta`, allows a certain tolerance in checking equality. `Assert.AreEqual(10.0F,10.0F,0.00F)` will pass because we have a tolerance of 0.0F. That is, both `Expected` and `Actual` values must be exactly equal to pass, and because 10 does indeed equal 10, this test would pass. The `Delta` parameter is used to set limits on what *may be considered* to be equal, thus for a low-tolerance test, `Assert.AreEqual(4.00F,3.999F,0.10F)` will pass, because 4.000 – 3.999 = 0.001. This is well within the tolerance limit—that is, much smaller than the maximum allowable difference of 0.1.
`Assert.AreEqual (double Expected, double Actual, double Delta)`	Performs the same as the `float` overload but takes three `double`s instead.
`Assert.IsNull(Object)`	If the passed in object is null, the test passes.
`Assert.IsNotNull(Object)`	If the passed in object is not null, the test passes.

Each of the methods in Table 9-1 also has an overloaded method with an additional parameter, `string Message`, which can be used to output a message to the screen in the event of a test failing, as shown in the following example:

```
Assert.IsTrue (bool expression, string Message)
```

TIP For projects with more than a handful of tests, it pays to use the overloads that take the `Message` parameter to output a useful message in the event of the test failing. This is particularly useful when you have multiple similar tests in a cross-platform project. As long as a unique message is used for each test, it should be easy to locate a failed test in the test source code.

In addition to these methods, a technique is available that allows you to check for expected exceptions, using the `ExpectedException` attribute. Use this attribute when you're testing your code's error handling, because it allows your code to throw an exception when appropriate without having the test fail. Use of the `ExpectedException` attribute is illustrated later in this chapter.

The Devil Is in the Delta

The inclusion of the `delta` parameter in the `float` and `double` overloads is an elegant refinement for equality testing. It allows real-world mechanics—where perfection may be impossible to achieve—to be tested in software.

Consider a digital micrometer that measures the diameter of a piston. The ideal thickness is 5.000, but any value in the range of 4.999 to 5.001 is considered to be acceptable. This is a tolerance of +/– 0.001, which is used for the `delta` parameter, as follows:

```
public void TestPiston()
{
    float idealDiameter = 5.000F;
    float pistonDiameter = 5.001F;
    float tolerance = 0.001f
    Assert.AreEqual(idealDiameter, pistonDiameter, tolerance);
}
```

As it stands, this test will pass. However, some results for this kind of test do not appear to work as expected, and this is due to hardware rounding errors. To illustrate, alter the `pistonDiameter` and `idealDiameter` as follows and run the test for each set:

```
idealDiameter = 5.000F; pistonDiameter = 4.999F; // pass
idealDiameter = 4.999F; pistonDiameter = 4.998F; // pass
idealDiameter = 4.998F; pistonDiameter = 4.997F; // pass
idealDiameter = 4.997F; pistonDiameter = 4.996F; // fail
```

Although the difference between the `pistonDiameter` and the `idealDiameter` is always the same—0.001—the tests do not return consistent results, and this is echoed further by similar value sets.

This flaw could be a potential source of errors and unexpected results in your test suites, but coping with this problem merely takes an adjustment to the interpretation of the parameters. The inline help for the `delta` parameter states that "[the `delta` parameter is] the maximum acceptable difference between the expected and the actual." You should adjust your *usage and understanding* of the parameter to instead be "The difference between the expected and actual must be below this value for the test to pass," followed by subtly altering the `tolerance` variable to suit, as follows:

```
// now test passes
tolerance = 0.0011; idealDiameter = 4.997F; pistonDiameter = 4.996F;
```

As a caveat, it's fair to say that without exhaustive testing, this technique cannot be guaranteed to be entirely reliable, and due to underlying processing techniques of the hardware, it is an issue that may never be resolved.

To demonstrate some of the main features of NUnit, it's time to dig out the `Person.cs` file from Chapter 5 and, in maintaining this chapter's dignity, change its namespace from `Crossplatform.NET.Chapter05` to `Crossplatform.NET.Chapter09`. To save you from looking, we reproduce the edited code for you, as follows:

```
//Filename: Person.cs
using System;

namespace Crossplatform.NET.Chapter09
{
    public class Person
    {
        public event EventHandler PersonChangedEvent;

        private string socialSecurityNumber;
        private string firstname;
        private string surname;
        private string email;

        public Person(string first, string surname, string ssn, string email)
        {
            this.firstname = first;
            this.surname = surname;
            this.socialSecurityNumber = ssn;
            this.email = email;
        }

        protected void RaisePersonChangedEvent(EventArgs e)
        {
            if (this.PersonChangedEvent != null)
                this.PersonChangedEvent(this, e);
        }
```

```
            public string Email
            {
                get{ return email; }
                set{ SetValue(ref this.email, value); }
            }

            public string Firstname
            {
                get{ return firstname; }
                set{ SetValue(ref this.firstname, value); }
            }

            public string SocialSecurityNumber
            {
                get{return socialSecurityNumber;}
                set{ SetValue(ref this.socialSecurityNumber, value); }
            }

            public string Surname
            {
                get{ return surname; }
                set{ SetValue(ref this.surname, value); }
            }

            //Simply properties' "set"implementation
            private void SetValue(ref string field, string value)
            {
                if(field != value)
                {
                    field = value;
                    RaisePersonChangedEvent(EventArgs.Empty);
                }
            }
        }
    }
```

The `Person` class has a simple constructor that initializes all the fields, which in turn are encapsulated in the usual manner by the use of properties. The first tests are for these constructors and illustrate the use of the `null` status tests. Now is the perfect time to create a new file to contain the tests. Following the plain and simple guidelines, we start with an appropriate namespace and filename to hold the tests, as follows:

```
//Filename PersonTest.cs
using System;
using NUnit.Framework;
using Crossplatform.NET.Chapter09;

namespace Crossplatform.NET.Chapter09.PersonTest
{
    [TestFixture]
    public class PersonTest
    {
        public PersonTest(){}

        [Test]
        public void TestObjectExist()
        {

            string email = "Mj.Easton@Crossplatform.NET";
            Person mj = new Person("Mj", "Easton", "111-222", email);
            Assert.IsNotNull(mj, "constructor fails");
        }
    }
}
```

NOTE The source code samples for this chapter can be found in the Downloads section of this book's Web site (`http://www.cross-platform.net`) and the Apress Web site (`http://www.apress.com`). The source code for this example can be found in the `Chapter_09\tests1` directory.

To run the tests, you first need to compile the `Person` class into a library, as follows:

```
C:\MS.NET> csc /target:library /out:Person.dll Person.cs
```

On Mono, use the following command:

```
mono@linux:~ % mcs /target:library /out:Person.dll Person.cs
```

Next, compile the tests into a library, making sure to reference your newly compiled `Person.dll` and the `NUnit.Framework.dll`, a copy of which should be placed in your working directory, as follows:

```
C:\MS.NET> csc /target:library /out:PersonTest.dll /r:NUnit.Framework.dll
 /r:Person.dll PersonTest.cs
```

For Mono, use the following command:

```
mono@linux:~ % mcs /target:library /out:PersonTest.dll /r:nunit.framework.dll \
> /r:Person.dll PersonTest.cs
```

To launch the GUI version of NUnit and load your test library from the command line, use the following command:

```
C:\MS.NET> NUnit-gui.exe PersonTest.dll
```

Figure 9-5 shows the freshly loaded tests, before they've been run.

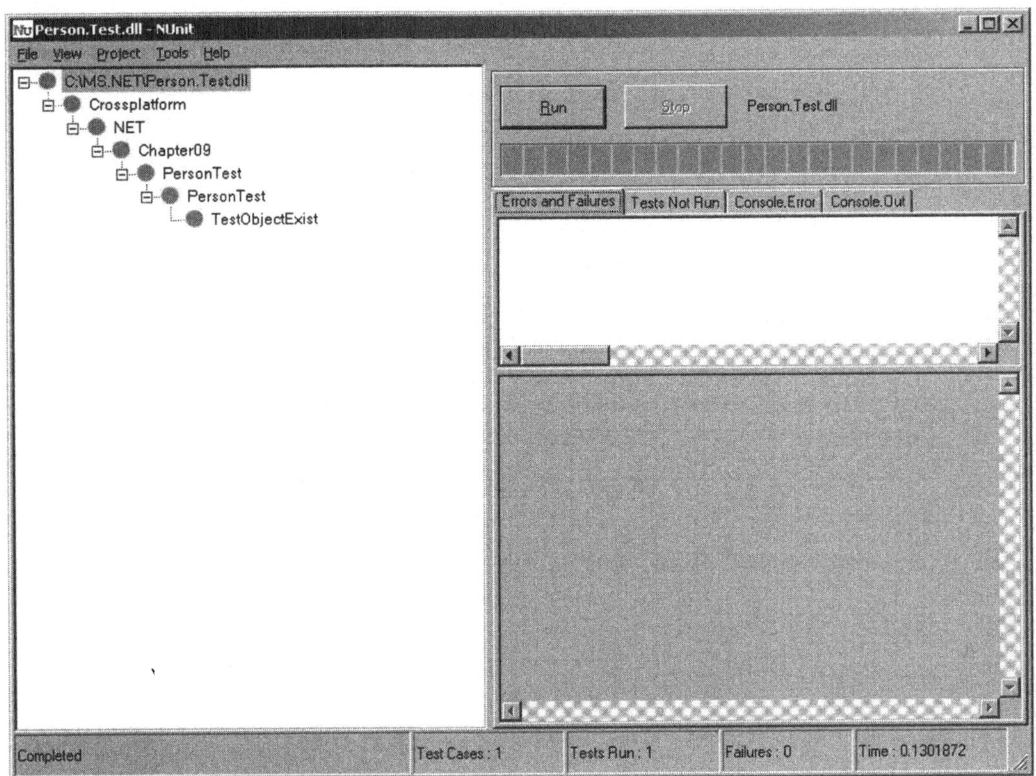

Figure 9-5. NUnit before the tests are run

Notice how the treeview has staggered the namespace elements, culminating in the `PersonTest` class, which was marked with `TestFixture` and the `Test` method `TestObjectExist()`.

Feel free to run the console-based version using `nunit-console.exe PersonTest.dll` and examine the XML file output at your leisure. The file output will be produced in the same folder as the `PersonTest.dll` file.

Now we can expand the test scenario. Some of the tests are trivial, purely to demonstrate the usage of the various NUnit `Assert` methods; note the use of the various overloads that take a message string as a parameter. Add the following tests into the `TestFixture PersonTest` class as follows:

```
Test]
public void TestObjectsEqual()
{
    string email = "Mj.Easton@Crossplatform.NET";
    Person mj = new Person("Mj", "Easton", "111-222", email);
    Person mj2 = new Person("Mj", "Easton", "111-222", email);
    Assert.AreEqual(mj, mj2, "Objects are not equal.");
}

[Test]
public void TestObjectsSame()
{
    string email = "Mj.Easton@Crossplatform.NET";
    Person mj = new Person("Mj","Easton","111-222",email);
    Person mj2 = mj;
    Assert.AreSame(mj, mj2, "Objects should be the same");
}
```

NOTE The source code for this example can be found in the `Chapter_09\tests2` directory at this book's Web site (`http://www.cross-platform.net`) and the Apress Web site (`http://www.apress.com`).

Recompile `PersonTest.dll`, and run the tests again. Note that `nunit-gui.exe` has some neat functionality. It watches for a new version of the currently loaded test DLL and reloads it automatically; this saves you from some pesky manual reloads. If all is well, `TestObjectsEqual()` will fail, as illustrated in Figure 9-6.

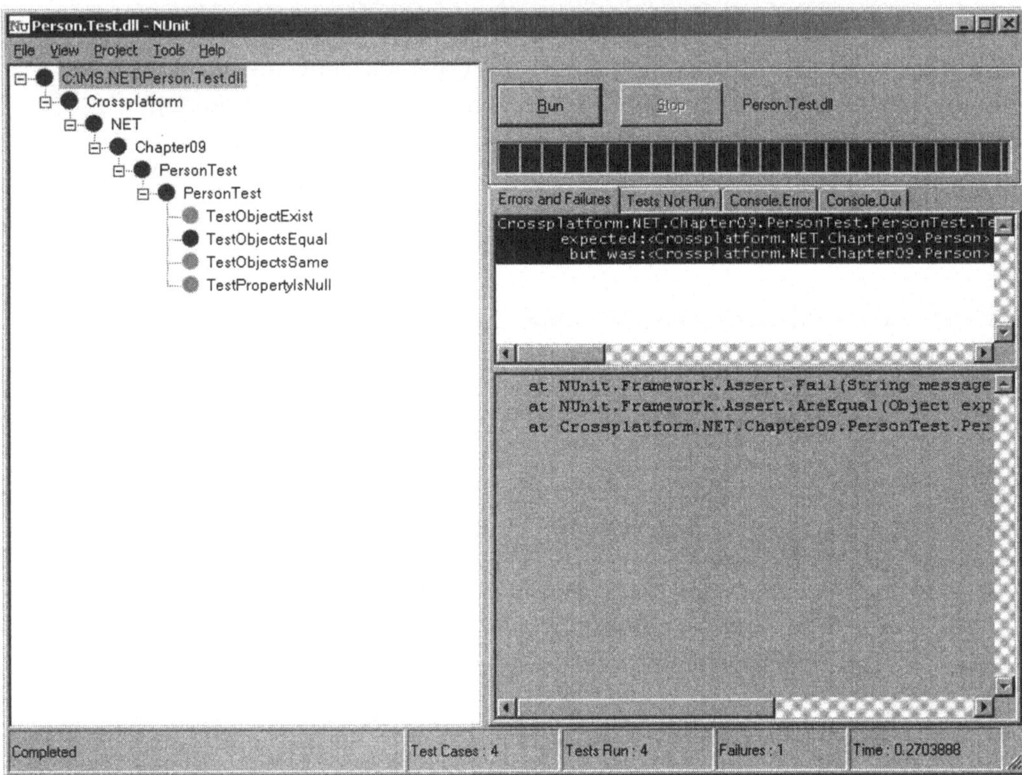

Figure 9-6. Failure message

Why does `TestObjectsEqual()` fail? `Person` derives from `Object`, a reference type, and by default, `Object.Equals()` compares references, and this is the method that is used by NUnit. If you want, you can override `Person.Equals()` to compare using value-based semantics as opposed to using a reference comparison.

For example, if the `SocialSecurityNumbers` of two instances have the same value, we can consider them equal. For good measure, we throw in additional sensible logic to determine whether two instances of `Person` can be considered to be equal. Alter the code in `Person.cs` as follows:

```
//Person.cs
//... snip snip
public override bool Equals(object o)
{
    bool returnValue = false;
    // cast our parameter to the correct type for comparison
    Person p = (Person)o;
    if(p.Firstname.ToUpper() == this.Firstname.ToUpper() &&
        p.Surname.ToUpper() == this.Surname.ToUpper() &&
        p.SocialSecurityNumber.ToUpper() == this.SocialSecurityNumber.ToUpper())
    {
            returnValue = true;
    }
    return returnValue;
}

public override int GetHashCode()
{
    return socialSecurityNumber.GetHashCode();
}
```

NOTE The source code for this example can be found in the Chapter_09\tests3 directory at this book's Web site (http://www.cross-platform.net) and the Apress Web site (http://www.apress.com).

The logic now states that two Persons may be considered equal if their first name, surname, and Social Security number are the same. As an added requirement that is enforced by the compiler, any class that overrides the default Equals() method must also override the default GetHashCode() method, because both methods are used behind the scenes if you place the class in any Hashtable type. The following code uses the System.String implementation of GetHashCode() on the Social Security number, because the Social Security number should be unique for each person.

Compile Person.cs into its own library, and recompile Person.Test.cs to reflect the changes in the Person.dll, as follows:

```
C:\MS.NET> csc /target:library /out:Person.dll Person.cs
C:\MS.NET> csc /target:library /out:PersonTest.dll /r:nunit.framework.dll
/r:Person.dll PersonTest.cs
```

Because our Person class now has revised logic for determining equality, the two instances of Person are now considered equal, and thus TestObjectsEqual() now passes.

At this point, you can take a breather as we reexamine our test code. In every Test() method so far, we've created at least one instance of Person and occasionally more than one instance. This makes for tedious coding, but happily, you can resolve the tedium. You can alter the PersonTest class to include some fields that can be initialized and cleaned up in two new methods, by marking these new methods with the Setup and TearDown attributes. The key point here is that the method names are of little importance; the attributes that are assigned to them are significant.

For the sake of cleanliness, we name these methods to match. Note how TestObjectExist() is now smaller and neater, as follows:

```
//Filename PersonTest.cs
// snip snip...

private Person mj;

[SetUp]
public void SetUp()
{

    string email = "Mj.Easton@Crossplatform.NET";
    this.mj = new Person("Mj", "Easton", "111-222", email);
}

[Test]
public void TestObjectExist()
{
    // this is now smaller and neater

    Assert.IsNotNull(this.mj, "constructor fails");
}
```

```
[TearDown]
public void TearDown()
{
    // clean up code here.  No cleanup needed
    // in this trivial example, so demo console stuff
    Console.WriteLine("This output is redirected to the screen...");
    Console.Error.WriteLine("... if you are running the GUI version");
}
```

NOTE The source code for this example can be found in the `Chapter_09\tests4` directory at this book's Web site (`http://www.cross-platform.net`) and the Apress Web site (`http://www.apress.com`).

The subtlety of `SetUp` and `TearDown` is that unlike the `Init()` and `Dispose()` style methods that you have probably mapped these attributes to in your head, the `SetUp` and `TearDown` methods are called *before and after each test* in your test fixture. This means that the state of `PersonTest.mj` is reset with each test that runs. So, for example, if `Test1()` alters the state of `mj.Email`, it will be reset by the time that `Test2()` starts executing. If you happen to overlook this fact while you are designing your tests, you may end up with unexpected results.

TIP In this example, the `Person` class is so trivial that you don't need any `TearDown` code, so we've taken the opportunity to demonstrate the NUnit feature of redirecting `Console.WriteLine()` and `Console.Error.WriteLine()` to the Standard Out and Standard Error tabs in the GUI.

It's time to flesh out `Person` a little more and put some meat on `Person`'s bones. You can add some validation for the e-mail addresses by checking that the value that is passed in to the `Email` property's `set` is a correctly formatted e-mail address. If the e-mail address is valid, accept it; if it's not valid, raise an exception and leave the old e-mail address in place.

The raising of the exception is crucial, because it allows you to see NUnit's `ExpectedException` attribute in action.

We now use the `IsEmail()` method that we introduced in Chapter 6 to carry out the validation. Alter the `Person` class as follows, remembering to add `System.Text.RegularExpressions` to the `using` list. In addition, we define a new `Exception` to be raised as a nested class in `Person`:

```
// Filename: Person.cs
using System;
using System.Text.RegularExpressions;
// snip snip...
public string Email
{
    get{return email;}
    set
    {
        if (this.isEmail(value))
        {
            email = value;
            this.RaisePersonChangedEvent(EventArgs.Empty);
        }
        else
        {
            throw new InvalidEmailException(value);
        }
    }
}

// snip snip...
private bool isEmail(string value)
{
    string emailExpr = @"^([a-zA-Z0-9_\-\.]+)@((\[[0-9]{1,3}\.[0-9]"+
                       @"{1,3}\.[0-9]{1,3}\.)|(([a-zA-Z0-9\-]+\.)+)"+
                       @")([a-zA-Z]{2,4}|[0-9]{1,3})(\]?)$";
    return (new Regex(emailExpr).IsMatch(value));
}

// snip snip...now for the Exception class
public class InvalidEmailException : System.Exception
{
    private string email;
    public InvalidEmailException(string email)
    {
        this.email = email;
    }
```

```
    public override string Message
    {
        get
        {
            if (this.email != null)
            {
                return base.Message + " " + this.email +
                       " is not a valid email address.";
            }
            else
            {
                return base.Message;
            }
        }
    }
}
```

You now need to test a couple of different things in the `Email` property's `set` method, such as whether it works when a valid e-mail address is passed in and whether it throws an exception when an invalid e-mail address is passed in.

In general, if an exception is raised during a test, NUnit considers the test a failure, although, as mentioned earlier in the chapter, the `ExpectedException` attribute can be used to declare that a test is explicitly expected to throw an exception. The `ExpectedException` attribute effectively negates the result of any `Assert` calls within a test method and allows the test's success to be determined by whether the specified type of exception is thrown.

NOTE For testing exception handling, you are still required to mark your method with the `Test` attribute. Also, note that the `ExpectedException` attribute has a parameter that lists the type of exception you expect to raise.

To test that the `Email` property correctly throws an `InvalidEmailException` when passed an illegal e-mail address, we add the following test to the `PersonTest` class:

```
[Test]
[ExpectedException(typeof(Person.InvalidEmailException))]
public void TestEmailException()
{
    // deliberately try to throw exception
    this.mj.Email = "mj#Snifferoo.com";
}
```

We also need to devise a test to check that when a faulty e-mail address is passed to the `Email` property, the original e-mail address remains intact. To achieve this, we need to trigger the exception and catch it within the test method to ensure that the test isn't automatically failed. We use the following code:

```
[Test]
public void TestEmailExceptionLogic()
{
    string bogusEmail = "mj#Snifferoo.com";
    string oldEmail = this.mj.Email;
    bool testWorking = false;
    string m = "Test failed as InvalidEmailException was not thrown";
    // deliberately try to throw exception
    try
    {
        this.mj.Email = bogusEmail;
    }
    catch(Person.InvalidEmailException e)
    {
        testWorking = true;
        // designed behavior is to leave old email
        // in event of new email being invalid
        Assert.IsTrue((oldEmail == this.mj.Email), e.Message);
       Assert.IsFalse((this.mj.Email == bogusEmail), "Bogus email was assigned");
    }
    finally
    {
        Assert.IsTrue(testWorking, m);
    }
}
```

NOTE The source code for this example can be found in the Chapter_09\tests5 directory at this book's Web site (http://www.cross-platform.net) and the Apress Web site (http://www.apress.com).

Testing private Methods

Because isEmail() is a helper method, it's declared with private scope. This means that to test it explicitly, we need to either change its scope or create a public method that forwards a call to the private implementation.

Making a method accessible to allow it to be unit-tested extricates us from the realms of blackbox testing, and it raises the question of whether testing private methods is a sensible thing. Although there are various schools of thought about the suitability of blackbox testing versus whitebox testing, it is reasonable to say that if the inner workings of a class cannot be adequately tested using only blackbox testing, it is justifiable to also test the class's private methods.

A good way to test private methods is to create an additional public wrapper method for the private method that is declared with the ConditionalAttribute. This ensures that the public method can be called only if the specified compilation symbol is declared in the calling class.

For example, the following TestIsEmail() method is declared with the Conditional attribute being passed DEBUG as a parameter. This means that it can be compiled into the Person class only when the DEBUG compilation symbol is declared.

```
// Filename: Person.cs
[System.Diagnostics.Conditional("DEBUG")]
public void TestIsEmail(string email, ref bool passed)
{
    passed = this.isEmail(email);
}
```

The PersonTest class can then contain test methods that explicitly test isEmail() by calling the TestIsEmail() method, as follows:

```
// Filename: PersonTest.cs
[Test]
public void TestIsEmailForTrue()
{
    string m = "IsEmail did not identify a valid address";

    bool passed = true;
    this.mj.TestIsEmail (this.mj.Email, ref passed);
    Assert.IsTrue(passed, m);
}

[Test]
public void TestIsEmailForFalse()
{
    string m = "IsEmail did not identify an invalid address properly";
    bool passed = false;
    this.mj.TestIsEmail ("Scooby.Don't", ref passed);
    Assert.IsFalse(passed, m);
 }
```

To recompile the `Person.cs` and `PersonTest.cs` classes, you can use the following commands, remembering to use the `DEBUG` compilation symbol if you want to include the `TestIsEmail()` method that is mentioned in the sidebar "Testing private Methods." Figure 9-7 illustrates the additional tests.

```
mono@linux:~ % mcs /target:library /d:DEBUG /out:Person.dll Person.cs
mono@linux:~ % mcs /target:library /d:DEBUG /out:PersonTest.dll \
> /r:NUnit.Framework.dll /r:Person.dll PersonTest.cs
```

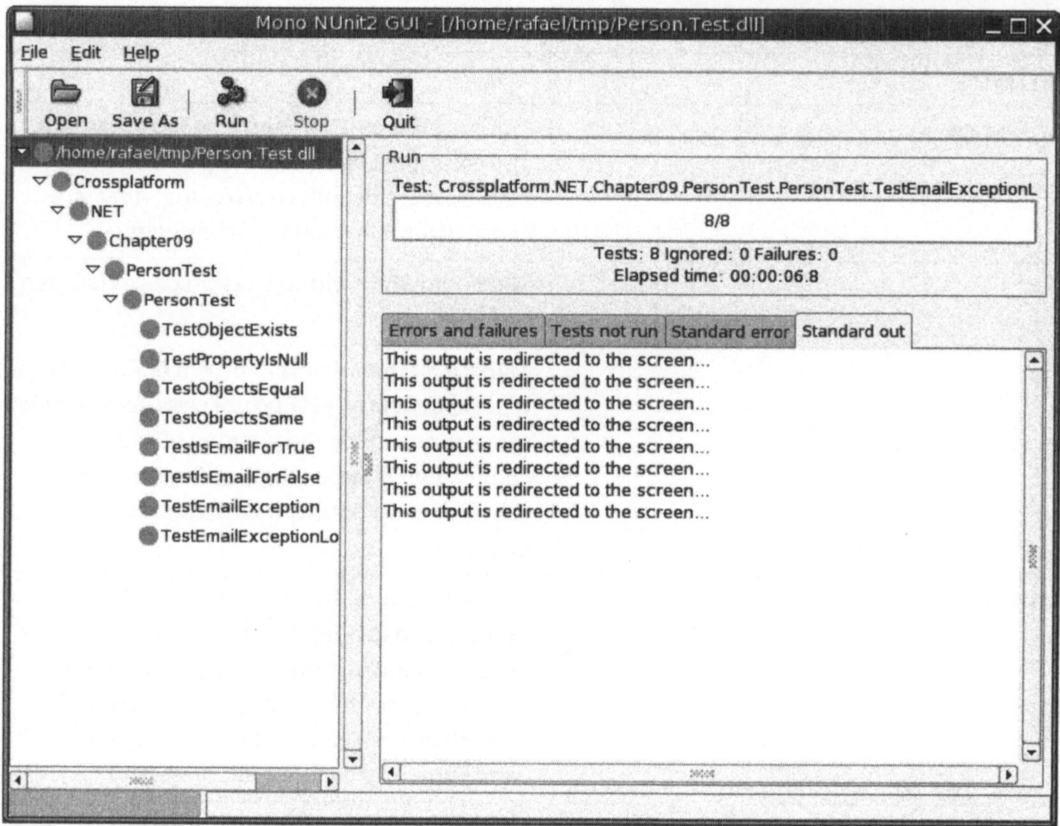

Figure 9-7. Revised and additional tests

Having so far introduced a few of the NUnit attributes, Table 9-2 shows a definitive list of all the attributes that are available within NUnit. All of these attributes are located in the `NUnit.Framework` namespace.

Who Watches the Watchmen?

Looking back at the `TestEmailExceptionLogic` code, you can see that an extra sneaky test checks that the test you have written is valid. Your test is required to throw the correct exception type, and additionally, you may have inadvertently attempted to set a correct e-mail address such as `bogusEmail = "jason.king@crossplatform.net"`.

Table 9-2. NUnit Attributes

Attribute	Usage
`TestFixture`	Marks a class as a container for `Test` methods. The class must be a public export and must have a `public` default constructor—that is, a constructor that takes no parameters.
`Test`	Marks a method within a `TestFixture` class as a test method.
`SetUp`	Marks a method that is to be run before every `Test` method in a `TestFixture` class. An example usage may include the opening of a database connection. If more than one `SetUp` method exists for a test fixture, that fixture will not be run.
`TearDown`	Marks a method that is to be called after every `Test` method in a `TestFixture` class. An example usage may include the closing of a database connection or other freeing of resources. If more than one `TearDown` method exists for a test fixture, that fixture will not be run.
`TestFixtureSetUp` and `TestFixtureTearDown`	These are similar to the more granular `SetUp` and `TearDown`, but they are executed only once per test fixture, as opposed to once per test.
`ExpectedException(Type ExceptionType)`	Marks a `Test` method as one that will throw an exception of a certain type. If the exception is thrown, the test passes; if the exception is not thrown, the test is considered a fail. Test will fail even if the thrown exception is a descendant of the expected exception. Furthermore, any additional tests that are defined with that particular `Test` will not affect the overall result. Therefore, an expected exception test will pass if the correct exception is thrown, even if the test also contains deliberate fails such as `Assert.IsTrue("boo" == "hiss")`.
`Suite`	Provided for backward compatibility. If you do not already use it, do not start.

Table 9-2. NUnit Attributes (Continued)

Attribute	Usage
`Ignore(string Reason)`	Marking a `Test` with `Ignore` will prevent the `Test` from being run. This should be used only as a temporary measure, and it is preferable to removing a test altogether and then forgetting to reimplement it. Ignored tests are listed in the Tests Not Run tab of the GUI. An example is as follows: `[Test][Ignore("Database not reindexed yet; come back later."]`

If you were tired when you wrote this test and made this mistake—and hadn't put in this failsafe—the test would pass and you would never know whether the logic worked correctly. Try it now with this deliberate usage of a correct e-mail address instead of an incorrect one.

Designing with Tests in Mind

Although choosing the right way to implement unit testing is something of a personal and project-dependent choice, one school of thought advocates test-based development, which holds that tests for a class or a method should be written before the class or method exists. As the theory goes, by writing the test first, you help clarify the expected functionality of the class and demonstrate how it will be used.

Regardless of whether writing tests before the code to be tested is right for you, it embodies an excellent software development principle: You should design systems in a way that facilitates easy testing. If code is written without considering how it can be tested, it's far too easy to create code that cannot be easily tested. With this goal in mind, it is time to revisit the Model-View-Controller (MVC) pattern that you learned about in Chapter 5 within this context of designing with tests in mind. Regardless of the variations in interpretation of this pattern, from a testing perspective, the pattern is ideal. By separating domain functionality from display functionality—that is, no more core logic is behind buttons—you are left with a system that is considerably easier to test. If all your domain logic and functionality live in the model, you can write tests for the model. However, if your domain logic is an integral part of the GUI, not only will you find testing unnecessarily difficult, but you will also need to duplicate the test—and the code that the test is targeting—for each GUI that you bolt on.

Testing the Model-View-Controller

As a starting point, we modify the source code for the Controller.cs, View.cs, and ConsoleView.cs classes from Chapter 5. For the sake of consistency, we convert their namespaces from Crossplatform.NET.Chapter05 to Crossplatform.NET.Chapter09, as we did earlier for Person.cs.

We can then compile the code for the model, view, and controller into a handy assembly, which in turn can be referenced by the following test code:

```
C:\MS.NET> csc /target:library /out:MVC.dll Person.cs Controller.cs
View.cs ConsoleView.cs
```

Having already written tests for the model, which in this case is Person, all that's left is to write some tests for the controller, the view, and the relationships and interactions between them.

The MVCTest class starts with some private fields to store the various elements of the MVC and has a public default constructor. Following this is the SetUp() method, which is used to initialize the relationships between the elements of the MVC and is called before each test is run, as follows:

NOTE The source code for this example can be found in the Chapter_09\testsMVC directory at this book's Web site (http://www.cross-platform.net) and the Apress Web site (http://www.apress.com)

```
//Filename MVCTest.cs
using System;
using NUnit.Framework;
using Crossplatform.NET.Chapter09;

namespace Crossplatform.NET.Chapter09.MVCTests
{
    [TestFixture]
    public class MVCTest
    {
        private Person model;
        private View view;
        private Controller controller;

        public MVCTest(){}
```

```
[SetUp]
public void SetUp()
{
     //Set up all objects, and their relationships
    this.model = new Person("Timothy",
                            "Ring",
                            "000-111",
                            "Timothy.Ring@Crossplatform.net");

    this.controller = new Controller(this.model);
    this.view = new ConsoleView(this.model, this.controller);
    this.controller.View = this.view;
}
```

To test the relationship between the controller and model, we create a test that checks that the usage of the controller is suitably reflected in the state of the model, as follows:

```
[Test]
public void TestControllerModelInteraction()
{
   string newEmail = "Power.Unlimited@crossplatform.net";
   this.controller.ChangeFirstname("Monty");
   this.controller.ChangeSurname("Burns");
   this.controller.ChangeEmail(newEmail);
   // this.controller.ChangeSSN("012-345");
   // string SSNPostChange = this.model.SocialSecurityNumber;
   Assert.AreEqual("Monty", this.model.Firstname, "C-M Firstname broken");
   Assert.AreEqual("Burns", this.model.Surname, "C-M Surname broken");
   Assert.AreEqual(newEmail, this.model.Email, "C-M email broken");
   // Assert.AreEqual("012-345", SSNPostChange, "C-M ssn broken");
}
```

Then, to test the relationship between the controller and the view, we create a basic test that checks whether the controller has a reference to a view, as follows:

```
[Test]
public void TestReferencesExist()
{
    string message = "Controller should have a view";
    Assert.IsNotNull(this.controller.View, message);
}
```

Finally, the `TestControllerModelViewInteraction()` method demonstrates the `Ignore` attribute, which tells the NUnit framework not to run the test. The method should check the whole round-trip, from controller to model to view, as follows:

```
        [Test][Ignore("Write wrappers and fill in tests")]
        public void TestControllerModelViewInteraction()
        {
            // test publicly exposed wrappers here
        }
    }
}
```

Because all the views that were created in Chapter 5 rely on `private` fields for storing controls such as labels, testing a view requires some design decisions about how, or indeed whether, these private fields should be tested. Earlier in this chapter, the conditional method `TestIsEmail()` was demonstrated as a simple way to test the `private isEmail()` method, and this idea could easily be extended to allow the creation of read-only `public` fields that similarly wrap those `private` members that require testing.

The crucial point in this decision is to consider whether a particular view is complex enough to warrant the creation of these wrapper methods and fields. For a busy form that reflects a complex model, perhaps a few hours spent bulking up the view with `public` wrappers and writing tests will save hours of manual inspection and screen blindness every time a change is made in the codebase.

For this simple MVC example, the complexity of the model and view is minimal, so we forgo testing the view and its relationship with the controller and model.

Although these tests are straightforward, their importance should not be underestimated, because they test the core concepts of the MVC example.

We now compile the test code and load it into NUnit to run the tests, and we make sure that everything is working as expected:

```
C:\MS.NET> csc /target:library /out:MVCTest.dll
/r:nunit.framework.dll /r:MVC.dll MVCTest.cs
```

Figure 9-8 shows the results of the MVC tests, complete with output from the `Ignore` attribute.

At this point, you should be all tested out. We finish this section by mentioning that because NUnit is being embraced by more programmers, its integration with other tools is likely to grow. As a starting point, the `ReadMe.pdf` file that is included with NUnit documents one such example, which is the integration of NUnit with Microsoft's Visual Studio. A number of open source projects are also working to enhance NUnit by creating additional features, such as automatic test creation, and many of these projects can be found at `http://www.sourceforge.net`.

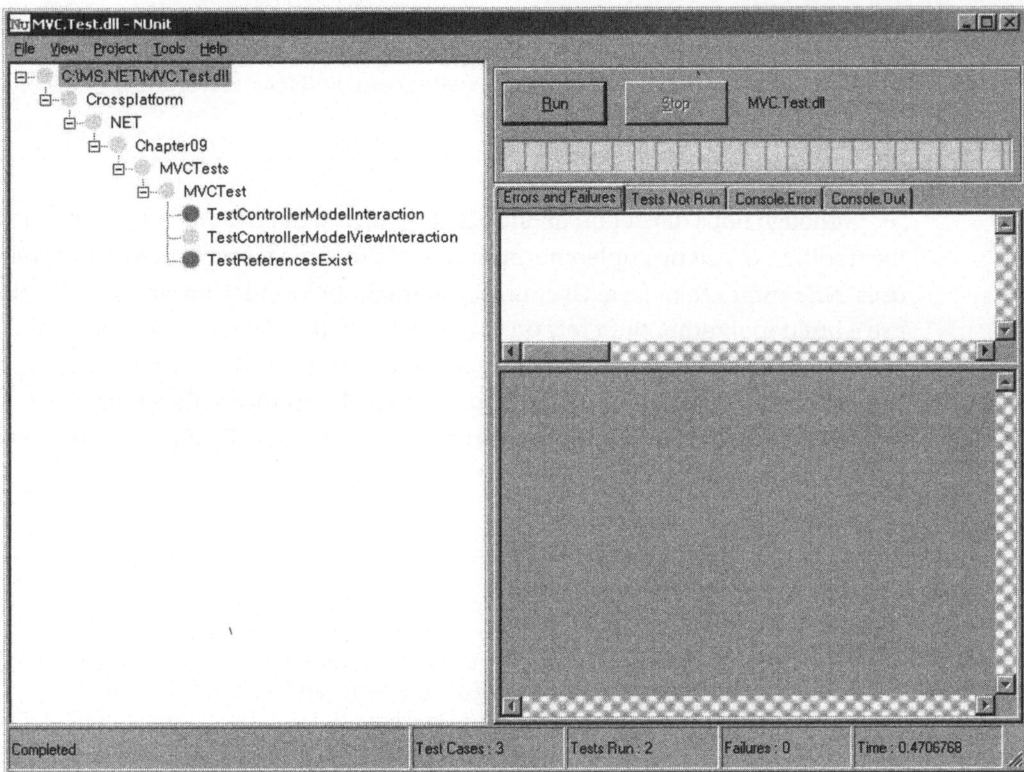

Figure 9-8. MVC tests running in the Windows GUI

Building a Brighter Future: NAnt

Simply put, NAnt is the .NET version of Ant, which is an XML-based build tool that is written in Java. Conceived under a flag of annoyance waved by James Duncan Davidson, Ant was developed in response to perceived inadequacies of other build tools, such as `make`, which depend heavily on the availability of certain operating system commands. Although previous build tools were excellent at using specific operating system features, they raised a number of problems for cross-platform development, because not all operating systems have the same set of commands available.

Ant was different because it no longer used operating system commands to carry out build tasks, but instead it relied on Java, which made it intrinsically cross-platform. Likewise, instead of using an esoteric text file format, Ant relies on XML configuration files that can be easily processed by software and humans alike.

TIP Ant is alive and kicking to this day. It is supported and maintained by a comprehensive team, and it can be found at `http://ant.apache.org`.

Although not a direct port of Ant, NAnt—which stands for *Not Ant*—continues the tradition of Ant by implementing many of the same features as Ant, but NAnt uses .NET rather than Java. Of course, you might be wondering why you should use a build tool rather than rely on your trusty old IDE. While compiling and building a project with a single menu command is intuitively easy and might suffice for small programs, for larger projects with significant development teams, it's essential that the system can be built automatically, ensuring that each build is performed in a reproducible fashion.

TIP For advocates of Visual Studio .NET who want to try NAnt, the good news is that a number of freely available tools can convert VS .NET solution files into NAnt build scripts. One such tool that we highly recommend is SLiNgshoT, which can be downloaded from `http://nantcontrib.sourceforge.net`.

More important, when you're developing cross-platform software, which increases the number of things that can go wrong during a build, using a unified build tool like NAnt can be essential. Not only does it allow you to test building your software with more than one CLI implementation, but it also reduces the need to type in complex command-line instructions, as we've done throughout the examples in this book.

By the end of this section, we will have investigated various techniques and approaches for using NAnt effectively. Some you may dismiss as not being suitable for yourself, and some may prove to be ideal for your purposes. Along the way, you will pick up enough knowledge of NAnt to make it work for you in a clear and manageable fashion. We guarantee that if NAnt doesn't make your cross-platform development life easier, you can send us your hat and we'll eat it!

Eating Your Hat

JK Ha ha! I remember a few years ago I came across a Web site called HatsOfMeat.com.

MJ Oh dear, I think can see what's coming here. . . .

JK Indeed, it was fantastic. If you ever wanted to wear a pork chop deer-stalker or a minced-meat baseball cap, this was the site for you! Amusing pictures, great commentary, sartorial diet advice.

MJ Sounds like a winner. Is it still live?

JK Nah, but if you Google the term *HatsOfMeat*, you should get some links to some sites that cache the contents.

MJ I must check it out. In the meantime, don't ever let me hear you use "Google" as a verb ever again!

NAnt is distributed with three other open source libraries: NUnit, NDoc, and SharpZipLib. As expected, each of these libraries has its own license details. We discussed NUnit earlier in the chapter, so what a boon it is to know that it integrates with NAnt. We'll overlook SharpZipLib and NDoc at this point, but suffice it to say that the former is a C# compression library and the latter is a documenting tool that is great for creating professional documentation for your .NET projects.

TIP You can find NAnt at `http://nant.sourceforge.net`, along with documentation and links to the licensing details. NDoc can be found at `http://ndoc.sourceforge.net`, and SharpZipLib can be found at `http://www.icsharpcode.net/OpenSource/SharpZipLib`.

NAnt Overview

NAnt is written in C# and allows you to run various tasks sequentially, or in an arbitrary order. NAnt currently only runs under Mono and Microsoft .NET CLIs, although open source support for Portable.NET is planned for the near future.

Portable.NET and CSAnt

While the world waits for the open source community to develop Portable.NET support for NAnt, an alternative build system, called CSAnt, ships with Portable.NET. Once again, CSAnt uses an XML file to denote build instructions, and it features some support for NAnt build files. Fortunately, CSAnt ships with a manual page—`man CSAnt`—and has further details listed under *Build Management* in the information page. This page can be accessed on UNIX-based systems using `info pnettools`.

To get a feel for NAnt's power, consider a project that needs to build a cross-platform library that works with .NET, Mono, and Portable.NET. It might be necessary to compile the source code with each of the CLI implementations, run unit tests against the library for each target CLI, and then package the resulting DLL in a ZIP file. Remember to delete any intermediate files in the process and push any updated source code to your source code repository. If you take a second to contemplate how many command-line shenanigans this process would involve, you should rest easy when we tell you that NAnt can do all of this—and much more.

With a few well-placed tags in a NAnt build script, you can perform a variety of tasks, including compilation of source code, interactions with the file system, file compression, and unit testing, to name but a few. Should you so desire, you can even create your own custom tasks. NAnt has so many features that it would take a small library to cover them all, so in this section, we concentrate on the core functionality from the perspective of cross-platform development.

Installation and Testing

NAnt is distributed as source code but also includes the latest executable file; it can be downloaded as a ZIP file from `http://nant.sourceforge.net`.

For a Microsoft .NET setup, installation involves a couple of additional steps: Unzip all the files into a new folder and set the system path to point to your `nant/bin` folder.

On Mono, you must rebuild NAnt: Unzip the NAnt files into a new folder, navigate to that folder, and use the following commands on a UNIX-based system:

```
mono@linux:~ % make clean
mono@linux:~ % make bootstrap
```

After building NAnt, you can drill down through the `build` folder until you find `NAnt.exe`. Typing **mono NAnt.exe –help** at the Mono command prompt should produce the console output shown in Figure 9-9.

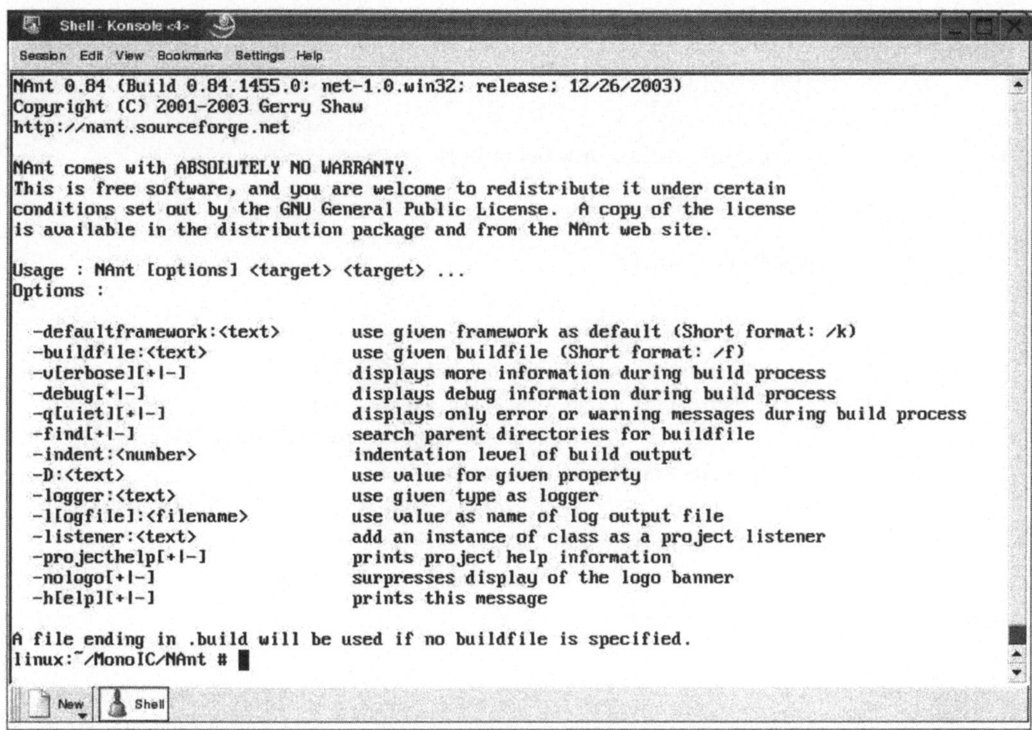

Shell - Konsole <4>
Session Edit View Bookmarks Settings Help
NAnt 0.84 (Build 0.84.1455.0; net-1.0.win32; release; 12/26/2003)
Copyright (C) 2001-2003 Gerry Shaw
http://nant.sourceforge.net
NAnt comes with ABSOLUTELY NO WARRANTY.
This is free software, and you are welcome to redistribute it under certain
conditions set out by the GNU General Public License. A copy of the license
is available in the distribution package and from the NAnt web site.
Usage : NAnt [options] <target> <target> ...
Options :
-defaultframework:<text> use given framework as default (Short format: /k)
-buildfile:<text> use given buildfile (Short format: /f)
-v[erbose][+|-] displays more information during build process
-debug[+|-] displays debug information during build process
-q[uiet][+|-] displays only error or warning messages during build process
-find[+|-] search parent directories for buildfile
-indent:<number> indentation level of build output
-D:<text> use value for given property
-logger:<text> use given type as logger
-l[ogfile]:<filename> use value as name of log output file
-listener:<text> add an instance of class as a project listener
-projecthelp[+|-] prints project help information
-nologo[+|-] surpresses display of the logo banner
-h[elp][+|-] prints this message
A file ending in .build will be used if no buildfile is specified.
linux:~/MonoIC/NAnt #
New
Shell

Figure 9-9. NAnt on Mono, proudly displaying its help

To get a feel for what NAnt is all about, we revisit the simple `GetInfo` program that was introduced in Chapter 2 and create a build script to make the `GetInfo.exe` executable file.

NOTE The source code for this example can be found in the `Chapter_09\buildGetInfo` directory at this book's Web site (`http://www.cross-platform.net`) and the Apress Web site (`http://www.apress.com`).

In case you have misplaced your `GetInfo` program, here it is again with an updated namespace to suit:

```
//Filename: GetInfo.cs
using System;

namespace Crossplatform.NET.Chapter09
{
    class GetInfo
    {
        static void Main()
        {
            GetInfo info = new GetInfo();
        }

        public GetInfo ()
        {
            Console.WriteLine("--------------------------------------");
            Console.WriteLine("Code in Main file.");
            Console.WriteLine("Operating system: " +
                                  Environment.OSVersion.Platform.ToString());
            Console.WriteLine("OS Version: " +
                                  Environment.OSVersion.Version.ToString());
            Console.WriteLine("Today's date is: " +
                                    DateTime.Today.ToString());
        }
    }
}
```

We use this program to demonstrate the simplest NAnt build script that you'll probably ever see. The file for GetInfo is aptly called GetInfo.build and uses the minimum number of features that you can get away with in a NAnt script. The script consists of some XML elements that combine to form the various features of a build script—elements that define and describe the NAnt project, along with, in this case, a single *target*, whose purpose is to build an executable file. For any task—such as <csc/>—to be executed, it must be contained within a <target/> element. Each <target/> may have one or more tasks, and each build file may have one or more targets. This concept of the multitarget build file is demonstrated later in the chapter. For this simple example, only one <target/> is necessary. The code is as follows:

```
<?xml version = "1.0"?>
<project name = "GetInfoBuild" default = "Build">
    <target name = "Build" description = "Builds the GetInfo.exe executable">
        <csc target = "exe" output = "GetInfo.exe">
            <sources>
                <include name = "GetInfo.cs"/>
            </sources>
        </csc>
    </target>
</project>
```

We'll examine all the elements that are used in this example a little later, so don't worry about them now—just feel satisfied that you have a working build tool.

Running the build script is simple, and NAnt automatically detects which platform it is running on to determine which compiler should be used for building the project. However, if you have more than one framework installed and you prefer to compile the project using a different CLI implementation, you can explicitly tell NAnt which platform you are targeting on the command line, as shown in Table 9-3.

Table 9-3. Command-Line Parameters for Targeting Specific CLI Implementations

CLI Implementation	Command-Line Parameter
Microsoft .NET 1.0	`-k:net-1.0`
Microsoft .NET 1.1	`-k:net-1.1`
Microsoft Compact Framework	`-k:netcf-1.0`
Mono 1.0	`-k:mono-1.0`

Although NAnt automatically searches the current working directory to try and locate a build file to run, you can also use the `-buildfile` command-line argument to specify the name of the script to run, as shown in the following command and as illustrated in Figure 9-10.

```
C:\MS.NET>\nant -k:net-1.1 -buildfile:GetInfo.build
```

TIP The `-buildfile` command-line option may be substituted with the shorter form of `-f`.

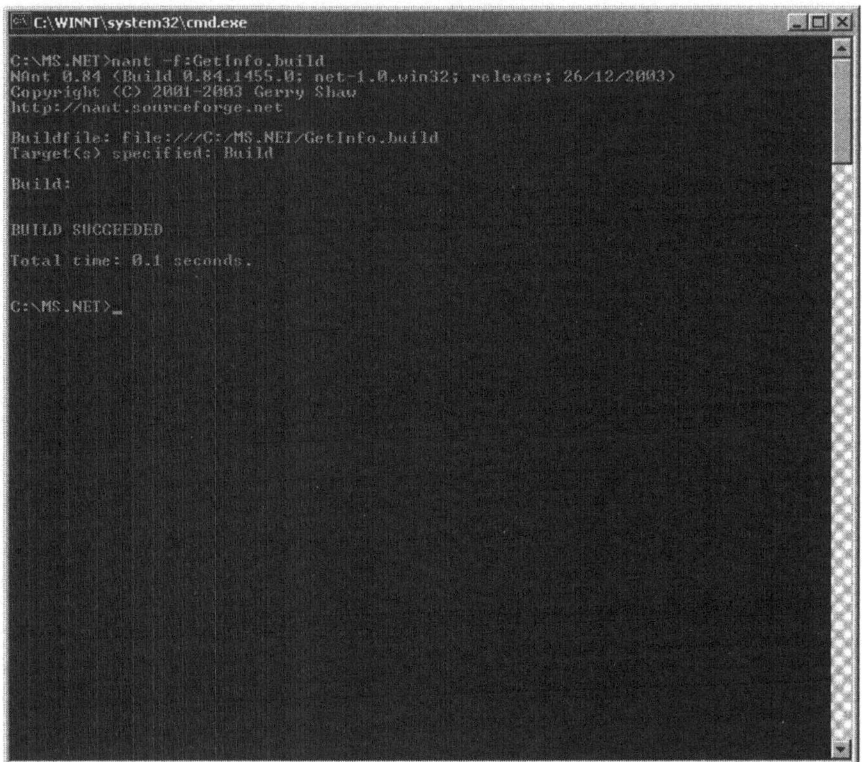

Figure 9-10. `GetInfo.cs` *built into an executable file*

Building a Strategy

Although on one level, NAnt is just a glorified compilation tool, on another level, it's a very powerful and extendable framework that can be used to carry out a number of different tasks, from compiling an assembly, to manipulating the file system, to managing source control, to packaging files in a ZIP file.

TIP While NAnt is packaged with numerous built-in tasks, a large library of external tasks written by other developers—such as Visual SourceSafe and StarTeam integration—is also packaged in the separate NAntContrib project, which is hosted at `http://nantcontrib.sourceforge.net`.

With so much functionality available, you might feel like a chimp in a banana plantation, but you don't have to gorge yourself on all the succulent fruit in a single sitting. Just as you take care with your architecture, class hierarchies, and coding standards, you should also take care with your build scripts. When a script is overly complicated, understanding it becomes a dark art, and inventing a complicated script is a good way of backing yourself into the corner labeled *Master Builder.*

Understandably, the more complex a project becomes, the more complex the script is likely to become. Hence, it is conceivable that one day you may cause some subtle bug that takes a lifetime to track down, or even worse, you might package your `MacMenu` class in your Windows distribution. In either event, the build file is often the last place that you'll look for errors, when perhaps it should be the first. With this in mind, a well-documented build script, complete with flow diagrams and clearly defined targets, is far easier to maintain than umpteen pages of XML.

As an introduction to the main features of NAnt, we start by building on our previous work and develop some scripts for the `Person` class and MVC demonstrated earlier in this chapter. To get the ball rolling, a suitable starting point for this jaunt is an examination of NAnt's `<project/>` element.

Script Purpose: Making Use of the <project/> Element

Before creating a build script, as with any coding task, you should define exactly what you wish to achieve. Is the script going to be used for building and testing code? Manipulating source control? Compressing and archiving? Distribution? Or is it going to encompass a combination of these?

Because you're just starting out with NAnt, we'll now just settle for building the `Person` class and running the unit tests that we created earlier in the chapter. Each build file contains a single project, and in turn, the project contains one or more `<target/>` elements, which define the tasks that NAnt must perform. The `<project/>` element has the following three attributes:

- `basedir`: The starting directory from which all path calculations are performed. This is an optional attribute, and it defaults to the current directory.
- `default`: The default `target` to use in the event that no `target` is specified on the command line.
- `name`: The project name, which is an optional attribute.

Additionally, `<project/>` can contain a `<description/>` element that is output when the build file is run with the `-projecthelp` command-line parameter.

TIP For those of you with multiple framework installations, as an alternative to using the `-k` command-line option to specify the target framework, you can include a `currentframework` property in the `<project/>` section of your build file. This property specifies the CLI to use when running the build script, as follows:

```
<property name="nant.settings.currentframework" value="net-1.1" />
```

NOTE The source code for this example can be found in the `Chapter_09\buildPerson` directory at this book's Web site (`http://www.cross-platform.net`) and the Apress Web site (`http://www.apress.com`).

As shown in the following code, the `Person.build` file is similar to our previous build file, although it also takes advantage of a `<description/>` element to help document the file and contains a couple of `<echo/>` elements, which direct NAnt to send some output to the standard output stream:

```
<?xml version="1.0"?>
<!-- Person.build-->
<!-- This is the format for an XML comment -->

<project name="Person " default="build">
    <description>Builds the Person.dll assembly.</description>

    <echo message="This project builds the Person class into a .NET assembly"/>
    <echo message = "Target framework is ${nant.settings.currentframework}" />
```

```
    <target name="build" description="Build Person.cs into Person.dll">
        <csc target="library" output="Person.dll">
            <sources>
                <include name = "Person.cs"/>
            </sources>
        </csc>
    </target>

</project>
```

To test the build file, open a console in your source code directory. Because you now might have more than one build file in your working directory, you need to use the `-buildfile` option to tell NAnt which file to use. Figure 9-11 shows the build command and the resulting screen output.

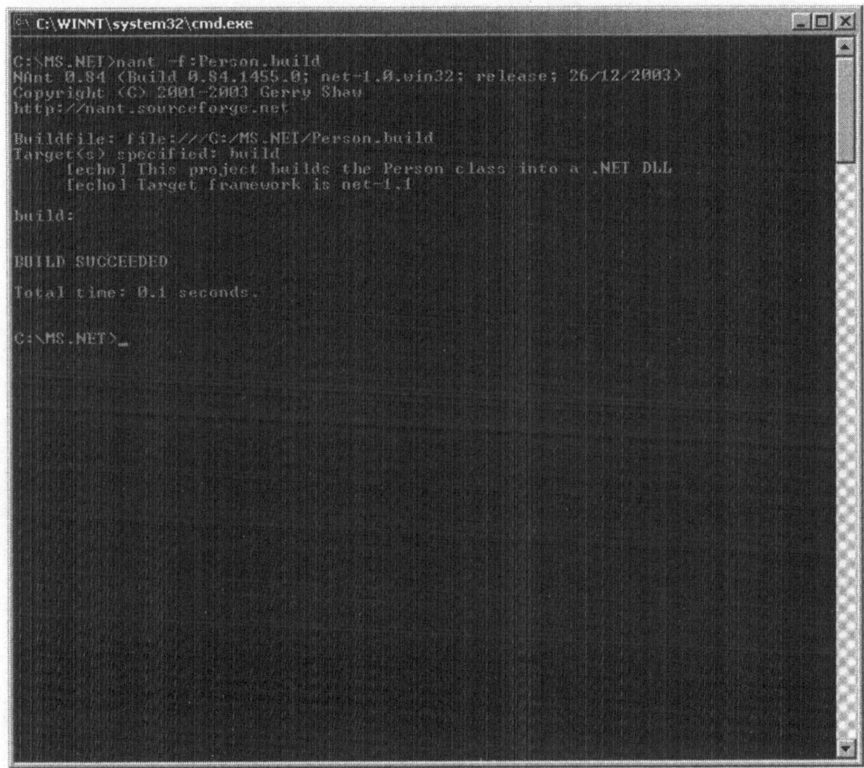

Figure 9-11. `Person.build`

Note how the second `<echo/>` element writes the setting for the `currentframework` property to the console.

Integrating NUnit in the Build Process

Now that we've looked at examples of building a library and an executable assembly, we'll steam ahead and see how unit testing can be made an integral part of the build process.

To demonstrate NAnt's ability to call other .build files by using the <nant/> element, we create three .build files: one for building the production assembly, Person.build; one for building the NUnit test assembly, PersonTest.build; and a third to direct the other two build scripts, Person.Subscript.Wrapper.build.

Because we already have the Person.build file, have a look at the PersonTest.build file, which contains the NAnt instructions for building the PersonTest.dll assembly. The PersonTest.build file is as follows:

```
<?xml version="1.0"?>
<!-- PersonTest.build-->

<project name="Person - build test" default="build">

    <echo message="This project builds the PersonTest.dll assembly"/>
    <echo message="Target platform is ${nant.settings.currentframework}"/>

    <target name="build"
            description="Produces PersonTest.dll for NUnit consumption">
        <csc target="library" output="PersonTest.dll">
            <sources>
                <include name = "PersonTest.cs"/>
            </sources>
            <references>
                <include name = "Person.dll"/>
                <include name = "nunit.framework.dll"/>
            </references>
        </csc>
    </target>
</project>
```

Although this is similar to the files that we've already looked at, you'll notice that the <csc/> task contains an extra <references/> element, which is used to specify the assemblies that are normally declared using the command-line compiler's /r option.

As you can imagine, writing a wrapper for calls to a compiler and specifying the various compiler flags and options is a complex business, and NAnt achieves this by using XML attributes for specifying the singular elements of a csc call, with nested elements specifying those options that can have many values.

The `<csc/>` task from `PersonTest.build` is functionally equivalent to issuing the following command:

```
csc /target:library /out:PersonTest.dll /r:nunit.framework.dll
/r:Person.dll PersonTest.cs
```

TIP A comprehensive guide to the use of `<csc/>` can be found in the `nant/doc/help` directory, which is distributed as part of the NAnt installation.

csc, cscc, and mcs: What's in a Name?

JK With each CLI implementation having a different C# compiler, the NAnt people must have had some real fun coding to cope with them all.

MJ I expect so. In the previous versions, there were separate tasks for calling `csc` and `mcs`, but now, thanks to the framework-targeting functionality, you don't need to worry about the different compilers—simply using `<csc/>` will do the job.

JK Neat! I wonder why they chose to use `<csc/>` as the task name, though.

MJ Indeed, perhaps `<compile/>` would have been a little easier on the eye.

JK Perhaps it's just a matter of time before NAnt makes that change.

VFE* YOU ARE INCORRECT. NANT MUST EVOLVE TO COPE WITH MANY LANGUAGES AND MANY FILENAME EXTENSIONS. A MORE COMPREHENSIVE PLAN **MUST** EVOLVE. . . .

MJ and JK We are swayed by your missive, oh Most Significant Bit!

*Voice from the Ether

You can now test the build file by using the following command, but don't forget to include a copy of `nunit.framework.dll` and `Person.dll` in the source code folder:

```
C:\MS.NET> nant -buildfile:PersonTest.build
```

Finally, we need a file to piece the steps together, `Person.Subscript.Wrapper.build`. Figure 9-12 illustrates the build file.

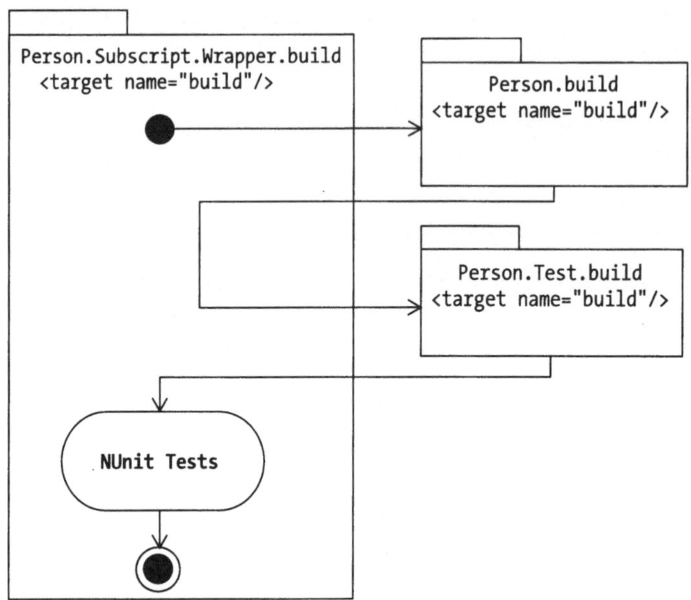

Figure 9-12. Activity diagram showing the `Person.Subscript.Wrapper.build` *script*

The `Person.Subscript.Wrapper.build` file is as follows:

```
<?xml version="1.0"?>
<!-- Person.Subscript.Wrapper.build-->

<project name="Person Sub-script Wrapper" default="build">

    <echo message="Calls Person.build and PersonTest.build and runs the tests."/>

    <target name="build"
        description="Builds Person.dll and PersonTest.dll from sub-scripts">

        <nant buildfile="Person.build"/>
        <nant buildfile="PersonTest.build"/>

        <nunit2>
            <test assemblyname="PersonTest.dll"/>
        </nunit2>

    </target>
</project>
```

The file begins by following the same format as shown before, but the default `<target/>` is now a bit more complex, because it contains a couple of `<nant/>` tasks to call the subscripts and an `<nunit2/>` task to run the unit tests.

Try running this new script using the following command, but don't be alarmed by the high console output from the NUnit tests:

```
mono@linux:~ % mono nant.exe -buildfile:Person.Subscript.Wrapper.build
```

NOTE The source code for this example can be found in the `Chapter_09\buildSubscriptWrapper` directory at this book's Web site (`http://www.cross-platform.net`) and the Apress Web site (`http://www.apress.com`).

Multitarget Build Files

As mentioned earlier in the chapter, the `<target/>` element acts as an entry point into the build file, and while we've so far concentrated on single target files, it's now worth looking at how multitarget build files can be used effectively.

A common feature of build files is a mechanism that removes old files that were created by a previous build. To add this feature to our earlier `Person.build` file, we simply include an additional `<target/>` named `clean`, as follows:

```
<?xml version="1.0"?>
<!-- Person.build-->

<project name="Person " default="build">

    <description>Builds and cleans Person assembly.</description>

    <target name="build" description="Build Person.cs into Person.dll">
        <csc target="library" output="Person.dll">
            <sources>
                <include name = "Person.cs"/>
            </sources>
        </csc>
    </target>
```

```
    <target name="clean"
         description="Deletes any leftover files in preparation for building">
        <echo message="Cleaning files"/>
        <delete file="Person.dll" failonerror="false"/>
    </target>

</project>
```

Because the `<project/>` element's `default` attribute is set to `build`, we can still build the `Person.dll` assembly by using the same command as before, but we now have the option to run the build file with the `clean` target by specifying the target name on the command line, as follows:

```
C:\MS.NET>\nant -f:Person.build clean
```

NOTE The source code for this example can be found in the `Chapter_09\buildCleanPerson` directory at this book's Web site (`http://www.cross-platform.net`) and the Apress Web site (`http://www.apress.com`).

Although this option to clean a previous build is not particularly useful for a simple build process like the one for `Person.dll`, for complex projects with numerous files that are spread across various directories, such a mechanism is imperative.

NOTE An astute reader might have noticed the `failonerror` attribute of the `<delete/>` task. This attribute, if set to `true`, would halt the script and produce a `build failed` message if the file were not successfully deleted.

Target Dependencies

Now that you've seen how a number of targets can be declared within a build file, we need to introduce the concept of *dependencies*, which are declared using the `depends` attribute of the `<target/>` task and can be used to ensure that a target isn't run until another has been run.

When one target depends on another target, NAnt automatically resolves the dependency and runs the targets in the desired order. All is not gold, however, and dealing with the dependencies for complex build files can be a great source of frustration if you don't have a clear plan of action.

To demonstrate some task dependencies in action, we revisit the `Person.Subscript.Wrapper.build` example, but instead of using three different files, we use a single build file, `Person.All.In.One.build`, as follows:

```
<?xml version="1.0"?>
<!-- Person.All.In.One.build-->

<project name="Person all in one" default="BuildAndTest">

    <echo message="Demonstrates task dependencies"/>
    <echo message="Target platform is ${nant.settings.currentframework}"/>

    <target name="BuildAndTest"
            description="Works through resolution of dependency"
            depends="test">
    </target>

    <target name="test"
            description="Runs the PersonTest.dll through NUnit"
            depends="personTest">

            <echo message="Running Nunit"/>
            <nunit2>
                <test assemblyname="PersonTest.dll"/>
            </nunit2>
    </target>

    <target name="personTest"
            description="Produces PersonTest.dll for NUnit consumption"
            depends="person">

            <echo message="Building test dll"/>
            <csc target="library" output="PersonTest.dll">
                <sources>
                    <include name = "PersonTest.cs"/>
                </sources>
                <references>
                   <include name = "Person.dll"/>
                   <include name = "nunit.framework.dll"/>
                </references>
            </csc>
    </target>
```

```
    <target name="person"
            description="Build Person.cs into Person.dll">

            <echo message="Building Person.dll"/>
            <csc target="library" output="Person.dll">
                <sources>
                    <include name = "Person.cs"/>
                </sources>
            </csc>
    </target>

</project>
```

NOTE The source code for this example can be found in the Chapter_09\buildAllInOne directory at this book's Web site (http://www.cross-platform.net) and the Apress Web site (http://www.apress.com).

The file's default target is BuildAndTest, and while it doesn't have any tasks of its own, it's useful in helping to illustrate the depends attribute.

BuildAndTest depends on test, test depends on personTest, and personTest depends on person. This is all straightforward, but for complex projects, resolving these dependencies by looking at the file alone can be a nightmare. This can be readily cured with a simple diagrammatic remedy, as illustrated in Figure 9-13.

In multitarget build files, you should be careful of circular dependencies, which occur when one <target/> relies on another <target/> that already relies on the first <target/>, as follows:

```
<?xml version="1.0"?>
<!-- CircularDependency.build-->
<project name="Deadlock " default="alpha">
    <target name="alpha" depends="omega">
        <echo message = "The Alpha..." />
    </target>
    <target name="omega" depends="alpha">
        <echo message = "...and the omega" />
    </target>
</project>
```

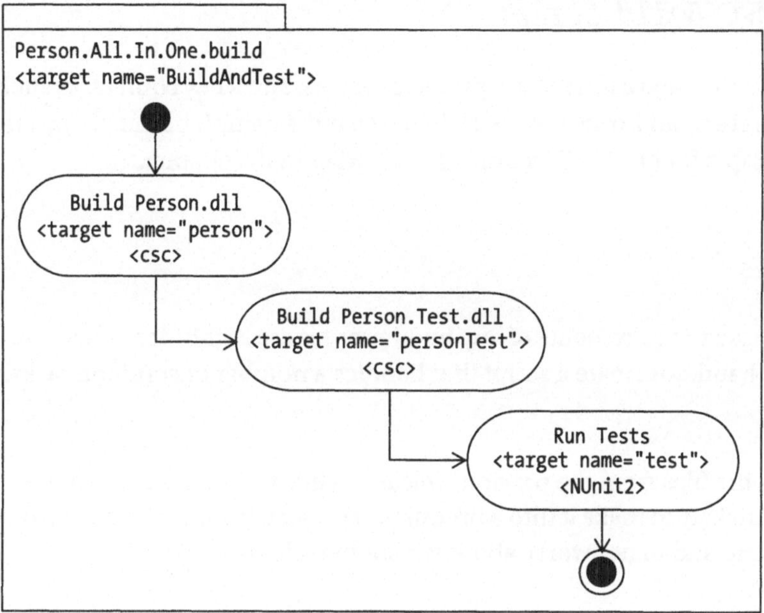

Figure 9-13. The `Person.All.In.One.build` *process*

NOTE The source code for this example can be found in the `Chapter_09\buildCircularDependency` directory at this book's Web site (`http://www.cross-platform.net`) and the Apress Web site (`http://www.apress.com`).

Luckily, NAnt automatically detects these dependencies and issues a warning message whenever you attempt to run such a build file.

When chaining a number of targets together, it's also likely that more than one `<target/>` will rely on the same `<target/>`, although NAnt can detect this and runs each `<target/>` only once during a build. If you need to explicitly run a `<target/>` more than once, use the `<call/>` task to override the default behavior.

A First MVC Build Script

Now that you've learned a little about projects, targets, and a few NAnt tasks such as `<csc/>`, `<delete/>`, and `<nunit2/>`, we'll look at a more complex example by creating some scripts for our MVC example from earlier in the chapter.

Script Goals

Although the exact requirements of any build process are highly dependent on the project at hand, we create a script that handles a number of common tasks, as follows:

- Deletes the files from the previous release. While this defies convention and is unlikely to make it into a production project, it allows us to keep our file system and to not worry about versioning releases.
- Builds the application assemblies.
- Builds the test assemblies.
- Executes all tests. If all the tests pass, the application and supporting files should be copied into a folder named `release`, and any of the temporary build files will be deleted.

Script Design

Although the MVC example doesn't require an extensive build solution, we demonstrate one approach to creating a modular build process by grouping the build logic for separate assemblies into their own build files, and we glue the whole lot together with a *meta-buildfile*. This provides a reasonably elegant solution that can encompass increasing complexity without overly complicating the build files, as illustrated in Figure 9-14.

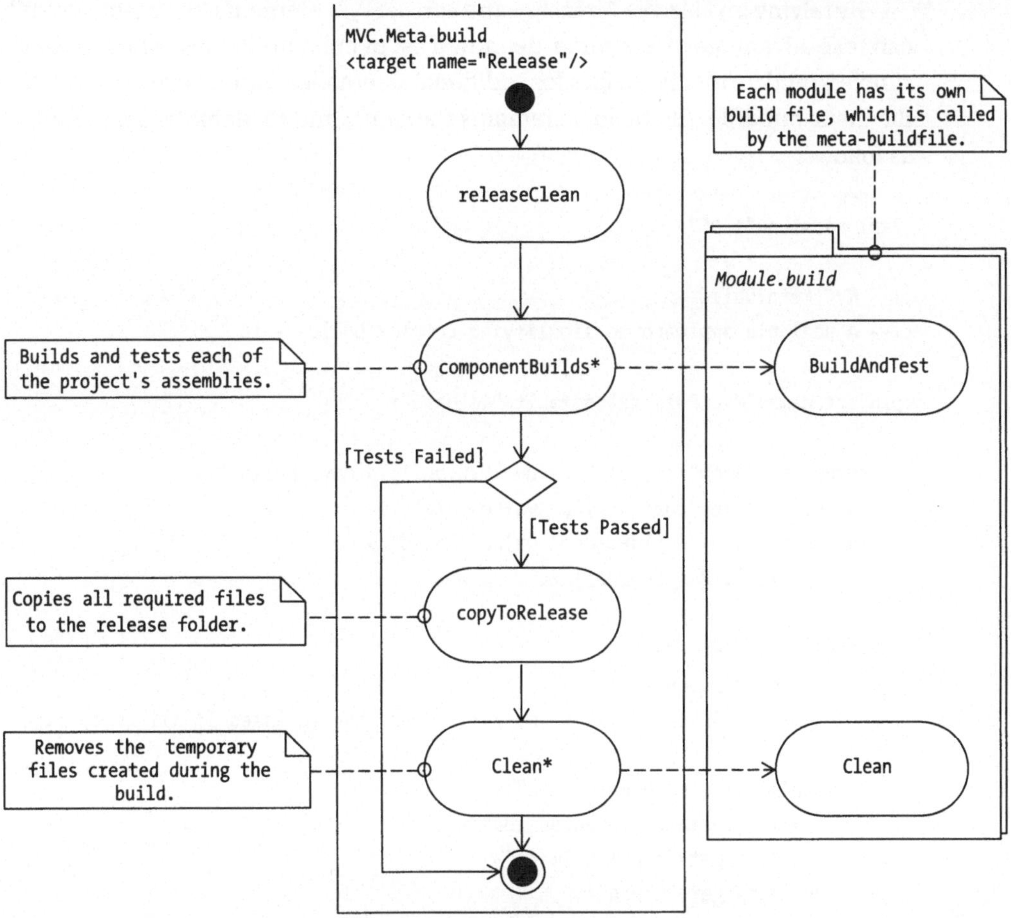

MVC.Meta.build
<target name="Release"/>

Each module has its own build file, which is called by the meta-buildfile.

releaseClean

Module.build

Builds and tests each of the project's assemblies.

componentBuilds*

BuildAndTest

[Tests Failed]

[Tests Passed]

Copies all required files to the release folder.

copyToRelease

Removes the temporary files created during the build.

Clean*

Clean

Figure 9-14. A script for gluing together all the elements of a release

NOTE The source code for this example can be found in the `Chapter_09\buildMVCMetaBuildFile` directory at this book's Web site (`http://www.cross-platform.net`) and the Apress Web site (`http://www.apress.com`).

By relying on NAnt's <foreach/> and <property/> elements, the meta-buildfile can take advantage of a comma-delimited list of child build files, which makes it simple to add further build files for additional assemblies without overcomplicating the meta-buildfile. All the logic remains the same, and readability is retained, as follows:

```
<?xml version="1.0"?>

<!-- MVC.Meta.build-->
<!-- A scalable approach to simplifying complex builds -->

<project name="MVC Release" default="Release">

    <property name="fileList" value="MVC.build,dummy1.build "/>
    <property name="currentFile" value=""/>
    <property name="BuildFolder" value="build"/>
    <mkdir dir="${BuildFolder}"/>

   <target name="Release"
           description =
                 "Deletes files, builds, tests, and releases if all tests pass">

        <call target="releaseClean"/>
        <call target="componentBuilds"/>
        <call target="copyToRelease"/>
        <call target="Clean"/>
    </target>

    <target name="componentBuilds"
            description="runs, builds, and tests in separate files">

        <echo message="Building components and testing..."/>
        <foreach item="String" in="${fileList}" delim="," property="currentFile">
            <nant buildfile="${currentFile}"
                      target="BuildAndTest"
                      inheritall="true"/>
        </foreach>
    </target>

    <target name="Clean"
            description="iterates through list of build files and calls clean">
```

```
        <echo message="Cleaning components..."/>
        <foreach item="String" in="${fileList}" delim="," property="currentFile">
            <nant buildfile="${currentFile}" target="Clean" inheritall="true"/>
        </foreach>
        <delete dir="${BuildFolder}"/>
    </target>

    <target name="releaseClean"
            description="deletes old release files">

        <delete dir="release" failonerror="false"/>
    </target>

    <target name="copyToRelease"
            description="copies files to release folder">

        <mkdir dir="release"/>
        <copy file="${BuildFolder}/mvcApp.exe"
                  tofile="release/mvcApp.exe"
                  overwrite="true"/>
    </target>

</project>
```

The file starts with some `<property/>` elements that are used for declaring variables to use during the build process. The `fileList` property contains a comma-delimited list of the build files that need to be built, `currentFile` is a loop variable that is used when iterating through `fileList`, and `BuildFolder` stores the name of a directory to build the assemblies in.

Next, the `Release` target contains some explicit calls to various targets within the meta-buildfile that have been implemented as a series of `<call/>` tasks, rather than a series of dependencies.

The `componentBuilds` target then demonstrates how to use the `<foreach>` element to iterate through the comma-delimited list that is stored in `fileList`. The loop steps through each string in the list of files and assigns the string's value to `currentFile`, which is passed to the `<nant/>` task by using NAnt's macro substitution, a feature that allows a property's value to be referenced by using `${}` notation. This same technique is subsequently used by the `Clean` target, which uses calls to a `<nant/>` task to call the `Clean` target in the child build files.

Managing Mayhem with a Building Contract

The technique of iterating through a list doesn't just simplify a build script, but also forces all the child build files to adhere to a standard—or to stick to implementing a contract. This means that once you understand how one child build file works, you have a head start on all the others.

In this case, our contract stipulates that each build file must have a `Clean` and a `BuildAndTest` target. To ensure that each of the child build files can share the meta-buildfile's properties, such as the `BuildFolder` property, the meta-buildfile uses the `inheritall` attribute of `<nant>`. If you were to define this property in each client, its value would override the meta-buildfile's property of the same name, and in effect, `inheritall` would appear to fail. As a consequence, if you want to use a child build file without using the meta-buildfile, you need to use the `-D` option on the command line, which initializes a new instance of the named property, as follows:

```
C:\MS.NET>nant -buildfile:MVC.build -D:BuildFile=build
```

Although the concept of a meta-buildfile and contracted child build files is restrictive, it brings with it a couple of significant advantages. Not only is the meta-buildfile much easier to extend, but also the child build files can be freely customized without affecting the complexity of any of the other build files. Furthermore, the nature of the partnership means that any common requirements or functionality can be moved into the meta-buildfile, as appropriate. Ah, chaos controlled!

The meta-buildfile's `fileList` property contains an extra filename, `dummy1.build`, which illustrates the concept. The `dummy1.build` file contains a template that conforms to the contract that we have established, but it doesn't have an actual payload. The `dummy1.build` file is as follows:

```
<?xml version="1.0"?>

<!-- dummy1.build-->
<!-- must implement iMVC.meta.build: -->
<!-- contract / interface targets: BuildAndTest, Clean -->
<!-- contract / interface properties: BuildFolder DO NOT DEFINE HERE-->

<project name="dummy1" default="BuildAndTest">

   <target name="BuildAndTest"
           description="cleans, builds source, and tests, and then runs tests">
   </target>
```

```
    <target name="Clean"
            description="Deletes files created by this module">
    </target>
</project>
```

TIP The comments at the start of each file help piece together the picture of a set of build files. Therefore, these comments are an excellent addition to the documentation that you produce for others to read.

Now that we've looked at a dummy contracted build file, it's time to look at the `MVC.build` file, which is shown in Figure 9-15.

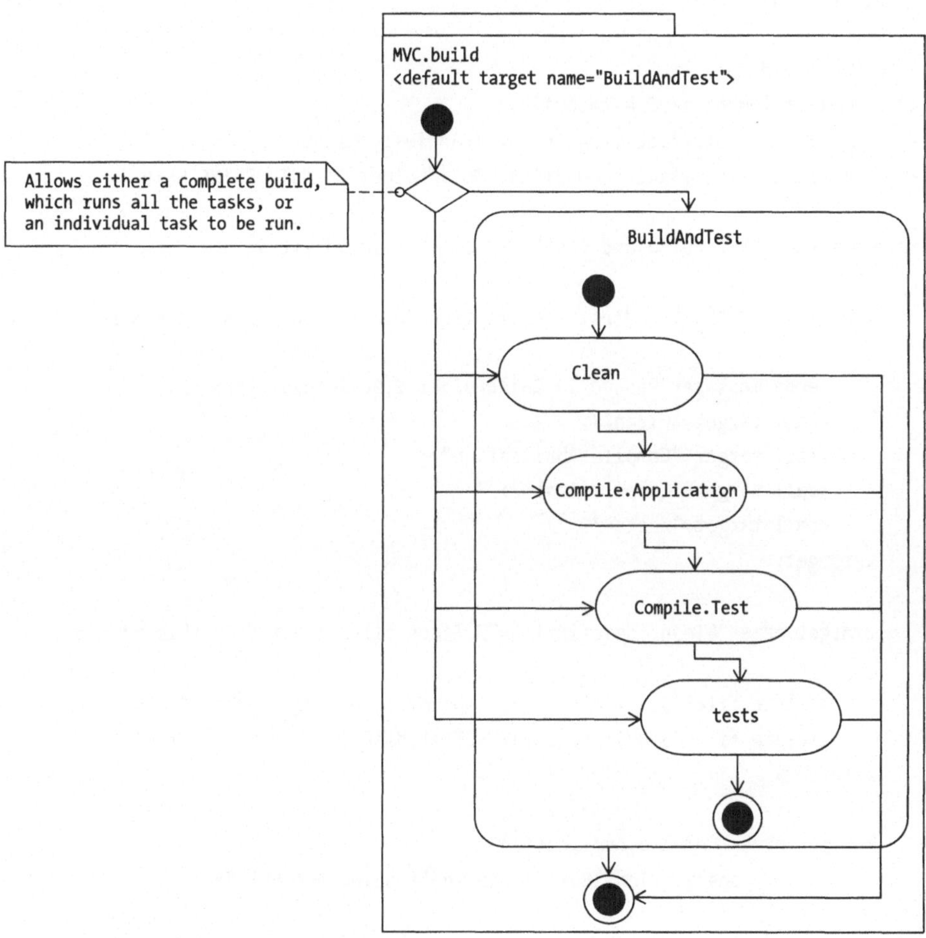

Figure 9-15. The contracted build file

NOTE The source code for this example can be found in the `Chapter_09\buildMVCMetaBuildFile` directory at this book's Web site (`http://www.cross-platform.net`) and the Apress Web site (`http://www.apress.com`).

As Figure 9-15 shows, the file's distinct actions have been split into their own targets, and the `BuildAndTest` target merely acts to chain together calls to the other targets. Of note are the naming conventions for the various targets: Public targets that conform to the contract are named with initial capitals, and internal helper targets are named in camel case. Taking a copy of `dummy1.build` and using these additional targets, the build file is then as follows:

```
<?xml version="1.0"?>

<!-- MVC.build-->
<!-- must implement iMVC.meta.build: -->
<!-- contract / interface targets: BuildAndTest, Clean -->
<!-- contract / interface properties: BuildFolder DO NOT DEFINE HERE-->

<project name="MVC Build and test" default="BuildAndTest">

    <target name="BuildAndTest" description="cleans, builds and tests">

        <echo message="Passed in BuildFolder=${BuildFolder}"/>
        <call target="Clean"/>
        <call target="Compile.Application"/>
        <call target="Compile.Test"/>
        <call target="tests"/>
    </target>

    <target name="Clean" description="Deletes files created by this module">

        <delete file="${BuildFolder}/SimpleMVC.exe" failonerror="false"/>
        <delete file="${BuildFolder}/MVCTest.dll" failonerror="false"/>
    </target>

    <target name="Compile.Application"
            description="Builds the application assembly">
```

```
    <csc target="exe" output="${BuildFolder}/SimpleMVC.exe">
        <sources>
            <include name="SimpleMVC.cs"/>
            <include name="Person.cs"/>
            <include name="View.cs"/>
            <include name="ConsoleView.cs"/>
            <include name="Controller.cs"/>
        </sources>
    </csc>
</target>

<target name="Compile.Test" description="Builds the test assembly">

    <csc target="library" output="${BuildFolder}/MVCTest.dll">
        <sources>
            <include name="MVCTest.cs"/>
        </sources>
        <references>
            <include name="${BuildFolder}/SimpleMVC.exe"/>
            <include name="nunit.framework.dll"/>
        </references>
    </csc>
 </target>

<target name="tests" description="runs the tests">

    <nunit2>
        <test assemblyname="${BuildFolder}/MVCTest.dll" failonerror="true"/>
    </nunit2>
 </target>
</project>
```

In our original specification for this script, we stated that the script should execute all tests, and if all tests pass, the application and any supporting files should be moved to a release directory, with all temporary files being deleted.

Running the meta-buildfile should produce the following results, in this order:

1. The build folder is created.

2. The executable and the test assemblies are built.

3. The tests are run.

4. If the tests succeed, the executable file is copied to the release folder.

5. The temporary files are deleted.

6. The meta-buildfile removes the build folder.

NOTE For the purposes of testing the meta-buildscripts and the child or contracted scripts, edit the `SimpleMVC.cs` program to use the `ConsoleView` rather than the `WindowsView` or `GtkView`.

Cross-Platform Build Projects

Now that you've seen a couple of different examples of NAnt being used to build assemblies, it's time to consider how it can be used specifically when working on cross-platform projects. While Chapter 2 and Chapter 7 both showed different ways to determine the platform at runtime, and Chapter 4 showed how the bridge pattern can be used to isolate platform-specific implementations, this section demonstrates that the ideal time to handle platform-specific details can be build time.

In this last section of the chapter, we offer up, for your delectation, an example of how build files can be structured as an important part of successful cross-platform projects.

The SimpleMVC.exe Program

As the dog returneth to the proverbial vomit, we once again visit our old friend, the MVC, and examine how to build and deploy a cross-platform application that uses this pattern.

We begin with a quick review of the code for the original `SimpleMVC.exe` program, which first appeared in Chapter 5:

```
//Filename: SimpleMVC.cs
using System;

namespace Crossplatform.NET.Chapter05
{
    public class SimpleMVC
    {
        public static void Main()
```

```
        {
            //Set up all objects, and their relationships
            Person timmy = new Person("Timothy",
                                      "Ring",
                                      "000-111",
                                      "Timothy.Ring@Crossplatform.net");

            Controller controlTim = new Controller(timmy);

            //Choosing the correct view can be done in a number of ways
            //as discussed throughout the book, notably Chapters 4 and 7
            //View watchTim = new ConsoleView(timmy, controlTim);
            //View watchTim = new WindowsView(timmy, controlTim);
            View watchTim = new GtkView(timmy, controlTim);

            controlTim.View = watchTim;
            ChangeDetails(controlTim);
        }

        private static void ChangeDetails(Controller controller)
        {
            controller.ChangeFirstname("Tim");
            controller.ChangeSurname("King");
            controller.ChangeEmail("Tim.King@crossplatform.net");
        }
    }
}
```

As you'll remember, although the example used a bridge pattern to work with different `View` implementations, we cheated a little and changed the application's source code to suit the particular view that we wanted to use. While that was acceptable back in Chapter 5, we can now do much better than that, by introducing an extra class, `ViewFactory`, which is responsible for creating the actual `View`.

NOTE The source code for this example can be found in the `Chapter_09\buildCrossplatform` directory at this book's Web site (`http://www.cross-platform.net`) and the Apress Web site (`http://www.apress.com`).

The ViewFactory Class

The sole responsibility of the ViewFactory class is to decide which View implementation to instantiate and to return an instance of the chosen implementation.

Because we want to choose the View implementation at compile-time, it's the perfect opportunity to use some conditional compilation to choose the View implementation, as shown in the following CreateView() method:

```
//Filename: ViewFactory.cs
using System;

namespace Crossplatform.NET.Chapter09
{
    public class ViewFactory
    {
        public static View CreateView(Person model, Controller controller)
        {
#if GTK
            return new GtkView(model, controller);
#elif SWF
            return new WindowsView(model, controller);
#else
            return new ConsoleView(model, controller);
#endif
        }
    }
}
```

This ensures that if the GTK compilation symbol is defined at compile-time, CreateView() will create instances of GtkView, or if SWF is defined, it will create instances of WindowsView. If neither of these compilation symbols is defined, CreateView() will fall back to the platform-agnostic ConsoleView.

The New SimpleMVC.exe Program

Now that we have the ViewFactory, we can change the SimpleMVC.cs file so that it defers the actual instantiation of the View to the ViewFactory, as follows:

```
//Filename: SimpleMVC.cs
using System;

namespace Crossplatform.NET.Chapter09
{
    public class SimpleMVC
    {
        public static void Main()
        {
            //Set up all objects, and their relationships
            Person timmy = new Person("Timothy",
                                      "Ring",
                                      "000-111",
                                      "Timothy.Ring@Crossplatform.net");

            Controller controlTim = new Controller(timmy);
            View watchTim = ViewFactory.CreateView(timmy, controlTim);

            controlTim.View = watchTim;
            ChangeDetails(controlTim);
        }

        private static void ChangeDetails(Controller controller)
        {
            controller.ChangeFirstname("Tim");
            controller.ChangeSurname("King");
            controller.ChangeEmail("Tim.King@crossplatform.net");
        }
    }
}
```

This beautifies the code from Chapter 5 somewhat by negating the need to manually change the code to work with different implementations of `View`. This is a good example of the maxim that ugly code is always the first to be pulled.

The SimpleMVC Build Files

Now that the `SimpleMVC` program relies on conditional compilation, we need to create some build files that can pass the requisite compilation symbols into the build process. The easiest way to do this with NAnt is to have a separate build file for each implementation choice, with each of these build files declaring different compilation symbols using the <csc/> task's define attribute. Figure 9-16 shows the relationships between the files in the project.

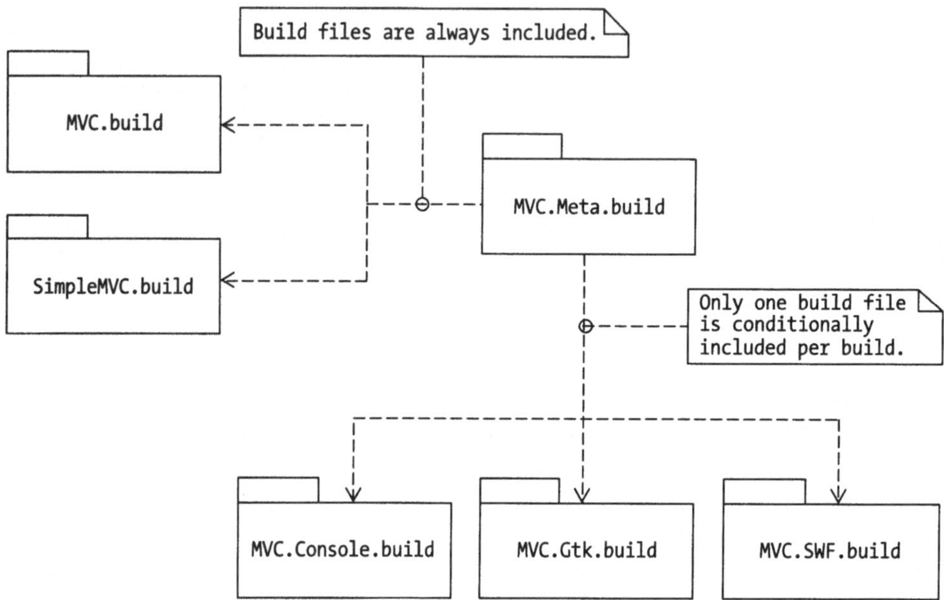

Figure 9-16. Cross-platform build files

As indicated in Figure 9-16, the key to getting this cross-platform build mechanism working is for the meta-buildfile *not* to call the application build file, as shown in previous examples, but to conditionally call the implementation-specific build files. That's all well and good, but the important question is "How can we do this within a build file?"

The secret is to use a <property/>, which in this case is called deploy. Because NAnt allows properties to be passed in on the command line, the deploy property acts as a parameter that is then used by the script to determine which implementation build file to use, as follows:

```
<?xml version="1.0"?>
<!-- MVC.Meta.build-->

<project name="MVC Release" default="Release">

    <property name="Deploy" value="Console"/>
```

The rest of the build file is similar to the ones that we've already seen, although the clever bit is the use of macro substitution in the `fileList` property, to pass in the value of the `deploy` property, as follows:

```
    <property name="fileList"
            value="MVC.build,MVC.${Deploy}.build,SimpleMVC.build"/>
    <property name="currentFile" value=""/>
    <property name="BuildFolder" value="build"/>

    <mkdir dir="${BuildFolder}"/>

    <target name="Release">
        <call target="componentBuilds"/>
    </target>

    <target name="componentBuilds">
        <echo message="Building components and testing..."/>
        <foreach item="String" in="${fileList}" delim="," property="currentFile">
            <nant buildfile="${currentFile}" target="Build" inheritall="true"/>
        </foreach>
    </target>
</project>
```

The `SimpleMVC.build` file is then a simple build file, which uses the value of the `BuildFolder` property when constructing the path to the build directory, as follows:

```
<?xml version="1.0"?>
<!-- SimpleMVC.build-->

<project name="MVC Build" default="Build">
    <target name="Build">
        <csc target="exe" output="${BuildFolder}/SimpleMVC.exe">
            <sources>
                <include name="src/SimpleMVC.cs"/>
            </sources>
            <references>
                <include name="${BuildFolder}/MVC.dll"/>
                <include name="${BuildFolder}/MVC.${Deploy}.dll"/>
            </references>
        </csc>
    </target>
</project>
```

Similarly, the MVC.build file uses the platform-agnostic files Controller.cs, View.cs, and Person.cs to build the MVC.dll assembly, as follows:

```
<?xml version="1.0"?>

<!-- MVC.build-->

<project name="MVC build" default="Build">
    <target name="Build">
        <csc target="library" output="${BuildFolder}/MVC.dll">
            <sources>
                <include name="src/Controller.cs"/>
                <include name="src/View.cs"/>
                <include name="src/Person.cs"/>
            </sources>
        </csc>
    </target>

</project>
```

Finally, we need a separate build file for each View implementation. Each build file is responsible for building a single assembly that does the following:

- Contains the code that is required to implement the platform-specific View
- Defines the required compilation symbol in the <csc/> task's define attribute so that the ViewFactory knows to create the correct type of View

Because each assembly creates only one type of view, the build files include just the source code for the particular view that they will create.

The build file that creates instances of GtkView includes the GtkView.cs file and defines the GTK compilation, as follows:

```
<?xml version="1.0"?>
<!-- MVC.Gtk.build-->

<project name="MVC Gtk build" default="Build">

    <target name="Build">
        <csc target="library" output="${BuildFolder}/MVC.Gtk.dll" define="GTK">
            <sources>
```

```
                <include name="src/ViewFactory.cs"/>
                <include name="src/GtkView.cs"/>
            </sources>
            <references>
                <include name="${BuildFolder}/MVC.dll"/>
                <include name="gtk-sharp.dll"/>
            </references>
        </csc>
    </target>
</project>
```

The build file for WindowsView is virtually the same, except that it includes the WindowsView.cs file instead of the GtkView.cs file and it defines the SWF compilation symbol instead of GTK, as follows:

```
<?xml version="1.0"?>
<!-- MVC.SWF.build-->

<project name="MVC Windows build" default="Build">
    <target name="Build">
        <csc target="library" output="${BuildFolder}/MVC.SWF.dll" define="SWF">
            <sources>

                <include name="src/ViewFactory.cs"/>
                <include name="src/WindowsView.cs"/>
            </sources>
            <references>
                <include name="${BuildFolder}/MVC.dll"/>
                <include name="System.Windows.Forms.dll"/>
            </references>
        </csc>
    </target>
</project>
```

Finally, the build file for ViewFactory includes ConsoleView.cs, and because the ViewFactory defaults to creating instances of ConsoleView, the build file doesn't need to define a compilation symbol in the <csc/> task, as follows:

```
<?xml version="1.0"?>
<!-- MVC.Console.build-->

<project name="MVC Console build" default="Build">
    <target name="Build">
        <csc target="library" output="${BuildFolder}/MVC.Console.dll">
            <sources>

                <include name="src/ViewFactory.cs"/>
                <include name="src/ConsoleView.cs"/>
            </sources>
            <references>
                <include name="${BuildFolder}/MVC.dll"/>
            </references>
        </csc>
    </target>
</project>
```

Now that we have all the files, we can build different versions of the application entirely according to our fancy. To build a version that uses `System.Windows.Forms`, we just need to pass in `SWF` as a property on the command line, as follows:

```
C:\MS.NET>\nant -buildfile:MVC.Meta.build -D:Deploy=SWF -k:net-1.1
```

To create a version that uses Gtk#, we can pass in `GTK` on the command line, as follows:

```
mono@linux:~ % nant.exe -buildfile:MVC.Meta.build -D:Deploy=Gtk -k:mono-1.0
```

So there you have it: a set of build files that can easily be used to build the `SimpleMVC.exe` application for different views, depending on the command line that is used to start the build process. Figure 9-17 shows the relationships between the various files in the SimpleMVC project.

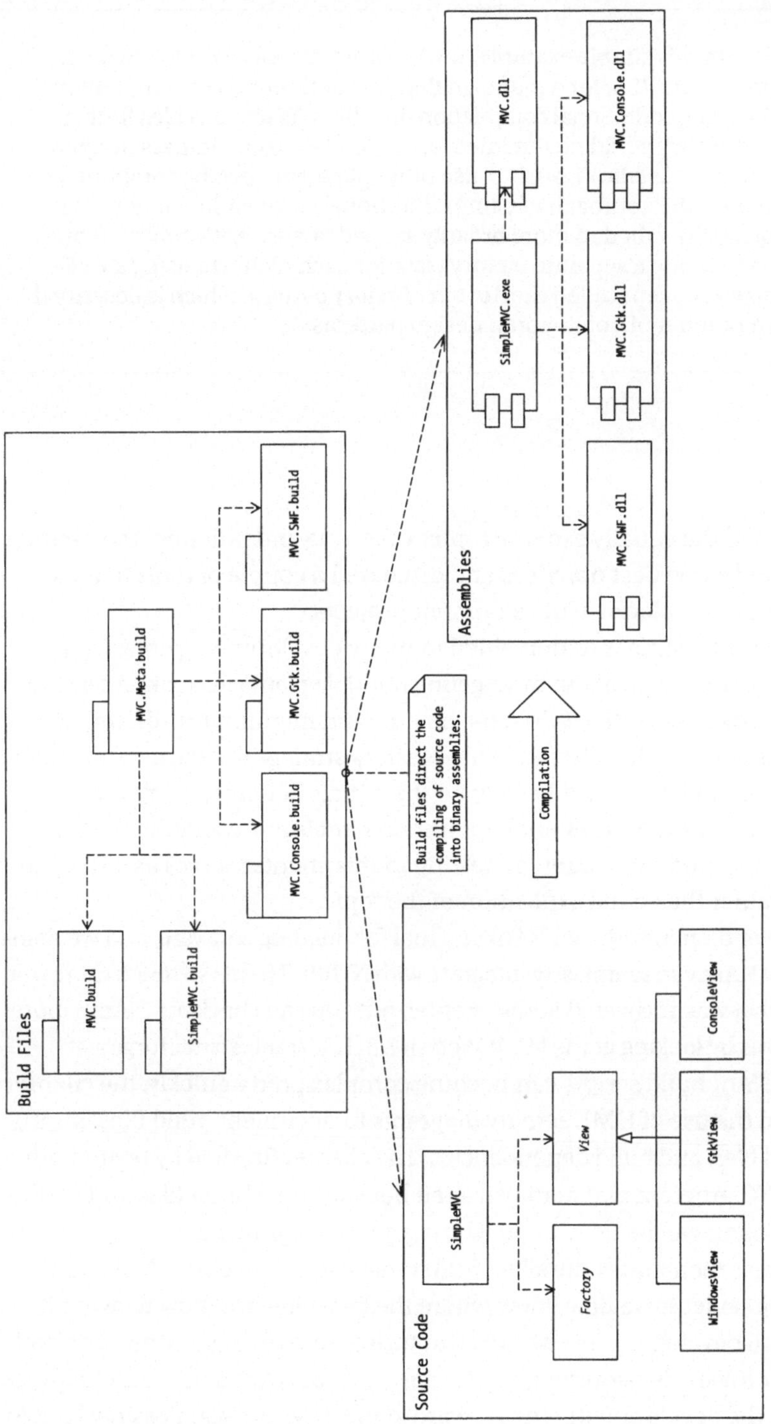

Figure 9-17. The relationships between the SimpleMVC project's files

TIP In this simple example, the `ViewFactory` was used to create an appropriate `View` for a platform that was determined at compilation time using conditional compilation directives. Taking this idea further, `ViewFactory` could be renamed and extended to encompass not just platform-specific `Views`, but also other platform-specific components. Because the approach of using conditional compilation directives is not ideally suited to more broadly scoped factories, it's common practice to create a separate factory class for each platform using a well-known concept called the *Abstract Factory* pattern, which is described in a number of books about design patterns.

Summary

Having traversed the equally exciting topics of testing and building, this chapter has investigated some best practices and discussed a couple of tools that can prove useful in cross-platform development projects.

Although unit testing is undervalued in many development projects, the intricacies that are brought about by targeting multiple platforms make a sensible unit testing strategy essential. While the chapter did mention test-driven development in passing, it didn't discuss related testing strategies, such as continuous integration, nor did it focus too heavily on the details of how to carry out a complex series of tests. A number of open source tools are available for more advanced testing, and the section on testing in this chapter serves as a stake in the ground, rather than a full exposition of the topic.

The chapter then introduced NAnt as a tool for building software, and we demonstrated how NAnt can seamlessly integrate with NUnit. There's so much more that NAnt can do that wasn't covered in the chapter, but you can check out NAnt's more esoteric features by looking at the NAnt Web site, `http://nant.sourceforge.net`.

Because NAnt build scripts can become complex pretty quickly, the chapter demonstrated the use of UML activity diagrams to document build files, multi-targeted build files, and build dependencies. The chapter finished by regurgitating the SimpleMVC program and demonstrated how multiple build files and conditional compilation can be used to build cross-platform projects.

So, are these techniques the silver bullet that slays the beast? Maybe and maybe not, but at least we now know where the beast is—and how to avoid its fangs. While all developers are used to structuring domain logic, structuring all elements of software development using tools such as NAnt and NUnit helps to not only shift the development ethos toward simplicity, but also possibly lead to quicker release times and more robust software—not bad for a couple of open source tools.

CHAPTER 10

Summary

"The saddest summary . . . contains three descriptions: could have, might have, and should have."

—Louis E. Boon, author

WHETHER YOU'VE TRAWLED your way through this book fastidiously or jumped gaily through the chapters like a drug-crazed gazelle, you're probably quite aware that the subject of .NET's cross-platform aspirations is far too big to be fully covered within this tome. It's certainly tempting to finish by mentioning the conspicuously absent material that we could've covered, the subsidiary topics that we might've mentioned, and numerous subjects that we should've espoused. Nonetheless, we'll instead follow the wise, albeit misappropriated, words of Louis E. Boon and avoid reminiscing on the book's shortcomings, instead opting to provide an opinionated glimpse into what the future holds for .NET as a cross-platform tool.

Although .NET is likely to always be considered first and foremost a Microsoft technology, as mentioned in Chapter 1, the technical heart of .NET, the Common Language Infrastructure, is in the hands of the international standards bodies, ECMA and ISO. This effectively means that .NET's future is at least partially in the hands of those who take due interest and can afford the standards bodies' membership fees. Even so, Microsoft, like most parents, is likely to do its utmost to keep .NET from harm's way and will continue to be the most influential party in .NET's future direction. With this in mind, and with due respect to the company that first brought us .NET, this chapter starts by considering how Microsoft is likely to influence the future development of .NET.

The Future of Microsoft .NET

Despite the corporate and strategic tendencies of technology companies to shroud their future developments in secrecy, Microsoft has been notably forthcoming with their short- and medium-term roadmap for .NET, as shown in Figure 10-1.

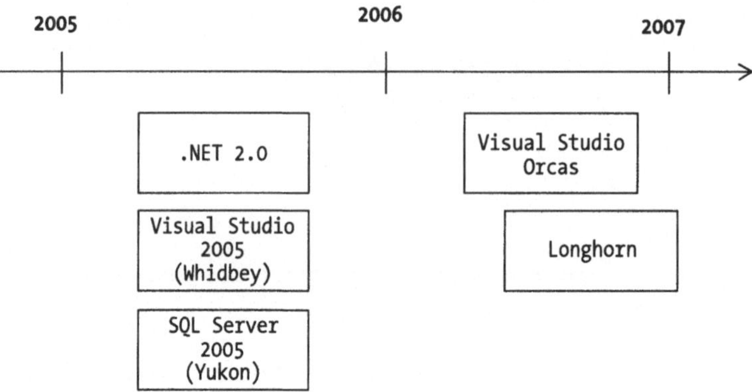

Figure 10-1. Microsoft's .NET roadmap

While there will undoubtedly be some twists in the tale—research and innovation being as important to Microsoft as money is to a miser—the roadmap gives a good overall indication of how .NET will mature on Windows. Although it's difficult to judge how Microsoft's roadmap will affect the other CLI implementations, it serves as a good indication of how the company must mature if it is to compete in the .NET arena with the relentless company from Richmond.

Microsoft .NET Framework 2.0

Following the groundbreaking entrance of .NET 1.0 and the subtle fixes and minor enhancements of 1.1, Microsoft .NET 2.0 will contain a number of major enhancements to the .NET CLR and the core .NET languages, and it will also contain a broad number of extensions across the .NET Framework Class Library.

NOTE One of the most eagerly anticipated changes in .NET 2.0 is the addition of *generics*, which are akin to a subset of C++ templates and allow strongly typed code to be written against types that will only be known at runtime. They essentially provide a code template that can be used with different types without requiring type casting.

It is interesting to note that the next version of Java is also promising to introduce generics. However, considering that C++ has had templates for a decade and ADA has had generics for over two decades, it begs the question of why two advanced development environments are implementing only a subset of the features that are available in C++ templates. Nonetheless, .NET 2.0 will herald in an age of maturity for .NET and includes a number of eagerly anticipated features, including the following:

- ASP.NET 2.0, which provides a slew of new features, including master pages, a number of new controls, and various features for enabling personalization and themes
- The `ObjectSpaces` namespace, which implements object-relational mapping and greatly simplifies the creation of business entity objects
- Numerous networking enhancements, including an FTP client, SSL streams, and some extensive security and versioning improvements to Remoting
- A variety of new Windows form controls, including layout containers that manage the placement of controls and bring Windows Forms in line with other GUI toolkits, such as GTK+
- A revamped XML namespace, including an implementation of the `XQuery` XML query language and a number of improvements to the existing types

With these powerful new features, .NET 2.0 will undoubtedly improve the lot for .NET developers on the Windows platform while serving as a reminder that Microsoft is seriously committed to pushing .NET as *the* development platform of choice for the discerning developer. It remains to be seen how many features from .NET 2.0 will make it into the ECMA standards, but it's a fair bet that the majority of new features won't make it to ECMA.

Visual Studio 2005

To complement the release of .NET 2.0, Microsoft is producing a new version of its popular IDE, Visual Studio 2005, which was formerly know as Whidbey.

Apart from containing a number of tools that integrate with the new .NET 2.0 features, Visual Studio 2005 will also include some exciting additional features, such as MSBuild, which is an XML-based build system that offers seamless integration with the Visual Studio user interface.

SQL Server 2005

Since it first bought the SQL Server technology from Sybase, Microsoft concentrated on giving it the Microsoft touch, which has involved the following items:

- Adding a modern, simple-to-use (and some would say abuse) administration interface
- Adding a number of powerful development and administration tools
- Modifying the core SQL engine to improve the database server's performance

With a considerable gestation period of 5 years, SQL Server 2005, which was previously known as Yukon, promises a number of special features. While the majority of these enhancements are not directly related to .NET development, one key feature is the ability of SQL Server 2005 to effortlessly interoperate with .NET, allowing the database server to directly host .NET code, akin to the way that Oracle and DB2 host a Java Virtual Machine.

SQL Server 2005's ability to host managed code is useful for two distinct reasons. First, it provides the ability to write complex functionality in SQL Server without resorting to Transact-SQL, and second, it allows code to be moved from .NET client applications into the database server, which is particularly useful for data-intensive operations, as shown in Figure 10-2.

SQL Server 2005's ability to tightly integrate with .NET means that it will provide more thorough support for .NET than any of the competing database servers, and it is therefore likely to further entrench SQL Server as the database server of choice on Windows. Because it will be available only for the Windows operating system, it is also fair to say that it will create a notable disparity between Windows and other operating systems.

Nonetheless, such tight integration between .NET and the database server is by no means essential, and data-intensive operations can be run on the database server with some judicious use of .NET Remoting, as shown in Figure 10-3.

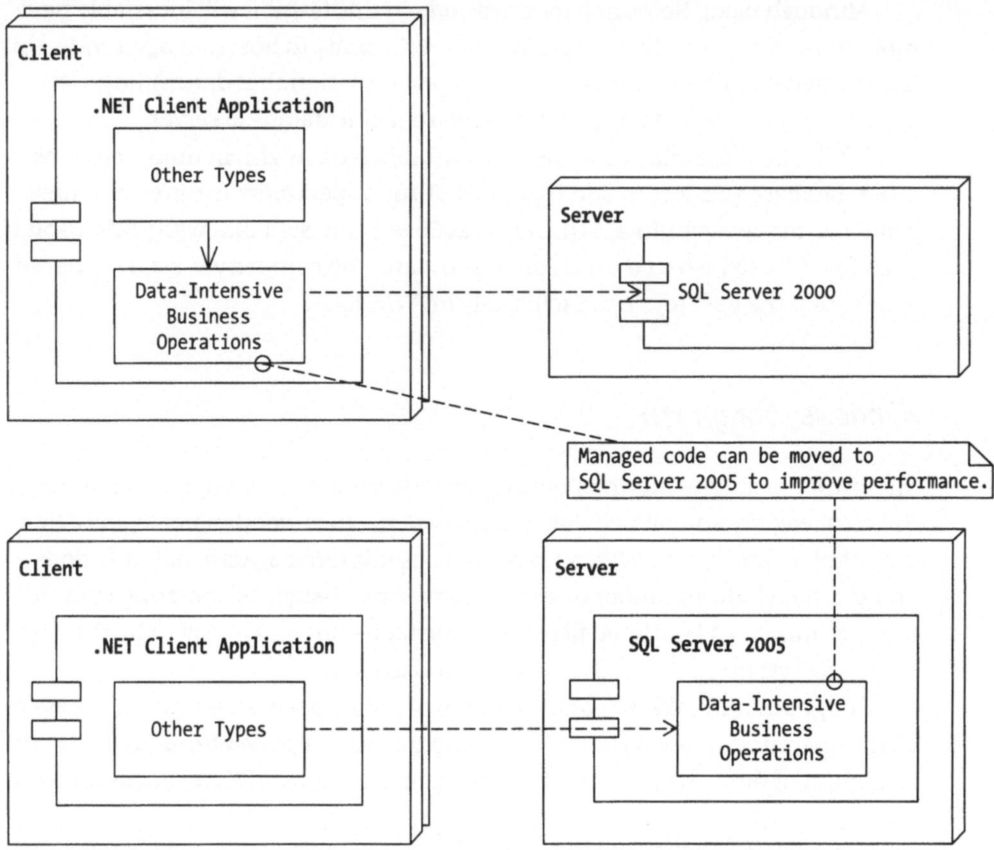

Figure 10-2. Moving .NET code into SQL Server 2005

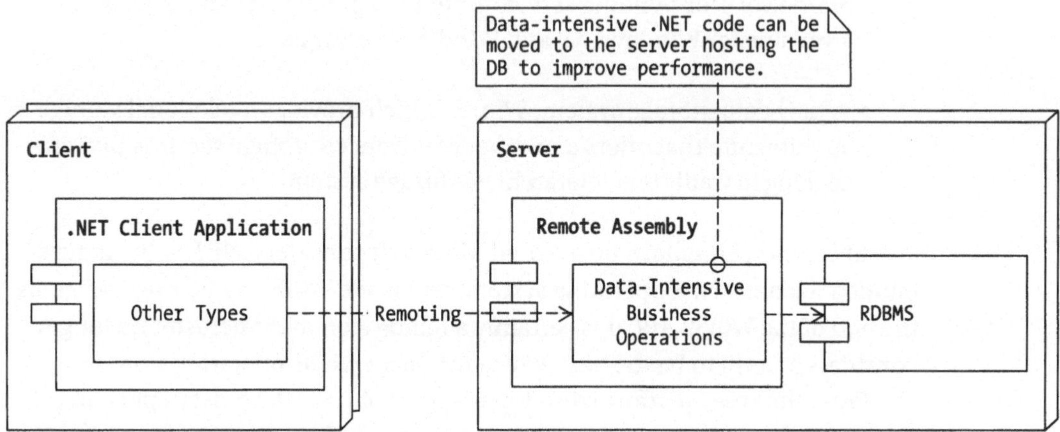

Figure 10-3. Moving .NET code onto the RDBMS host to improve performance

Although using Remoting to move code in this fashion will invariably be more time consuming than using SQL Server's ability to host managed code, this has the benefit of being a generally applicable solution that doesn't impose a dependency between an application and a specific database server.

While the portability of Mono and Portable.NET might, in time, convince other database vendors to add tighter .NET interoperability features into their products, in the meantime, SQL Server 2005 is a sure sign that while Microsoft is keen for .NET to be based on an open standard, the company is even keener to ensure that the best toys run exclusively on Windows.

Windows Longhorn

Microsoft's next-generation operating system, Windows Longhorn, is possibly the most eagerly anticipated computing system since wooden beads were first mounted on an abacus. With a brand-new user interface, Aero, not only does Longhorn include a number of advanced features—such as operating system transactions and a relational file storage system—but it's also set to be the first operating system that uses .NET as its standard API.

Longhorn's API, WinFX, offers a range of namespaces that provide access to all the operating system's functionality and that can be called from .NET with the minimum of fuss. The three main components of the WinFX API are as follows:

- A new GUI toolkit, Avalon, which is vector based and founded on an XML-based declarative programming language, XAML

- A new communication infrastructure, Indigo, which provides a powerful framework for building service-oriented applications and will also be available for Windows XP and Windows Server 2003

- A new data-storage system, WinFS, which provides a relational storage architecture that offers a number of advanced storage services that are lacking in traditional hierarchical storage systems

In essence, Longhorn proves that Microsoft considers .NET to be mature enough to control the operating system, and while WinFX by no means signals the end of the Win32 API, it is certainly a telling sign that Microsoft no longer considers a C API to be the best way to interact with its operating systems.

From the cross-platform developer's point of view, the most important point about Longhorn is that with the extensive range of features offered by WinFX, Longhorn will almost certainly be the most feature-rich environment in which to run .NET applications. Although many of WinFX's features will be available to all CLI implementations running on Longhorn, and some features will undoubtedly be ported to other operating systems, Microsoft is keenly positioning Longhorn as the ideal operating system for .NET applications. Not only is the company keeping the best toys, but it also wants the best playroom.

NOTE As mentioned in Chapter 5, an open source equivalent to Avalon's markup language, XAML, already exists in the form of MyXaml. Although it remains to be seen how much compatibility will exist between MyXaml and XAML, MyXaml is an excellent example of the open source community responding to future innovations in the Microsoft camp.

The Bigger Picture: The Microsoft .NET Framework

As the canonical CLI implementation, Microsoft's .NET Framework is likely to be the only CLI implementation that many organizations will consider for the foreseeable future, and it's rapidly becoming the de facto development tool for Windows-based projects.

With very good performance and a vast array of extensions that are above and beyond the ECMA CLI, the .NET Framework is the implementation that other CLI implementations will be measured by, and it is also the technical strategy that will drive Microsoft for the next couple of decades.

Although it's extremely unlikely that Microsoft would ever want to trade Windows dominance for .NET dominance, .NET does give Microsoft the option of one day releasing a commercial, cross-platform implementation of .NET. More likely, perhaps, is that as .NET is increasingly used for Microsoft applications and as the cross-platform CLI implementations mature, Microsoft will easily be able to port slimmer versions of its applications to other platforms.

The Cross-Platform Future of .NET

With .NET set to continue in a steady flux of evolution, it's something of a moving target for the open source community, which has led some industry commentators to openly wonder whether the open source CLI implementations will ever provide a commercially viable alternative to Microsoft .NET. As Mono wizard Jonathan Pryor notes, "The way to portability is restraint. It's difficult to be portable while making use of the latest-and-greatest on all platforms. . . ." What this boils down to is that while the cross-platform CLI implementations might lag certain Microsoft innovations, because the CLI implementations already implement the core ECMA CLI features and the most frequently used extensions, they already serve as practical alternatives to Microsoft .NET.

Of course, one of the greatest facets of open source development is that it's not held back by commercial restraints, and it's therefore quite typical of the open source movement that both the Mono and PNET project teams have already started implementing features from the .NET Framework 2.0. Couple this with numerous other open source projects that are implementing features not present in Microsoft .NET, and it's apparent that open source .NET software is useful in the cross-platform context, and it enhances the capabilities of Windows-based projects.

If we take a moment to consider some of the up-and-coming Microsoft-led .NET innovations, it's readily apparent that the future of .NET lies juxtaposed between the Microsoft and open source camps:

- **Visual Studio 2005's Managed Extensions for C++**: Prior to Visual Studio 2005, Microsoft's Managed Extensions for C++ couldn't easily be compiled into purely managed code, whereas PNET has had the ability to compile C code into pure managed code since 2003. With ECMA currently ratifying C++/CLI, a standard binding will soon exist between C++ and the CLI, which will be a big step in making C++ a viable language for cross-platform .NET development.

- **Visual Studio 2005's build tool, MSBuild**: While MSBuild will undoubtedly be promoted as Microsoft's preferred build system for .NET, its reliance on XML and its use of tasks as the atomic build unit are, in essence, very similar to NAnt, which has been around for 3 years—or 4 years, if you consider its Java antecedent, Ant.

- **.NET 2.0's Object Relational Mapping framework, ObjectSpaces**: Although ObjectSpaces serves as Microsoft's first foray into Object Relational Mapping (ORM), as mentioned in Chapter 6, the open source community has already produced a broad variety of different ORM frameworks for .NET, a number of which have a reputable Java heritage.

- **Windows Longhorn's user-interface toolkit, Avalon**: While Avalon contains a number of interesting features, one prominent feature is the use of layout containers. Not only are layout containers popular in other non-Microsoft GUI toolkits, but they've also been available in .NET since 2002, courtesy of Gtk#. As mentioned earlier, MyXaml is already available as an open source alternative to Avalon's markup language, XAML.

Perhaps it's worth remembering that while the different CLI implementations share a significant breadth of functionality and a will to innovate, at any one time, they can each provide a different set of features. Above all: "The way to portability is restraint."

The Future of Mono

As the most prominent open source CLI implementation, it is highly likely that the future success of Mono will be used to measure the open source and cross-platform success of .NET. With Mono's roadmap therefore being heavily loaded with expectation, it makes sense to discuss some things that are currently not on the roadmap.

First, there are currently no plans to implement some of the namespaces that are architecturally dependent on Windows, such as `System.Management` and `System.EnterpriseServices`. It's possible that these features will be added in due course, but because they heavily rely on Windows services, it's perhaps more likely that Mono will implement equivalent features in an architecturally sound manner. Also, a couple of architecturally sound features, such as Code Access Security, aren't featured on the roadmap, but they'll almost certainly be implemented in due course.

The Mono philosophy for missing features is when a contributor is prepared to implement these features, the Mono project will accept the contributor with open arms, but in the meantime, Mono will get along quite sufficiently without the features.

TIP For an up-to-date look at Mono's roadmap, browse to `http://www.go-mono.com/mono-roadmap.html`.

Similarly, while Mono has very much been designed as a cross-platform CLI, it is currently only supported fully on the *x*86, PowerPC, and SPARC architectures, with the Mono's interpreter, `mint`, being available for use on other hardware platforms. We have no definite word on when support will be added for other hardware platforms, but it goes without saying that in the future, Mono will invariably provide support for other hardware platforms. There's no reason why it won't, one day, be available for the majority of modern hardware platforms. The future of Mono is presented in Figure 10-4.

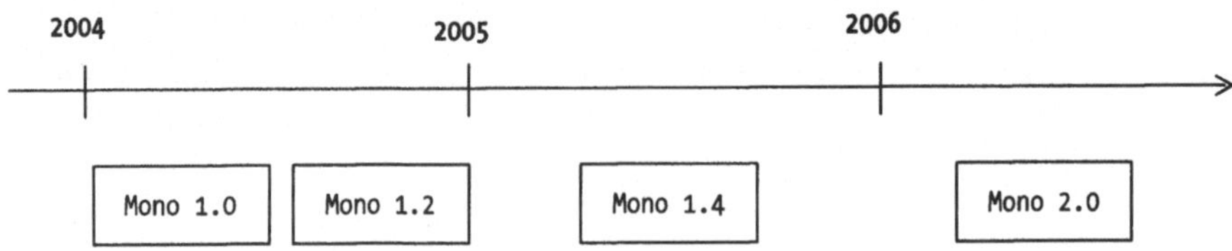

Figure 10-4. The Mono roadmap

Although version 1.0 of Mono is generally considered as the first production release of Mono, the majority of Mono's functionality has been stable since much earlier releases. Like many open source projects, new Mono versions are released frequently. This generally allows bugs to be fixed much quicker than for commercial products.

While one criticism that's occasionally leveled at Mono is that it can't compete with Microsoft .NET's stability, its frequent releases and the open availability of its source code break the reliance on a third party for bug fixing and make it easier for proactive developers to deal with bugs firsthand.

CAUTION It's worth remembering that Mono's version numbers will change independently of Microsoft .NET's version numbers; just because an application runs on Microsoft .NET 1.0, there's no guarantee that it will run on Mono 1.0, and vice versa.

Mono 1.0

The Mono 1.0 release aims to be the first production-ready open source .NET implementation. While it doesn't implement all the functionality from the Microsoft .NET Framework 1.1, it can be considered as roughly equivalent. In particular, version 1.0 will contain the following production-ready components:

- The Mono VM, supporting JIT compilation and Ahead Of Time compilation (or prejitting) for *x*86, PowerPC, and SPARC architectures. The `mint` interpreter allows Mono to run on other architectures.
- An IL assembler and disassembler.
- The Mono C# compiler.
- The core .NET libraries: `mscorlib.dll`, `System.dll`, and `System.Xml.dll`.

- A number of other essential libraries, such as `System.Data.dll`, `System.Web.dll`, `System.Web.Services.dll`, `System.Drawing.dll`, and `System.DirectoryServices.dll`.
- Java integration using IKVM, which was demonstrated in Chapter 8.
- Gtk# for creating GUI applications.
- An Apache integration module for Web applications.

Additionally, Mono 1.0 will provide a number of preview features such as generics, the Mono Basic compiler, and an implementation of `System.Windows.Forms`. Although these preview items won't be stable enough to rely on in-production systems, they ably demonstrate some of the up-and-coming features from the world of Mono.

Mono 1.2

The second major release of Mono will serve the following two purposes:

- It will contain the features that are not stable enough to make it into Mono 1.0, such as `System.Windows.Forms` and the VB .NET compiler.
- It will implement some of the core features from the .NET Framework 2.0, such as generics and ASP.NET 2.0.

NOTE Although its release date may move, Mono 1.2 is currently due to ship before Microsoft .NET 2.0. Although the majority of Mono 1.2's additions are features that are implemented in Microsoft's .NET Framework 1.1, the possibility of Mono implementing generics before Microsoft is a testament to the extraordinary speed with which open source software can move.

Mono 1.4

The third major release of Mono will complete the features that are not stable enough to be released in Mono 1.2, including the additional features from the .NET Framework 2.0 and numerous performance enhancements.

Mono 2.0

Mono 2.0 is included on the Mono roadmap more as a show of intent than as an actual planned release. While certain features from Longhorn might be included in Mono in due course, Mono will most likely grow to encompass technologies that are not part of the Microsoft game plan.

The Bigger Picture: Mono

Apart from being one of the most exciting open source projects in existence, Mono is frequently seen as the proof that .NET is suitable for cross-platform development.

Although it has publicly been debated whether Microsoft might attempt to strangle Mono with patent or copyright lawsuits, the very existence of Mono boosts the overall utility of .NET as a technology and flatters Microsoft by proving the CLI's versatility. The fact that Mono also offers a dual-stack approach to its functionality, as shown in Figure 10-5, offers some defense against the possibility of lawsuits, because compatibility with the .NET Framework is only a part of Mono.

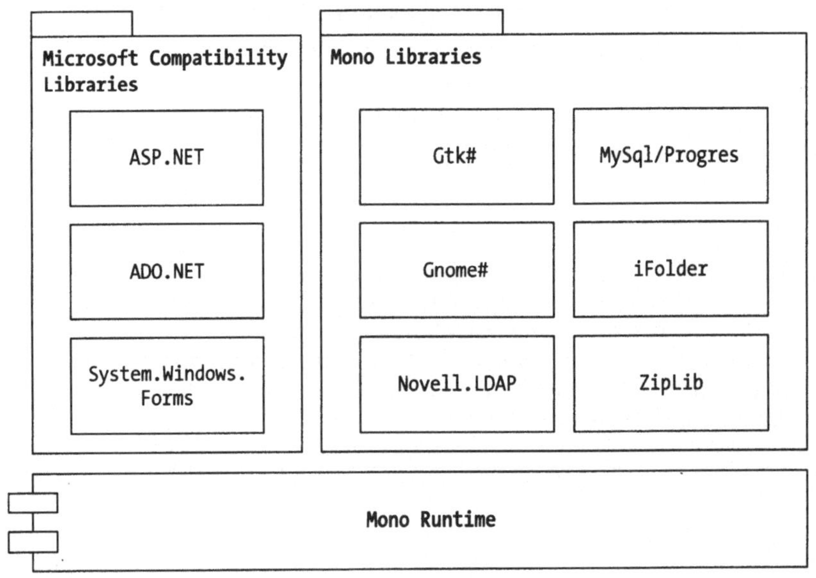

Figure 10-5. The Mono stacks

With good JIT and AOT performance, and functionality that almost matches Microsoft's .NET Framework, Mono is likely to be the most popular open source and cross-platform CLI implementation for the foreseeable future.

Additionally, as the open source community overcomes its hang-ups with .NET, Mono is likely to consume an increasing number of smaller open source .NET projects and could take on a momentum that far exceeds its current pace. There have even been discussions about using Mono to reimplement one of the premiere desktop managers for UNIX-based systems, GNOME. While such a move is not to everybody's taste—with many GNOME advocates threatening to bail rather than embrace a technology with its heritage in Richmond—it's nevertheless indicative of Mono's potential to revitalize the UNIX family of operating systems by providing a coherent, object-oriented infrastructure on which to build.

The Future of Portable.NET

Although Portable.NET's future plans are not as clearly specified as Microsoft's and Mono's, as part of the dotGNU meta-project, Portable.NET's stated goal is as follows:

> *"... to be for webservices and for C# programs what GNU/Linux is rapidly becoming for desktop and server applications: the industry leader and provider of Free Software solutions."*

Although no explicit roadmap is available for PNET, it goes without saying that in its push to provide a free and ubiquitous environment for .NET applications and Web services, the PNET runtime will continue to be enhanced through a number of frequent releases. Although PNET's development team is notably lean, as Mono progresses, PNET's `ml-pnet` package will continue to evolve, meaning that PNET's functionality will continue to lag Mono's only slightly.

The Bigger Picture: Portable.NET

One common question from developers who are new to cross-platform .NET projects is "Why are two different open source projects working on CLI implementations?" Because Mono is the better known of the two projects, it's often wrongly assumed that using Mono is preferable to using PNET, but choosing the right open source CLI implementation is not that straightforward.

To better understand PNET's likely role in the future, you should consider PNET's CLI implementation and the overall project separately.

The PNET Runtime

One of the most popular criticisms aimed at PNET is that because the `ilrun` runtime uses interpretation rather than compilation, it's too slow for carrying out any real work. While it's true that PNET's runtime performance is generally slower than that of Mono and Microsoft's .NET Framework, it's significantly faster than Mono's interpreter, `mint`.

Coupling this with dotGNU's newly released `libjit` library, which implements a cross-platform, virtual machine–agnostic JIT compilation library, PNET will soon be able to take advantage of JIT compilation, just like Mono and Microsoft .NET.

Although Mono is going to increasingly support JIT and AOT compilation on more platforms, in the meantime, PNET's interpreted nature is going to make it the preferred runtime on platforms for which Mono doesn't yet support JIT and AOT compilation. Because `libjit` can automatically fall back on interpretation if a code generator doesn't exist for a particular machine architecture, PNET will probably maintain its position as the most easily portable CLI implementation.

TIP Celebrating the fact that performance alone doesn't maketh a CLI implementation, PNET includes the `pnetmark` package, which contains a variety of assemblies that can be used for benchmarking a CLI implementation.

Another advantage that is touted by PNET advocates is that because PNET's compiler, `cscc`, is written in C, it can easily be compiled on a machine with a C compiler. In comparison, because Mono's `mcs` compiler is written in C#, it requires an existing CLI implementation to compile, creating a technical version of the infamous chicken-and-egg scenario.

One final advantage of the PNET runtime is that it has good profile support, which makes it relatively straightforward to build slimmer CLI implementations. While PNET's profile support is not particularly useful for desktop or server applications, it is potentially a very useful feature for creating CLI implementations for embedded systems, where efficient resource management is essential.

The PNET Project

Because the PNET project offers a number of features that aren't available in other CLI implementations—such as a C compiler, a curses wrapper, and a crafty implementation of `System.Windows.Forms`—PNET will most likely also be used to complement the functionality that's available in other CLI implementations.

For example, because PNET's C compiler and `libc` implementation, `pnetC`, are unique among the CLI implementations, PNET is the perfect tool for compiling C programs into assemblies that can then be used with any CLI implementation. Indeed, given the breadth of open source software that is written in C, PNET will prove itself to be an indispensable tool for porting existing software to .NET.

Final Thoughts

Whether you're an experienced cross-platform developer or a .NET junkie, we hope this book has given you a good idea of .NET's capabilities as a cross-platform tool. Given that .NET is still in its early ascendancy on Windows, and that the open source community is generally suspicious of anything related to Microsoft, it will likely be some time before .NET is widely considered as the rich cross-platform tool that it is. However, with the current excess of energy and excitement going about .NET across the industry, there's no better time to start using .NET as a cross-platform development tool.

While the book has purposefully concentrated on using .NET as a cross-platform tool, consider that as the open source CLI implementations mature further, .NET is going to become a highly suitable platform for developing software that is specifically targeted at a single platform. Noting that one of Ximian's aspirations in starting the Mono project was to create a powerful, high-level development environment for GNU/Linux, .NET will play a key role in Windows' future, and it will be a useful facet in the modernization of other operating systems.

Similarly, while many of Microsoft's corporate competitors have been slow to respond to .NET, they are now in the position of having to improve their .NET strategies. Apart from creating suitable .NET APIs for their products, many software vendors will find that integrating .NET closely into their products is a pivotal part of their product's future. With both Mono and PNET being embeddable, there's no reason software vendors can't host CLI environments in their products in a similar way to SQL Server 2005 .NET integration. In the long term, this is likely to create a highly fertile environment in which .NET can evolve further.

Of course, .NET is by no means a cross-platform panacea, and because managed code doesn't perform quite as well as native code, languages such as C and C++ will remain the tools of choice for performance-based development. With C APIs being the de rigueur form of cross-platform code, tools such as PNET will undoubtedly go a long way in reducing the distance between C and .NET.

Although many other popular cross-platform languages are available—such as Python and PHP— .NET's language agnosticism will help to bind these languages closer together. Similarly, excellent open source tools such as `whirl2il`—which is a work in progress that will eventually provide an IL backend for the languages that are supported by the GCC compiler—will in time help make IL ubiquitous. As the natural barrier between different languages is reduced, the most fashionable applications will most likely be ported to run on the CLI.

In the business application domain, .NET's only real competitor is Java, and as was mentioned in Chapter 8, Java and .NET are so similar that it's difficult to ridicule one without insinuating the other. While vendors of Java tools have traditionally rallied together to appear as a reasonable alternative to Microsoft, they are all very aware that the commonalities between Java and .NET make porting their tools to .NET a highly lucrative opportunity and an easy way to broaden their markets.

Java certainly has the advantage of maturity over .NET, but .NET has the advantage of a more modern runtime environment. While Java nuts currently laugh at .NET's cross-platform aspirations, .NET geeks bemoan Java's lack of open standards.

With Java having proved the business context for virtual execution environments, .NET is now helping to prove the irrelevance of language syntax. The youthful .NET has a lot to learn from the successes of Java, but by the same token, Java can learn from the technical innovations of .NET. While Sun's and Microsoft's legal departments might plan otherwise, all indications are that it will be difficult to stop Java and .NET from becoming closer, and tools such as IKVM already demonstrate the technical differences to be minimal. Although it's too early to see exactly what effects these platforms will have on each other, it's conceivable that both will evolve until a single virtual machine appears to unite them.

Indeed, one of the most exciting catalysts in the adoption of .NET has been the wealth of open source projects that are written in Java, which have proven to be ideal for porting to .NET. This migration of projects has not only helped .NET to reach a level of maturity that belies its age, but it has also helped bring along a number of tried and tested best practices. While this book has mentioned two of these tools, NUnit and NAnt, these are only the beginning of the story, and many more projects are already available for .NET or are currently in production.

TIP For a more thorough exposition on Java projects that have made it to .NET, please visit this book's Web site at `http://www.cross-platform.net`.

In an era when every other software vendor is trumpeting the advantages of software as a service, .NET is perfectly positioned to become one of the essential tools for building Web services and to reduce the choice of underlying operating systems to a purely infrastructural decision. As .NET promises to cross-pollinate the innovations of the world's largest software monopoly with the hopes and dreams of the open source community, .NET shouldn't just be viewed as yet another capricious development tool but rather as a sure sign that the software industry is putting away the childish one-upmanship of its past and is finally reaching a hitherto unknown maturity.

APPENDIX A

The Unified Modeling Language

THROUGHOUT THIS BOOK, we use diagrams that are almost exclusively based on the Unified Modeling Language (UML), which we hope will help clarify and soften the book's sometimes dry text. More importantly, by including UML, we can proudly refer to ourselves as the authors of a picture book.

For those of you who haven't already come across UML, it is a nonproprietary technique for modeling software. In the words of its creators, the so-called Three Amigos—Rumbaugh, Jacobson, and Booch:

> *"UML is a general-purpose visual modeling language that is used to specify, visualize, construct, and document the artefacts of a software system."*[1]

NOTE A great book for learning how to apply UML in your everyday work is Martin L. Shoemaker's *UML Applied: A .NET Perspective* (Apress, 2004).

One of UML's undeniable strengths is that even for those without prior knowledge of UML, it is easy to grasp the meaning of a UML diagram without explicit knowledge of the problem domain. Nonetheless, understanding some of UML's intricacies is a little trickier, and we therefore include this perfunctory overview for those readers who have not yet mastered one of the most important development tools since the introduction of punch cards.

UML Diagrams

UML clearly defines a number of different diagram types, each of which can be useful for documenting particular aspects of a software system. Although UML is

1. J. Rumbaugh, I. Jacobson, and G. Booch, *The Unified Modeling Language Reference Manual* (Reading, MA: Addison-Wesley, 1999).

far vaster than we can cover in this short introduction, you should get a feel for the expressiveness of the language and gain enough knowledge to understand the diagrams that are presented within the text.

When using UML, one of the most important considerations is to get the relevant points across concisely, which means choosing the correct diagram types for specific situations and using the right level of detail to display the concepts. In practice, this also means that elements from different types of diagram are frequently shown in the same model to reduce the number of diagrams that are needed to document the system.

While some modelers prefer to throw everything into a diagram, you should find that our diagrams contain just enough detail to demonstrate the concepts being portrayed, without being overtly formal or unnecessarily thorough.

Structural Diagrams

Structural diagrams classify the different entities in a system and the relationships between the entities. They are useful for understanding the concepts, implementation, and user requirements of a system.

Class Diagrams

The *class diagram* is one of the most important diagrams for object-oriented software and shows classes, the class members, and the relationships between different classes.

A class diagram is comprised of one or more classes and the relationships between them. As illustrated in Figure A-1, classes are displayed with named rectangles, and the relationships between classes are shown using various types of lines.

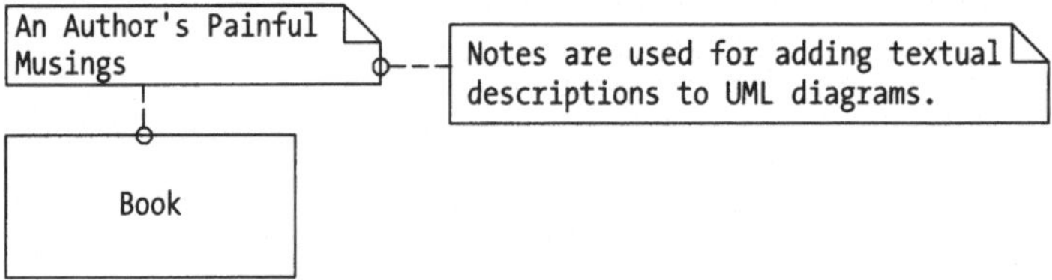

Figure A-1. A simple class

If required, classes can be shown with their members' details, with each type of member being separated with horizontal lines. The number and type of parameters and return types can be optionally shown, and visibility can be shown using a minus sign (–) for *private* members, a plus sign (+) for *public* members, and a hash sign (#) for *protected* members.

Figure A-2 shows the simple Author class complete with members.

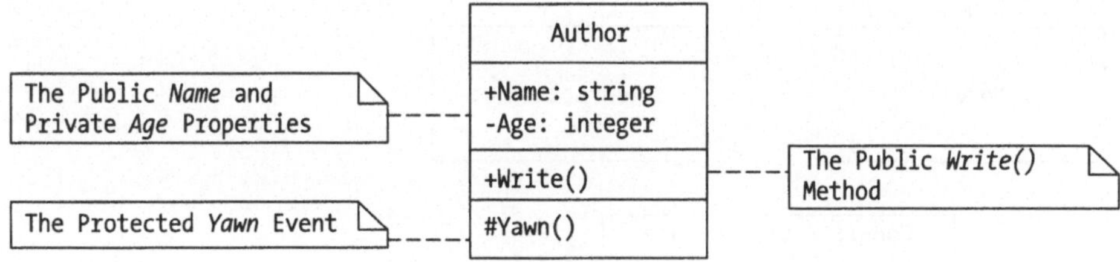

Figure A-2. A simple class with member details

Various types of relationships between classes can be shown in a variety of ways. The most common relationship between classes is the *association* relationship, which is indicated with a solid line and represents a link that exists between two classes.

Figure A-3 shows the relationship between the Author and Book classes.

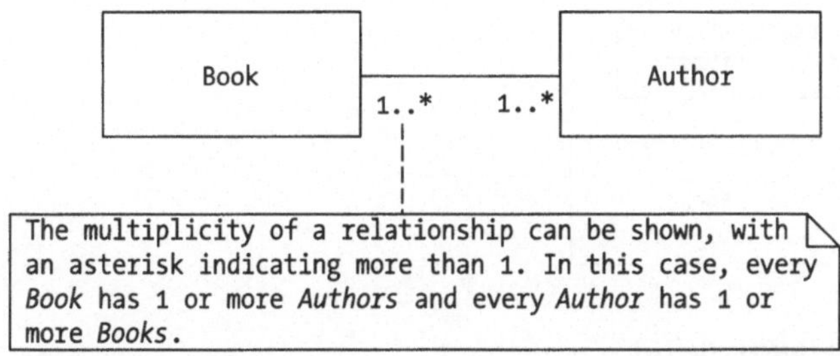

Figure A-3. An association between classes

The *generalization* relationship, which is also known as specialization, indicates class inheritance and is shown with a solid line tipped with a hollow arrow, with the arrow pointing toward the superclass.

Figure A-4 demonstrates generalization by showing how the Book class is specialized by the Novel and Nonfiction classes.

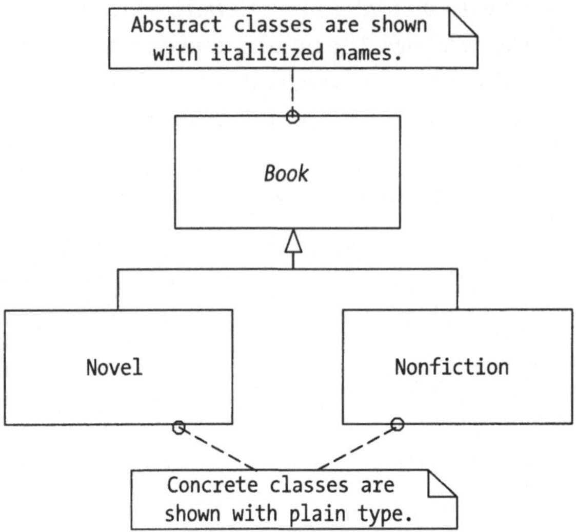

Figure A-4. A simple inheritance hierarchy

The *aggregation* relationship indicates that one class is part of another class, but instances of the class exist as entities outside of instances of the aggregating class. Aggregation is shown using a solid line with a hollow diamond on the aggregating class, as shown in Figure A-5.

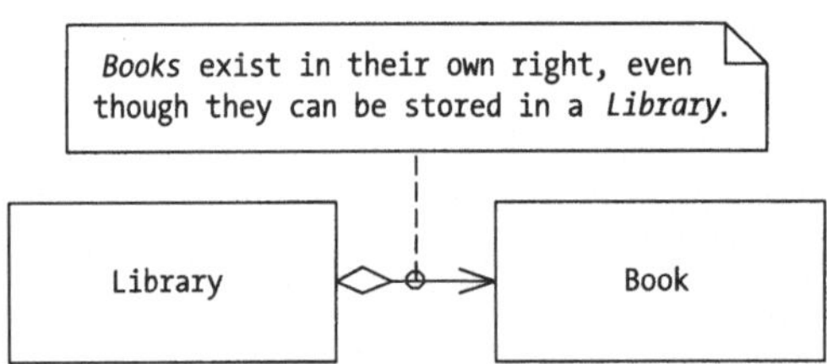

Figure A-5. An aggregation relationship

The *composition* relationship is a stronger form of aggregation, where instances of one class are composed of instances of other classes. Composition differs from aggregation because instances of the subordinate class do not exist as separate entities outside of the instances of the composing class. Composition is shown with a solid line and a solid diamond, as demonstrated in Figure A-6.

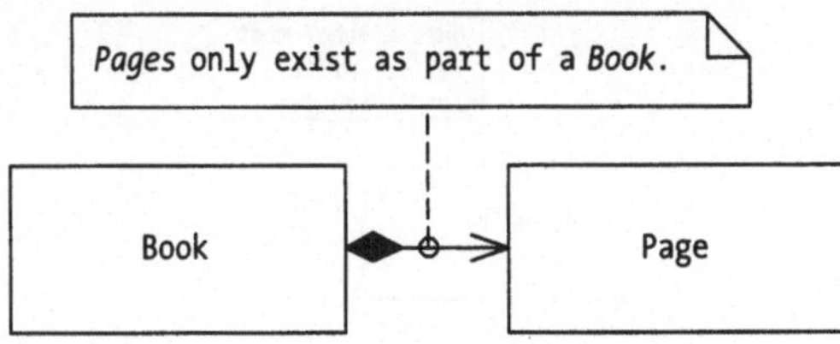

Figure A-6. A composition relationship

Interfaces can be displayed by using either a stereotyped class (a rectangle marked with <<interface>>) or by using a lollipop. The implementation of an interface by a class, *interface realization*, can be shown by connecting the lollipop to the class or by connecting the class to the stereotyped representation via a dotted line with a hollow arrow.

The two representations of interfaces are shown in Figure A-7.

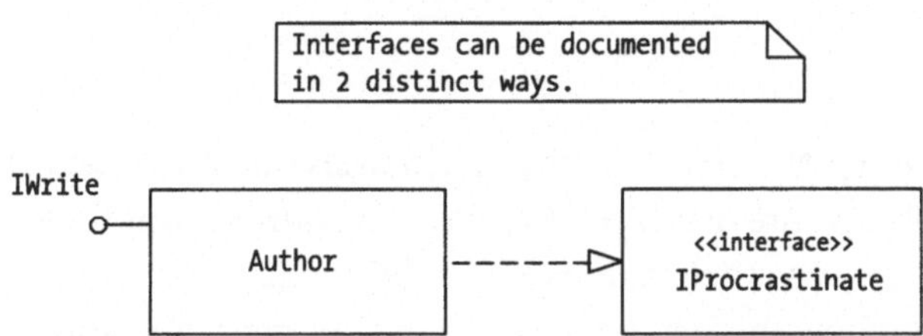

Figure A-7. The two different ways of displaying an interface

When the various elements are considered together, class diagrams become excellent for documenting the static structure of object-oriented software. Figure A-8 aggregates the previous seven diagrams into a simple class diagram.

Because they can encompass a broad range of detail, class diagrams can be useful for displaying different system perspectives, including the high-level concepts of the problem domain, the initial design of a solution, and the detailed implementation of a solution.

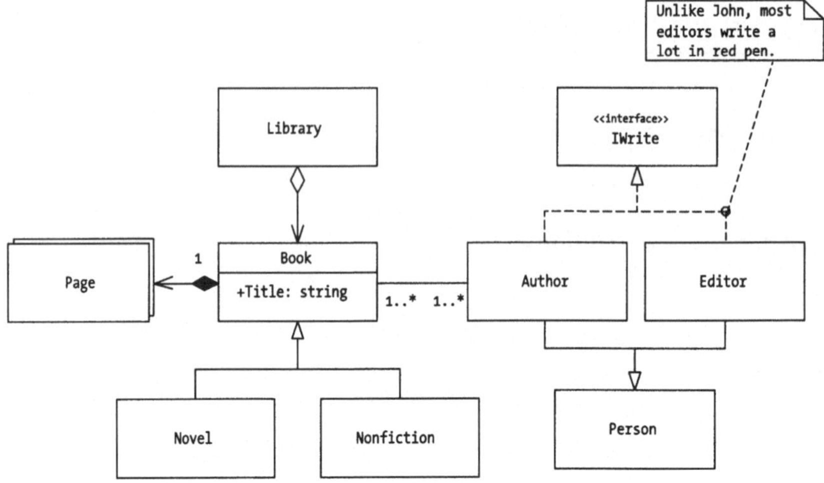

Figure A-8. A class diagram

Object Diagrams

A variation of the class diagram is the *object diagram*, which shows the system at a particular point in time. Objects are displayed in named rectangles, but they can be differentiated from classes as their names are underlined.

Because object diagrams show the system at runtime, they generally only contain association relationships as the other types of relationship indicate design aspects of the system. Figure A-9 shows a simple object diagram for this book.

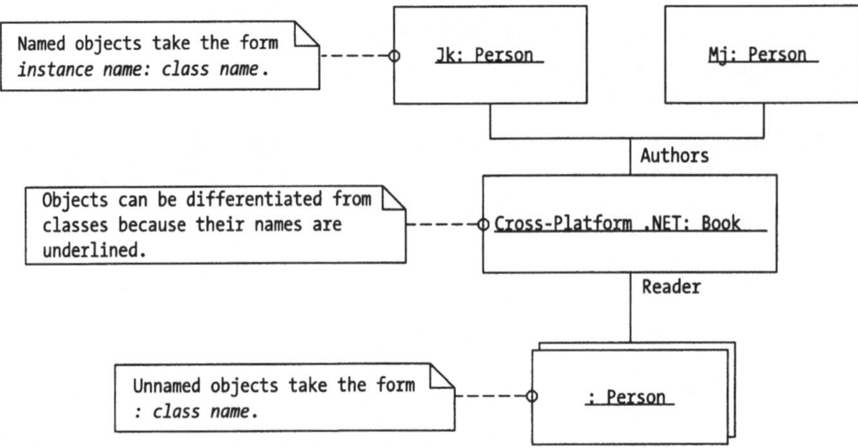

Figure A-9. An object diagram for this book

Object diagrams are useful for demonstrating the static relationships between instances of classes at runtime. In some situations, it's useful to extend object diagrams by adding some details of the system dynamics, in which case the object diagrams become *collaboration* diagrams, as described later in this appendix.

Component Diagrams

Component diagrams are used to show the deployable units of a system and the dependencies that exist between the different software entities. Components are represented as rectangular boxes with two rectangular teeth protruding from the left side. Dependencies between the different components are represented with a dotted line, as shown in Figure A-10.

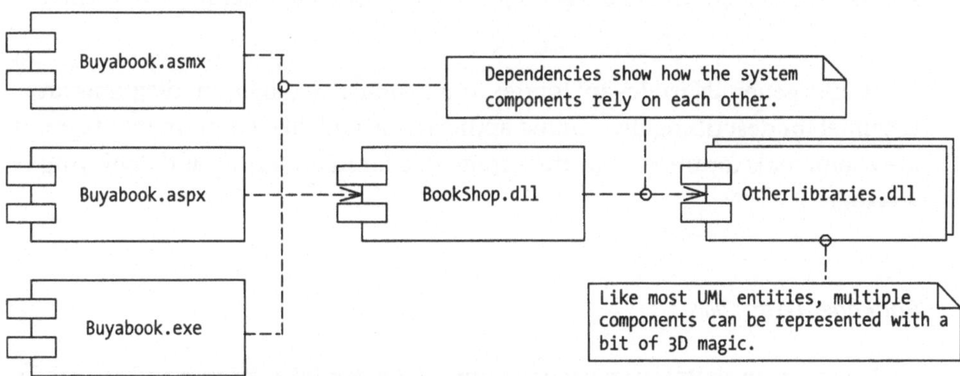

Figure A-10. A component diagram for a book-selling application

Component diagrams are highly useful for describing how a system is implemented as separate physical units. They act as important guidelines for system deployment and maintenance.

Deployment Diagrams

Closely coupled to component diagrams are *deployment diagrams*, which show how the system's components are distributed over different machines, or *nodes*. Nodes represent a physical machine, or computer, and are shown as a box, usually containing a number of components. The communication protocol that is used between different nodes is often shown with a solid line connecting the nodes. Figure A-11 shows how certain components from the previous component diagram can be displayed on a deployment diagram.

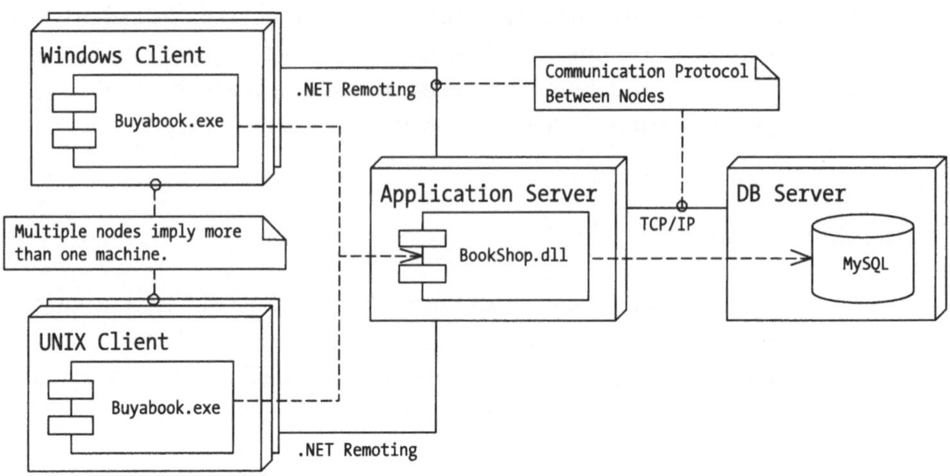

Figure A-11. A deployment diagram for the three-tier book-selling application

While generally irrelevant for desktop systems, deployment diagrams are essential for describing distributed applications and, like component diagrams, are useful tools for those who are responsible for maintaining and deploying a system.

Package Diagrams

Packages are an abstraction used to group other model elements and are used to simplify diagrams. Packages are represented by folders and can be used in any UML diagram to simplify the diagram, as shown in Figure A-12, which is a simplified version of the component diagram in Figure A-10.

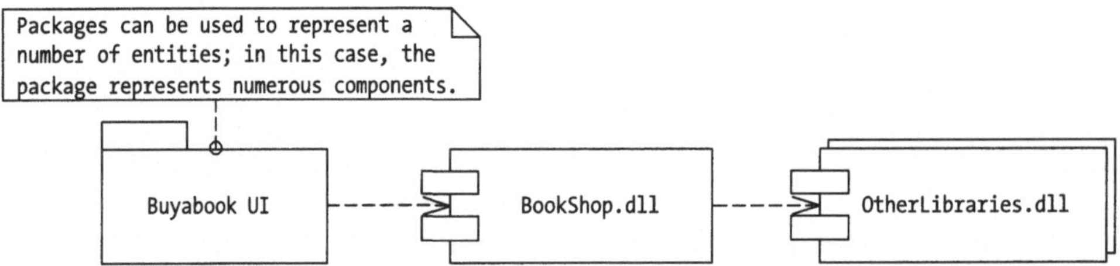

Figure A-12. A revised component diagram for the book-selling application

In some cases, a UML diagram might be abstract enough to only contain packages, and although they are not an official type of UML diagram, these types of diagrams are generally known as a *package diagrams.* Figure A-13 shows how a high-level package diagram could represent a book-dealing system.

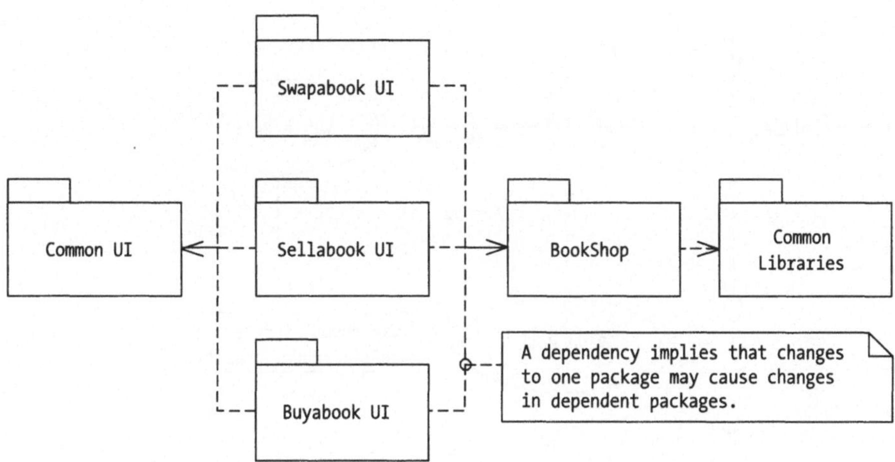

Figure A-13. The packages for a book-dealing system

Use Case Diagrams

Use case diagrams can be used to document system requirements. They show the system's users, the system's functionality, and the relationships between the two. The user roles are called *actors* and are displayed with a stick man; the functionality is broken into units of functionality called *use cases*, which are represented by an oval; and the relationships between user roles and use cases are *associations* and are shown with a straight line. A simple use case diagram, depicting use cases related to books, is shown in Figure A-14.

Use case diagrams are generally used in the analysis phase of software development and provide a high-level view of what the system does and how it interacts with human users and other systems. The fact that this book contains no use case diagrams suggests that the examples don't have demanding sets of requirements and that we, as authors, have not carried out much in the way of analysis.

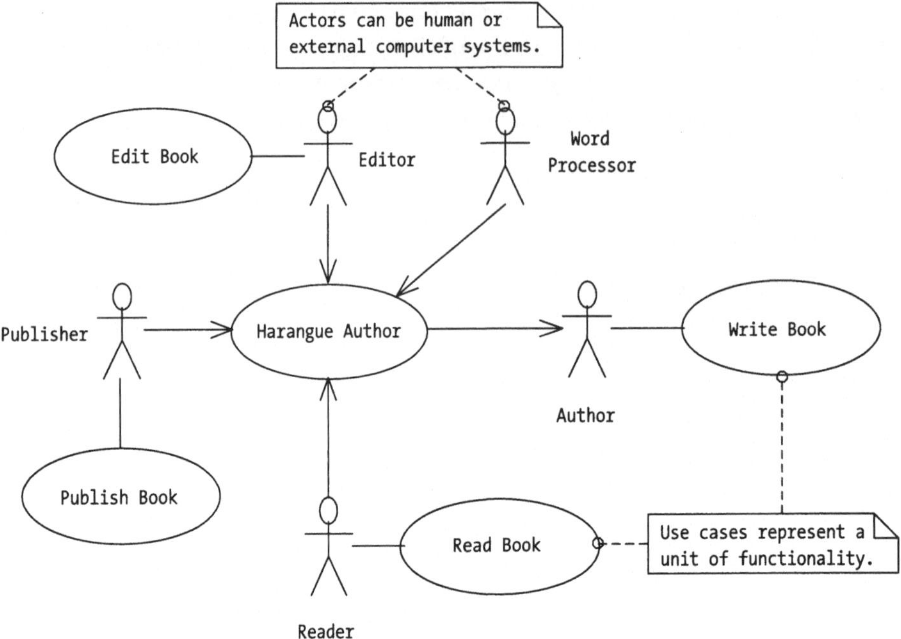

Figure A-14. A use case diagram, showing the life of an author

Dynamic Diagrams

In contrast to the fixed nature of the structural diagrams, *dynamic diagrams* show the behavior of a system over time and are useful tools for documenting the active parts of a system.

State Machine Diagrams

State machine diagrams display the various states or modes that a system goes through, the transitions between these states, and the events that cause the transitions.

NOTE State machine diagrams were known as *Statechart* or *State* diagrams prior to UML 2.

States are used to indicate that the system is in a particular mode and are represented by rounded rectangles. Transitions between states are shown with solid arrows. They are frequently annotated with details of the event that caused the transition, a guard condition that dictates when the transition occurs, and the action that occurs when the transition fires. These annotations take the form *event* [*condition*] / *action* and are illustrated in the state machine diagram in Figure A-15.

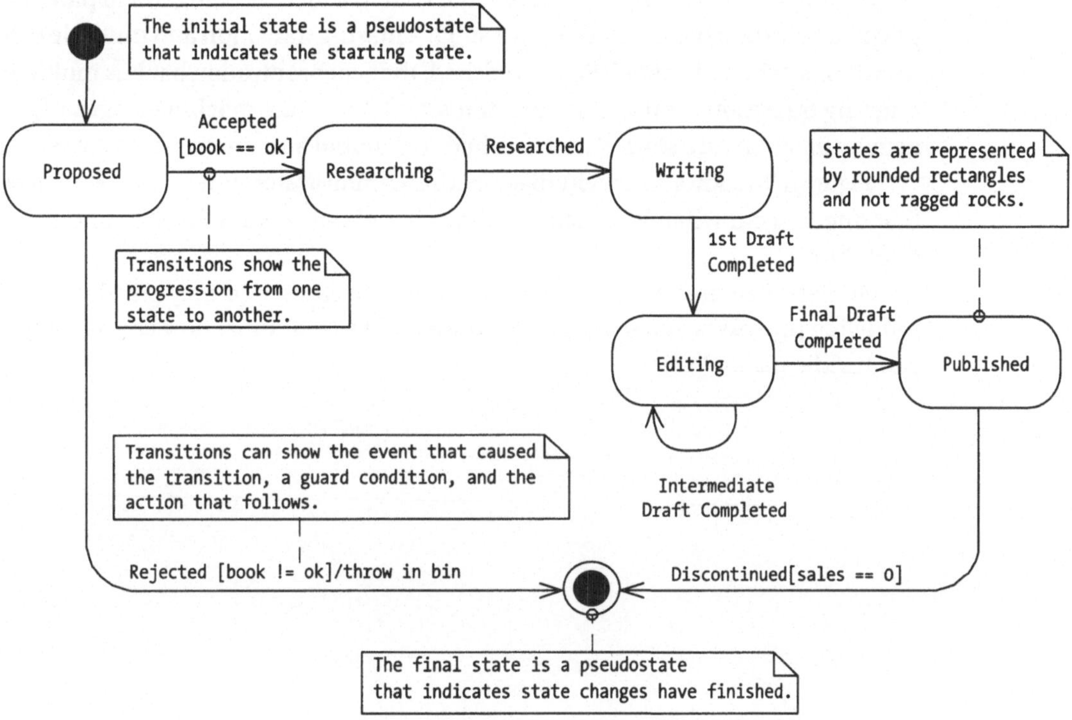

Figure A-15. A simplified state machine diagram for the book-writing process

State machine diagrams are typically used to model single classes and are useful for modeling classes with complex internal behaviors.

Activity Diagrams

Highly reminiscent of state diagrams, *activity diagrams* show the high-level sequencing of activities through a system.

The fundamental entity in an activity diagram is called an *activity* or an *activity state* and is a state of action that is also represented with a rounded rectangle. Transitions between activities indicate that an activity has finished and are shown as a solid arrow.

Conditional branches are indicated by *branches*, which are hollow diamonds with a single transition entering and multiple transitions exiting. Each exiting transition can optionally be annotated with a guard condition. The opposite of a branch is a *merge*, which is a hollow diamond with multiple entering transitions and a single exit transition.

Parallel activities can be shown by using a synchronization bar, which is shown as a thick black line. To indicate the start of activities being run in parallel, a synchronization bar is shown with a single entering transition and multiple exit transitions. When the parallelism is finished, the synchronization bar has multiple entering transitions and a single exit transition. Like state machine diagrams, activity diagrams are started and finished with initial and final pseudostates.

Figure A-16 shows an activity diagram that demonstrates some of the sequences that might occur when you place an order for a book at your favorite online bookshop.

Activity diagrams are often used to model use cases, and they are ideal for modeling processes and workflow because, unlike traditional flow charts, they can handle parallelism.

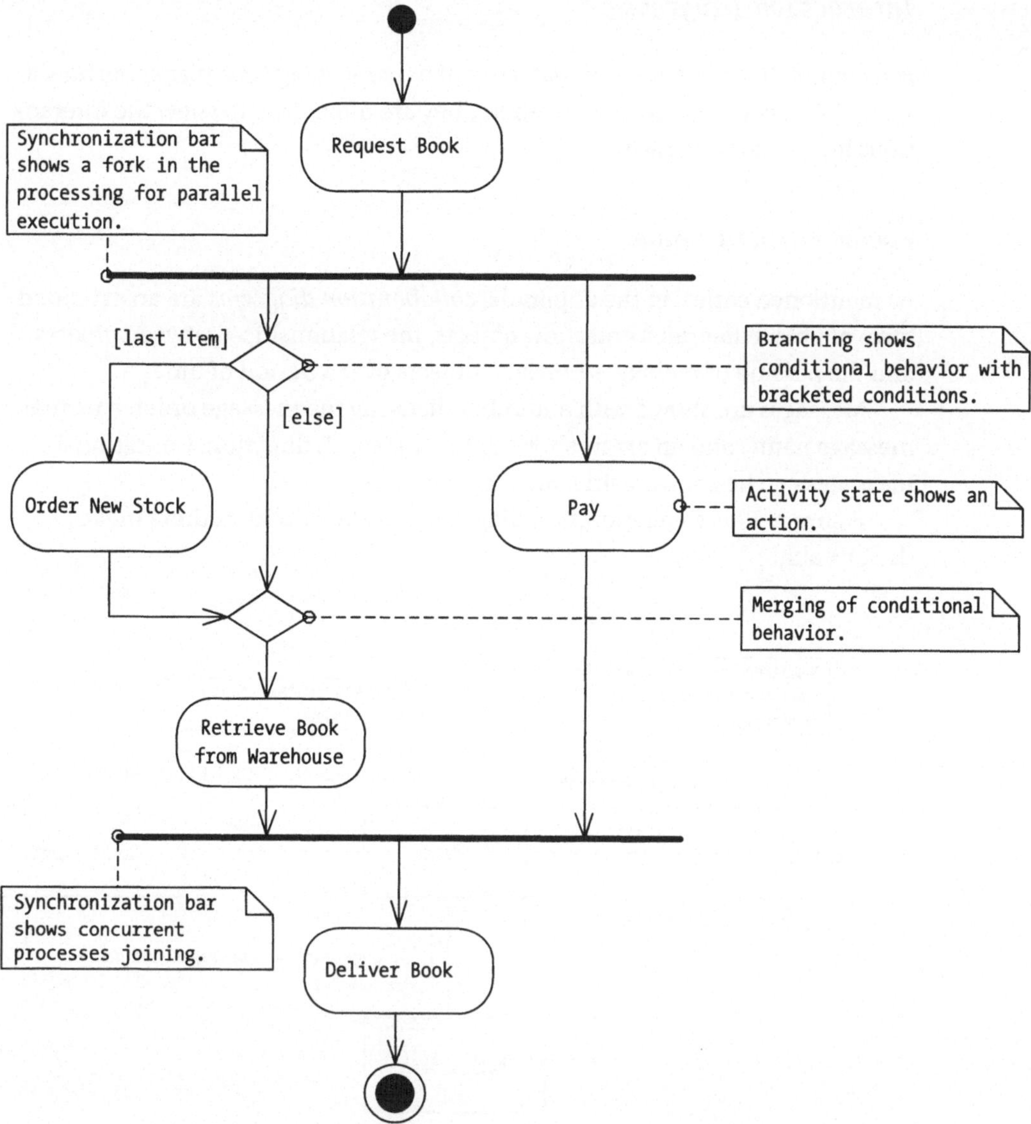

Figure A-16. An activity diagram showing a customer ordering a book

Interaction Diagrams

Interaction diagrams are a subcategory of dynamic diagrams that show how a group of objects collaborate together. They are often used to show the interactions for a single use case.

Collaboration Diagrams

As mentioned earlier in the appendix, *collaboration diagrams* are an extended form of object diagrams and show objects, the relationships between objects, and the passing of messages between objects over a period of time.

Messages are shown with a number dictating the message order, a textual message name, and an arrow showing the message's direction. Conditional messages can be shown with a bracketed guard.

Figure A-17 is a collaboration diagram that shows how authors make their wealth.

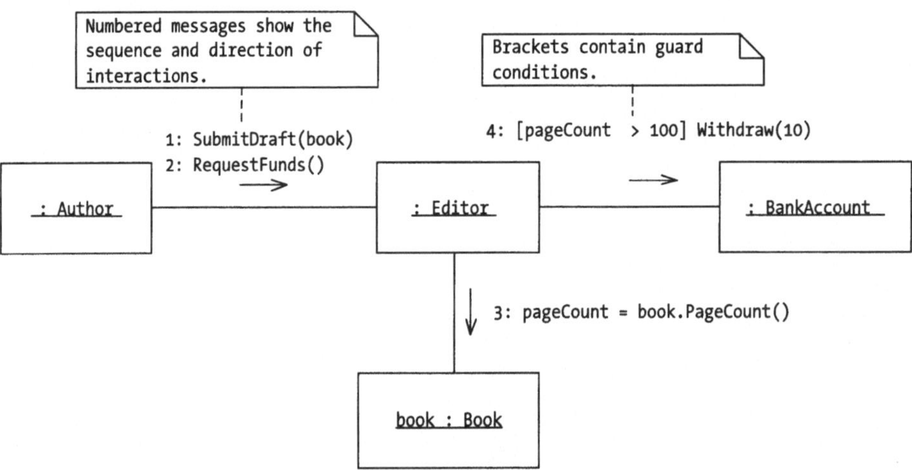

Figure A-17. A collaboration diagram of an author making ends meet

Because collaboration diagrams couple the interaction between objects with the static relationships between objects, they are useful for documenting simple interactions while maintaining a degree of structural detail.

Sequence Diagrams

Sequence diagrams also show object interactions, but unlike collaboration diagrams they concentrate on the flow of control between objects.

Objects are shown at the top of a dashed line, called a *lifeline*, which represents the life of the object during the interaction. Messages are shown as arrows between the lifelines of objects, with the order of messages running from top to bottom. The lifeline is optionally shown with a hollow activation box to show when the object is *active*, which would be equivalent to a procedure being on the stack for a procedural interaction.

Figure A-18 contains a sequence diagram showing the same interaction that was depicted in Figure A-17.

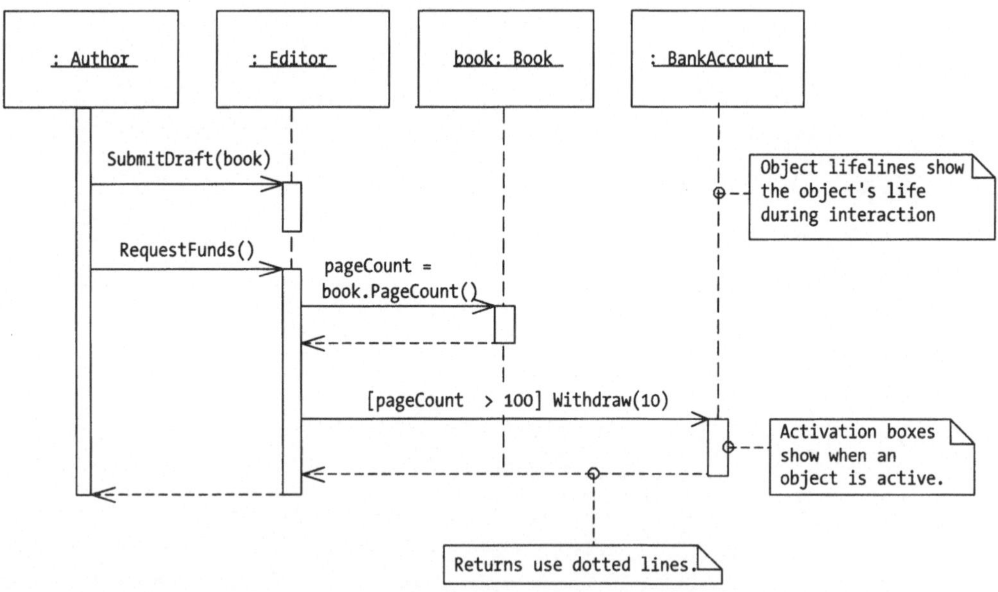

Figure A-18. A sequence diagram of an author making a living

Because sequence diagrams explicitly show the succession of interactions between objects, they are more useful than collaboration diagrams for showing more complex interactions between objects.

Further Reading

While we hope this terse coverage of UML is fine for the purpose of reading this book, a sound knowledge of UML is becoming increasingly essential for professional software development. With the UML standards continually evolving, we have not mentioned a number of important intricacies and extensions, and a good place to start learning more about UMLis the official UML Web site (`http://www.uml.org`).

APPENDIX B

.NET Framework Map

THE FIRST PART of this appendix provides a list of the types as defined in the ECMA standards for the CLI. This is followed by a series of figures that illustrate how the various namespaces relate to the categorizations that are found in Chapter 4: CLI Defined, Architecturally Sound, and Architecturally Dependent.

Kernel and Compact Profiles

Figure B-1 shows the ECMA CLI Defined profile and the types that are found within this profile.

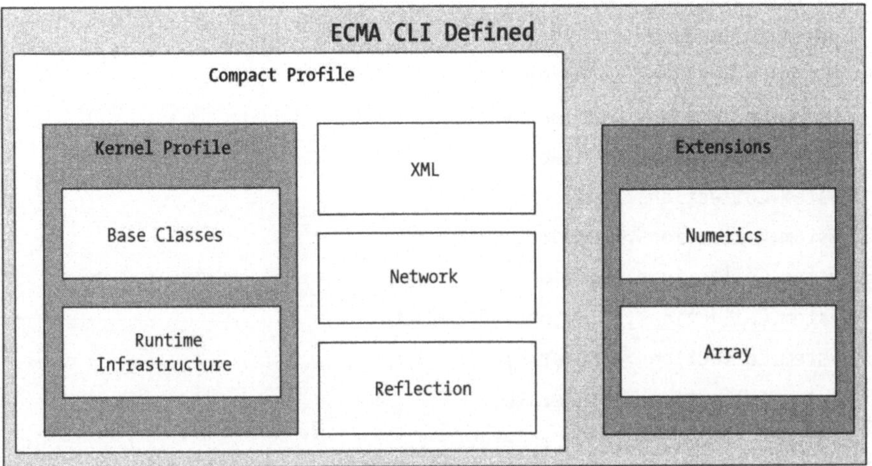

Figure B-1. The ECMA CLI Defined libraries and profiles

Base Class Library (147 Items)

System.ApplicationException
System.ArgumentException
System.ArgumentNullException
System.ArgumentOutOfRangeException
System.ArithmeticException
System.Array
System.ArrayTypeMismatchException
System.AsyncCallback
System.Attribute
System.AttributeTargets
System.AttributeUsageAttribute
System.Boolean
System.Byte
System.Char
System.CharEnumerator
System.CLSCompliantAttribute
System.Collections.ArrayList
System.Collections.Comparer
System.Collections.DictionaryEntry
System.Collections.Hashtable
System.Collections.ICollection
System.Collections.IComparer
System.Collections.IDictionary
System.Collections.IDictionaryEnumerator
System.Collections.IEnumerable
System.Collections.IEnumerator
System.Collections.IHashCodeProvider
System.Collections.IList
System.Console
System.Convert
System.DateTime
System.Delegate
System.Diagnostics.ConditionalAttribute
System.DivideByZeroException
System.DuplicateWaitObjectException
System.Enum

System.Environment
System.EventArgs
System.EventHandler
System.Exception
System.ExecutionEngineException
System.FlagsAttribute
System.FormatException
System.GC
System.Globalization.DateTimeFormatInfo
System.Globalization.DateTimeStyles
System.Globalization.NumberFormatInfo
System.Globalization.NumberStyles
System.Globalization.UnicodeCategory
System.IAsyncResult
System.ICloneable
System.IComparable
System.IDisposable
System.IFormatProvider
System.IFormattable
System.IndexOutOfRangeException
System.Int16
System.Int32
System.Int64
System.InvalidCastException
System.InvalidOperationException
System.InvalidProgramException
System.IO.Directory
System.IO.DirectoryNotFoundException
System.IO.EndOfStreamException
System.IO.File
System.IO.FileAccess
System.IO.FileLoadException
System.IO.FileMode
System.IO.FileNotFoundException
System.IO.FileShare
System.IO.FileStream
System.IO.IOException
System.IO.MemoryStream

System.IO.Path
System.IO.PathTooLongException
System.IO.SeekOrigin
System.IO.Stream
System.IO.StreamReader
System.IO.StreamWriter
System.IO.StringReader
System.IO.StringWriter
System.IO.TextReader
System.IO.TextWriter
System.MarshalByRefObject
System.NotImplementedException
System.NotSupportedException
System.NullReferenceException
System.Object
System.ObjectDisposedException
System.ObsoleteAttribute
System.OutOfMemoryException
System.OverflowException
System.Random
System.RankException
System.SByte
System.Security.CodeAccessPermission
System.Security.IPermission
System.Security.Permissions.CodeAccessSecurityAttribute
System.Security.Permissions.EnvironmentPermission
System.Security.Permissions.EnvironmentPermissionAccess
System.Security.Permissions.EnvironmentPermissionAttribute
System.Security.Permissions.FileIOPermission
System.Security.Permissions.FileIOPermissionAccess
System.Security.Permissions.FileIOPermissionAttribute
System.Security.Permissions.PermissionState
System.Security.Permissions.SecurityAction
System.Security.Permissions.SecurityAttribute
System.Security.Permissions.SecurityPermission
System.Security.Permissions.SecurityPermissionAttribute
System.Security.Permissions.SecurityPermissionFlag

System.Security.PermissionSet

System.Security.SecurityElement

System.Security.SecurityException

System.Security.VerificationException

System.StackOverflowException

System.String

System.SystemException

System.Text.ASCIIEncoding

System.Text.Decoder

System.Text.Encoder

System.Text.Encoding

System.Text.StringBuilder

System.Text.UnicodeEncoding

System.Text.UTF8Encoding

System.Threading.Interlocked

System.Threading.Monitor

System.Threading.SynchronizationLockException

System.Threading.Thread

System.Threading.ThreadAbortException

System.Threading.ThreadPriority

System.Threading.ThreadStart

System.Threading.ThreadState

System.Threading.ThreadStateException

System.Threading.Timeout

System.Threading.Timer

System.Threading.TimerCallback

System.Threading.WaitHandle

System.TimeSpan

System.Type

System.TypeInitializationException

System.UInt16

System.UInt32

System.UInt64

System.UnauthorizedAccessException

System.ValueType

System.Version

Runtime Infrastructure Library (41 Items)

System.AppDomain
System.AssemblyLoadEventArgs
System.AssemblyLoadEventHandler
System.BadImageFormatException
System.CannotUnloadAppDomainException
System.EntryPointNotFoundException
System.FieldAccessException
System.IntPtr
System.MemberAccessException
System.MethodAccessException
System.MissingFieldException
System.MissingMemberException
System.MissingMethodException
System.ParamArrayAttribute
System.Reflection.Assembly
System.Reflection.DefaultMemberAttribute
System.Runtime.CompilerServices.DecimalConstantAttribute
System.Runtime.CompilerServices.IsVolatile
System.Runtime.CompilerServices.MethodImplAttribute
System.Runtime.CompilerServices.MethodImplOptions
System.Runtime.CompilerServices.RuntimeHelpers
System.Runtime.InteropServices.CallingConvention
System.Runtime.InteropServices.CharSet
System.Runtime.InteropServices.DllImportAttribute
System.Runtime.InteropServices.FieldOffsetAttribute
System.Runtime.InteropServices.GCHandle
System.Runtime.InteropServices.GCHandleType
System.Runtime.InteropServices.InAttribute
System.Runtime.InteropServices.LayoutKind
System.Runtime.InteropServices.MarshalAsAttribute
System.Runtime.InteropServices.OutAttribute
System.Runtime.InteropServices.StructLayoutAttribute
System.Runtime.InteropServices.UnmanagedType
System.RuntimeFieldHandle
System.RuntimeMethodHandle
System.RuntimeTypeHandle

System.TypeLoadException
System.TypeUnloadedException
System.UIntPtr
System.UnhandledExceptionEventArgs
System.UnhandledExceptionEventHandler

Networking Library (57 Items)

System.Collections.Specialized.NameValueCollection
System.Net.AuthenticationManager
System.Net.Authorization
System.Net.CredentialCache
System.Net.Dns
System.Net.DnsPermission
System.Net.DnsPermissionAttribute
System.Net.EndPoint
System.Net.GlobalProxySelection
System.Net.HttpContinueDelegate
System.Net.HttpStatusCode
System.Net.HttpVersion
System.Net.HttpWebRequest
System.Net.HttpWebResponse
System.Net.IAuthenticationModule
System.Net.ICredentials
System.Net.IPAddress
System.Net.IPEndPoint
System.Net.IPHostEntry
System.Net.IWebProxy
System.Net.IWebRequestCreate
System.Net.NetworkAccess
System.Net.NetworkCredential
System.Net.ProtocolViolationException
System.Net.ServicePoint
System.Net.ServicePointManager
System.Net.SocketAddress
System.Net.SocketPermission
System.Net.SocketPermissionAttribute
System.Net.Sockets.AddressFamily

System.Net.Sockets.LingerOption
System.Net.Sockets.MulticastOption
System.Net.Sockets.NetworkStream
System.Net.Sockets.ProtocolType
System.Net.Sockets.SelectMode
System.Net.Sockets.Socket
System.Net.Sockets.SocketException
System.Net.Sockets.SocketFlags
System.Net.Sockets.SocketOptionLevel
System.Net.Sockets.SocketOptionName
System.Net.Sockets.SocketShutdown
System.Net.Sockets.SocketType
System.Net.TransportType
System.Net.WebClient
System.Net.WebException
System.Net.WebExceptionStatus
System.Net.WebHeaderCollection
System.Net.WebPermission
System.Net.WebPermissionAttribute
System.Net.WebProxy
System.Net.WebRequest
System.Net.WebResponse
System.Uri
System.UriBuilder
System.UriFormatException
System.UriHostNameType
System.UriPartial

Reflection Library (27 Items)

System.Globalization.CultureInfo
System.Reflection.AmbiguousMatchException
System.Reflection.Binder
System.Reflection.BindingFlags

System.Reflection.ConstructorInfo
System.Reflection.EventAttributes
System.Reflection.EventInfo
System.Reflection.FieldAttributes
System.Reflection.FieldInfo
System.Reflection.MemberInfo
System.Reflection.MethodAttributes
System.Reflection.MethodBase
System.Reflection.MethodInfo
System.Reflection.Module
System.Reflection.ParameterAttributes
System.Reflection.ParameterInfo
System.Reflection.ParameterModifier
System.Reflection.PropertyAttributes
System.Reflection.PropertyInfo
System.Reflection.TargetException
System.Reflection.TargetInvocationException
System.Reflection.TargetParameterCountException
System.Reflection.TypeAttributes
System.Security.Permissions.ReflectionPermission
System.Security.Permissions.ReflectionPermissionAttribute
System.Security.Permissions.ReflectionPermissionFlag
System.Void

XML Library (18 Items)

System.Xml.Formatting
System.Xml.NameTable
System.Xml.ReadState
System.Xml.WhitespaceHandling
System.Xml.WriteState
System.Xml.XmlConvert
System.Xml.XmlException
System.Xml.XmlNamespaceManager

System.Xml.XmlNameTable

System.Xml.XmlNodeType

System.Xml.XmlParserContext

System.Xml.XmlReader

System.Xml.XmlResolver

System.Xml.XmlSpace

System.Xml.XmlTextReader

System.Xml.XmlTextWriter

System.Xml.XmlUrlResolver

System.Xml.XmlWriter

Extended Libraries

Extended Numerics (5 Items)

System.Decimal

System.Double

System.Math

System.NotFiniteNumberException

System.Single

Extended Array (1 Item)

System.Array

Cross-Platform Categorization of Namespaces

Figure B-2 shows the namespaces that are defined by the ECMA CLI standards.

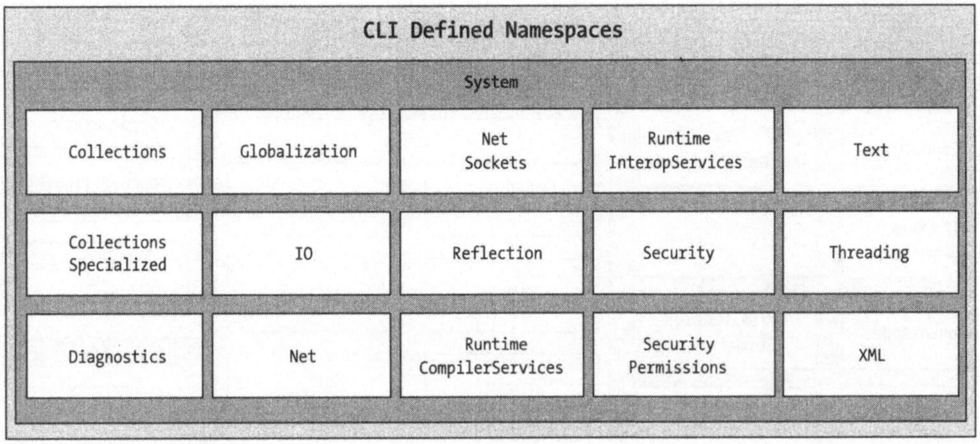

CLI Defined Namespaces

System

Collections
Globalization
Net Sockets
Runtime InteropServices
Text
Collections Specialized
IO
Reflection
Security
Threading
Diagnostics
Net
Runtime CompilerServices
Security Permissions
XML

Figure B-2. The CLI Defined namespaces

Figures B-3 and B-4 illustrate those namespaces that fall into the Architecturally Sound categorization.

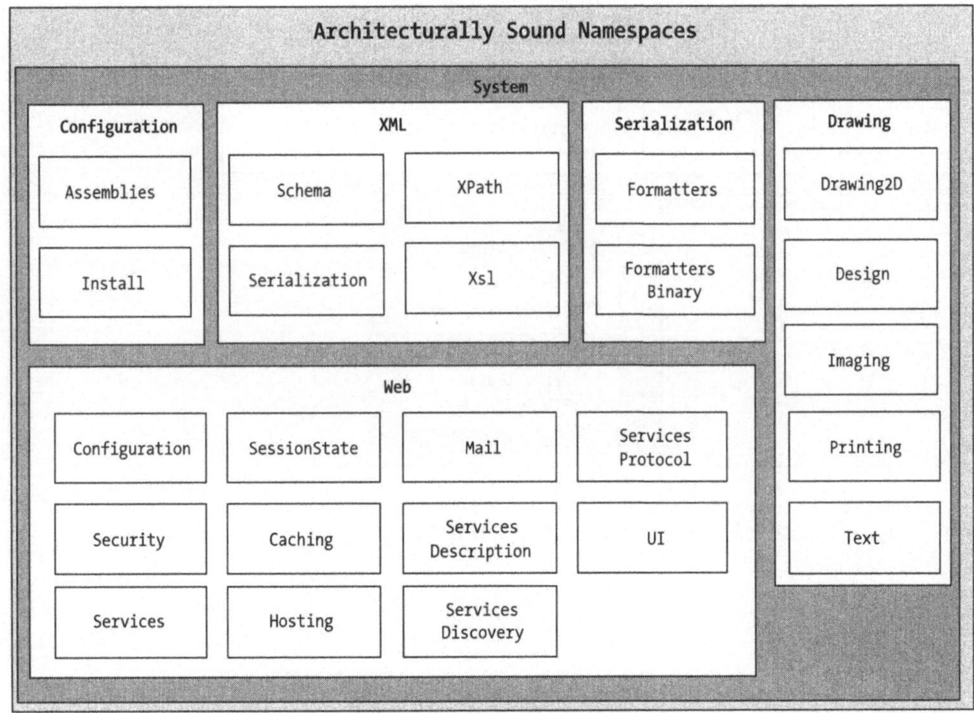

Figure B-3. The Architecturally Sound namespaces (Part 1)

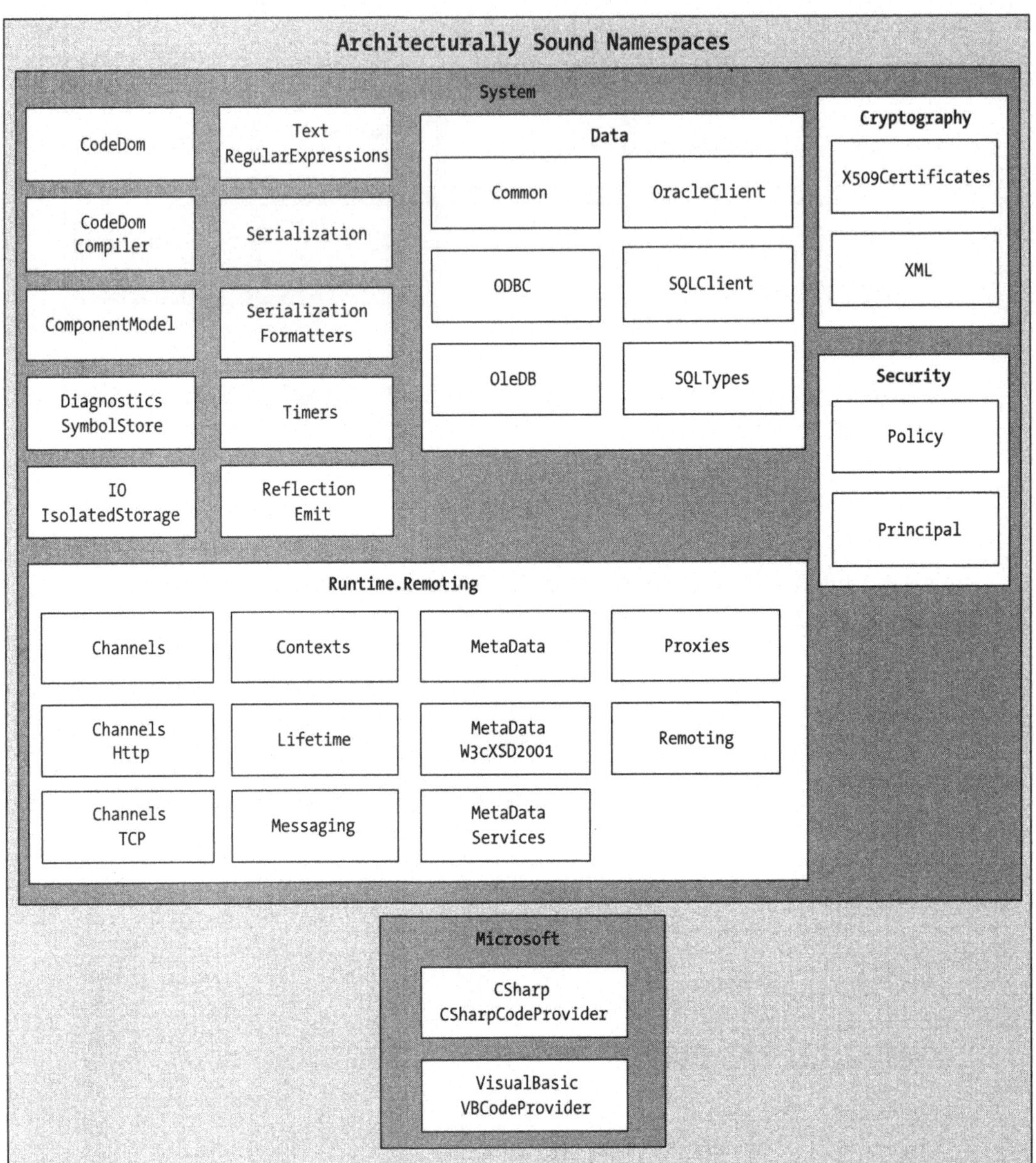

Figure B-4. The Architecturally Sound namespaces (Part 2)

Figure B-5 depicts those Architecturally Dependent namespaces where careful choices must be made.

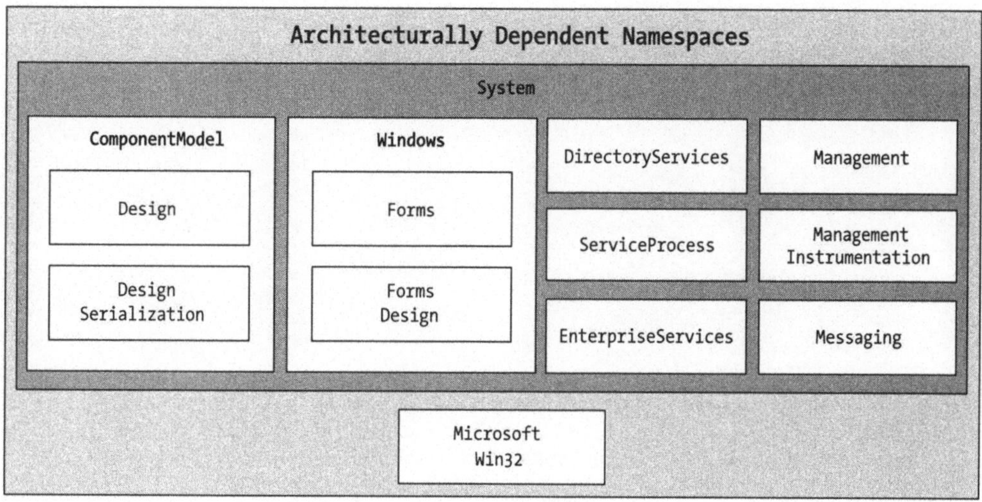

Figure B-5. The Architecturally Dependent namespaces

APPENDIX C

Additional Portable.NET Features

Apart from implementing a large swath of common .NET facilities, Portable.NET also contains a number of extra features that are not available in the other CLI implementations, as listed in Table C-1. The data in this table is based on the following versions: pnet-0.64, pnetlib-0.6.4, pnetC-0.6.4, ml-pnet-0.6.4, treecc-0.3.0, and pnetcurses-0.0.2.

Table C-1. Portable.NET Assemblies

Assembly Name	Description
cstest.dll	Unit-testing framework.
DotGNU.Images.dll	Image-loading and -saving routines for various formats, including BMP, JPEG, and PNG.
DotGNU.SSL.dll	Secure Socket Layer support routines, used by System.Net.dll.
DotGNU.Terminal.dll	Routines that augment the .NET version 1.2 extended console.
I18N.dll, I18N.CJK.dll, I18N.MidEast.dll, I18N.Other.dll, I18N.Rare.dll, I18N.West.dll	Localization handling, used internally by mscorlib.dll.
ICSharpCode.SharpZipLib.dll	Compression and decompression routines.
libc.dll & libm.dll	IL equivalents of the libc and libm libraries that are typically found in UNIX C systems. They contain the libraries for the C PNET compiler.
Libpthread.dll	Contains an API for functions and data structure classes relating to POSIX Threads.
OpenSystem.C.dll	Low-level C support routines, used internally by libc.
OpenSystem.Platform.dll	Platform-dependent type definitions.

Table C-1. Portable.NET Assemblies (Continued)

Assembly Name	Description
`System.Drawing.Postscript.dll`	Drawing toolkit for Postscript.
`System.Drawing.Win32.dll`	Drawing toolkit for Win32.
`System.Drawing.Xsharp.dll`	Drawing toolkit for X Windows.
`Xsharp.dll`	C# binding for the X11 libraries. This is not generally intended to be called directly from user code, and it implements the low-level X Windows functionality that is used by `System.Drawing.Xsharp.dll`.

Table C-2 shows those libraries that have been sourced from the Mono project. As a rule, these are particularly easy to spot, due to their Mono moniker. These can be found in the `ml-pnet` package.

Table C-2. Libraries Contributed by the Mono Project

Library Name
`PEAPI.dll`
`Custommarshalers.dll`
`ISymWrapper.dll`
`Mono.Cairo.dll`
`Mono.Data.DB2Client.dll`
`Mono.Data.MySql.dll`
`Mono.Data.PostgreSqlClient.dll`
`Mono.Data.SqliteClient.dll`
`Mono.Data.SybaseClient.dll`
`Mono.Data.TdsClient.dll`
`Mono.Data.Tds.dll`
`Mono.Directory.LDAP.dll`
`Mono.GetOptions.dll`
`Mono.Posix.dll`
`Mono.Security.dll`

Table C-2. Libraries Contributed by the Mono Project (Continued)

Library Name
Mono.Security.Win32.dll
Novell.Directory.Ldap.dll

Apart from containing additional assemblies, Portable.NET also contains a number of tools, some of which are useful only when developing with PNET, but some of which deserve a place in any self-respecting .NET developer's toolkit. These tools are described in Table C-3.

Table C-3. Portable.NET Tools

Tool Name	Description
al	Alias for ilalink.exe
clrwrap	Assists with automatically launching IL programs under UNIX systems
csant	XML-based build tool
cscc	The Portable.NET compiler
csdoc	Converts C# source code into XML documentation
csdoc2hier	Prints a class hierarchy diagram from XML documentation
csdoc2html	Converts XML documentation into HTML
csdoc2texi	Converts XML documentation into Texinfo
cssrc2html	Pretty-print C# source code in HTML
csunit	Unit-testing front-end
ilalink	The PNET IL stand-alone linker
ilasm	The PNET IL assembler
ildasm	The PNET IL disassembler
ildd	Prints assembly dependencies for an IL binary
ilfind	Finds definitions within an IL binary
ilheader	Generates C header files for accessing C# libraries
ilnative	Prints native methods P/Invoke and internalcall

Table C-3. Portable.NET Tools (Continued)

Tool Name	Description
`ilranlib`	Stub program that simulates `ranlib` for IL binaries
`ilrun`	The Portable.NET loader and runtime engine
`ilsize`	Prints code and metadata size information for an IL binary
`ilstrip`	Strips debug symbols from an IL binary
`ilverify`	Stand-alone bytecode verifier
`resgen`	Converts resources between various formats

APPENDIX D

Additional Mono Features

TABLE D-1 SHOWS a list of additional namespaces that can be found under `mcs/classes`.

Table D-1. Additional Mono Namespaces

Namespace	Description
`ByteFX.Data`	Managed data provider for the MySQL database (license: LGPL).
`Commons.Xml.Relaxng`	Support to validate XML using RelaxNG schemas.
`I18N*.dll`	Internationalization support. These libraries are sourced from the Portable.NET project but currently are not used in the Mono project. For a full list of Portable.NET's internationalization libraries, see Appendix C.
`ICSharpCode.SharpZipLib`	Compression/Decompression Library, supports `BZip2`, `GZip`, `Tar`, and `Zip`.
`Mono.Cairo`	Managed wrappers around the Cairo graphics drawing API.
`Mono.CSharp.Debugger`	Support library for debugging C# under the Mono debugger.
`Mono.Data`	Offers a factory of data providers to allow coding an application once for many databases.
`Mono.Data.DB2Client`	Data provider for the DB2 database.
`Mono.Data.MySql`	Deprecated: Wrapping data provider for the MySQL database; uses `ByteFX.Data.MySqlClient` instead.
`Mono.Data.PostgreSqlClient`	Deprecated: Wrapping data provider for the PostgreSQL database; uses `Npgsql` instead.
`Mono.Data.SqliteClient`	Data provider for the Sqlite database.

Table D-1. Additional Mono Namespaces (Continued)

Namespace	Description
Mono.Data.SybaseClient	Managed provider for the Sybase database.
Mono.Data.Tds	Managed base classes for the TDS protocol that is used by Mono.Data.SybaseClient, Mono.Data.TdsClient, and Mono's implementation of System.Data.SqlClient.
Mono.Data.TdsClient	Experimental: Managed unspecific data provider for databases using TDS.
Mono.Directory.LDAP	Minimal wrapped support for Generic LDAP/Directory Services
Mono.GetOptions	Contains useful types for reading and handling command-line parameters in an object-oriented fashion.
Mono.Globalization	No longer used; an XML-based store of language and culture information relating to English and country names, calendar and date/time formats, and so on.
Mono.Http	Support for additional HTTP features such as gzip compression and authentication. Used by xsp for ASP.NET.
Mono.PEToolkit	A range of classes for reading the binary .NET portable executable format files.
Mono.Posix	Partial wrapping of POSIX APIs.
Mono.Security	Many classes for security-related algorithms.
Mono.Security.Win32	Many classes for security-related algorithms, available only in Windows, because it wraps CryptoAPI functionality.
Novell.Directory.Ldap	Managed support for Novell eDirectory LDAP/Directory Services.
Npgsql	Managed data provider for the PostgreSQL database.
PEAPI	Classes for writing .NET portable executable format files.

Index

Symbols

A

B

C

D

E

F

G

H

I

M

N

O

P

Q

R

S

U

V

W

X